Negotiating Exclusion in Early Modern England, 1550–1800

This edited volume examines how individuals and communities defined and negotiated the boundaries between inclusion and exclusion in England between 1550 and 1800. It aims to uncover how men, women, and children from a wide range of social and religious backgrounds experienced and enacted exclusion in their everyday lives.

Negotiating Exclusion takes a fresh and challenging look at early modern England's distinctive cultures of exclusion under three broad themes: exclusion and social relations; the boundaries of community; and exclusions in ritual, law, and bureaucracy. The volume shows that exclusion was a central feature of everyday life and social relationships in this period. Its chapters also offer new insights into how the history of exclusion can be usefully investigated through different sources and innovative methodologies, and in relation to the experiences of people not traditionally defined as 'marginal'.

The book includes a comprehensive overview of the historiography of exclusion and chapters from leading scholars. This makes it an ideal introduction to exclusion for students and researchers of early modern English and European history. Due to its strong theoretical underpinnings, it will also appeal to modern historians and sociologists interested in themes of identity, inclusion, exclusion, and community.

Naomi Pullin is Assistant Professor of Early Modern British History at the University of Warwick.

Kathryn Woods is Dean of Students at Goldsmiths, University of London.

Routledge Research in Early Modern History

The Political Discourse of the Polish-Lithuanian Commonwealth
Concepts and Ideas
Anna Grześkowiak-Krwawicz

Manila, 1645
Pedro Luengo

The Polish-Lithuanian Commonwealth
History, Memory, Legacy
Edited by Andrzej Chwalba and Krzysztof Zamorski

German Imperial Knights
Noble Misfits Between Princely Authority and the Crown, 1479–1648
Richard J. Ninness

The Scramble for Italy
Continuity and Change in the Italian Wars, 1494–1559
Idan Sherer

Artistic and Political Patronage in Early Stuart England
The Career of William Herbert, Third Earl of Pembroke, 1580–1630
Brian O'Farrell

Bringing the People Back In
State Building from Below in the Nordic Countries ca. 1500–1800
Edited by Knut Dørum, Mats Hallenberg and Kimmo Katajala

Negotiating Exclusion in Early Modern England, 1550–1800
Edited by Naomi Pullin and Kathryn Woods

Islamic Thought Through Protestant Eyes
Mehmet Karabela

For more information about this series, please visit: https://www.routledge.com/Routledge-Research-in-Early-Modern-History/book-series/RREMH

Negotiating Exclusion in Early Modern England, 1550–1800

Edited by Naomi Pullin and Kathryn Woods

NEW YORK AND LONDON

First published 2021
by Routledge
52 Vanderbilt Avenue, New York, NY 10017

and by Routledge
2 Park Square, Milton Park, Abingdon, Oxon, OX14 4RN

Routledge is an imprint of the Taylor & Francis Group, an informa business

© 2021 Taylor & Francis

The right of Naomi Pullin and Kathryn Woods to be identified as the authors of the editorial material, and of the authors for their individual chapters, has been asserted in accordance with sections 77 and 78 of the Copyright, Designs and Patents Act 1988.

All rights reserved. No part of this book may be reprinted or reproduced or utilised in any form or by any electronic, mechanical, or other means, now known or hereafter invented, including photocopying and recording, or in any information storage or retrieval system, without permission in writing from the publishers.

Trademark notice: Product or corporate names may be trademarks or registered trademarks, and are used only for identification and explanation without intent to infringe.

Library of Congress Cataloging-in-Publication Data
Names: Pullin, Naomi, 1987- editor. | Woods, Kathryn, 1988- editor.
Title: Negotiating exclusion in early modern England, 1550-1800 / edited by Naomi Pullin and Kathryn Woods.
Description: New York, NY : Routledge, 2021. |
Series: Routledge research in early modern history |
Includes bibliographical references and index.
Identifiers: LCCN 2020053859 (print) | LCCN 2020053860 (ebook) | ISBN 9780367338862 (hardback) |
ISBN 9780429322631 (ebook) | ISBN 9781000359084 (adobe pdf) | ISBN 9781000359121 (epub)
Subjects: LCSH: Marginality, Social--England--History. |
Social status--England--History. | Social role--England--History. |
England–Social conditions.
Classification: LCC HN400.M26 N44 2021 (print) |
LCC HN400.M26 (ebook) | DDC 305.50942--dc23
LC record available at https://lccn.loc.gov/2020053859
LC ebook record available at https://lccn.loc.gov/2020053860

ISBN: 978-0-367-33886-2 (hbk)
ISBN: 978-0-367-34827-4 (pbk)
ISBN: 978-0-429-32263-1 (ebk)

Typeset in Sabon
by MPS Limited, Dehradun

Contents

List of Figures	vii
Acknowledgements	viii

Introduction: Approaching Early Modern Exclusion
and Inclusion   1
NAOMI PULLIN AND KATHRYN WOODS

PART I
Exclusion and Social Relations   25

1 Domestic Exclusions: The Politics of the Household
in Early Modern England   27
BERNARD CAPP

2 The Language of Exclusion: 'Bastard' in Early
Modern England   44
KATE GIBSON

3 Women and Religious Coexistence in Eighteenth-
Century England   68
CARYS BROWN

4 Failed Friendship and the Negotiation of Exclusion
in Eighteenth-Century Polite Society   88
NAOMI PULLIN

vi *Contents*

PART II
The Boundaries of Community   **115**

5 The Negotiation of Inclusion and Exclusion in the
   Westminster Infirmary, 1716–1750   117
   KATHRYN WOODS

6 Defining the Boundaries of Community?:
   Experiences of Parochial Inclusion and Pregnancy
   Outside Wedlock in Early Modern England   141
   CHARMIAN MANSELL

7 Hunting, Sociability, and the Politics of Inclusion
   and Exclusion in Early Seventeenth-Century
   England   161
   TOM ROSE

PART III
Exclusions in Ritual, Law, and Bureaucracy   **179**

8 Failing at Patriarchy: Gender, Exclusion, and
   Violence, 1560–1640   181
   SUSAN D. AMUSSEN

9 They 'Know as Much at Thirteen as If They Had
   Been Mid-Wives of Twenty Years Standing': Girls
   and Sexual Knowledge in Early Modern England   200
   SARAH TOULALAN

10 Inscription and Political Exclusion in Early Modern
    England   221
    NICHOLAS POPPER

   Afterword   240
   ANDREW SPICER

   Contributors   249
   Index   252

List of Figures

4.1 Elizabeth Carter. Engraving after Sir Thomas Lawrence 1808. Yale Center for British Art. Accession Number: B1977.14.9839.   96

4.2 Mary Hamilton (later Dickenson). Engraved frontispiece to *Mary Hamilton: Afterwards Mrs. John Dickenson: At Court and at Home* (1925). Yale Center for British Art. Reference Number: DA483 D5 A4 1925 (LC).   98

4.3 Letter from Mary Hamilton (Dickenson) to Mary Sharpe (Beauvoir) Dated 24 August 1789. John Rylands Library, University of Manchester, Mary Hamilton Papers, HAM/1/22/54.   108

7.1 *Anne of Denmark* (1574–1619) by Paul Van Somer (1617). Royal Collection Trust / © Her Majesty Queen Elizabeth II 2020. RCIN 405887.   170

7.2 *Charles I and Henrietta Maria Departing for the Chase* by Daniel Mytens (c.1630–1632). Royal Collection Trust / © Her Majesty Queen Elizabeth II 2020. RCIN 404771.   171

8.1 STC 10408.6, Anon., *English Customs. 12 Engravings of English Couples with Verses* (London, 1628), Image 9, 'Well Worth to Scurge, So Weake A Patch'. Used by Permission of the Folger Shakespeare Library.   192

Acknowledgements

Perhaps somewhat ironically for a book about exclusion, the volume stands as a testament to the value of inclusion, collaboration, kinship, friendship, and community. This volume developed from a two-day conference in May 2017 on the theme of 'Cultures of Exclusion in the Early Modern World: Enemies and Strangers, 1600–1800', where early versions of some of these essays were presented. We thank Warwick's History Department, Humanities Research Centre, European History Research Centre, The British Society for Eighteenth-Century Studies, and The Royal Historical Society, for funding this conference. We are grateful to those who attended the conference whose work does not feature in this volume.

We would very much like to thank Warwick's history department for providing the intellectual and physical space to enable this event to happen. We would especially like to thank Mark Philp, Penny Roberts, and Mark Knights, who provided crucial advice that helped shape the intellectual scope and discussions of the conference and, subsequently, the book. Valuable feedback on an early draft of the introduction was also provided by the Centre for the History of Medicine Work-in-Progress Seminar. Both of us were also supported by various people in the development of our individual chapters, and we acknowledge them in full in our chapter notes. Especial thanks need to be extended to the Leverhulme Trust for providing the funding and space for Naomi to pursue this project as an early career fellow.

We realise now our great fortitude in having found in one another a great friendship and fruitful collaborative working partnership. Our friendship has also enabled us to keep the project on track despite the challenges of institutional moves, heavy workloads, home relocations and renovations, and motherhood. Finally, we would like to acknowledge all the loving support offered by our families, without which this book would not have been possible. They have been there to provide encouragement, and daily lessons on the value of inclusion, kindness, community, and respect for difference.

Introduction
Approaching Early Modern Exclusion and Inclusion

Naomi Pullin and Kathryn Woods

In his *Dictionary of the English Language,* Samuel Johnson defined *exclusion* as the act of shutting out or denying admission, of denying privilege, and of being in a state of 'rejection', not 'reception'.[1] Although the word *exclude,* derived from the Latin *exclūdĕre,* had been widely used from the fifteenth century, 'exclusion' did not enter the English language until the early 1600s, first appearing in the works of Walter Raleigh and Francis Bacon.[2] It was and remains a slippery and unstable concept. However, it has generally entered the modern lexicon as a negative term or process where access is denied, or where a group or individual is refused certain rights or privileges. In a modern context, there is often a tendency to regard its antonym *inclusion* as a more positive concept, but to *include* in an early modern sense meant to 'enclose, encircle, to shut'.[3] This compelling paradox – that inclusion is achieved only through exclusion, and that being in a state of exclusion could be motivated by an active process of inclusion – forms the central premise of this volume. In a number of permutations, it asks: who made decisions about who to include or exclude? How were the boundaries between inclusion and exclusion determined? In what ways did experiences of social inclusion or exclusion map onto the 'desires and dilemmas of ordinary life'?[4]

The objective of this edited collection is to examine early modern England's distinctive cultures of exclusion to uncover how people negotiated, articulated, and came to terms with their lived experiences. It takes a fresh and challenging look at the conditions that created the exclusion and marginalisation of particular individuals and groups. It also examines how a multiplicity of linguistic, cultural, social, religious, legal, political, and institutional structures shaped people's experiences. The ways in which those who found themselves outside wider sociocultural norms used exclusion to mould and negotiate an identity for themselves is another central question of this volume. Focusing on England in the period between 1550 and 1800, this book illustrates that exclusion was not just experienced by marginal and deviant groups. It shows that in the course of their lives, most people would have

2   Naomi Pullin and Kathryn Woods

experienced exclusion in one form or another. In doing so, it challenges our historical understanding of what it meant to be an 'insider' and 'outsider' in early modern England. It also demonstrates that the boundaries between inclusion and exclusion were more porous and complex than traditional scholarship has suggested.

This book posits exclusion as a core but often overlooked facet of social interaction. To a great extent, existing scholarship on exclusion has aimed to chart general trends across medieval and early modern Europe.[5] This volume, by contrast, concentrates only on England. This geographical focus has been chosen not to suggest English exceptionalism, but instead to offer deeper insights into how exclusion was negotiated by those who operated within a similar socio-economic, religious, and political context. England provides a fitting case study for examining shifting cultures of early modern exclusion because it was a country where significant social and political changes occurred between 1550 and 1800, resulting in major redefinitions of relationships between ruler and ruled; state and society; believers and the Established Church; and individuals and their communities. The individual chapters that comprise this volume explore exclusion in a range of cultural contexts and situations: from unmarried mothers in the South Western counties of England to the archives of the Tower of London, and from law courts to disorderly households. One thing our chapters share is a focus on the exclusionary experiences of individuals and groups traditionally overlooked in the historiography of marginality and not necessarily conceived as 'outsiders'.[6] The volume is not intended to be comprehensive, but instead charts some attitudes and practices of exclusion, and explores how and why they were regarded as necessary within the prevailing socio-cultural norms of early modern England. It is intended to foster further research and teaching on this theme. With this in mind, this introductory chapter maps some of the ways that exclusion and inclusion have been explored in early modern scholarship, and in other related disciplines.

Inclusion and Exclusion in History

History has the power to be both inclusionary and exclusionary. Historians are situated in time and place and, deliberately or not, impose an intellectual agenda on what they choose to study and what they choose to overlook. It is also a contextually rooted discipline, and its enquiries are often tied to broader political, social, and commercial agendas. Many of the questions about exclusion that underpin this volume are a product of contemporary concerns about social inclusion and exclusion, and how they play out in state and political structures, power relations, and in interpersonal relationships. Another challenge for historians is produced by the inclusions and exclusions of the archive.

Introduction 3

Indeed, as chapters by Nicholas Popper and Sarah Toulalan in this collection show, long before historians reach the archive, multiple decisions about what is important and deserving to be preserved for posterity have already been made, causing significant parts of history – and certain people's histories – to be lost or distorted along the way.[7]

The exclusionary tendencies of history first started to be recognised in the 1960s. Producing this questioning were various social and political movements, including the civil rights movement, second-wave feminism, student protests, and the rise of gay and disability rights campaigning. Historians began to turn against what came to be termed 'Whiggish History'; histories which principally concerned themselves with the actions and lives of the upper or ruling classes, and the actions and deeds of 'great men'. In a 1966 article, E.P. Thompson proposed: 'It is one of the peculiarities of the English that the history of the "common people" has always been something other than – and distinct from – English History Proper'.[8] Through his own historical writing, which came to form the basis of a new field of 'history from below', Thompson wrote:

> I am seeking to rescue the poor stockinger, the Luddite cropper, the "obsolete" hand-loom weaver, the "Utopian" artisan, and even the deluded follower of Joanna Southcott, from the enormous condescension of posterity ... Their aspirations were valid in terms of their own experience; and, if they were casualties of history, they remain, condemned in their own lives, as casualties.[9]

The same historical moment also gave rise to a range of new histories that attempted to recover the experiences of those who had previously been considered marginal. In early modern scholarship, research coalesced around the historical experience of Jews, the poor, witches, religious minorities, and patients.[10] For example, in *Witchcraft in Tudor and Stuart England* (1971), Alan Macfarlane identified how neighbourhood disputes underpinned many accusations of witchcraft. In particular, he highlighted the impact of charity refusal in the demonisation of poor and marginal women within their communities.[11] To get at the historical experience of marginal groups, historians also began to make use of previously overlooked archival sources. For instance, chapters included in Roy Porter's edited volume *Patients and Practitioners* (1985), examined a variety of non-conventional sources to uncover early modern patient experiences, including self-help and advice guides, patient letters, and popular magazines.[12] Since the 1990s, the historiography of marginal groups has evolved in many different directions, notably including work on sexual 'deviants', vagrants, lepers, and travellers.[13] Bill Donovan's research into traveller communities in Portugal, for example, showed how their autonomy from early modern power structures caused civil and religious officials to identify them as 'potential threats to the public order'.[14] More recent work on marginal groups has explored the experiences of people of colour, Muslims, and immigrants in Europe, as well as those with disabilities and divergent gender and sexual identities.[15]

As this historiography has evolved, historians have attempted to uncover the mechanisms that led to the marginalisation of particular groups in early modern Europe. In their edited collection *Fear in Early Modern Society* (1997), William G. Naphy and Penny Roberts posit that fear – caused by the spread of disease, crime, harvest failure, or tragedy – often served to unite society against a common enemy. This resulted in the creation of scapegoats; a role that marginal groups and societal outsiders often filled, thereby justifying their persecution.[16] Scholars have also identified convergence in the way that different marginal groups were characterised. In her study of the relationship between witchcraft and leprosy, Mary Douglas pinpointed similarities in the stereotypical characteristics associated with these two very different groups, which included sexual deviance, criminality, anti-social behaviour, and pollution.[17]

Taking cues from Douglas, more recent studies have continued to investigate the shared experiences of European marginals. For example, the introduction to *The Place of the Social Margins, 1350–1750* (2017), draws attention to the significance of conceptual and physical space in creating societal 'insiders' and 'outsiders' in medieval and early modern Europe.[18] Such studies, which look at particular European contexts, have provided deeper insights into how national and ethnic traditions informed the characterisation and treatment of minority groups. In his study of premodern Italy, Derek Duncan writes: 'In depictions of space and society, a common palate of tones was utilized in different styles and traditions to produce distinct but related images of marginality'.[19]

A rich historiography of persecution and toleration has developed alongside the history of marginal groups, revealing how religion operated in the creation of societal insiders and outsiders. Published in 1987, Robert Moore's influential study on the rise of Europe as a persecuting society provided an important framework for questioning the origins of religiously motivated persecution. Moore argued that as a result of a programme of consolidation and centralisation starting around 1100, the church became more intolerant of deviant behaviour. Religious outsiders were thus increasingly presented as a threat to the social order.[20] Although Moore's thesis has its critics, the idea that the rise of persecution was a by-product of the development of religious structures and institutions has subsequently been employed by numerous scholars of early modern Europe to explain the intensification of persecution after the Reformation.[21] Indeed, the rise of religious pluralism following the religious transformations of the sixteenth century was a marked moment

Introduction 5

in the history of social relations because it presented a radical challenge to the prevailing politico-religious hierarchy. It meant that those who dissented from the Established Church divided neighbourhoods and endangered social harmony, but also threatened the salvation of their communities.

Although it remained an unpopular concept throughout our period, from the mid-seventeenth century onwards, toleration became a common rallying call for dissenting groups. In the words of historian Andrew Pettegree, it was the cry of 'the disappointed, the dispossessed, or the seriously confused', or as he puts it another way, 'a loser's creed'.[22] Historians have tended to treat persecution and toleration discreetly. However, Alexandra Walsham has influentially shown that far from being mutually exclusive, 'persecution' and 'toleration' were processes and practices that oscillated along a continuum.[23] For some religious denominations, persecution was key to their social and theological identity. A prime example is the Quakers, who regarded persecution as 'a necessary, even a somewhat welcome element of their being'.[24] Giovanni Tarantino and Charles Zika have similarly used their recent edited collection *Feeling Exclusion: Religious Conflict, Exile and Emotions in Early Modern Europe* (2019), to show the affective consequences of the European Reformations for individuals and communities. Employing approaches from the history of emotions, they show how language, gesture, and visual and material objects can be powerful tools for understanding the psychological and visceral consequences of religious change.[25]

Historical studies of multiconfessionalism in early modern Europe have demonstrated that whilst many authorities regarded confessional unity as essential to political stability, persecuting states not only embraced religious coexistence but came to regard it as essential to political survival.[26] Although religious fragmentation was a feature of Christianity long before the sixteenth century, in the years following the Reformation, the rise of religious pluralism as a permanent feature of parochial life produced a number of intriguing dilemmas for everyday communal relations. The scholarship has thus produced explorations of the different sorts of negotiations that took place within and between faiths at this time. Questions about whether people could coexist in peace when their basic beliefs were irreconcilable underpin Benjamin J. Kaplan's *Divided by Faith: Religious Conflict and the Practice of Toleration in Early Modern Europe* (2010). Here Kaplan reveals the various strategies particular communities and localities in early modern Europe adopted in order to prevent religious conflict and violence. He cites, for example, the remarkable case of the Catholics and Lutherans in the German town of Goldenstedt sharing their parish church for religious services.[27]

Early modern English historians have also explored episodes of informal acceptance in the absence of official religious toleration.

William Sheils, for example, has analysed the place of Catholics in Yorkshire, the Midlands, and London to unpick the nature of inter-confessional social interactions. He persuasively demonstrates how harmonious relationships could exist between Protestants and Catholics, even at times of intense political turmoil.[28] Other studies have focused on the specific moral dilemmas that devout Protestants and Catholics might have faced in their day-to-day encounters. For example, Walsham shows that the shared meals and leisure activities that were central to early modern neighbourhood relations naturally led to crises of conscience about the types of interchange it was acceptable to have with one's religious enemies.[29] The Act of Toleration was passed in 1689. Although this act formally recognised religious Dissenters, it did not mark a fundamental change in their community positioning. Rather the acceptance religious minorities encountered in their communities and society at large was continually negotiated and contingent on a range of social, economic, and political factors across the period. The tension between maintaining an authentic religious identity and sustaining relationships with people of different faiths is a theme that Carys Brown explores in her chapter in this volume, which focuses on the social activities of eighteenth-century female Protestant Dissenters.[30]

Negotiations within community life did not only rest on religious belief. Social structures played an equally fundamental role in determining who was included and excluded. It is well-established that early modern society was highly hierarchical, and that factors such as class, status, gender, age, health, and confessional identity determined an individual's experiences, opportunities, and life chances.[31] Research on perceptions of the poor within rural and urban settings has illustrated how complex ties of kinship, deference, and subservience created barriers to accessing wealth and political power. In the words of John Walter and Michael J. Braddick, social inequalities rested not only on material issues but also on 'the ways in which the social world was imagined and described'.[32] Pressures within parish communities were often heightened during times of economic hardship and had a noticeable impact on the poor and those who were dependant on charitable relief. The 'shame of pauperization', Steve Hindle has argued, was symbolically represented in the late seventeenth-century practice of 'badging of the poor'; where all poor persons and their families receiving parish relief were required to wear a badge with a 'P' in 'an open and visible manner'. Although these badges served a marker of validity, indicating that their wearers had been deemed 'deserving' and thus worthy of relief, they also marked recipients of charity as different from their rate-paying neighbours, which could create exclusion and social ostracism.[33]

The rituals and customs that underpinned early modern rural life had a vital place in ensuring community cohesion. As Roy Porter has argued,

Introduction 7

this was a time when '[s]ubjects were set into the social strata not primarily by choice, or by 'faceless' bureaucracy and paper qualification ... but rather by their personal connections with others, especially authority figures: fathers, masters, husbands, parsons, patrons'.[34] Shame, in this context, was a fundamental force. In the absence of formal state structures, the mechanisms that operated within localities to instil social expectations had a dialectical role in marking out those who failed to conform to expected social norms, whilst also facilitating the re-inclusion of certain individuals and groups within local communities. Social rituals such as the charivari, skimmington, public penance, and punishments like the scold's bridle, whipping, branding, and the stocks, acted as rituals of longer-term accommodation that simultaneously maintained social structures and enabled social healing after moments of disruption.[35]

Many of the social rituals described above were concerned with policing and maintaining patriarchal norms. Patriarchy was an ideological system that underpinned early modern European society and produced inequalities between men and women. It also informed the ideals of behaviour that were expected of both sexes, which were then carried across almost all realms of private and public life. Reinforced by Christian theology, law and legal practice, and medicine, patriarchy promoted the idea of women as the 'weaker sex', causing their exclusion from many aspects of power, public life, and knowledge.[36] For example, women found it notoriously difficult to secure a conviction for rape if there was no evidence except their word alone. As Bernard Capp has argued, courts and juries were influenced by prejudicial views that women were 'untrustworthy, libidinous, and swayed by passions such as malice and revenge'.[37] Sarah Toulalan, in her chapter in this volume, offers further insights into this situation in her examination of young girls' testimonies in sexual abuse trials. Toulalan shows how depositions only tended to be believed if the girl involved displayed an appropriate level of ignorance according to her age.[38]

Patriarchy glued men and women to certain behavioural expectations and, as scholarship since the 1980s has shown, both men and women had to negotiate their place within patriarchal structures.[39] Important work by Alexandra Shepard, Karen Harvey, and Elizabeth Foyster, among others, has focused specifically on issues of masculinity and demonstrates how patriarchal ideals of honour circumscribed the behaviour of men and affected their status within the household and community.[40] This has provided historians with the opportunity to explore how gendered experiences varied according to factors of age, religious background, marital status, rank, and nationality. These scholarly developments are reflected in the way gender is approached in many of the chapters in this volume, most notably by Bernard Capp, Carys Brown, Tom Rose, Sarah Toulalan, Susan Amussen, and Naomi Pullin.

8 Naomi Pullin and Kathryn Woods

From the mid-seventeenth century, a range of socio-economic developments, including demographic changes, commercialism, and urbanisation, contributed to shifts in traditional community organisation and core social structures. This social transformation fundamentally changed the fabric of communities and the contexts in which social inclusion functioned and operated. London, in particular, experienced massive expansion. In 1700 it was the largest city in Europe with around 575,000 inhabitants, and by 1800 its population had swelled to around 900,000.[41] The effect of all these demographic shifts was the decline of what Laslett termed 'face-to-face' society.[42] This had important implications for a culture dependent on honour, trust, and interpersonal credit. These processes also led to the emergence of new structures of social organisation including, state bureaucracy, the rise of new sorts of 'professionals', as well as new charitable, intellectual, social, and medical institutions. As Kathryn Woods's chapter in this volume shows, in the early eighteenth century, societal concerns around socio-economic change coalesced. This resulted in the establishment of new institutions, like the Westminster Infirmary (1719), which were sites where the concerns of authorities and ordinary people were, and had to be, negotiated in relation to contemporary social, gendered, and religious mores.[43]

The consequences of this more complex social structure are important for understanding a number of facets of exclusionary culture as it evolved over our period. The anonymity of towns, and the constant influx of people whose social status and backgrounds were uncertain eroded traditional hierarchies. Indeed, the place of the stranger in early modern urban centres remains an understudied area, but it is clear that for individuals trying to access sites of polite sociability social acceptance was not guaranteed. As Hannah Greig has shown in her work on the eighteenth-century elite, spaces that enhanced social mixing, particularly in urban centres like London, at once encouraged greater informality, whilst also enhancing social distinction. For example, although men and women from a range of social classes may have participated in public settings like pleasure gardens and theatres, these were arenas that also 'cement[ed] interpersonal acquaintances and consolidate[d] group networks'.[44] The constraints of late seventeenth- and early eighteenth-century ideals of sociability have been widely recognised, especially when more sophisticated notions of 'politeness' became a way of ensuring that the leisured upper ranks of society could assert their superiority. However, in the words of Keith Thomas, politeness, as an elite form of social distancing, was not just intended to remove oneself from 'the vulgar, but also from the worlds of commerce, provincialism and nonconformity'.[45] This challenge raised obvious tensions between the individual and social self, the individual and society, and exclusive and inclusive behaviours.

The increasing openness of urban society had the paradoxical effect of restricting access to 'polite' spaces and elite social circles, which were often exclusive and highly dependent on intrinsically intangible factors such as dress, manner, decorum, and connection. Valérie Capdeville's work on eighteenth-century gentlemen's clubs, for instance, contrasts the original openness of coffeehouse sociability with the conviviality of club life, as they increasingly restricted members and often became private institutions.[46] Practices of social exclusion were not only determined by socio-economic worth, but also by gender. For example, the coffeehouse, a key early site of the metropolitan 'public sphere', was a primarily masculine space. This stood in tension with the fact that women and ideas about femininity were increasingly regarded as central to the performance of polite sociability.[47] Indeed, as Naomi Pullin's chapter shows, it is easy to regard activities that centred around social bonding as inclusive. Yet the constraints of politeness also caused tensions because its social norms and codes were as likely to create anxiety and foster new forms of exclusion and marginality.[48]

Political changes had an equally profound effect on the structure of social relations and definitions of mainstream versus marginal culture. In many ways, political tension and conflict characterised the experiences of many early modern English men and women. The impact of the European Reformations, combined with the unprecedented violence and uncertainty of the Civil Wars and Interregnum in the 1640s and 1650s, disrupted traditional hierarchies and created a fundamental crisis in social relations at the state and community level. At the same time, the collapse of royal control over the Established Church, alongside the emergence of an unregulated press, led to widespread sectarianism, new political ideas, and gave rise to an atmosphere of factionalism and division. As Brian Cowan has recently argued, these changes were integral to the creation of party political factionalism between Whigs and Tories, and the development of their own separate cultures and communities, which thrived in the decades after the Restoration of the monarchy in 1660.[49] One striking symbolic manifestation of how political unease and factionalism could quickly turn into crisis came with the so-called 'Exclusion Crisis' that took hold of parliament from 1679, as Whig supporters in parliament fought to bar the future James II – a practising Catholic – from succeeding the throne. This was exclusion of the highest order.[50]

The political crises of the seventeenth century marked a fundamental transformation in how power and authority were determined. Nevertheless, it was not only moments of conflict that shaped how inclusion and exclusion from political life were experienced and negotiated. Historiography concerning the political involvement of those groups excluded from the 'political nation' has demonstrated the malleability of the early modern English political system, and its ability to include people beyond the enfranchised classes.[51] Andy Wood's research on memory and custom has shown how moments of tension, like riot, emerged in response to perceived injustices in the exclusion of the poor from processes of community government. This is clearly evidenced in contemporary debates over land use and enclosure.[52] Although there were deep-seated political tensions, it is possible to argue that this same system had underlying flexibility that created opportunities for inclusion as well as exclusion. Tim Harris's edited collection *The Politics of the Excluded, 1500–1850* (2001), for instance, illustrates that the majority of Englishmen and women possessed political opinions, and were able to voice them in a range of forums and settings. As he argues, far from being excluded from politics, ordinary people were 'included, either in a formal, institutionalized way, or in an extra-institutional sense'.[53]

Theories of Inclusion and Exclusion

'One of the greatest difficulties faced in trying to analyse social exclusion', as sociologist John Hobcraft reminds us, 'is that of finding a working definition of what comprises social exclusion'.[54] In the last decade, historians have begun the work of finding an analytical framework for the study of exclusion, to explore its distinct historical trends and issues. In his chapter, 'Reflection on Insiders and Outsiders' in *At the Edges of Liberalism* (2012), Steven Aschheim attempted to 'provide some kind of general conceptual and historical framework for thinking about the categories of "insiders" and "outsiders" and for rendering explicit some of the assumptions and problems regarding these notions that usually remain implicit in treatments of this subject'.[55] In developing their essays for this volume, the contributors have been invited to read Aschheim's chapter in order to consider how their subject-matter intersects with broader theories of social inclusion and exclusion. By approaching exclusion in this way, this volume seeks to address, at least in part, a tantalising question posed by Aschheim: how are modern variants in definitions and formulations of inclusion and exclusion 'differentiated from their premodern predecessors and examples'?[56]

In asking our contributors to consider these theoretical issues when developing their chapters, we were conscious that we were presenting them with a challenge. The application of theory to history has never been seamless, and historians often reject the subjection of their historical sources to theory. Core to this issue is the idea of historical rationality or objectivity; something that has remained a dominant concept in early modern studies that, in many instances, has seen off challenges produced by social constructivism and the linguistic turn. Nevertheless, theory can be a useful means of thinking about how exclusion operated as a structure and practice and was experienced by early modern people. In the following discussion, various theoretical approaches to inclusion, exclusion, and social organisation will be considered to provide an overview of some useful frameworks for thinking around the issues raised in the volume's chapters.

Introduction 11

This discussion is not comprehensive but instead aims to underscore how the theories of exclusion presented in sociology, social anthropology, and modern and early modern historical scholarship can provide useful ways of approaching inclusion and exclusion.

As the sociologist David Sibley has provocatively suggested: 'The human landscape can be read as a landscape of exclusion'.[57] Questions about the roles played by inclusion and exclusion in the structures and organisation of societies have long been core to the social sciences. In his *Division of Labour Within Societies* (1893), Émile Durkheim, the father of French sociology, proposed that societies were formed through social solidarity and that in order to achieve cohesion, societies were at least determined in part by those who they chose to exclude. For Durkheim, this sort of social organisation, based on levels of dependency and social stratification, was a uniquely 'modern' phenomenon. Indeed, he explicitly contrasted the 'mechanical solidarity' of pre-industrial societies – where he suggested that entire communities shared the same tasks, values, and beliefs – with 'the functional interdependency' of more complex industrial societies. Durkheim therefore argued that the rise of the modern period was accompanied by essential changes that created groupings and divisions centred around labour-based solidarity.[58]

A core and long-lasting critique of Durkheim has been his tendency to overlook the complexity of pre-modern communities and non-Western societies.[59] Despite this valid criticism, Durkheim's thesis still provides a useful framework for thinking about how group and social cohesion produce experiences of exclusion. The value of such an approach was underscored by David Pocock's sociological study of the caste system in 1950s Gujarat, India. Here, Pocock argued that inclusion and exclusion were the results of structural processes at work at every level of society, including the family. 'To speak of inclusion', he wrote, 'is to recognise at once its corollary exclusion'.[60] In more recent times, sociologists have become interested in how social hierarchies and systems of social positioning might form an ideological 'landscape of exclusion', and how they connect to the exercise of social, economic, and political authority.[61]

These issues have also been of interest to early modern scholars, particularly to enable exploration of the concept of community. This research has drawn attention to the 'habitus' of different early modern communities to understand the processes of inclusion and exclusion better. The French sociologist Pierre Bourdieu defined habitus as the ideological framework of perception, reinforced by memory experiences and socialisation, which predisposes individuals to certain attitudes, feelings, and routine behaviours.[62] Early modern and eighteenth-century scholarship concerning social relations has shown the significance of ideology, especially religion – but also science and empiricism – in creating a shared sense of belonging and collective identity within communities and beyond borders. For historians, Benedict Anderson's influential concept of

12 Naomi Pullin and Kathryn Woods

'imagined communities', which explicates how individual and community mentalities can become connected to political movements and structures, has played a role in this discussion.[63] As in the case of Durkheim, Anderson's theory has been criticised for being too focused on 'national' state formation; making it inapplicable to the early modern period. In fact, the overtly political and nationalistic focus of this theory of community caused some early modernists to reject the term and concept of 'community' altogether, positing it as a uniquely modern phenomenon.[64]

Yet, since the 2000s, scholars of early modern Europe have increasingly reconciled themselves to the concept of community – both real and imagined – to explore how groups organised to create belonging through shared ideological expression. This scholarship has provided a useful critique of theoretical concepts of community by illustrating the contradictions inherent in its construction. There are times when these might be more obvious in early modern contexts. For example, in *Communities in Early Modern England* (2000), Alexandra Shepard and Phil Withington argue that community was highly significant for early modern people and denoted a sense of belonging and cohesion. This was despite, as they suggest, the rhetorical and idealised codes of community shifting in their application over time and having varied meanings for the individual people involved.[65] Expanding on this, Michael J. Halvorson and Karen E. Spierling have warned of the danger of attempting to define community by imposing 'too great a clarity, simplicity, or transparency on the operations of any particular community'.[66] Such research has shown that community formation was a continuous process in the pre-modern period when societies and groups were perpetually in flux. A pertinent question for this research has been how multiple identities and ideologies were accommodated to create shared communities and values.

Early modern research into community has also been shaped by the theories of the nineteenth-century German sociologist Georg Simmel. According to Simmel, community is best understood 'as collections of overlapping entities or "circles" that meet one another at points of common interest, dispute or compromise'.[67] This theory provides a useful framework for understanding why the boundaries between insider and outsider are – and were in the period considered in this volume – often blurred, and how outsiderism was (and is) created. As Aschheim points out, the very definition of outsider suggests the existence of a meaningful connection with an 'inside'. He writes: 'there are no centers without margins, insides without outsides; the inside is constituted by constructing the outside.'[68] It is now widely recognised that early modern people could simultaneously identify with a range of communities, and that allegiance with a particular religious or civic community did not destroy shared social, economic, or political interests. But if people were capable of identifying themselves as members of multiple communities, there remains the question of what happened when different types of community allegiance came into conflict. This is a crucial yet historically neglected issue. Further research will be required to understand how people came to choose the community groups and 'interests' with which they aligned at particular historical moments, whilst simultaneously maintaining other aspects of their religious, political, and social identities.[69]

Influenced by Simmel and Durkheim, various studies have illustrated the significance of marginalisation, disagreement, and conflict to community formation. One strand of this scholarship has examined how the pressures for group cohesion could have serious implications for both marginal groups and those who seemed to be following communal expectations and adhering to social norms. In these scenarios, we can see how attempts to build positive relationships had exclusionary consequences. On some occasions, groups may have deliberately excluded themselves to reinforce their social bonds and mark themselves out as distinct. In other instances, marginal groups have been shown to have deliberately emphasised their differences from mainstream society in order to carve out a place for themselves within its culture and customs. Tim Hitchcock, for example, has shown how poor Londoners in the eighteenth century 'faked' disease and disability in pursuit of charity, and had to walk a fine line between cajoling 'without threatening' while also presenting 'a compelling case for charity'.[70]

A second strand of research has interrogated how seemingly negative behaviours could benefit collective community identity. Gossip, to take one example, is a particularly useful illustration of how an act that might have been cruel and destructive in its intent, could also serve as a force for solidifying group cohesion.[71] Likewise, drawing from anthropology, studies by David Sabean and Gregory Hanlon have underscored how envy and hatred, as much as love, held communities together.[72] 'What is common in community', writes Sabean:

> is not shared values or common understanding so much as the fact that members of a community are engaged in the same argument ... in which alternative strategies, misunderstandings, conflicting goals and values are threshed out.

The existence of community clearly did not preclude conflict. In fact, as Sabean suggests, conflict was intrinsic to how social relations were constructed. In a number of ways, this approach connects to many of the exclusionary behaviours and attitudes explored in the essays in this collection. This is because they draw attention to the fact that exclusion was central to how early modern communities were constructed, whilst also underscoring how inclusion and exclusion were continually in dialogue with one another.

Chapter Overview

This volume – the first collection to focus on the language, processes, practices, and experiences of exclusion beyond the experiences of marginal or 'deviant' groups – provides fresh perspectives on familiar themes in early modern English history. It also showcases emerging early modern research into the agency and experience of female children and nonconformist women within their communities; enmity and its various functions within male and female sociability; the stigmatising uses of violent language; and the various ways that groups, traditionally regarded by scholars as 'marginals', integrated with aspects of mainstream society. To attend a complex range of exclusionary and inclusionary experiences during this period, the chapters are organised into three sections: 'Exclusion and Social Relations', 'The Boundaries of Community', and 'Negotiating Exclusions in Ritual, Law, and Bureaucracy'. These sections are not mutually exclusive, and there is significant overlap in the topics and questions discussed between chapters. This is because, as is often the case with early modern social and cultural history, it is almost impossible to distinguish between social and gendered experiences, and broader political, economic and social changes, and institutional developments. Many of the chapters within the collection also consider the exclusion and experience of similar sorts of individuals and groups, including women, children, the poor, and religious minorities.

Part I engages with and reflects upon the various ways historians might approach themes of social inclusion and exclusion from different relational perspectives, including within the household and family, neighbourhood, and in friendships. Bernard Capp's chapter 'Domestic Exclusions' opens the volume with an assessment of how disgruntled or manipulative individuals from inside and outside seventeenth-century English households set out to marginalise or exclude other family members. There is a specific focus on the breakdown of familial boundaries as a result of extra-familial interlopers through a detailed examination of the activities of two sisters, Mehetabel Pigeon and Elizabeth Jones. Over the course of a decade, they contrived to rid themselves of their husbands, gain possession of their estates, and insert themselves into the family and business affairs of the ageing London dyer Wessell Goodwin. The complexities of familial social relations are also explored in Chapter 2 by Kate Gibson. This chapter interrogates the ways in which language was used to express and categorise forms of social exclusion, using the word 'bastard' as a case study. In investigating the meanings and uses of the term 'bastard', as it was employed in different contexts, Gibson adopts an original method of linguistic analysis to explore the changing vocabulary of illegitimacy. The chapter draws upon a range of legal and religious texts, personal writings, and legal proceedings to explore the contexts in which illegitimacy mattered, and how language choice varied according to the socio-economic status, gender, and personal circumstances of the author.

Exclusion might have been felt most acutely within the home or family, but it was highly contingent on other factors, as explored in the last two chapters of this section. Carys Brown's chapter 'Women and Religious Coexistence in Eighteenth-Century England' considers the activities of women within their broader communities. Women, as Brown notes, 'were considered to be important guardians of community reputation and moderators of polite society in early eighteenth-century England'.[73] In her chapter, Brown explores the complex place of women from Presbyterian and Independent backgrounds within their local communities in eighteenth-century England. At the centre of this discussion is the question of how far Dissenting women experienced a 'double exclusion' from their communities and wider public life on the basis of both their gender and religious affiliation. While acknowledging the extent to which religion disabled such women from adhering to conventional gender norms surrounding sociability and polite behaviour, Brown also emphasises a number of distinctive ways in which female Dissenters might also be integrated within the social life of their wider communities. Women's roles as gatekeepers to social manners are further explored in the closing chapter of this section. Chapter 4, by Naomi Pullin, examines failed friendship in the polite society of late eighteenth-century London. Here, Pullin uses a case study of an instance of failed friendship involving Mary Sharpe, a wealthy heiress, and her female acquaintances – the courtier Mary Hamilton, and the bluestocking Elizabeth Carter – to explore the limits of inclusion within elite women's friendships. Despite the growth of spaces for sociability in the late seventeenth and eighteenth centuries, access to friendship, as Mary Sharpe's personal history reveals, was not straightforward and required constant negotiation. Politeness, Pullin concludes, was not only a code of conduct to which fashionable women were expected to adhere but also a mechanism for gauging the failure of female acquaintances in particular contexts, especially surrounding the thorny issue of marriage.

In Part II, 'The Boundaries of Community', the focus of the collection moves from interpersonal to broader social and communal relationships. Kathryn Woods's discussion of the early activities and culture of the Westminster Infirmary in Chapter 5, reminds us that debates surrounding the inclusion and exclusion of certain groups and individuals were woven into the fabric of so-called 'Enlightened' medical institutions in the early eighteenth century. Woods provides a number of examples of how donors, trustees, physicians, and patients negotiated the structures, rules, and processes of the Infirmary in its early years. The negotiation of the boundaries of inclusion and exclusion in a parochial context is similarly underscored in Chapter 6. Here, Charmian Mansell employs

16 *Naomi Pullin and Kathryn Woods*

church court depositions of the dioceses of Exeter, Gloucester, Winchester, and Bath and Wells between 1550 and 1650, to show a range of experiences and perceptions of illegitimate pregnancy in early modern England. It provides a significant revision to the prevailing scholarship on illegitimacy by showing how single mothers were not routinely excluded from community life but were able to re-negotiate their place within their communities of settlement after giving birth. In fact, Mansell's analysis offers surprising evidence of how communities made deliberate choices to financially and morally support such women, and how mothers who had born children out of wedlock continued to participate in parish life actively.

Chapter 7 in this section, Tom Rose's 'Hunting, Sociability, and the Politics of Inclusion and Exclusion in Early Seventeenth-Century England', shifts the focus away from structures of exclusion and urban contexts to examine the exclusionary facets of rural-based hunting sociability. This chapter shows how 'community' was created through seventeenth-century elite hunting culture. This type of sociability, Rose argues, enabled the formation of shared culture among powerful, principally male, elites. Yet, Rose also illustrates how the line between inclusion and intrusion was sometimes thin, as evidenced in a case study of the Catholic hunting party that exploited the hunting hospitality of the Puritan Sir Thomas Hoby to abuse and emasculate their host. Rose's research also underscores the ways in which elite women were more fully included in hunting sociability than the wider discourse on hunting culture at this time suggests. Far from being excluded, he shows how elite women used hunting to aid their husbands and families in establishing and maintaining friendships, political alliances, and patronage networks.

Many of the chapters included in Parts I and II of the volume deal with social relationships, whilst also touching upon how the exclusions that resulted were informed by the underlying structures and hierarchies at play in early modern English society. Part III explores in more detail how the potential for exclusion was embedded in ritual, legal, and bureaucratic frameworks. Building upon her established body of research on early modern gender relations, in Chapter 8 Susan Amussen explores the tensions of masculinity within seventeenth-century patriarchal culture. She shows how men's performance of patriarchy could be challenged or inverted through ritual violence, which she examines in various physical, non-verbal, and verbal dimensions. Such acts of violence, she suggests, were 'both a cause of patriarchal disorder, and a tool for enforcing order'.[74] By investigating how gender norms were policed in this period, the chapter sheds new light on the regulation of men's behaviour in the period before 1640. Central to Amussen's argument is the view that 'credit' given to men was an important tool of social and political control and that 'failed patriarchs were a greater source of anxiety than

Introduction 17

disorderly women', as demonstrated in responses to insults, charges of cuckoldry, and in verse libels.[75]

The final two essays in this volume are the two that most explicitly engage with exclusion within legal and bureaucratic settings. Chapter 9 by Sarah Toulalan focuses on seventeenth- and eighteenth-century legal structures, showing how exclusion from sexual knowledge caused challenges in securing prosecutions in trials for rape and sexual assault of girls between the ages of ten and fourteen held at the Old Bailey. Since knowledge of sex for women in this period was only expected to be legitimately learned after marriage, girls were not expected to know or talk about sex. This created problems in the courtroom where, to secure a conviction, girls had to describe the encounter. As Toulalan shows, the language used in the depositions varied greatly according to the age of the victims and often codified their innocence about bodies and matters relating to sex. Indeed, a girl's admission of sexual knowledge, or an indication that she was knowledgeable in such matters, could undermine her testimony as it could suggest a potential lack of modesty and be indicative of previous sexual experience. In seeming contrast but dealing with similar issues about how knowledge was produced and used in bureaucratic procedures, Nicholas Popper's chapter explores hierarchies within knowledge creation and production. This is achieved through examination of the practices involved in the collection, transcription, storage, and production of official political records held in the Tower of London in the seventeenth century. Like many of the chapters in this volume, this chapter reveals the place of women within a setting from which they were theoretically excluded, as it emphasises their role as political record-keepers and preservers of the physical space of the archive. It also shows the ways in which statesmen of the period deliberately devised certain bureaucratic methods of record-keeping – especially the transcription of documents like patents, inquisitions, warrants, and other legal judgements – to tighten their grasp on power and use political history for their own purposes. Control over the archive, Popper argues, was deliberately used to exclude certain groups and individuals from matters relating to governance.

Collectively, these chapters show that similar inclusionary and exclusionary practices and processes were negotiated in a range of spaces, settings, and relationships in early modern England. The breadth of approaches for analysing exclusion employed in this volume – social, legal, religious, linguistic, medical, and political – shed new light on how 'outsiderism' was created and negotiated in this context. A volume of this length can never be comprehensive and involves its own exclusions. Nevertheless, by focusing on the experiences of a much broader range of groups and individuals who might not have been identified as 'marginal' or 'deviant' within their own communities or by historians, the chapters in this book show that exclusion and marginalisation were distinct processes.

18 Naomi Pullin and Kathryn Woods

It is through exploring the differences and connections between marginalisation and exclusion that a more nuanced and complex pattern of early modern social relations can be identified and begun to be understood. The contributions in this volume simultaneously bring together gender, social relations, language, and social status as important lenses of focus for exclusionary attitudes, experiences, and behaviours, whilst also adding substantively to our collective and ongoing conversations about social and community life in early modern England and beyond.

Notes

1 Samuel Johnson, *A Dictionary of the English Language* (London, 1755), n.p.
2 According to the *Oxford English Dictionary,* the word 'exclusion' derives from the Latin *exclusiōn-em, meaning* to shut out. It is first attributed to Walter Raleigh's *History of the World* (1614), vol. i, ch. 6, 'The most high God is also an infinite God, not only by exclusion of place, but by the dignitie of nature'. It was used in a secular sense by Francis Bacon in his *History of the Reign of King Henry VII* (1622), 93: 'To have the disposing of the Marriage of Britaine with an exception and exclusion, that he should not marry her himselfe.' 'exclusion, n.'. June 2020. Oxford University Press www.oed.com/view/Entry/65828. Accessed 26 July 2019.
3 See Johnson's entry for 'Inclusion' in his *Dictionary,* n.p.
4 Keith Thomas, *The Ends of Life: Roads to Fulfilment in Early Modern England* (Oxford: Oxford University Press, 2009), 5.
5 See for example: Andreas Gestrich, Lutz Raphael, and Herbert Uerlings (eds), *Strangers and Poor People: Changing Patterns of Inclusion and Exclusion in Europe and the Mediterranean World from Classical Antiquity to the Present Day* (Frankfurt am Main: Peter Lang, 2009); Stephen J. Milner (ed.), *At the Margins: Minority Groups in Premodern Italy* (Minneapolis: University of Minnesota Press, 2005); William G. Naphy and Penny Roberts (eds), *Fear in Early Modern Society* (Manchester: Manchester University Press, 1997); T. Nichols (ed.), *Others and Outcasts in Early Modern Europe: Picturing the Social Margins* (Ashgate, 2007); Andrew Spicer and Jane L. Stevens Crawshaw, *The Place of the Social Margins, 1350–1750* (Abingdon and New York: Routledge, 2017); and Giovanni Tarantino and Charles Zika (eds), *Feeling Exclusion: Religious Conflict, Exile and Emotions in Early Modern Europe* (Abingdon and New York: Routledge, 2019).
6 Derek Duncan provides a good overview of how marginality cannot be equated with minority status in 'Margins and Minorities: Contemporary Concerns?' in Milner (ed.), *At the Margins,* 22–6.
7 Nicholas Popper, 'Inscription and Political Exclusion in Early Modern England', 221–39; and Sarah Toulalan, 'They "Know as Much at Thirteen as If They Had Been Mid-Wives of Twenty Years Standing": Girls and Sexual Knowledge in Early Modern England', 200–20.
8 E.P. Thompson, 'History from Below', Times Literary Supplement (7 April 1966), 279.
9 E.P. Thompson, 'Preface to 1963 Edition', in *The Making of the English Working Class* (Harmondsworth: Penguin, 2013), 12.
10 Robert Jütte, *Poverty and Deviance in Early Modern Europe* (Cambridge: Cambridge University Press, 1994); Steve Hindle, *On the Parish?: The Micro-Politics of Poor Relief in Rural England 1550–1750* (Oxford: Oxford

Introduction 19

University Press, 2004); Paul Slack, *Poverty and Policy in Tudor and Stuart England* (London: Longman, 1988); A.L. Beier, *Masterless Men: the Vagrancy Problem in England, 1560–1640* (London and New York: Methuen, 1985); Brian Levack, *The Witch-Hunt in Early Modern Europe* (London & New York: Longman, 1995); Roy Porter, *Mind-Forg'd Manacles: A History of Madness in England from the Restoration to the Regency* (London: Athlone Press, 1987).

11 Alan Macfarlane, *Witchcraft in Tudor and Stuart England: A Regional and Comparative Study* (New York: Harper and Row, 1970), 165–6, 174–76, 196–7.

12 Roy Porter (ed.), *Patients and Practitioners: Lay Perceptions of Medicine in Pre-Industrial Society* (Cambridge: Cambridge University Press, 1985).

13 On sexual deviants see: Caroline Bingham, 'Seventeenth-Century Attitudes Toward Deviant Sex', *Journal of Interdisciplinary History*, 1 (1971), 447–68; Alan Bray, *Homosexuality in Renaissance England* (London: Gay Men's Press, 1982); Katherine Crawford, *European Sexualities, 1400–1800* (Cambridge: Cambridge University Press, 2007), esp. 189–231; Katherine O'Donnell and Michael O'Rourke (eds), *Queer Masculinities, 1550–1800: Siting Same Sex Desire in the Early Modern World* (Basingstoke: Palgrave Macmillan, 2006). On vagrants see: Beier, *Masterless Men*; David Hitchcock, *Vagrancy in English Culture and Society, 1650–1750* (London: Bloomsbury, 2016); and Jütte, *Poverty and Deviance*. On lepers see: Pater Lewis Allen, *The Wages of Sin: Sex and Disease, Past and Present* (Chicago: University of Chicago Press, 2000), esp. 29–40; Malcolm Barber, 'Lepers, Jews and Moslems: The Plot to Overthrow Christendom in 1321', *History*, 66 (1981), 1–17; and Mary Douglas, 'Witchcraft and Leprosy: Two Strategies of Exclusion', *Man*, 26 (1991), 723–36. On traveller communities see: Bill M. Donovan, 'Changing Perceptions of Social Deviance: Gypsies in Early Modern Portugal and Brazil', *Journal of Social History*, 26 (1992), 33–53; Ian Hancock, 'The Roots of Inequality: Romani Cultural Rights in their Historical and Social Context', *Immigrants & Minorities*, 11 (1992), 3–20; David Mayall, 'Egyptians and Vagabonds: Representations of the Gypsy in Early Modern Official and Rogue Literature', *Immigrants & Minorities*, 16 (1997), 55–82; and John E. Morgan, '"Counterfeit Egyptians": The Construction and Implementation of a Criminal Identity in Early Modern England', *Romani Studies*, 26 (2016), 105–128.

14 Donovan, 'Changing Perceptions of Social Deviance', 33–53.

15 On people of colour and Muslims in Europe see: Jerry Brotton, *This Orient Isle: Elizabethan England and the Islamic World* (Penguin, London, 2016); T.F. Earle and K.J.P. Lowe (eds), *Black Africans in Renaissance Europe* (Cambridge: Cambridge University Press, 2005); Imtiaz Habib, *Black Lives in the English Archives, 1500–1677: Imprints of the Invisible* (London: Routledge, 2007); and Miranda Kauffman, *Black Tudors: The Untold Story* (London: Oneworld, 2018). On disabilities and mental illness see fn. 8 above: Laura Carnelos, 'Street Voices. The Role of Blind Performers in Early Modern Italy', *Italian Studies*, 71 (2016), 184–96; Emily Cockayne, 'Experiences of the Deaf in Early Modern England', *Historical Journal*, 46 (2003), 493–510; Richard H. Godden and Asa Simon Mittman, *Monstrosity, Disability, and the Posthuman in the Medieval and Early Modern World* (Cham, Switzerland: Palgrave Macmillan, 2019); and Allison P. Hobgood and David Houston Wood (eds), *Recovering Disability in Early Modern England* (Columbus, OH: Ohio State University Press, 2013). On sexual and gender identities see fn. 11 above: Ari Friedlander, Melissa Sanchez, and Will

Stockton (eds), 'Desiring History and Historicizing Desire', special issue of *Journal for Early Modern Cultural Studies*, 16 (2016), 1–149; E.L. McCallum (ed.), *The Cambridge History of Gay and Lesbian Literature* (Cambridge: Cambridge University Press, 2014), esp. Parts II and III; Cathy McClive, 'Masculinity on Trial: Penises, Hermaphrodites and the Uncertain Male Body in Early Modern France', *History Workshop Journal*, 68 (2009), 45–68; and Valerie Traub, *Thinking Sex with the Early Moderns* (Philadelphia: University of Pennsylvania Press, 2016). On immigrants see: Steven King and Anne Winter (eds), *Migration, Settlement and Belonging in Europe, 1500–1930s: Comparative Perspectives* (New York: Berghahn Books, 2013), esp. 29–80; Stana Nenadic, *Scots in London in the Eighteenth Century* (Lewisburg, PA: Bucknell University Press, 2010); and Jacob Selwood, *Diversity and Difference in Early Modern London* (Farnham: Ashgate, 2010).

16 Naphy and Roberts, *Fear in Early Modern Society*, 3.
17 Douglas, 'Witchcraft and Leprosy', 723–36.
18 Jane L. Stevens Crawshaw, 'Introduction' in Spicer and Stevens Crawshaw, *The Place of the Social Margins*, 1–17.
19 Duncan, 'Margins and Minorities', 1–2.
20 R.I. Moore, *The Formation of a Persecuting Society: Authority and Deviance in Western Europe 950–1250* (Oxford: Blackwell Publishing, 1987).
21 David Nirenberg provides a particularly extensive critique of Moore's structuralist approach to persecution and violence in *Communities of Violence: Persecution of Minorities in the Middle Ages* (Princeton and Oxford: Princeton University Press, 1996), 231–50.
22 Andrew Pettegree, 'The Politics of Toleration in the Free Netherlands, 1572–1620', in Ole Peter Grell and Bob Scribner (eds), *Tolerance and Intolerance in the European Reformation* (Cambridge: Cambridge University Press, 1996), 198.
23 Alexandra Walsham, *Charitable Hatred: Tolerance and Intolerance in England, 1500–1700* (Manchester: Manchester University Press, 2006).
24 Richard L. Greaves, 'The "Great Persecution" Reconsidered. The Irish Quakers and the Ethic of Suffering', in Muriel C. McClendon, Joseph P. Ward, and Michael MacDonald (eds), *Protestant Identities. Religion, Society, and Self-Fashioning in Post-Reformation England* (Stanford: Stanford University Press, 1999), 212.
25 Giovanni Tarantino and Charles Zika, 'Introduction: Feeling Exclusion, Generating Exclusion', in Tarantino and Zika (eds), *Feeling Exclusion*, 1–3.
26 Thomas Max Safely, 'Multiconfessionalism: A Brief Introduction', in Thomas Max Safely (ed.), *A Companion to Multiconfessionalism in the Early Modern World* (Leiden: Brill, 2011), 12–3.
27 Benjamin J. Kaplan, *Divided by Faith: Religious Conflict and the Practice of Toleration in Early Modern Europe* (Cambridge, MA: Belknap Press, 2007), 198–234.
28 William J. Shiels, '"Getting On" and "Getting Along" in Parish and Town: English Catholics and their Neighbours', in Benjamin J. Kaplan, Bob Moore, Henk van Nierop, and Judith Pollmann (eds), *Catholic Communities in Protestant States: Britain and the Netherlands, c.1570–1720* (Manchester: Manchester University Press, 2009), 67–83.
29 Alexandra Walsham, 'Supping with Satan's Disciples: Spiritual and Secular Sociability in Post-Reformation England', in Nadine Lewycky and Adam Morton (eds), *Getting Along? Religious Identities and Confessional*

Relations in Early Modern England – Essays in Honour of Professor W. J. Sheils (Farnham: Ashgate, 2012), 29–55.

30 Carys Brown, 'Women and Religious Coexistence in Eighteenth-Century England', 68–87.

31 Susan D. Amussen, *An Ordered Society: Gender and Class in Early Modern England* (New York: Columbia University Press, 1993); Susan D. Amussen and David Underdown (eds), *Gender, Culture and Politics in England, 1560–1640: Turning the World Upside Down* (London and New York: Bloomsbury, 2017); Michael J. Braddick and John Walter (eds), *Negotiating Power in Early Modern Society: Order, Hierarchy and Subordination in Britain and Ireland* (Cambridge: Cambridge University Press, 2010); Anthony Fletcher, *Gender, Sex and Subordination in Early Modern England* (New Haven: Yale University Press, 1995); Steve Hindle, Alexandra Shepard, and John Walter (eds), *Remaking English Society: Social Relations and Social Change in Early Modern England* (Woodbridge: The Boydell Press, 2013); and Keith Wrightson, *English Society 1580–1680*, second edition (London: Routledge, 2003).

32 Braddick and Walter (eds), *Negotiating Power*, 1.

33 Hindle, *On the Parish?*, 433–45.

34 Roy Porter, *English Society in the Eighteenth Century* (Harmondsworth: Penguin, 1982), 21.

35 See for example, Susan D. Amussen, 'Punishment, Discipline, and Power: The Social Meanings of Violence in Early Modern England', *Journal of British Studies*, 34 (1995), 1–34; Martin Ingram, 'Charivari and Shame Punishments: Folk Justice and State Justice in Early Modern England', in Herman Roodenburg and Petrus Spierenburg (eds), *Social Control in Europe* (2 vols, Columbus, OH: Ohio State University Press, 2004), ii. 288–308; and David Underdown, 'The Taming of the Scold', in Anthony Fletcher and John Stevenson (eds), *Order and Disorder in Early Modern England* (Cambridge: Cambridge University Press, 1985), 116–36.

36 Sara Mendelson and Patricia Crawford, *Women in Early Modern England, 1550–1720* (Oxford: Clarendon, 1998), 15–74.

37 Bernard Capp, *When Gossips Meet: Women, Family, and Neighbourhood in Early Modern England* (Oxford: Oxford University Press, 2003), 6.

38 Toulalan, 'Girls and Sexual Knowledge', 200–20.

39 Especially influential were: Joan W. Scott, 'Gender: A Useful Category of Historical Analysis', *American Historical Review* 91 (1986), 1053–75; and Natalie Zemon Davis, '"Women's History" in Transition: The European Case', in *Feminism and History* (Oxford: Oxford University Press, 1996), 79–104.

40 Elizabeth A. Foyster, *Manhood in Early Modern England: Honour, Sex and Marriage* (London: Longman, 1999); Karen Harvey, *The Little Republic: Masculinity and Domestic Authority in Eighteenth-Century Britain* (Oxford: Oxford University Press, 2012); and Alex Shepard, *Meanings of Manhood in Early Modern England* (Oxford: Oxford University Press, 2006). A good overview of the historiography of masculinity in early modern England is provided in Tim Reinke-Williams, 'Manhood and Masculinity in Early Modern England', *History Compass*, 12 (2014), 685–93.

41 Roy Porter, *London: A Social History* (London: Penguin Books, 1996), 98.

42 Peter Laslett, *The World We Have Lost* (London: Methuen, 1965), 1–21; Peter Laslett, 'The Face-to-Face Society' in Peter Laslett (ed.), *Philosophy, Politics and Society*, Fifth Series (Oxford: Blackwell, 1956), 157–84.

43 Kathryn Woods, 'The Negotiation of Inclusion and Exclusion in the Westminster Infirmary 1716–1750', 117–40.
44 Hannah Greig, *The Beau Monde: Fashionable Society in Georgian London* (Oxford: Oxford University Press, 2013), 90.
45 Keith Thomas, *In Pursuit of Civility: Manners and Civilization in Early Modern England* (New Haven and London: Yale University Press, 2018), 29.
46 Valérie Capdeville, 'Club Sociability and the Emergence of New 'Sociable' Practices', in Valérie Capdeville and Alain Kerhervé (eds), *British Sociability in the Long Eighteenth Century: Challenging the Anglo-French Connection* (Woodbridge: The Boydell Press, 2019), 53–64.
47 The importance of women to eighteenth-century sociability is outlined in Lawrence E. Klein, 'Gender, Conversation and the Public Sphere in Early Eighteenth-Century England', in Michael Worton and Judith Still (eds), *Textuality and Sexuality: Reading Theories and Practices* (Manchester: Manchester University Press, 1993), 100–115.
48 Naomi Pullin, 'Failed Friendship and the Negotiation of Exclusion in Eighteenth-Century Polite Society', 88–114.
49 Brian Cowan, "Restoration", England and the History of Sociability', in Capdeville and Kerhervé (eds), *British Sociability in the Long Eighteenth Century*, 10, 16–24.
50 Mark Knights, *Politics and Opinion in Crisis, 1678–81* (Cambridge: Cambridge University Press, 1994); and Jason McElligott (ed.), *Fear, Exclusion and Revolution: Roger Morrice and Britain in the 1680s* (London and New York: Routledge, 2016).
51 Tim Harris, *The Politics of the Excluded, c. 1500–1850* (Basingstoke: Palgrave, 2001), 1.
52 Andy Wood, 'Custom, Identity and Resistance: English Free Miners and their Law, c. 1550–1800', in Paul Griffiths, Adam Fox, and Steve Hindle (eds), *The Experience of Authority in Early Modern England* (Basingstoke: Macmillan, 1996), 249–85.
53 Harris, *The Politics of the Excluded*, 1.
54 John Hobcraft, 'Social Exclusion and the Generations', in Phil Agulnik, John Hills, Julian Le Grand, and David Piachaud (eds), *Understanding Social Exclusion* (Oxford: Oxford University Press, 2002), 62.
55 Steven E. Aschheim, *At the Edges of Liberalism: Junctions of European, German and Jewish History* (2012), 145.
56 Ibid., 145.
57 David Sibley, *Geographies of Exclusion: Society and Difference in the West* (London: Routledge, 1995), ix.
58 Émile Durkheim, *The Division of Labour in Society*, trans. W.D. Halls (Basingstoke: Macmillan, 1984), xvi–xvii.
59 Sibley, *Geographies of Exclusion*, 35–6.
60 David Pocock, 'Inclusion and Exclusion: A Process in the Caste System of Gujarat', *Southwestern Journal of Anthropology*, 13 (1957), 28.
61 See for example Sibley, *Geographies of Exclusion*, iv, see also ix–xviii.
62 Pierre Bourdieu, *The Logic of Practice*, trans. Richard Nice (Cambridge: Polity, 1990), 52–65.
63 Benedict Anderson, *Imagined Communities: Reflections on the Origin and Spread of Nationalism* (London & New York: Verso, 1991).
64 The critique of early modern 'community' is surveyed in Alexandra Shepard and Phil Withington (eds), *Communities in Early Modern England: Networks, Place, Rhetoric* (Manchester: Manchester University Press, 2000), 1–15.

Introduction 23

65 Ibid., 1–15.
66 Michael J. Halvorson and Karen E. Spierling (eds), *Defining Community in Early Modern Europe* (Aldershot: Ashgate, 2008), 1.
67 Halvorson and Spierling (eds), *Defining Community in Early Modern Europe*, 7; Georg Simmel, *Conflict: The Web of Group Affiliations* (New York and London: Free Press: Collier Macmillan, 1964).
68 Aschheim, *At the Edges of Liberalism*, 147.
69 Barbara B. Diefendorf, 'Reflections on Community and Identity', *French Historical Studies: Forum on Communities and Religious Identities in the Early Modern Francophone World, 1550–1700*, 40 (2017), 386.
70 Tim Hitchcock, 'Cultural Representations: Rogue Literature and the Reality of the Begging Body', in Carole Reeves (ed.), *A Cultural History of the Human Body in the Age of Enlightenment* (London: Bloomsbury, 2014), 180.
71 The paradoxical elements of gossip were influentially outlined in Max Gluckman, 'Papers in Honor of Melville J. Herskovits: Gossip and Scandal', *Current Anthropology*, 4 (1963), 307–16. Markman Ellis has recently discussed its application to studies of eighteenth-century sociability in 'The Tea-Table, Women and Gossip in Early Eighteenth-Century Britain', in Capdeville and Kerhervé (eds), *British Sociability in the Long Eighteenth Century*, 69–87.
72 Gregory Hanlon, *Confession and Community in Seventeenth-Century France: Catholic and Protestant Coexistence in Aquitaine* (Philadelphia: University of Pennsylvania Press, 1993), 90; and David Sabean, *Power in the Blood: Popular Culture and Village Discourse in Early Modern Germany* (Cambridge: Cambridge University Press, 1984).
73 Brown, 'Women and Religious Coexistence', 68.
74 Susan Amussen, 'Failing at Patriarchy: Gender, Exclusion and Violence, 1560–1640', 182.
75 Ibid., 184.

Part I

Exclusion and Social Relations

1 Domestic Exclusions
The Politics of the Household in Early Modern England

Bernard Capp

Contemporaries liked to imagine the household as a well-ordered society, bound together by love and duty. This ideal, as they were well aware, was often far removed from reality. The prescriptive conduct books of the period, such as William Gouge's *Of Domesticall Duties* (1622), spelt out the all too common failings of husbands, wives, children, and servants, and the tensions they generated. This essay shows how such tensions, in a variety of contexts, could lead to an unwanted wife, child, stepchild, sibling, or occasionally husband, being marginalised or driven out. Social exclusion was a phenomenon that possessed a significant domestic dimension. The essay focuses on two remarkable cases, both of which underline the particular threat to domestic order when a family head proved unable to assert his authority. In the first case, this resulted in a struggle between the head's second wife and her stepson, each attempting to exclude the other from influence and authority within the household. In the second, a man's adult children were gradually excluded from his home and business by two scheming women who were not even related to him by blood or kinship. And eventually, the father found himself excluded too. Collectively, these remarkable tales of domestic exclusion underline the potentially unstable nature of marital arrangements and family structures in seventeenth-century England.

Exclusionary Contexts

The most common contexts for domestic exclusion were fourfold: a breakdown in relations between a father and his adult offspring; friction between siblings, often over inheritance; a failing marriage; and tensions within a second (or subsequent) marriage, between an adult and his or her stepchildren. In the first scenario, an angry father might disinherit a son or daughter, often for defying or ignoring him over the choice of a marriage partner, or for converting to Catholicism or a nonconformist movement.[1] In one such case, young William Serjeant was 'turnd out of doores' by his angry father in 1668 for joining the Quakers, and the

28   Bernard Capp

Bristol Quaker community was left to find him a home.[2] Siblings frequently quarrelled over their father's will, sometimes while he was still alive. A furious dispute erupted in 1589 over the affairs of John Dampire, an elderly Somerset villager described as 'very simple and easy to be seduced'. His son Thomas had pressured him into giving him a substantial part of his estate, outraging his other son, who discovered that little would now remain for him. Dampire had wanted to be generous to both sons, but Thomas's sharp practice had effectively excluded that possibility.[3] Failing marriages, a third frequent context, could often lead to domestic violence or adulterous liaisons. An unfaithful wife would usually try to conceal her affair, but an unfaithful husband might go further, driving his wife away or allowing another woman to usurp her role as a housekeeper or even her place in the marital bed.[4] Such behaviour was found at all levels of society. Sir Richard Grenville, who sued for divorce in 1632, had allegedly given his wife Mary a black eye, called her a whore, and 'excluded her from governing the house and affaires within dore'. One of his kinswomen now 'ordered and ruled all things'. Mary, who had brought him a considerable fortune, had retaliated by mocking him as a 'petty fellow' not worth ten groats when they wed, 'and sung unseemly songs to his face to provoke him'. A hostile witness called her 'domineering' and 'imperious', but it was Mary who was excluded from her wifely functions and the freedom of her house, and now lived, she said, in fear of her life.[5] At the other end of the social hierarchy, we hear of a heartless Sussex villager who made his wife sleep in a spare room and locked her out of the house while he had sex with their maidservant.[6]

Stepfamilies, the fourth context, were a common feature of early modern society, the product of high mortality rates and remarriage. Many reconstituted families developed satisfactory relationships, but tensions were common, and the unkindness of stepparents was proverbial.[7] The safety and welfare of young children were often at risk, while older children worried about their inheritance. Would a stepmother turn their father against them? Would a stepfather overturn the arrangements their own father had made for them? Those adults who viewed their stepchildren as an unwelcome burden responded with cruelty or neglect, a pattern we again find at all levels of society. In some cases, unwanted stepchildren were literally excluded, pushed out and sometimes left to fend for themselves. In desperation, some turned to crime to survive.[8] Robert and Margaret Buckley took a very different course, petitioning the Privy Council in 1638 to tell their sorry tale. Their father, Sir Richard Buckley (or Bulkeley) of Beaumaris, had been a wealthy landowner, but after his death, his widow married a family servant, Thomas Cheadle, and soon fell completely under his sway. Cheadle then claimed that the children were illegitimate and drove them out, placing them in 'mechanick Trades' under new names. When Robert later appealed to his mother for relief, Cheadle had him imprisoned and uttered dire threats if he ever claimed the family name.[9]

Adolescents and young adults were not always passive victims, and family dynamics could be complex. If both partners brought children into the new marriage, tensions might erupt from day one between the stepsiblings. In one Sussex family in the early 1600s, the two sets of children hated each other so much that the parents were forced to maintain separate households to keep the peace. Older children might never accept unwanted stepparents, and sometimes found ways to undermine their position. A stepmother might find herself vulnerable, for example, if her husband had to be away for an extended period. In one Cheshire case, a father left his son in charge of the estate and directed him to provide well for his stepmother. Instead, he seized the opportunity to reduce her to destitution.[10] Very occasionally, we find a stepfather similarly targeted, as in the case of Daniel Town, an Anglican minister in Yorkshire. Town and his second wife, a widow with adult children, proved ill-matched and 'did woefully disagree', whereupon her two sons threatened to kill him. In 1672 they contrived to have him imprisoned, and when he was released and returned home, he was attacked by four men and dumped in the street, with wounds that may have proved fatal.[11]

These stories, and many others like them, provide glimpses of domestic exclusion in a range of forms and contexts. The remainder of this essay focuses on two striking cases, both hitherto overlooked, which enable us to reconstruct the family dynamics of exclusion in far greater depth and add new dimensions to our understanding of inclusion and exclusion in the seventeenth-century household.

The Pagitts: Son Versus Stepmother

In the early 1630s James Pagitt, a successful London lawyer, was the rather ineffective head of a troubled household. Though its problems never reached the courts, his son Justinian kept a notebook which gives us a detailed, if partisan, account of a struggle over several years between him and his stepmother, each seeking to undermine and marginalise the other.[12] Justinian was a law student, dividing his time between home and his rooms in the Middle Temple. He and his younger brother were not seriously threatened by their stepmother, for he was already in his early twenties and there were no half-siblings to endanger his inheritance. But he believed that his stepmother was abusing her position as wife and housekeeper, and neglecting her responsibilities to her husband and stepsons. In response, he compiled a comprehensive dossier of her offences, each catalogued with precise details of time, place, and witnesses. He complained, for example, that she would order the maid to buy only the cheapest meat at the market, some of it already rotten and stinking,

30   Bernard Capp

to save housekeeping money which she then kept for herself. The house was dirty, and the hall was dark because she would not buy candles for the lanterns. Though her own clothes were well maintained, she took little care of the household linen or her husband's and stepchildren's clothes, and the laundress complained she was not allowed sufficient soap to wash them properly. The servants were often directed to leave the cleaning and cooking and spend their time spinning, carding, and knitting, to make money which his stepmother then kept for herself. The cook complained she was not even allowed time to wash the platters. Pagitt's stepmother had a generous housekeeping budget of £3 a week, but misled her husband and told him that she needed more. When he wanted to invite a guest for dinner, she would claim that she did not have enough money to cater for such an occasion. Disgusted by her fraudulent devices, Pagitt wanted to see every item of expenditure set down precisely in an account book.

We only have Pagitt's version of the domestic situation. Some of his material came from his own observation, some from the servants, and some from neighbours. The servants passed on stories to their friends, which Pagitt feared was undermining the family's good name. The maid, for example, told how she was directed to buy stale butter by the pennyweight, 'which the Neighbours jeer at to my fathers disgrace'. The notebook also throws incidental light on a very different dimension of these household tensions. Pagitt often reflected on spiritual and religious matters, and how well he was obeying all Ten Commandments. He acknowledged that the Fifth Commandment (to honour and obey parents) applied equally to stepparents, and feared that he might be committing a sin whenever he criticised or confronted his stepmother. On the other hand, he fretted, when he failed to challenge her, she behaved still worse, so silence might also be a sin. Pagitt was also fully aware of the material issues at stake in this situation. One section of the notebook is headed, 'Inconveniences which might arise to me if I should inform my father concerning my mothers etc'. The 'etc.' suggests that he was unsure how to categorise his mother's misconduct. Moreover, she would obviously retaliate by telling his father lies about him, and he would no longer have his clothes washed or mended. But in the next section, headed 'Inducements to me to inform against her', he reflected that his stepmother could hardly treat him worse than she already did. And if she was suffered to carry on, she would control his father so tightly that it would become impossible ever to free him. Pagitt eventually decided to pass over small matters in silence, but speak out on major abuses. He would try to please his father in all things, to protect his own position. And if necessary, he could make his own laundry arrangements.

Pagitt insisted that his concern was solely for his father, abused by a devious woman betraying her duties as wife and housekeeper. A recurring marginal note reads, 'Provides for herself. Neglects her husband'.

He presented his own mistreatment as a secondary issue, but it clearly rankled. He was certain that she was trying to turn his father against him, and feared being marginalised or excluded. When he reported her failings to his father, she did indeed retaliate with stories about his own minor misdeeds. Pagitt believed that she wanted to push him away, almost literally. She suggested, for example, that he should always live in the Middle Temple in term-time, not at home. And when their father thought of spending the vacation at his country house, she told him that Justinian would rather stay behind. That was untrue, and he saw it as a blatant device to exclude him. James Pagitt remains an enigma. Justinian fretted about his father's health, and worried about him sleeping in damp bed-linen. Though he never criticised his 'poor father', his comments suggest a man who was failing in his duty to govern his household and maintain good order within it. His father seems to have longed for domestic harmony, but was either unable or unwilling to assert his authority as head of the household. After listening to his wife's and son's complaints against each other, he grumbled weakly that 'These things will make us a weary of one another'.

Pagitt's notebook, which offers a rare insight into the dynamics of a London household, does not reveal how the contest ended. After one clash with his stepmother, Pagitt's father told him, 'We are so wearied and troubled with you'. The 'we' is suggestive, and his stepmother may have prevailed. When he married in 1635, Pagitt probably established his own household, which would have defused the situation. His father died three years later. Pagitt, who went on to forge a successful legal career, would have insisted that he had merely been trying to make his stepmother discharge her domestic responsibilities. But if he was not seeking to displace her, he was clearly attempting to reduce her influence over his father, and undermine her standing and authority. No woman would have tolerated a stepson meddling in the housekeeping as Pagitt did. He listened to servants' gossip, and sometimes countermanded the orders she had given them. He even took it upon himself to draw up plans for a better housekeeping regime, urging his father, for example, to appoint a regular day each week for mending clothes and scouring the plate. His father, he admitted, considered his interventions inappropriate and divisive. We can only speculate how much his father understood of the struggle being waged around him.

The Goodwins: Usurpation and Exclusion

The politics of the Pagitt family are relatively simple compared to those in the household of Wessel Goodwin, a prosperous dyer in Southwark. Goodwin's tragic-comic story, the main focus of this essay, matches the most outlandish plots of Ben Jonson's city comedies. It also directs our attention to a less familiar dimension of domestic exclusion: the *trepan*, a

32 Bernard Capp

term newly in vogue in the mid-seventeenth century, used to describe a conspiracy to trap and cheat a victim, usually to extort money. Over almost a decade from the later 1640s, two scheming sisters devised a far more ambitious trepan, to rid themselves of their unwanted husbands, insinuate themselves into Goodwin's household, drive out his children, and seize possession of his business, money, and property. Their machinations were spelled out in detail in two pamphlets by Goodwin's son-in-law, Samuel Vernon.[13] The women repudiated his account, but did not respond in print. They preferred litigation, and launched a succession of mainly vexatious suits. Interventions by family members, the parish minister, separatist pastors, local magistrates, and even commissioners appointed by Oliver Cromwell, achieved almost nothing. The story ends with three husbands ejected, two of them ruined, Goodwin dead, and his children and grandchildren ousted and impoverished. Vernon entitled his second pamphlet *The Trepan*, and promised to reveal '*many notable devices Belonging to the Art of Trepanning*'.[14]

This is a story of multiple domestic exclusions, from both within and without. Wessel Goodwin was born about 1589, married a Leicestershire gentlewoman named Ellenor Armstrong, and had a daughter and three sons. By the time his wife died, early in 1648, he had built up a substantial business, judged 'one of the best Dyers trades in England', with a stock estimated at £2200. Ellenor had brought him a good portion, and was described as a pious, prudent, and faithful wife.[15] The marriage had been unhappy, however. The narrative refers to her melancholy, and the 'private unkindnesses with which she long strugled'. One unusual bone of contention was Goodwin's 'ravenous appetite' for music, especially lutes and lute-music. He had a room full of instruments that he was unable to play, and paid for expensive lessons that consisted mainly of listening to the tutor play. His enthusiasm became so obsessive that as his wife lay on her deathbed, she begged for the music to stop so that she could at least 'dye out of the noise of it'. Her request was ignored.[16]

This curious detail is relevant because the lute-teacher's wife was Mehetabel Jones, one of the scheming sisters. Her name is that of an obscure Old Testament figure (Genesis 36:39), and in Hebrew signifies 'God does good', which suggests a puritan family background. It was to prove singularly inappropriate. Like her husband, Mehetabel and her sister Elizabeth had frequented Goodwin's house. He had become infatuated with Mehetabel, and the sisters undermined his marriage by telling him that his wife failed to show him proper respect.[17] It was a large household. Goodwin's daughter Sarah, married to a tradesman named Samuel Vernon, lived in Bishopsgate, but his sons were still living at home, along with servants and apprentices. The eldest son, Andrew, married not long before his mother's death, and father and son established a business partnership. Andrew, as the better accountant, kept the books and the cash, and looked after the 'street business', leaving his

Domestic Exclusions 33

father to 'follow the trade within doors'. Initially all went well. But a few months after his wife's death, Goodwin declared that the house needed a guide, and announced that he had found a godly woman who would make him an excellent wife. This was Mehetabel, who, of course, was unfortunately already married. Goodwin had allegedly promised to marry her even before his wife's death.[18]

Mehetabel Jones, born in 1611, was the daughter of John Thorold (d.1628/9), a Lincolnshire gentleman, by his second marriage. She had married the music-teacher Edward Jones in London in 1634, and they lived with their children in Paul's Alley, off Redcross Street, near Cripplegate. Her sister Elizabeth shared their lodgings, along with her husband, John Pigeon, a lieutenant in Cromwell's own regiment. Another sister was married to a minister, Dr Francis Walsal, rector of Sandy, Bedfordshire; and yet another to a schoolmaster in Berkshire. Their brother Edward lived in Lincolnshire.[19] The sisters were outwardly models of piety. Mehetabel belonged to the Baptist congregation led by William Kiffin, while Elizabeth Pigeon was a member of Hanserd Knollys's Baptist church, which met for some time in Bishopsgate.[20] The narrative identifies Elizabeth as 'the great architect of all this villany', and supplies a character sketch worth quoting:

> She is one that can transforme her self into an Angell of light, and having her tongue tipt with Scripture, can with teares, sighes, gesture at command, set off what she would have believed, as Gospell, ... no sport to her like catching credulous persons with her faire Saint-like expressions, making sure prey of all that she can thus draw into her toyles; and so implacable, that when she hath once got an advantage, nothing shall satisfie her but the utmost rigour, which she will rise at midnight to prosecute.[21]

The narrative supplies a short account of Elizabeth's married life to illustrate her manipulative genius. She had persuaded her first husband, a prosperous apothecary, to make a will leaving her everything. Though he made another will on his deathbed, she had it nullified by claiming that he had died *non compos mentis*. She urged Pigeon to make a similar will, and when he refused, launched a campaign that provides the most comical element in this story. She allegedly plied him each day with viper wine (an aphrodisiac) 'compounded with provocative drugs', while refusing sexual relations. The strategy backfired by triggering a physical and mental collapse, but Pigeon eventually gave way, and 'made over to her all his estate, which was very great' in a trust. These events belong to the mid-1640s. Their marriage was always turbulent, and Elizabeth would sometimes desert him for several weeks or a month.[22] Not long after the establishment of the Commonwealth in 1649, she urged him to draw up and publish a declaration denouncing the new government.

34 Bernard Capp

For a serving officer, this would have been reckless, even treasonable, and the narrative suggests that it was a cynical device to ruin and be rid of him.[23] Whatever the truth, the marriage did not survive. Elizabeth persuaded her pastor, Hanserd Knollys, to draw up a bill of divorce (or more accurately, separation), and Pigeon was persuaded to sign it. They were briefly reconciled again, but Elizabeth then began a liaison with a merchant in Clapham. Pigeon was away on military service in Jersey in 1650, and when he returned, she accused him of having contracted the pox, and claimed to fear for her life. Knollys attempted to mediate again, without success, and told Pigeon that a separation would now be the best solution. Pigeon, indignant, ordered him to leave, whereupon Elizabeth shouted derisively, 'Mr Knowles, take him with you'. A brawl erupted. Knollys punched Pigeon in the face, Pigeon thrust him away, Knollys summoned 'many rude persons' to assist, and a general melee ensued. The narrative concedes that Pigeon had flown into a rage, and had left his wife with a 'strange black face'. She put her injury to good use. She and Knollys applied to Cromwell, now Lord General, and succeeded in having her husband court-martialled, cashiered, and briefly imprisoned. Henceforth the couple lived apart, and Pigeon left London.[24]

If Elizabeth Pigeon was to prove the driving force behind the Goodwin saga, Mehetabel had the starring role. Through her husband, the lutenist, she had become a close friend of Wessel Goodwin, and after his wife's death he became besotted. He visited her house almost every day, 'spending his time in dalliance with her', and gave her substantial sums of money. He bought clothes for her and her children and took them for trips by coach in the country, 'for whole weeks together'. One day Pigeon found them kissing and cuddling, and said in disgust that it was a bawdy-house, whereupon Elizabeth retorted that Goodwin was a suitor to Mehetabel, and that she would make it a match. 'Mr Jones', she added, 'was no longer her sisters husband before God, but had forfeited his right in her'. Though Jones was not a member of his church, Hanserd Knollys took it upon himself to draw up a bill of divorce, and delivered it to him as he was giving a lute-lesson at the Ram Inn in Smithfield. Jones, astonished, threatened to kick him down the stairs. When he returned home, Mrs Pigeon hurled abuse at him, whereupon he drove her out of the house, 'with kicks in the breech'. She took revenge by entering a lawsuit for £500 against him in her husband's name, but without his knowledge, and did not rest till he was lodged in the Counter. Her design was not only revenge, but to force Jones to set his hand to the bill of divorce, which he eventually did, 'or to something equivalent'. Mehetabel broke the news to Goodwin by 'throwing herself into his arms, saying, Mr Goodwin, Mr Jones and I am [sic] parted for ever, and you must keep me. The poore deluded old man being overjoyed, takes her in his armes, tells her, it was the best newes to him that ever came to towne, and that he would provide for her'.[25]

Domestic Exclusions 35

Jones was released, probably in return for accepting the divorce. It was agreed that Mehetabel would leave the house, with her husband keeping their five children and the household goods. Two weeks later, however, when he was out teaching pupils, she returned with her maid and stripped the house of all the linen and goods of value, leaving him 'with all his children in an empty house'. Jones was soon driven by Mehetabel to accept a new set of conditions. He made over his entire estate to her, through a trust, and moved to Norwich, 'stript of wife, children, estate' and with only the clothes on his back.[26]

The focus of the exclusion story now switches to the Goodwin family itself. It was said that Wessel Goodwin was at Mehetabel's house 'night and day', though 'all the towne rings of their scandalous converse'. Appeals and complaints from his children, neighbours, and the parish minister, William Cooper of St Olave's, Southwark, were all brushed aside.[27] The economic fallout from Goodwin's infatuation was also becoming apparent. He was seriously undermining the business by giving substantial sums of money to Mehetabel, throwing the business accounts into confusion. Mehetabel strengthened her position further by arranging a marriage between Goodwin's youngest son, James, a 'weak headed' schoolboy of seventeen, and one of her daughters, aged about fifteen. This created a formal bond between the two families, which provided her with legitimate grounds for being at Goodwin's house so often. The girl was so small that she looked no more than nine, which meant, Mehetabel explained, that 'she hath the more need of a guide'. The sisters both now moved into Goodwin's dye-house, 'bringing all their children and retinue with them', and began to use their position to turn him against his older children.[28]

The next part of the plan was to drive out Goodwin's eldest son, Andrew, his business partner. The sisters persuaded Goodwin to hire another accountant, who was allegedly bribed to undervalue the business and ruled that Andrew was entitled to only £150, blaming him for its decline. In November 1653, the sisters presented him with a note ordering him to quit the house within two weeks. He refused. So, a few days later, when he was out, they brought in a smith and directed him, in Wessel Goodwin's name, to break open the counting-house. They took away all the papers and money, and rifled the trunk in Andrew's chamber. And when the two weeks were up, they entered an action in Goodwin's name against his own son. Sergeants and bailiffs, summoned at 1 a.m., smashed their way into his chamber with a crowbar, and arrested him. All this was done at dead of night, the narrative explains, because otherwise the sisters 'might have been by the neighbours throwne into the ditch headlong'. Andrew countered with a legal move of his own but was outmanoeuvred by Elizabeth and her 'Secretary and fast friend', a scrivener named Henry Coleborn. The sisters now pressed for final victory. Wessel Goodwin was persuaded to confess a judgement

36   *Bernard Capp*

'for all that he hath in the world' to Coleborn, dubbed 'the man midwife' in these transactions. Mrs Pigeon thereupon turned Goodwin and his servants out of his house and took possession, before witnesses, of his entire estate 'for the use of Mr Henry Colborne formally, and for her self and Sister Jones virtually [i.e. in reality]'.[29] Goodwin had been stripped of his home and his business.

In the event, Goodwin was soon permitted to return, albeit now in the humble capacity of a journeyman to Henry Coleborn. Far from being distraught at this humiliation, the narrative reports, 'he proclaims to all comers that he had rather be Mrs Pigeons Journyman, then to be Master of all without his two women'. His sons and daughter were forbidden the house, except 'the young traitor James', who was firmly under the sisters' control.[30] The family fought back. They petitioned Southwark magistrates, and secured a hearing at which Goodwin was severely reprimanded and warned to 'forsake the scandalous company of these women'. But the proceedings were adjourned, and when they were resumed a week later several new justices attended. Justice Gold of Clapham (Elizabeth Pigeon's close friend) insisted that she was 'a most Angelical woman', and that 'the whole army of England should maintaine the reputation of these Gentlewomen'. Goodwin's family, told to produce their witnesses, explained that many were willing to testify, but wanted a direct summons, fearing retribution at the hands of 'these Litigious women'. Most of the witnesses lived near the sisters in Redcross Street, in the city, and as this lay outside the jurisdiction of the Southwark justices, the proceedings went no further.[31] The churches proved similarly impotent. After several warnings, the sisters were expelled from their Baptist congregations. Goodwin was admonished by William Cooper, minister of St Olave's, and the parish Elders, and eventually barred from the sacrament. None of this had any effect.[32]

The pamphlet did not identify its author, printer or publisher, testimony to the fear the litigious sisters had aroused. The author was later revealed as Samuel Vernon, Goodwin's son-in-law and the sisters' most determined adversary. Lacking the sisters' own version of events, we have to read Vernon's pamphlet against the grain to explore how they might have explained and justified their behaviour. The pamphlet never suggested that Wessel Goodwin had been coerced into any of his actions. And while the family called him 'deluded' and a 'pittifull weak man', it did not claim he was senile or mad. The narrative accepts that the business was in serious decline, though it insists that Wessel was mainly responsible, not his son. It concedes, however, that Andrew was so demoralised by his wife's death and his father's irresponsible behaviour that he 'gave up himselfe to melancholly and carelesse stupidity, [and] that he let his bookes run into some disorder'.[33]

John Pigeon had clearly cooperated in compiling the printed narrative, in which his wife appears as the villainous mastermind and he as her

Domestic Exclusions 37

innocent victim. But for some time, he had gone along with her designs, and had even drawn up one of the wills that Wessel Goodwin had been persuaded to sign.[34] Vernon calls him 'cholerick' by nature, and he was certainly no stranger to violence. The brawl at his lodgings had seen him fly into a blind rage. On another occasion, when the sisters and Goodwin were celebrating having rid Mehetabel of her husband, Pigeon had responded with 'blowes to correct their folly, and thrust them all down staires headlong'. And when Goodwin was assaulted and 'grievously beaten' one night on his way home, most people suspected that Pigeon or Edward Jones was responsible. Goodwin, embarrassed, pretended that he had been trampled by a horse.[35] As for Jones, we know that he had kicked Mrs Pigeon out of the house, literally, if under extreme provocation. His wife later claimed that he had 'committed folly' with other women, a charge the narrative brushes aside as a lie to cover her own scandalous relationship.[36]

The bookseller George Thomason acquired his copy of the *Narrative* on 9 December 1654.[37] It was not the first edition, and the original may have appeared at the end of 1653. An appendix explains that the sisters had exploited the anonymity of the tract to claim that 'all is lies and slanders'. In rebuttal, the text now supplied the names and addresses of witnesses ready to substantiate all the allegations.[38] The author also took the opportunity to update Mehetabel's story. Around Christmas 1653, Edward Jones had returned to London, despite his wife's vow to have him gaoled should he ever do so. While he was with his children, the sisters sent to enter an action against him for £400 in the name of a Mr Mountague, a schoolmaster in Berkshire. Jones was arrested as he left the house, and carried away to the Wood Street Counter. The next day, Mrs Pigeon went to the Counter and entered four more actions against him, in the name of several parties, to the value of £1000. All these actions appear to have been wholly vexatious, and the latter four were soon dropped. Mountague, who was married to another of the sisters, probably knew nothing of the suit entered in his name until Mehetabel asked him to own it. When it came to trial in February 1654, Elizabeth's counsel told her it would certainly fail. But they concocted a new claim, that some years earlier Mountague had maintained Mehetabel and her children, because Jones had run away and left them destitute. Swearing on oath to this story, Mrs Pigeon secured a verdict for Jones to pay Mountague £60. Having no such funds at his disposal, he remained in prison where, the narrative ends gloomily, he would probably die.[39]

The Goodwins: The Sequel

The second pamphlet, *The Trepan*, appeared in 1656, also anonymously. Thomason dated his copy 20 July. Another edition later the same year

38   Bernard Capp

carried Samuel Vernon's name, and reported that the sisters were now Quakers. One disgusted reader, perhaps a Quaker, scrawled a note on his copy that they had not been Quakers when they committed their cheats, 'whatsoever they are now'.[40]

The Trepan provided a résumé of the story, and brought readers up to date on subsequent developments. The sisters had intimidated Andrew by entering a suit against him for £1000, letting it hang fire, and shifting between friendliness and abuse in their dealings with him. Wessel Goodwin had been left to run the business as a mere hired hand. Mrs Pigeon had returned to her lodgings near Redcross Street, partly to escape abuse from the neighbours in Southwark, returning occasionally in a hackney to check on the business. Mehetabel, also back in Redcross Street, had allegedly begun to fear she had been used by her sister 'only as a bait to catch old Mr Goodwin, whilst Mistress Pigeon caught the estate'. When Goodwin visited them, he was greeted now with sharp words instead of endearments.[41] Henry Coleborn, Mrs Pigeon's ally, and the trustee of both Goodwin's and Pigeon's estates, had fallen sick and died. She had dealt with this setback by summoning her brother Edward Thorold from Lincolnshire and persuading the dying Coleborn to assign both trusts to this 'shallowe harmless creature'.[42] Soon afterwards, John Pigeon had reappeared after an absence of four years, 'like one from another world'. Moved by the cries of Goodwin's children against his wife, the narrative reports, he had resolved to try once more to 'yoke this untamed Heifer'. One day he appeared outside her house with a coach, four horses and half a dozen servants, 'and having sufficient authority, enters this Dragons den'. Seizing his wife, he carried her away to his house in the country, 'all the street looking on, and rejoycing at the riddance'. The nature of his 'authority' is unclear, but predictably Elizabeth spurned his suggestion of reconciliation. A justice thereupon drew up a new deed of separation, which restored Pigeon's lands, and £500 in money, and left Elizabeth free to return to London and live apart.[43] It was a significant success for Pigeon, though the narrative does not present it as such.

Goodwin's children sought a different remedy, by petitioning Cromwell, now Lord Protector. He appointed a small body of commissioners to investigate, made up of Southwark magistrates and the minister of St Olave's. They questioned Goodwin, the sisters, and other parties, and established that the facts were much as alleged. Wessel Goodwin fell ill early in the proceedings, and died on 31 December 1655. His death triggered a bizarre new clash, over responsibility for the burial. Though Goodwin left not a penny, for all was now in Mrs Pigeon's hands, his children agreed to take charge of the arrangements. But Sarah Vernon, his daughter, declared that 'If we bury him, we will know how he came by his death', and demanded an autopsy. The family suspected that the sisters had hastened his death lest he should inadvertently reveal their secrets to the commissioners, as had happened on the first day. Mrs Pigeon refused to allow them access to the body, ignoring a magistrate's order, and had the two elder sons arrested for trespassing on the dye-house. With the body already nailed in its coffin, there was deadlock over when or how a burial could take place. But when the doctors ruled that it was now too late for an autopsy, Mrs Pigeon reversed her stance and decided on an elaborate funeral, to convince the neighbourhood that she had nothing to hide. She invited all the chief inhabitants of Southwark, including the commissioners, and promised to distribute seventy or eighty gold rings. In the event, only one of the commissioners attended, Samuel Highland, a separatist pastor as well as justice. Goodwin's family refused to take part, though they attended the body at the grave. It arrived by coach with Mrs Pigeon, along with a prominent city attorney named John Hat, allegedly there to 'awe the people'. It was a necessary precaution, for she had been mobbed and abused in the street on several occasions. Even so, onlookers hurled abuse and 'kennel-dirt'. Had Goodwin's children lifted a finger, the author claimed, she might well have been lynched. Mehetabel remained at the dye-house, not venturing to attend. Had she appeared, it was said, she might have been 'sent to gage the depth of the mud in the mill-pond'.[44]

The commissioners then resumed their investigation. John Hat's 'Guild-hall Rethorike' proved to no avail, and the commissioners found the complaints justified. They proposed a composition: Elizabeth Pigeon would restore the estate to the Goodwin family, with an account of all her receipts and outgoings. Her charges would be covered, and she would be awarded £100. She rejected the proposal with scorn, insisting that the estate was legally hers. The commissioners thereupon submitted their report to Cromwell. The text, reproduced in Vernon's pamphlet, affirmed the existence of a marriage contract between Goodwin and Mehetabel, and condemned the sisters in forthright terms. It recommended that 'something exemplarily penal be inflicted upon these Women', to deter others, and noted that the petitioners were destitute and in no condition to 'wage Law'.[45] *The Trepan* also published an attestation from William Kiffin's church, describing its dealings with Mehetabel. She had responded to admonitions with a mixture of tearful contrition, deceit, and defiance, claiming that several 'learned Divines' had assured her that she was freed from 'her first Husband by the Law of God'. Her obstinacy and 'Scandalous Conversation' had discredited the church, and it had eventually expelled her.[46]

On 14 March 1656, Cromwell referred the report to the Privy Council, expressing his 'high resentment' over the affair. There it lay for several weeks. But on 29 April, the Council decided to take no further action and leave the Goodwins to pursue their case through the courts. Lacking the funds to do so, they appealed plaintively 'to the Great Judge of Heaven and Earth'.[47]

40 *Bernard Capp*

There the story ends. But the pamphlet also reproduces a dozen letters found in Goodwin's study after his death, mostly from Mehetabel, along with several locks of her hair. One letter, written for Goodwin to copy and send in his own name, damned his children and excluded them from all business decisions. The first letter was from the women's elder sister Lydia, wife of the Bedfordshire minister, in which she addressed Goodwin as 'brother' [-in-law], implying that the family recognised him and Mehetabel as husband and wife. Whenever Goodwin was asked whether he was married or contracted to Mehetabel, he gave evasive answers, though he had admitted it to Edward Jones.[48] The pamphlet also prints some verses that Mehetabel had sent Goodwin. Even religious verse by early Baptist women is rare; humorous verse is surely unique. In one rhyming verse Mehetabel returns thanks for his gift of a bottle of 'Sage-Ale' and blames the modest quality of her lines on its effects. Another verse had accompanied a bracelet she had sent Goodwin. 'Many other parcels of her venerious Poetry I finde', Vernon added sternly, 'but being hob-nayl tattered stuffe I omit'. Mehetabel's verses, dismissed sarcastically as 'inchanting Madrigals' or 'Ribaldry Rhymes', add a startling new dimension to early Baptist history.[49] So does the sisters' enjoyment of drink. We hear of Mehetabel making 'pye-ale' for Goodwin, while Vernon referred to the sisters 'revelling with their Sage-ale, and Marmalade'.[50] Elizabeth Pigeon, for her part, had allegedly called for 'a filthy bawdy song' at a gathering in Islington.[51] The second edition of *The Trepan* includes a postscript addressed to John Hat, the lawyer, asking how he will defend himself when he appears before God's tribunal. Another postscript, mysteriously in Spanish, is addressed to 'Sennor Juan Gold', and marvels that a man of his understanding could be deceived by two such diabolical women. Was John Gold, the magistrate who had defended 'Angelical' Mrs Pigeon at the Southwark inquiry, perhaps a merchant trading with Spain? Might this have been an attempt to undermine his business reputation?[52]

Jacobean city comedies generally end with the wrongdoers exposed and punished, and order restored. This story, by contrast, ended with the adventurers largely victorious. Vernon commented ruefully that it exemplified 'the sublime Art of Trepanning, to gull a man of an Estate of 2000*l*' and fool him into being grateful.[53] His family had been ruined, Elizabeth Pigeon remained in possession of the dye-house, and Edward Jones had lost his wife, children, and property. Why the Privy Council declined to act remains unclear. Perhaps it noted that the sisters still had some champions, such as Hat and Gold, and that Samuel Highland had refused to sign the Report. He found the fraud proved, but questioned the allegations of sexual promiscuity.[54] What emerges most clearly is the sisters' ability to manipulate Goodwin and outmanoeuvre their opponents, including their unwanted husbands, and their skill in waging law. The Southwark magistrates achieved little, partly because they had no authority within the

Domestic Exclusions 41

city, where the sisters and most of the witnesses lived. The narrative also underlines the deeply unsettled state of marriage following the Civil War. The church courts had disappeared, and the legal situation sank into confusion after 1653, in the wake of the Act prohibiting church marriage.[55] The local churches proved as ineffective as the local magistrates, lacking any disciplinary powers beyond suspension and expulsion. Hanserd Knollys, one of the foremost separatist leaders of the time, appears in a less than flattering light. Despite having no legal authority, he had taken it upon himself to pen divorce bills for both sisters, one of whom did not even belong to his congregation.

This essay has underlined the multiple contexts of domestic exclusion, the variety of forms it could take, and the range of actors potentially involved. Exclusion was not restricted to angry parents or warring spouses. In the case of Justinian Pagitt, a stepmother stood accused of surreptitiously excluding her husband from the government of the household, and trying to exclude Pagitt from his father's affections and from the house itself. The extraordinary story of Wessel Goodwin shows family members excluded from their own home and business by manipulative outsiders, scheming sisters who also contrived to rid themselves of their unwanted husbands. Contemporaries relished stories of trickery and fraud, staple fare of jestbooks and city comedies alike. At the same time, they deplored the disruption and breakdown of family order, especially at the hand of outsiders. The Goodwin pamphlets read today like a Jonsonian city comedy, but for most of those involved, they were a chronicle of ruined lives. Domestic exclusion was a sobering reminder of the fragility of family structures in early modern England.

Notes

1 Felicity Heal and Clive Holmes, *The Gentry in England and Wales 1500–1700* (Basingstoke: Macmillan, 1994), 81–3; and Bernard Capp, *The Ties that Bind. Siblings, Family and Society in Early Modern England* (Oxford: Oxford University Press, 2018), 8–9, 22, 24, 26–7, 125.

2 Russell Mortimer (ed.), *Minute Book of the Men's Meeting of the Society of Friends in Bristol 1667–1686*, Bristol Record Society, 26 (1971), 6, 7, 8–10, 14.

3 Claire Cross (ed.), *The Letters of Sir Francis Hastings 1574–1609*, Sussex Record Society, 69 (1969), 44–5.

4 Laura Gowing, *Domestic Dangers* (Oxford: Oxford University Press, 1996); Frances Dolan, *Dangerous Familiars. Representations of Domestic Crime in England 1550–1700* (Ithaca, NY: Cornell University Press, 1994); Bernard Capp, *When Gossips Meet* (Oxford: Oxford University Press, 2003); and Joanne Bailey, *Unquiet Lives. Marriage and Marriage Breakdown in England, 1660–1800* (Cambridge: Cambridge University Press, 2003).

5 S.R. Gardiner (ed.), *Reports of Cases in the Court of Star Chamber and High Commission*, Camden Society, NS, 39 (1886), 265–8.

6 Capp, *When Gossips Meet*, 92.

42 Bernard Capp

7 Stephen Collins, 'British Stepfather Relationships, 1500–1800', *Journal of Family History*, 16 (1991); William Gouge, *Of Domesticall Duties* (1622), 580–2.

8 Heal and Holmes, *Gentry*, 83–4; Capp, *Ties*, 90–110.

9 The National Archives, SP 16/378, f.19; cf. Heal and Holmes, *Gentry*, 74, 85.

10 Capp, *Ties*, 102, 105–6.

11 Oliver Heywood, *Autobiography, Diaries, Anecdote and Event Books* (4 vols, Brighouse and Bingley, 1881–1885), iii.192.

12 The following discussion is based on BL, Harleian MS 1026, fos. 77–82. See the entry for 'Justinian Pagitt (1611/12–1668), Lawyer and Diarist', in *The Oxford Dictionary of National Biography (ODNB)* (Oxford, 2004) https://doi.org/10.1093/ref:odnb/66665.

13 [Samuel Vernon], *A Brief Relation of the Strange and Unnatural Practices of Wessel Goodwin* [and others] (London, 1654); Samuel Vernon, *The Trepan: Being a True Relation. Full of Stupendious Variety, of the Strange Practises of Mehetabel the Wife of Edward Jones, and Elizabeth Wife of Lieutenant John Pigeon* (London, 1656).

14 Vernon, *Trepan*, title page.

15 *Brief Relation,* 1–3, 24.

16 Ibid., 1–2.

17 Ibid., 3; *Trepan, sig.* A2v–3.

18 *Brief Relation*, 3. Andrew married Marie Tarleton on 20 January 1647/8: W.H. Challen, 'Transcription of the Marriages at St. Olave, Southwark, 1583–1755' (Typescript, 1927, in the British Library), 112. His mother's death, stated as 1647, must therefore have been in 1647/8.

19 A.R. Maddison (ed.), *Lincolnshire Pedigrees*, Harleian Society, 50–2 (4 vols, 1902–1904), iii. 985; J.L. Chester (ed.), *Allegations for Marriage Licences Issued by the Bishop of London 1611 to 1828*, Harleian Society, 26 (1887), 215; *Brief Relation*, 32–3; *Trepan*, 8, 20–1. Elizabeth and Pigeon were married by the prominent Independent Nathaniel Homes, whom she later dismissed as 'a knave': *Trepan*, 9.

20 *Brief Relation*, 4. See the entries for 'William Kiffin (1616–1701), Particular Baptist Minister and Author' and Hanserd Knollys (1598–1691), Particular Baptist Minister and Author' in *ODNB* https://doi.org/10.1093/odnb/9780192683120.013.15521 and https://doi.org/10.1093/ref:odnb/15756.

21 *Brief Relation*, 4; *Trepan*, 31–5.

22 *Brief Relation*, 4–6, 15.

23 Ibid., 16; cf. *Trepan*, 9.

24 *Brief Relation*, 15–18; *Trepan, sig.* A3v.

25 *Brief Relation*, 6–8, 12.

26 Ibid., 7, 9–11, an account modified in *Trepan*, 2–3.

27 *Brief Relation*, 12–13.

28 Ibid., 12, 18–19.

29 Ibid., 19–22, 25; *Trepan, sig.* A4–v.

30 *Brief Relation*, 22.

31 Ibid., 22–3.

32 Ibid., 12, 23; *Trepan*, 15, 18–19, 24.

33 *Brief Relation*, 12, 19–20.

34 *Trepan, sig.* A3; for his other wills see *Brief Relation*, 10, 19; *Trepan*, 29.

35 *Brief Relation*, 8–9, 17–18; *Trepan*, 33.

36 *Brief Relation*, 7, 10.

37 Wing B4636; BL, E818(19).

Domestic Exclusions 43

38 *Brief Relation*, 31.
39 Ibid., 28, 31–3.
40 BL, E884 (1), Wing V253B; BL, shelfmark 1419.c.30, Wing V254.
41 *Trepan*, 6–7.
42 Ibid., 7–8.
43 Ibid., 8–9.
44 Ibid., 9–14; see entry for 'Samuel Hyland [Highland] (fl. 1638–1663), Distiller and Political Activist', in *ODNB* https://doi.org/10.1093/ref:odnb/107135.
45 *Trepan*, 14–17. The report was signed by Christopher Searle, William Cooper, Cornelius Cook, and John Hardwick. Cook and Hardwick were Surrey justices, and the three laymen served on numerous militia and assessment committees.
46 Ibid., 18–19. It was signed by George Gosfright, William Warren, Kiffin, William Angel, John Sowdin, and John Battey. Angel, Sowdin and Warren (the navy contractor) served on militia committees in 1659.
47 Ibid., 17, 19; *Calendar of State Papers, Domestic, 1655–1656*, 301.
48 *Trepan*, 20–1, 26; *Brief Relation*, 10.
49 *Trepan*, 30–1.
50 *Brief Relation*, 11, 13, 30.
51 *Trepan*, 33–4.
52 Ibid., 33–8.
53 Ibid., 28.
54 Ibid., 19.
55 Christopher Durston, *The Family in the English Revolution* (Oxford: Basil Blackwell, 1989), chapter 4; Bernard Capp, *England's Culture Wars. Puritanism and Reformation and its Enemies in the Interregnum, 1649–1660* (Oxford: Oxford University Press, 2012), 28, 31, 147–9.

2 The Language of Exclusion
'Bastard' in Early Modern England

Kate Gibson

[I]n the house of one Samuel Scholsy ... in Skeldersgate in the Cityy of Yorke, [I] then and there heard the [plaintiff] John Avyard and Christopher Wright d[efendan]t in the same rooms at very high language one with thother and amongst other words this [witness] well remembers that ... Christopher Wright called ... John Avyard Rogue bastardly rogue and bastard ... Christopher Wright swore with much anger and passion.[1]

I dined today at the Chaplains table, St. James's, with Dr. Gretton. The Company consisted of a Mr. Turner of Lincolnshire, – Mr Williams who married a natural daugr of Lord Pembroke, – the Revd. Mr. Freind, nephew to the Primate of Ireland, Mr. Walton.[2]

These extracts illustrate variations in the language used to refer to individuals born outside of marriage in early modern England, and differences in the meaning and intent of such language depending on the context.[3] In the first extract, Christopher Wright sought to slander John Avyard by using the word 'bastard' as an insult, emphasising his illegitimacy to cast doubt on his worth in the community. In the second, the society artist Joseph Farington included the word 'natural' as a pertinent aspect of Mrs Williams' social identity, alongside geographical origin and kinship. Although Mrs Williams's attribution as a 'natural daugr of Lord Pembroke' appears more benign than Wright's description of Avyard as a bastard, this was not necessarily the case. This was because it identified Mrs Williams as belonging to a birth category that was legally and socially disadvantaged throughout the early modern period.

This chapter argues that language provides significant evidence of the perception of illegitimate individuals and their position in seventeenth- and eighteenth-century English society. It suggests that stigmatisation and exclusion was part of the illegitimate experience, but in more nuanced ways than scholars have previously acknowledged.[4] Indeed, the precise term used, whether bastard, illegitimate, or natural – to give only three synonyms in contemporary usage – conveyed a particular moral judgement and differentiated one type of illegitimacy from another. Analysis of the language used in printed texts, correspondence, life-writing, and defamation cases, shows that descriptors varied according to socio-economic status and type of parental relationship. Changes in language use also suggest that by the end of the eighteenth century, bastard had become a pejorative term used to describe primarily the poor, or children whose parents' relationship was considered particularly immoral. In contrast, middling and elite children were generally referred to as natural, a word with much more positive associations.

Language is a crucial way of marking someone out as different. Words can express enmity through the language of insult, and labels can signify a person's position as an outsider in a given community. Sociologists have argued that the connotations of particular 'stigma terms' are used to associate a person with undesirable characteristics and therefore create a rationale to facilitate exclusion.[5] According to sociologists Bruce Link and Jo Phelan, labelling allows 'the identification of difference, the construction of stereotypes, ... [and] the separation of labeled persons into distinct categories'.[6] Social and cultural historians have provided evidence of this process at work in early modern England, where linguistic labels were integral to how contemporaries expressed moral judgement and thought about social categories such as socio-economic status and gender.[7] Robert Jütte's work on poverty, for example, suggests that language was an evaluative tool through which contemporaries expressed gradations in their perceptions of different types of poverty.[8] Historians of gender and sexuality have also found that language conveyed moral attitudes. Multiple studies of defamation have shown that language was a powerful tool in policing socially disruptive sexual behaviour.[9] In his research on the language of adultery, David Turner argues that such language became increasingly socially specific over the eighteenth century, with words such as 'whore' becoming associated with poverty and street-walking, and as a violation of politeness rather than religious sin.[10] This chapter suggests that the language of illegitimacy underwent a similar shift in this period, as certain words became more associated with poverty. Although morality remained important, particularly in judgements of parental promiscuity, it became more closely connected with socio-economic status. Word choice was dictated, in part, by a sense that certain words were no longer appropriate for use in polite society. This chapter is, therefore, part of a growing historiography that points to much wider changes in how language was used to police morality in the burgeoning culture of politeness in eighteenth-century England.[11]

Existing research on the stigma of early modern illegitimacy has not considered the significance of language in any depth.[12] Richard Adair, in his leading study on this subject, concedes only that 'without any doubt some level of stigma existed' due to 'the long and ubiquitous persistence of the term "bastard" as a term of abuse', but he does not interrogate how frequently bastard was employed in everyday usage.[13]

46 Kate Gibson

I argue here that the existence of bastard as a pejorative should not be taken as straightforward evidence of blanket stigmatisation. This is because it was only one of many synonyms for illegitimacy, including natural or base-born – which frequently appear in parish registers – as well as multiple colloquial terms, such as merry-begotten or chance child, that often feature in popular literature and ego-documents.[14] This chapter explores the purpose of this wide vocabulary of illegitimacy and the mechanisms that governed the choice of employing one word over another. Critical language analysis of printed texts, life-writing, correspondence, and defamation cases provides new evidence for the everyday operation of stigma across the lifecycle of illegitimate individuals and allows for comparison of experience according to gender and socio-economic status.

In using such a variety of sources, not generally utilised in the existing scholarship on illegitimacy, this chapter will explore the contexts in which it mattered, and how language choice varied according to author, purpose, and audience. For the most part, historians have measured the stigma of illegitimacy through the levels of community support provided for unmarried mothers, as documented in poor law or Foundling Hospital records.[15] These sources tend to emphasise illegitimacy as a facet of poverty, focus only on a child's early life, and produce a picture of shame as imposed by church or state. By examining and comparing the language used in multiple source types we can get a much deeper understanding of how the stigma of illegitimacy worked as a social practice between individuals, as well as a disadvantage imposed by the law. Sources such as correspondence or life-writing provide an indication of language use in everyday life, in situations largely outside of or tangential to official record-keeping, and in relation to a much broader range of individuals from different social classes. In addition, the language of defamation indicates the reputational impact of illegitimate status. Although much scholarship has considered the defamation used against unmarried parents, it remains unclear how far insults directed towards illegitimate children fitted into wider patterns of slander.[16] For example, bastard does not work in the same way as other common insults such as 'thief' or 'whore' as it is an involuntary state unconnected to an individual's past actions. Yet, as we shall see, it was prosecuted as an insult in certain circumstances. The ways in which language was used to identify and 'other' illegitimate individuals provides crucial evidence of early modern attitudes towards sexual transgression and social difference.

Labels were particularly important to the identification and categorisation of illegitimate individuals because illegitimacy was a slippery concept that depended on subjective social and cultural categorisation to function as a means of exclusion. As a legal category, illegitimacy could vary according to definitions of marriage. As a social category, it relied on community perceptions of the longevity, propriety, and relative

The Language of Exclusion 47

sinfulness of the parental relationship. The particular word used to describe an individual's illegitimacy was therefore crucial in assigning illegitimate status and communicating the particular circumstances of their birth. Illegitimate individuals were excluded from communities through laws that decreed they had no legal father, no right to inherit property, and no claim to parish settlement by virtue of their familial relationships.[17] Illegitimacy was associated not only with moral transgression but also economic dependence, and was consequently a matter of concern for the whole community.[18] The labelling of someone as illegitimate was thus significant because it was associated with loss of social and legal status.

The first part of the chapter considers the range of synonyms for illegitimacy in use in early modern England, as well as the legal background of these terms, and their connotations in printed texts, such as dictionaries, which informed their everyday application. The discussion then examines the various social uses of the terms used to describe illegitimacy in twenty-one life-writing and correspondence collections produced between 1660 and 1830. The final part of the chapter examines defamation cases heard in the York church courts between 1660 and 1834, available in the York Cause Papers Database.[19] The cases have been previously used in studies of the defamation of unmarried parents, but the experience of illegitimate individuals has not been considered.[20] The words chosen, and their perceived impact, provides crucial evidence of the extent to which illegitimacy was considered damaging to reputation.

The Vocabulary of Illegitimacy

A wide vocabulary of illegitimacy existed in early modern England, originating from a legal need to categorise individuals according to birth circumstances. Classical and medieval texts used a range of Greek, Roman, and Hebrew terms to denote separate classes of illegitimacy, including female adultery (*nothus*), prostitution (*mamzer*), or concubinage (*naturales*). Although precise definitions fluctuated, these multiple categories were usually conflated into two: children whose parents' relationship involved unconcealed casual fornication and violated civil or religious law, such as adultery, incest, or rape (*spurious*); or children whose parents could have married each other, including those who engaged in pre-marital sex or were in long-term unmarried cohabitation (*naturales*).[21] These distinctions reflected ecclesiastical concerns over the relative sinfulness of certain types of relationship but were also practically necessary in Roman and canon law, under which a child could be legitimated if their parents later married.

Following the Reformation, canon law was rejected in favour of English common law, under which children could not be legitimated by later parental marriage.[22] With the absence of any legal need to

48   *Kate Gibson*

differentiate between types of illegitimacy, common law simply distinguished legitimate from illegitimate and the terminology consequently lost its specificity; bastard, a term that only emerged in the eleventh century, became the most common synonym.[23] The legal theorist Sir William Blackstone stated in his *Commentaries on the Laws of England* (1765) that 'Children are of two sorts; legitimate, and spurious, or bastards'. Blackstone used spurious as a synonym of bastard, not as a separate legal category, and throughout his text used illegitimate, spurious, and bastard interchangeably.[24] John Brydall's *Lex Spurorium* (1703), a legal text with a secondary moral motive to 'deter Men and Women from ever pursuing unlawful and exorbitant Embraces', adopted similar terminology.[25] Although Brydall was clearly familiar with Latin texts, quoting the same definitions of spurious and naturales used by classical authors, like Blackstone, he used bastard as an umbrella term, identifying *nothus* as one of 'The several sorts of Bastards', and stating that 'in the Common Law, are all termed by the Name of *Bastards*'.[26]

Bastard also appeared as the preferred term for illegitimacy in legislation from the seventeenth century onwards. Elite divorce acts and the poor laws, the two primary types of illegitimacy legislation in this period, both described the children of elite adultery as 'Bastards, and spurious Issue', and referred to the pauper 'putative Fathers of Bastard Children'.[27] In legal contexts, the socio-economic status of the parents did not alter the terminology employed. By the early eighteenth century, bastard had become the dominant legal term in England, creating a binary definition between legitimate and illegitimate, and obscuring the nuances of the original Roman categories. This partly reflected the legal reality that all children born outside of marriage were subject to the same legal disadvantages.[28]

However, examples from non-legal texts suggest that the use of bastard as a catch-all term to express the binary definition of legitimate versus illegitimate was not reflected in other contexts, particularly as the eighteenth century progressed. In seventeenth-century religious texts such as the King James Bible, bastard was the word of choice. The two most quoted biblical passages that made reference to illegitimate children were Deuteronomy 23:2 and Solomon 4:3, both of which made their exclusion explicit by deploying the word bastard. Deuteronomy, for example, stated that 'A bastard shall not enter into the congregation of the Lord', whilst the Wisdom of Solomon described how 'the multiplying brood of the ungodly shall not thrive, nor take deepe rooting from bastard slips'.[29] However, in eighteenth-century biblical commentaries and translations, bastard was often reserved as a term to describe the children resulting from the most transgressive sexual relationships. Presbyterian minister Matthew Henry stated that the label of bastard did not apply to 'all that were born of Fornication, or out of Marriage', but rather to 'all that were of those *incestuous* mixtures which are forbidden

The Language of Exclusion   49

... *unlawful Marriages*, and *unlawful Lusts*'.[30] The word bastard, in Henry's view, therefore referred not to children born to two single people, but to the children of incest, adultery, or prostitution. This distinction was not denominationally specific, appearing in Anglican, Dissenting, and Catholic texts. The Anglican Methodist John Wesley, for example, referred to a '*Son of a harlot* – That is, a bastard', whilst the version of Deuteronomy in the Catholic Rheims-Douai and Challoner Bibles substituted bastard for 'mamzer, that is to say, one borne of a common woman'.[31] As Naomi Tadmor argues, eighteenth-century Bible translators deliberately chose words familiar to their readers, 'that made sense to people at that time and invoked certain notions and ideas'.[32] This suggests that writers chose the word bastard to accompany religious mandates for the exclusion and sinfulness of illegitimate children because it was understood to primarily mean those born in the most transgressive of circumstances. This implies a more sympathetic attitude towards the children of parents who later married or had previously good reputations. Yet, this also meant that when bastard was used, its pejorative links with the additional sins of adultery and incest were often emphasised.

Published reference works outside of ecclesiastical and legal texts also used bastard as if it had further pejorative connotations beyond simply denoting someone born outside of marriage. Eighteenth-century dictionaries grouped bastard with its closest synonyms base-born and spurious, alongside other pejorative words conveying poor moral standards. Lexicographers defined base as 'mean; vile ... disingenuous; illiberal; ungenerous', and bastard as something corrupted, polluted, or counterfeit. To bastardize was 'to adulterate ... marr, spoil'.[33] Similar definitions were given to the word 'adulterine', defined by Nathan Bailey as 'Forged, counterfeited, sophisticated; also bastardly', implying that a bastard was a child not born simply to unmarried parents, but to adulterous ones.[34] This meaning is evidenced in the broad application of bastard in printed books and newspapers to describe adulterated or inferior versions of concepts or objects, such as 'bastard sugar', 'bastard r[h]ubarb', or 'bastard pleurisy', all of which closely and dangerously resembled their legitimate counterparts.[35] The anatomist Thomas Bartholin likewise used the language of illegitimacy to differentiate 'true ribs' from '*bastard Ribs* ... so called ... because they are lesser, softer, shorter'.[36] The existence of this transferable meaning of bastard suggests that the labelling of a child in this way conveyed inferiority and lesser value. It also implied that the parental relationship was one of deception: a form of fakery connected to the fear of imposter heirs and doubtful paternity.[37] This meaning was made explicit in Thomas Blount's *Glossographia* (1656), a key text that influenced many later lexicographers. Here, spurious was defined as: 'born of a common woman, that knows not his Father, base-born, counterfeit'.[38] The label spurious

50   *Kate Gibson*

and its synonyms base-born and bastard therefore alluded to illegitimacy in its most negative aspects, to mean children born to promiscuous or adulterous women who were unsure of their child's paternity.

Aside from bastard, and its closest synonyms, the other most commonly used word for illegitimacy was natural.[39] Its association with illegitimacy likely derived from the Roman legal term *naturales*: a child born to parents who were eligible to marry and who therefore had the potential to become legitimate under Roman (not English) law.[40] Under the Roman definition these children were not the products of adultery or prostitution, but of long-term, quasi-marital relationships considered as 'special' or 'induced by pure affection'.[41] The range of secondary meanings attached to the word natural in the early modern period indicates that this positive emotional association continued. John Ash's *New and Complete Dictionary of the English Language* (1775) defined natural as: 'beloved by nature ... tender, affectionate in temper; unaffected, easy; illegitimate, base born'.[42] Samuel Johnson also noted in his *Dictionary* its association with affection alongside notions of genuineness: 'unaffected; according to truth and reality'.[43] This was strikingly different from the association of bastard with falseness.

At the same time, natural also carried a secondary biological meaning referring to the genitals, or 'natural parts', and inherited attributes. Philosophers such as John Locke and Jean-Jacques Rousseau also closely associated the word natural with an idealised, virtuous state of human existence that stood in opposition to the corruption and artifice of civilisation.[44] A natural child was therefore a child of the body rather than of man-made legal marriage, conveying a message of known paternity and omitting all suggestion of sin or diminished value. Evidence from early modern printed texts thus clearly indicates that although there was a legal binary of illegitimate and legitimate, which could be conveyed through the word bastard, a wider vocabulary was adopted in non-legal texts to express gradation in the relative sinfulness, longevity, and affection of the parental relationship, as well as the inferior status of the child, and the certainty of paternity. The continued usage of this wide vocabulary of illegitimacy suggests that, in social practice, illegitimate children were perceived and treated differently according to their specific parental background.

The Experience of Illegitimacy

Seventeenth- and eighteenth-century life-writing and correspondence contained multiple references to illegitimate individuals. Authors from a range of socio-economic, religious, and occupational backgrounds often explicitly identified those born outside marriage, displaying considerable knowledge of parental relationship histories. Identification occurred through labels – single adjectives or nouns such as bastard or natural – or

The Language of Exclusion 51

by providing context, such as explicitly noting that parents were not married. As I have shown elsewhere, illegitimacy was considered integral to an individual's identity and often specifically mentioned alongside age or occupation.[45] However, the precise wording varied considerably according to the relative socio-economic status of the author and subject, and the type of parental relationship. Moreover, socio-economic status became increasingly significant in determining language choice over the eighteenth century.

The twenty-one diaries and correspondence collections examined here were drawn from across the social scale. Ten collections were written by authors from the peerage, gentry, and metropolitan elite, including gentleman Horace Walpole and noblewoman Lady Mary Wortley Montagu. Three authors were part of the provincial middling sort, such as the yeoman Richard Gough and excise officer John Cannon. A further three writers, including mill mechanic Benjamin Shaw, occupied the porous boundary between skilled lower-middling and labouring groups. The source base also includes five collections of pauper letters from Essex, eight hundred letters in total, that provide the perspectives of overseers and unmarried parents claiming relief. Sources written by individuals from across the social spectrum have been selected for analysis, because socio-economic status had such an impact on how illegitimate children were treated. Under the poor law, the illegitimate children of poor parents were subject to community investigation into their paternity and maintenance, whereas the children of wealthier parents could avoid state involvement altogether. Class belonging was also demonstrated through adherence to certain moral values, as Margaret R. Hunt argues.[46] Comparison of texts produced by authors of different socio-economic status corrects a common historiographical assumption that illegitimacy 'was very much an offence of the poor and obscure', and that stigmatisation was only a top-down manifestation of class antagonism.[47] Socio-economic status certainly affected the treatment of illegitimates, but analysis of the ways in which elite and middling groups referred to those of their *own* class, as well as to the poor, reveals a much greater level of complexity in attitudes towards sexual morality, family, and reputation.

The purposes of the texts varied. Some authors, such as Benjamin Shaw, intended to write family histories, while others, including overseer and shopkeeper Thomas Turner, sought to document their professional and personal lives. All of these texts were, in some way, exercises in self-fashioning, and words were chosen to convey specific messages about the author and their subject(s). Many pauper correspondents, for example, chose language strategically to present themselves as worthy of relief.[48] Authors from different backgrounds encountered illegitimacy in varying capacities: personally, in their own families and social circles, and professionally, as clerks or poor law officials. Often authors experienced

52 Kate Gibson

illegitimacy in both contexts. For example, Thomas Turner policed illegitimacy amongst his neighbours as a poor law overseer whilst also providing a home for his illegitimate nephew.[49] None of the authors discussed here were themselves illegitimate but several were, or were accused of being, the parents of illegitimate children.[50] Word choice may have been influenced by whether or not authors felt that their own reputation was damaged by association with illegitimacy.

The words chosen to describe illegitimate individuals changed over the eighteenth century as morality became more closely connected to socio-economic status. Male authors writing before 1750 tended to use bastard or base as their primary labels to describe children of all socio-economic backgrounds, and very rarely used natural. In the 1660s, the only specific word used by Samuel Pepys to refer to illegitimates, ranging from royalty to his own niece, was bastard.[51] Viscount Percival similarly used bastard to refer to illegitimate individuals in his own social class, using natural only once.[52] The excise officer John Cannon (d. 1743) employed slightly more variety, but continued to choose words associated with maternal promiscuity: 'base', 'bastard' and 'whoresbird child'.[53] Bastard was similarly the word of choice for yeoman Richard Gough, who applied it as a blanket label to rich and poor alike, as well as to children from incestuous or adulterous relationships, or what Gough refers to as 'lewdnesse'.[54] In the earlier half of the period, bastard primarily acted as a shorthand to differentiate illegitimate from legitimate. It was not based on socio-economic status and had the effect of associating all illegitimate children of any background with the undesirable and immoral qualities of bastard.

These authors did not convey a gradation in the moral judgement of illegitimacy through the label they chose to employ, but rather through their decision to use a label altogether. For example, Gough never used any label to refer to a child of doubtful legitimacy, including foundlings or children of alleged marriages. Instead, he preferred to explain their birth circumstances using contextual description.[55] He demarcated between parental marriages he considered to be legal and those that were alleged, stating in one case that when Sarah Tyler 'was found to bee with child ... she said (and some believed,) [she] was married to Robert Outram'.[56] Prior to the 1753 Marriage Act, which tightened marriage regulations by requiring the publication of banns and a ceremony in an Anglican church, contemporaries may have been reluctant to stigmatise the children of informal marriages or promised betrothals, recognising that sex with an intention to marry was less morally and socially transgressive than promiscuous or adulterous relationships.[57] Gough's avoidance of a label does not mean that he viewed these children as legitimate, but that he lacked a specific word to capture the nuances of their parents' relationship.

By the mid-eighteenth century, elite and middling authors increasingly adopted the word natural to refer to illegitimate children from their own

The Language of Exclusion 53

social class. Bastard became increasingly specific and evaluative and was reserved primarily as a pejorative term or to describe the poor. In the 1750s, shopkeeper Thomas Turner's word of choice was natural, which he primarily used to refer to children of his own socio-economic status who were not receiving poor relief, including his nephew.[58] He only used bastard in specific poor law contexts.[59] For example, he labelled pauper Elizabeth Day's child as 'a bastard, [who] would not belong to this parish', only when discussing its poor law status with the parish clerk.[60] Horace Walpole and his high-status correspondents, in letters penned between 1733 and 1797, used bastard in only three ways: to refer to historical or foreign royal illegitimates, when discussing inheritance in a legal context, or to refer to the poor. When describing members of their own class in social situations, they used natural, regardless of the type of parental relationship or the validity of the marriage.[61] For example, the artist Joseph Farington specifically noted whether elite children were adulterine or whether their parents lived together, but always referred to them by the same label, natural.[62]

Among elites, the more sympathetic use of natural was not specific to individuals with illegitimate relatives. Farington had no illegitimate connections but nevertheless followed the same linguistic pattern as Walpole, who had numerous illegitimate family members. By using the word natural, with all its positive connotations, elites sought to exempt themselves from the most socially and economically transgressive aspects of illegitimacy: a child born to promiscuous parents, with an unknown father, and dependent on the poor law for maintenance. In practical and economic terms, elite illegitimacy was less damaging because their children were, for the most part, privately maintained, and this was consciously reflected in word choice.[63] The association of natural with a loving, monogamous relationship was also significant to the elite's self-presentation of their extra-marital sexual activities. As I have shown elsewhere, extra-marital sex between upper middling and elite couples was often considered to have been motivated by love and unhappy mercenary marriages, whereas lower status couples were considered to be lustful and unfeeling. Moreover, under the tenets of sensibility, a behavioural model that had become dominant in English culture by 1770, a superior capacity for feeling was associated with gentility and virtue.[64] By suggesting that their children were the products of loving relationships of known paternity, elites were consciously distancing them from the most immoral aspects of illegitimacy.[65]

When bastard was used to describe elite illegitimacy, albeit rarely, it was specifically in a pejorative sense. The kept mistress of Admiral Thomas Pye, Anna Maria Bennett, for instance, feared that a reluctant potential lodger viewed her children as a 'Parcel of Bastards'.[66] Walpole reported that Lady Isabella Finch, of the royal bedchamber, refused to present an illegitimate distant relative at court, or as 'Lady Bel called it

54   *Kate Gibson*

publishing a bastard at Court'. Walpole presented this as a slur and sympathetically counselled his correspondent to 'think on the poor girl' who had been excluded.[67] Bastard was only very rarely used to refer to an elite child, and its utility as a pejorative rested on its associations with particularly immoral and poverty-stricken illegitimacy, rather than on the general stigmatisation of illegitimacy.

The adoption of the word natural during the eighteenth century was not echoed by lower-status authors. Throughout the period, these authors tended to avoid the common labels of bastard or natural, in favour of contextual description or terms highlighting the accidental nature of illegitimacy. The Lancashire metalworker Benjamin Shaw was related to many of the illegitimate individuals he mentioned in his account and was well-acquainted with their birth circumstances. In his autobiography and family history Shaw explicitly noted a child's illegitimacy thirty-four times, but primarily using contextual description. He used a label only in five instances. Shaw's preferred label was 'chance children', echoed by other lower-status autobiographers, such as John Clare and Thomas Johnson, who used words like 'misfortune' and 'fate's chance-ling'.[68] A typical usage in Shaw's text is this reference to his uncle who, in 1796, 'married [Esther] Richmond ... she had a child by chance before'.[69] Lack of labelling does not suggest that Shaw considered illegitimacy irrelevant, neither does it reflect a greater flexibility among the lower-classes about the definition of marriage. In fact, Shaw usually specified that parents were not married, and that he did not consider them as such, and referred to the births of his own illegitimate grandchildren as matters of 'misfortune', 'grief & trouble'.[70] Illegitimacy to Shaw was still a category of difference that he viewed negatively, but his preference for contextual identification reflected his understanding of the myriad ways in which an illegitimate birth could arise – not least through poverty, the death of a prospective husband or sexual assault. It may also indicate a more general reluctance to share labels used by elites to denigrate the poor.[71] Lower-status authors did not link the word bastard to the poor law but used it sparingly as a moral pejorative. Shaw, for instance, used the term only once, to describe the child of his brother-in-law Benjamin Leeming, a cheat and a thief who was 'Constantly Poor' as 'he did not like work'. In this case, its use conveyed Shaw's moral judgement on Leeming's wastefulness in fathering a child dependent on the parish, rather than his sexual activity or the worthiness of the child itself.[72]

Socio-economic distinctions are most apparent in the Essex pauper letters. Here, overseers, lawyers, and members of the clergy, usually drawn from the middling sort, only used the word bastard, never natural. The lawyer William Brittlebank relayed maintenance payments from his client, an unmarried father, to the Chelmsford overseers for 'the bastard child of Sarah Facey', using the word as an identifier to specify the recipient and purpose.[73] Bastard was the preferred term

The Language of Exclusion 55

to describe the legal and economic status of the child under the poor law, and did not necessarily imply additional immorality. For example, clergyman George Turner referred to the 'bastard child' of one of his parishioners whilst providing an otherwise glowing moral reference, stating that the family were 'very industrious', the girl had been 'very decently brought up, & I know nothing against her character'.[74]

However, the pauper letters also show that the lower-status families of illegitimate children rarely used bastard or any label, even though they were also writing in a poor law context. One letter stated that: 'Mary Smith formerly Mary Adams humbly Solicits your Assistance for Fredrick Adams her Son whom she had before she Married Smith & the Child was Passed to Upminster from Cripple-Gate'.[75] Mary gave as much information as possible about Frederick's status and identity in order to demonstrate his entitlement to relief, showing her familiarity with the law, but nevertheless avoided specific labels. Mary may have been trying to evade the negative connotations of bastard with parental promiscuity and implicitly present herself as a member of the morally deserving poor. The single usage of bastard by a pauper correspondent was pejorative. Reputed father, gardener Henry Blomfield, complained of his insolvency and loss of social credit in paying for 'this Cursed Bastard'.[76] He may have explicitly chosen this word to imply that he had been falsely accused of paternity by a promiscuous woman, or to express his frustration at being unable to pay the maintenance that the parish demanded. In general, though, the poor rejected the value-laden association of bastard with poverty, casual sex, and doubtful paternity, and instead implemented their own taxonomy that emphasised the variability of individual circumstance.

There were some gender differences in the way illegitimacy was described and discussed. In the sources examined here, women from across the social hierarchy rarely used the term bastard. Lady Bessborough, herself the mother of adulterine illegitimate children, used a label only once, referring to the character Frederick in Elizabeth Inchbald's 1798 play *Lover's Vows* as a 'natural child'. As Frederick is the heroic son of a baron, this usage reflects his class. Lady Bessborough's other references to illegitimacy are generally euphemistic, referring to the '*secret* of [her stepnephew's] birth'.[77] Lady Mary Wortley Montagu, writing around fifty years earlier, used only one label, in itself euphemistic – a 'false child' – to denote a child of an adulterous woman. Otherwise, Montagu preferred to state the context of parental relationships.[78] In the Essex pauper letters, Mrs Stapleton, a householder looking for a domestic servant, referred only to 'the child' of her servant Sarah, never using bastard even though she was writing to the master of Chelmsford workhouse about Sarah's rights under the poor law.[79] This was in contrast to Mrs Stapleton's male peers – lawyers, clergymen, and parish officials – who overwhelmingly used the term bastard. None of the

56 *Kate Gibson*

mothers claiming poor relief used the word bastard either, although in this case this seems to reflect the general reluctance among the labouring poor to use such a pejorative label. Women without legal education or parish office may have felt no need to use specific legal terminology, particularly as bastard may have been perceived as an offensive term. Notably, there was also little difference in the terminology employed in life-writing and correspondence to distinguish the gender of an illegitimate individual. It is not always clear whether the children being discussed are male or female, perhaps because gender was irrelevant to the legal or economic status of illegitimate children.

Women and higher status authors may have been reluctant to use certain labels due to constraints imposed by emerging notions of politeness and civility in the later seventeenth and eighteenth centuries.[80] Turner argues that during this period a 'widening gulf between "genteel" and "vulgar" modes of expression' led to the increasing use of euphemisms with positive connotations, evident in the rebranding of the language used to describe elite adultery as 'gallantry'.[81] Robert Shoemaker has observed a similar trend in the decline of defamation, linking it to a distaste among respectable women and the middling sort of using insulting words in public. Slander was increasingly seen as impolite and reflected badly on 'the character of the gossiper, not the person defamed'.[82]

There is evidence that public identification of illegitimate individuals was similarly regarded as vulgar and as displaying a lack of sympathy that might impugn the virtue and gentility of the speaker. Jonas Hanway, supporter of the Foundling Hospital, thought that from 'common people … we must often expect to hear the words "foundling son of a b–"'. He counselled that the foundling reply '"who is my father or mother I know not, but surely yours were very bad people, or they would have taught you better, than to reproach me"'.[83] Similarly, James Boswell's father warned him that his landlady Mrs Brown was illegitimate but added, 'I mention this to you in confidence; don't speak of it. Mrs Brown may be a good woman notwithstanding this *macula natalium* [stain on her birth], so it should not be published'.[84] Boswell himself used euphemisms such as 'dear innocent', 'a young friend', and even 'Edward the Black Prince' to refer to his own mistress's pregnancies, perhaps as way of signalling his refinement by following the codes of the polite London society that he hoped to infiltrate.[85] Refraining from labels with connotations of poverty and maternal promiscuity, in favour of euphemistic or more sympathetic terms such as natural, may have been regarded as both an act of charity and genteel restraint.[86]

Perceptions of morality and an author's personal relationship with the illegitimate individual had some impact on word choice, particularly when it came to making judgements about paternity and maternal promiscuity. John Cannon's attitudes towards illegitimacy were coloured by

The Language of Exclusion 57

an incident in his twenties when a maidservant, Ann Heister, with whom he had been having sex, became pregnant. He distanced himself from responsibility by suggesting that Ann was promiscuous and accused her of forcing him to marry her so he could 'father [another man's] bastard'. Cannon's choice of bastard neatly conveyed his belief in female duplicity and also showed that he disputed his own paternity of the child.[87] Authors from a range of backgrounds who were certain of an illegitimate individual's parentage, and in some cases their own blood ties to them, were much more likely to use non-pejorative terms such as natural or chance child. Horace Walpole, for example, was clear that his illegitimate nieces were his brother's biological children and included them within instrumental and affective expressions of kinship.[88] His use of the word natural to describe them, with its connotations of biological connection and known paternity within a loving and monogamous, albeit extra-marital relationship, signalled to his contemporaries that he acknowledged and valued them as his relatives and social peers.

Bastard, by contrast, could be deployed to express shame and the dis-avowal of responsibility and kinship, particularly amongst those from the upwardly mobile middling sort whose vulnerability and economic insecurity may have made them more sensitive to matters that might damage their family's collective reputation.[89] Samuel Pepys feared that 'we [the Pepys family] are like to receive some shame about the business of my brother's bastard', when his brother Tom fathered a child, Elizabeth, on his maidservant shortly before his death.[90] To Pepys, Elizabeth was a bastard because her parents had engaged in a transgressive master-servant relationship. Moreover, Tom, prior to his death, had clandestinely arranged for her to be adopted by a pauper couple, thereby associating her with the additional connotations of poverty and avoidance of paternal acknowledgement.[91] Although Samuel also engaged in extra-marital sex, he was discreet and sensitive to public opinion as he worked his way up in government office. Rather than acknowledge Elizabeth as a Pepys, he safeguarded his hard-won position by paying Elizabeth's foster parents money to ensure their secrecy. Samuel satisfied himself 'that neither we nor any of our family should be troubled with the child ... and that if the worst came to the worst, the parish must keep it.' Samuel's usage of bastard to describe his brother's illegitimate child thus conveyed the family's wish to disown her and his willingness to have her brought up as a pauper.[92]

The shopkeeper Thomas Turner was also judgemental of illegitimacy within his own class. Indeed, when the wife of his friend and fellow parish officer Thomas Davy had a bridal pregnancy, he complained that they were 'two people whom I should the least have suspected of being guilty of so indiscreet an act'.[93] These moral standards did not always result in the linguistic discrimination of a child as a bastard. Although Turner referred pejoratively to his half-sister as a 'vagabond', he always referred to her illegitimate son Philip as natural.[94] This perhaps reflects

58   *Kate Gibson*

Turner's certainty of their blood relationship, but also underscores the Turner family's acknowledgement and financial support of Philip.[95] Turner was thus linguistically separating Philip from the parish bastards, whilst also defending the family's financial reputation.

Illegitimacy as Defamation

The word bastard carried obvious negative connotations, but it is not clear whether it was used and perceived as an insult causing specific reputational damage. In the York Cause Papers, accusations of being the parent of an illegitimate child were common, comprising seventy-five per cent of all defamation cases, but accusations of *being* illegitimate were strikingly rare.[96] Only thirteen of 1,249 defamation cases between 1660 and 1834 involved an individual accused of being illegitimate. This small number is not symptomatic of the general eighteenth-century decline in defamation, as between 1517 and 1660 there were only eight cases. This suggests that the reputational damage of illegitimacy, and the desire to stigmatise illegitimates in this way, remained fairly constant even when the power of insulting words was in general decline.[97] York was not unusual. Illegitimacy insults did not occur in sufficient numbers for historians to include them in their defamation studies of other English courts.[98] This paucity also does not reflect the particular jurisdiction of the church courts where defamation was generally only actionable if it 'maliciously imputed a spiritual crime that fell under ecclesiastical jurisdiction'.[99]

Although being illegitimate was not a spiritual crime, several legal manuals considered calling someone a bastard a matter that could be prosecuted in ecclesiastical and civil courts. The barrister John March stated that 'calling of a man a Bastard, a Heretique, a Schismatique, an Advowterer [Adulterer], a Fornicator, [or] calling of a woman a Whore' were all actionable by imputing a moral crime and causing material damage.[100] Bastard was particularly grievous if it jeopardised inheritance or caused 'loss of a man's advancement' and could be prosecuted alongside other generally 'reproachful Words' such as 'Dog', 'knave', or 'filthy fellow'.[101] In practice, as J.A. Sharpe suggests, the law was flexible enough to allow the prosecution of any insult considered sufficiently damaging.[102] Moreover, defamations associated with illegitimacy were generally brought by the reputedly illegitimate individual alone, with no mention of their parents' reputations. Only one case, from 1692, involved parent and child as joint plaintiffs, when Richard Rimer stated that 'Hannah Byfield was a whore … and … that one George Byfields … was a Bastard'.[103] This suggests that illegitimacy was believed to have a personal reputational impact on the child, not just their parents.

Bastard was the most common slander term, but it could be used in several ways. In seven cases, bastard appeared alongside other slanders

The Language of Exclusion 59

such as 'rogue', 'thief' or 'son of a whore', and was often combined with them as the adjective 'bastardly'.[104] A particularly creative combination was 'bastardly rogue & fornicator of the pew'.[105] It was used as a general pejorative conveying immorality, lowliness, and corruption similar to alternative meanings of base discussed above. Other synonyms, such as spurious, were entirely absent, despite their similarly negative connotations to bastard. Natural appeared only once: as a compound insult of 'natural son of a whore and a Right Real Bastard'.[106] Bastard was clearly the most effective insult, perhaps because of its implications of poverty and doubtful paternity, which could thus defame both an individual and their entire family. Following Laura Gowing's argument that sexual insults were not about sex but the patriarchal control of women, bastard implied that a person's male relatives had been unable to control the women in their household. It might also indicate that moral failings were hereditary.[107] This is reflected in one compound insult from 1684, when Joshua Fenwick accused John Thorp of being 'a Bastard and the son of a whore and yt all his Relations were whores and theeves'. In this case bastard was deployed as an apparently effective insult in a dispute over the non-payment of wages. Fenwick used the slander in multiple ways, calling Thorp a 'bastardly curr' and 'bastardly rogue' as well as simply 'bastard'.[108]

The gender and status of litigants suggest that illegitimacy accusations had specific reputational consequences. Men were much more likely to be accused of being illegitimate or to bring defamation cases on these grounds: in nine out of the thirteen cases brought before the courts at York between 1660 and 1834, both litigants were male, and only one plaintiff was female. Similar proportions – six out of eight involving at least one male litigant – were found between 1517 and 1659. This evidence stands in contrast to other studies of early modern defamation, which show that most litigants were female.[109] Litigants, in cases of defamation for illegitimacy, were also likely to be of higher status than litigants in other types of defamation suits, who were generally from lower and middling socio-economic backgrounds.[110] Eight cases (forty-six per cent) involved at least one litigant who was described as 'gentleman' and two of these cases involved baronets.[111] An illegitimacy defamation case was more than twice as likely to involve a person described as 'gentleman' than any other type of defamation in York in this period.[112] It might thus be suggested that illegitimacy insults were most effective against propertied men, who had more to lose from its potential impact on inheritance. In 1715, gentleman John Murgatroyd reportedly called Sir William Lowther 'a son of a whore or son of a bitch, a lousy Baronett and a stubborn Rascall'. This was part of a long-running dispute over Lowther's estates, so the insult was deployed specifically to attack Lowther's economic and political legitimacy.[113]

Bastard was undoubtedly a pejorative term but was either not commonly used or not considered sufficiently damaging to warrant

60   *Kate Gibson*

prosecution unless it also importuned a person's socio-economic status through inheritance. Among other social groups alternative insults were more common. It was seemingly more effective to call a woman a whore, for instance, than a bastard. This may have been because other defamation terms, such as thief, knave, or whore, implied individual moral failing on the part of the individual concerned, while in cases of illegitimacy, the fault lay with their parents. As noted earlier, such public insults may also have reflected badly on the accuser, and defamations based on accusations of bastardy alone may have been seen as unjust. Instead, the insulting power of bastard, particularly as an adjective or combined insult, came from its association with being base, or low. Although these negative connotations may have contributed to a general perception of illegitimates as inferior, it does suggest that the charge of being a bastard alone was insufficiently damaging. As David Garrioch argues, insults rely on communal consensus.[114] The striking rarity and specific target of illegitimacy defamations suggest that communities did not openly ostracise illegitimate individuals, and illegitimacy was not sufficiently linked to unworthiness of character to warrant its broad usage and prosecution as an insult.

Conclusion

By the mid-eighteenth century, a vocabulary of illegitimacy existed, in which specific words – most notably bastard and natural – were used to identify and differentiate between types of illegitimacy. The frequency and consistency with which authors identified illegitimate individuals suggests that there was a desire to categorise those born out of wedlock and mark them out in some way as different. Language was both descriptive and evaluative. Although a binary definition of legitimate and illegitimate was legally necessary, the existence of a wide vocabulary suggests there was a moral desire to differentiate between types of illegitimacy. By choosing a particular word, authors conveyed opinions of an individual's socio-economic status, the relative sinfulness of their parents' relationship, the certainty of paternity, and their inclusion or exclusion from the family or peer group. A range of terminology allowed contemporaries to differentiate between different types of illegitimacy, suggesting that some birth circumstances, particularly poverty, were stigmatised more than others.

Language use changed over time to become more focused on socio-economic status. Strikingly, seventeenth-century texts showed less variation in language. Here, bastard was used to describe individuals of any class or parental background, suggesting that they were perceived as equally inferior. Any uncertainty over illegitimate status, such as alleged marriage, was expressed through the avoidance of labels in preference for contextual description. Yet, by the mid-eighteenth century middling

The Language of Exclusion 61

and elite authors increasingly differentiated poor illegitimates from those of their own social class using labels. The word natural was used to elevate middling and elite illegitimates by suggesting that they were privately maintained, and that their parents had been in long-term, emotionally attached, and morally more legitimate relationships. Bastard and its most negative connotations were reserved for individuals whose illegitimacy had the greatest communal impact: those dependent on poor relief, or associated with maternal promiscuity and uncertain paternity. The reluctance of poor authors to use words such as bastard about other poor illegitimates suggests that labelling conveyed a moral judgement based on the social-economic status of the subject being described.

Individuals may have chosen certain labels in order to display their own status and adherence to signifiers of politeness, echoing wider shifts in the language of insult and sexuality observed by Shoemaker and Turner.[115] By using the term natural, a person signified their own sensibility through their distaste for pejorative language, and, when referring to illegitimate relatives or friends, demonstrated that their family and peer group included a better type of illegitimate than the bastards of poor families. In turn, by avoiding the word bastard, labouring parents could consciously imply that their child's illegitimacy was the product of intended marriage or misfortune, rather than wilful immorality, and therefore worthy of relief. Accordingly, changes in the language of illegitimacy do not necessarily reflect a growing perception that extra-marital sex was less sinful, but rather that the sexual activities of certain social groups were perceived as less sinful or morally problematic than others.

Evidence of the language of illegitimacy calls for a reconsideration of approaches to defamation. Although contemporaries seemed more reluctant to use pejorative language such as bastard in life-writing and correspondence, it remained the word of choice in insults. Illegitimacy slanders buck the trend of defamation cases more generally; they affected higher-status men more than women and, although numbers were limited, showed no decline over the eighteenth century. The consistency of their numbers across the period testifies to the embedded nature of stigma towards illegitimate individuals in early modern society. The word bastard, in particular, clearly implied a person was of inferior value to their legitimate counterpart and was considered to have a sufficiently negative impact to warrant prosecution, perhaps because it also suggested the additional slanders of poverty and maternal prostitution. Illegitimacy evidence suggests that defamation did not just decline, as historians have argued, but rather that it was deployed in increasingly specific ways.

These findings indicate that language was a key means of identifying and excluding certain groups, and that linguistic analysis can be a fruitful means of measuring stigma amongst groups whose experience is

62   Kate Gibson

otherwise difficult to find in traditional sources. Linguistic comparison certainly suggests that historians should more carefully consider the impact of socio-economic status on perceptions of illegitimacy. This chapter has shown that there was a spectrum of attitudes that varied according to the socio-economic status of the individuals involved, and that attitudes changed over the period. The stigma of illegitimacy was not only experienced by the poor – identifying an elite child as natural still involved differentiation and stigmatisation – but poverty carried additional stigmas such as the implication of maternal promiscuity, economic dependence, and doubtful paternity, all neatly encapsulated in the word bastard. This chapter's investigation of the language of illegitimacy indicates that there is much more to be gleaned from the sources on the experience of this marginalised group in early modern society.

Notes

1 Borthwick Institute of Archives (hereafter BIA): CP.H.3107, Witness statement of Michael Brown, cordwainer, in Christopher Wright vs John Avyard (1671).
2 Kenneth Garlick, Angus Macintyre, Kathryn Cave, and Evelyn Newby (eds), *The Diary of Joseph Farington* (6 vols, New Haven: Yale University Press, 1978–1998), i. 141, 12 January 1794.
3 I refer to these individuals using the word 'illegitimate' to ensure consistency for the reader. No pejorative meaning is intended. Other synonyms appear according to contemporary usage.
4 Richard Adair, *Courtship, Illegitimacy and Marriage in Early Modern England* (Manchester: Manchester University Press, 1996), 90.
5 Erving Goffman, *Stigma: Notes on the Management of Spoiled Identity* (Harmondsworth: Penguin, 1968), 15.
6 Bruce Link and Jo Phelan, 'Conceptualizing Stigma', *Annual Review of Sociology*, 27 (2001), 367.
7 Penelope J. Corfield (ed.), *Language, History and Class* (Oxford: Basil Blackwell, 1991); Judith Spicksley, 'A Dynamic Model of Social Relations: Celibacy, Credit and the Identity of the "Spinster" in Seventeenth-Century England', in Henry French and Jonathan Barry (eds), *Identity and Agency in England, 1500–1800* (Basingstoke: Palgrave Macmillan, 2004), 106–46.
8 Robert Jütte, *Poverty and Deviance in Early Modern Europe* (Cambridge: Cambridge University Press, 1994), 10–12.
9 David Garrioch, 'Verbal Insults in Eighteenth-Century Paris', in Peter Burke and Roy Porter (eds), *The Social History of Language* (Cambridge: Cambridge University Press, 1988), 104–19; J.A. Sharpe, *Defamation and Sexual Slander in Early Modern England: The Church Courts at York* (York: Borthwick Papers, 1980), 15–19; Laura Gowing, *Domestic Dangers: Women, Words, and Sex in Early Modern London* (Oxford: Oxford University Press, 1996), 62–4.
10 David M. Turner, *Fashioning Adultery: Gender, Sex and Civility in England, 1660–1740* (Cambridge: Cambridge University Press, 2002), 42, 44–5, 48.
11 Robert Shoemaker, 'The Decline of Public Insult in London, 1660–1800', *Past & Present*, 169 (2000), 97–131.

The Language of Exclusion   63

12 Kate Gibson, 'Experiences of Illegitimacy in England, 1660–1834', unpublished PhD thesis (University of Sheffield, 2018), 25–7. The exception is work on the medieval period, see Sara McDougall, *Royal Bastards. The Birth of Illegitimacy 800–1230* (Oxford: Oxford University Press, 2017), 22–65.

13 Adair, *Courtship*, 90.

14 R.J. Hetherington, 'Synonyms for Bastard', *The Midland Ancestor*, 36 (1975), 15–6.

15 Alysa Levene, Thomas Nutt, and Samantha Williams (eds), *Illegitimacy in Britain, 1700–1920* (Basingstoke: Palgrave Macmillan, 2005); Tanya Evans, *'Unfortunate Objects': Lone Mothers in Eighteenth-Century London* (Basingstoke: Palgrave Macmillan, 2005); Patricia Crawford, *Parents of Poor Children in England, 1580–1800,* (Oxford: Oxford University Press, 2009); Samantha Williams, *Unmarried Motherhood in the Metropolis, 1700–1850* (Basingstoke: Palgrave Macmillan, 2018).

16 Neither of the two most significant works on sexual slander consider the labelling of the child themselves: Gowing, *Domestic Dangers*, 59–67; Alexandra Shepard, *Meanings of Manhood in Early Modern England* (Oxford: Oxford University Press, 2003), 152–85.

17 William Blackstone, *Commentaries on the Laws of England*, fourth edition (4 vols, Oxford, 1770), i. 459.

18 Gibson, 'Experiences of Illegitimacy', 291–2.

19 'Cause Papers in the Diocesan Courts of the Archbishopric of York, 1300–1858', BIA, University of York https://www.dhi.ac.uk/causepapers/. Accessed 30 September 2019.

20 Other studies that have used the Cause Paper Database include: Sharpe, *Defamation*, passim; and Fay Bound Alberti, '"An Angry and Malicious Mind"? Narratives of Slander at the Church Courts of York, c.1660–c.1760', *History Workshop Journal*, 56 (2003), 59–77.

21 As McDougall notes, the precise definitions were complex and changeable, so I have privileged the definitions also cited in early modern texts. McDougall, *Royal Bastards*, 22–3; John Witte, *The Sins of the Fathers: The Law and Theology of Illegitimacy Reconsidered* (Cambridge: Cambridge University Press, 2009), 52–3, 89–91.

22 Richard Burn, *Ecclesiastical Law*, second edition (4 vols, London, 1767), i. 110.

23 For the French medieval origins of bastard see McDougall, *Royal Bastards*, 44–9.

24 Blackstone, *Commentaries*, i. 434.

25 John Brydall, *Lex Spuriorum: Or, The Law Relating to Bastardy* (London, 1703), preface.

26 Brydall, *Lex Spuriorum*, 2–3, 6–10. Brydall quotes early medieval scholar Isidore, who is discussed in McDougall, *Royal Bastards*, 29. A similar binary definition appears in other legal texts, for example: Burn, *Ecclesiastical Law*, i. 108–20.

27 The former was a stock phrase, see for example, divorce bills for 17 February 1730 and 23 March 1747 in 'Harper Collection of Private Bills, 1695–1814', *UK Parliamentary Papers*. For poor law usage, see 18 Eliz. c. 3 (1576); 6 Geo. 2. c. 31 (1733) and 49 Geo. 3. c. 68 (1809).

28 Witte, *Sins of the Fathers*, 109.

29 Deuteronomy 23:2; Wisdom of Solomon 4:3, *King James Version* (London, 1611).

30 Matthew Henry, *An Exposition of All the Books of the Old and New Testament*, third edition (6 vols, London, 1721–25), i. 471–2;

64   Kate Gibson

Simon Patrick, *A Commentary Upon the Historical Books of the Old Testament*, third edition (2 vols, London, 1727), i. 804; Samuel Horsley, *Biblical Criticism on the First Fourteen Historical Books of the Old Testament* (4 vols, London, 1820), i. 203, 763.

31 John Wesley, *Explanatory Notes upon the Old Testament* (3 vols. Bristol, 1765), i. 838–9; *The Holie Bible Faithfully Translated into English* (Douai, 1609–10); Richard Challoner, *The Holy Bible Translated from the Latin Vulgat* (Dublin, 1750–52). In this, the Catholic texts were following the multiple legal categories remaining in Catholic canon law.

32 Naomi Tadmor, *The Social Universe of the English Bible: Scripture, Society and Culture in Early Modern England* (Cambridge: Cambridge University Press, 2010), 17, 26.

33 Samuel Johnson, *A Dictionary of the English Language*, sixth edition (2 vols, London, 1785); Nathan Bailey, *An Universal Etymological English Dictionary*, twenty-sixth edition (Edinburgh, 1789); John Ash, *The New and Complete Dictionary of the English Language* (2 vols, London, 1775), i. 103–4.

34 Bailey, *Dictionary*, n.p.

35 *Oracle and Public Advertiser*, no. 19928, 21 May 1798; Stephen Blake, *The Compleat Gardeners Practice, Directing the Exact Way of Gardening* (London, 1664), 117; Steven Blankaart, *A Physical Dictionary; In which, All the Terms Relating Either to Anatomy, Chirurgery, Pharmacy, or Chymistry, Are Very Accurately Explan'd* (London, 1684), 207.

36 Thomas Bartholin, *Bartholinus Anatomy Made From the Precepts of His Father, and From the Observations of All Modern Anatomists* (London, 1668), 353.

37 Margot Finn, Michael Lobban, and Jenny Bourne Taylor, 'Introduction: Spurious Issues', in Margot Finn, Michael Lobban, and Jenny Bourne Taylor (eds), *Legitimacy and Illegitimacy in Nineteenth-Century Law, Literature and History* (Basingstoke: Palgrave Macmillan, 2010), 2–3.

38 Thomas Blount, *Glossographia: Or A Dictionary, Interpreting All Such Hard Words* (London, 1656).

39 This is based on usage in the life-writing and correspondence sources examined for this study. Natural is noted as a synonym for bastard in the dictionaries by Coles and Bailey. Elisha Coles, *An English Dictionary Explaining the Difficult Terms that are Used in Divinity, Husbandry, Physick, Phylosophy, Law, Navigation, Mathematicks, and Other Arts and Sciences* (London, 1676), n.p.; Bailey, *Dictionary*, n.p.

40 McDougall, *Royal Bastards*, 28.

41 Justinian law of Novel 74, cited in Witte, *Sins of the Fathers*, 59–60; *Decretales D. Gregorii Papae IX. Suae Integritati Un Cum Glossis Restitutae* (Rome, 1584), cited and translated in McDougall, *Royal Bastards*, 22.

42 Ash, *Dictionary*, 639.

43 Johnson, *Dictionary*, n.p.

44 'natural, n.1', *OED Online* (Oxford: Oxford University Press, 2018); Richard Whatmore, 'Luxury, Commerce and the Rise of Political Economy', in James A. Harris (ed.), *The Oxford Handbook of British Philosophy in the Eighteenth Century* (Oxford: Oxford University Press, 2013), 575–98.

45 Gibson, 'Experiences of Illegitimacy', 220–2.

46 Margaret R. Hunt, *The Middling Sort: Commerce, Gender, and the Family in England, 1680–1780* (Berkeley: University of California Press, 1996), 14, 216.

The Language of Exclusion 65

47 Keith Wrightson and David Levine, *Poverty and Piety in an English Village: Terling, 1525–1700*, second edition (Oxford: Clarendon, 1995), 128. For more on this see Gibson, 'Experiences of Illegitimacy', 43–4.
48 Joanne Bailey, '"Think wot a mother must feel": Parenting in English Pauper Letters, c.1760–1834', *Family and Community History*, 13 (2010), 5–19; Thomas Sokoll, 'Writing for Relief: Rhetoric in English Pauper Letters, 1800–1834', in Andreas Gestrich, Steven King, and Lutz Raphael (eds), *Being Poor in Modern Europe: Historical Perspectives, 1800–1940* (Oxford: Lang, 2006), 91–113.
49 Naomi Tadmor, *Family and Friends in Eighteenth-Century England* (Cambridge: Cambridge University Press, 2001), 186.
50 For more on the self-identification of illegitimate individuals, see Gibson, 'Experiences of Illegitimacy', 238–47.
51 R.C. Latham and W. Matthews (eds), *The Diary of Samuel Pepys* (11 vols, London: G. Bell, 1970–83), supplemented by the digital version held by Project Gutenberg https://goldin.shinyapps.io/Search_Pepys/. Accessed 4 February 2018. iii. 191, 290; v. 142, 154; viii. 183.
52 R.A. Roberts (ed.), *Manuscripts of the Earl of Egmont, Diary of Viscount Percival, afterwards First Earl of Egmont* (3 vols London, 1920–23), i. 192–3, 196, 202; ii. 223–4; iii. 49, 247–8.
53 John Money (ed.), *The Chronicles of John Cannon, Excise Officer and Writing Master* (2 vols, Oxford: Oxford University Press, 2010), i. 20, 104; ii. 340. Entries in the printed edition were checked against a copy of the original in Shropshire Record Office: DD/SAS C/1193/4, 'Memoirs of the Birth, Education Life and Death of: Mr. John Cannon'.
54 Richard Gough, *The History of Myddle*, ed. by David Hey (Harmondsworth: Penguin, 1981), 221.
55 Ibid., 139, 181–3, 190–1, 207, 256.
56 Ibid., 181.
57 John R. Gillis, *For Better, For Worse: British Marriages, 1600 to the Present* (Oxford: Oxford University Press, 1985), 97, 110. For a contrary assessment of the scale of informal marriage, see Rebecca Probert, *Marriage Law and Practice in the Long Eighteenth Century* (Cambridge: Cambridge University Press, 2009), 72, 122, 250.
58 David Vaisey (ed.), *The Diary of Thomas Turner, 1754–1765* (Oxford: Oxford University Press, 1984), 77, 125, 181, 294.
59 Ibid., 56, 110, 135, 158, 266, 268.
60 Ibid., 135.
61 W.S. Lewis (ed.), *The Yale Edition of Horace Walpole's Correspondence* (48 vols, New Haven: Yale University Press, 1937–83, online edition), ii. 306; xviii. 506–7; xxv. 91, 570–1; xxxvi. 25–6, 69, 77.
62 *Joseph Farington*, xi. 2347; viii. 3015.
63 Gibson, 'Experiences of Illegitimacy', 74.
64 G.J. Barker-Benfield, *The Culture of Sensibility: Sex and Society in Eighteenth-Century Britain* (Chicago, 1992), xix, 215; Janet Todd, *Sensibility: An Introduction* (London, 1986), 3, 7.
65 Gibson, 'Experiences of Illegitimacy', 53–59.
66 City of Westminster Archives Centre: 36/72, Anna Maria Bennett to Sir Thomas Pye, July 1785.
67 *Walpole's Correspondence*, xix. 389, Horace Walpole to Horace Mann, 10 April 1748.
68 Alan G. Crosby (ed.), *The Family Records of Benjamin Shaw, Mechanic of Dent, Dolphinholme and Preston, 1772–1841* (Record Society of

66   Kate Gibson

Lancashire and Cheshire, 1991), 90; Eric Robinson (ed.), *John Clare's Autobiographical Writings* (Oxford: Oxford University Press, 1983), 2; Jacob Simon, 'Thomas Johnson's The Life of the Author,' *Furniture History*, 39 (2003), 15–6. Similar language appears in Foundling Hospital petitions and Yorkshire slang, see Evans, *'Unfortunate Objects'*, 109–12; Gillis, *For Better, For Worse*, 129–30.

69 Crosby (ed.), *Benjamin Shaw*, 14.

70 Ibid., 19, 20, 29, 37, 52, 56, 58, 74, 89, 91, 104, 115.

71 For more on the particular vulnerabilities of labouring women to illegitimate pregnancy through 'frustrated courtship' or assault, see John Gillis, 'Servants, Sexual Relations and the Risks of Illegitimacy in London, 1801–1900', *Feminist Studies*, 5 (1979), 158–63; Cissie Fairchilds, 'Female Sexual Attitudes and the Rise of Illegitimacy: A Case Study', *The Journal of Interdisciplinary History*, 8 (1978), 627–67; Nicholas Rogers, 'Carnal Knowledge: Illegitimacy in Eighteenth-Century Westminster', *Journal of Social History*, 23 (1989), 355–75.

72 Ibid., 87.

73 Essex Record Office (hereafter ERO): D/P 94/18/42, William Brittlebank to the Chelmsford overseers, 1 September 1828.

74 ERO: D/P 178/18/23 George Turner to the St Peter's Colchester overseers, 9 April 1825.

75 Thomas Sokoll (ed.), *Essex Pauper Letters, 1731–1837* (Oxford: Oxford University Press, 2006), Mary Smith to the Upminster overseers, 5 January 1814, 622.

76 ERO: D/P178/18/23, Henry Blomfield to the St Peter's Colchester overseers, 30 July 1821.

77 Castalia Countess Granville (ed.), *Lord Granville Leveson Gower, Private Correspondence, 1781–1821* (2 vols, London: John Murray, 1916), i. 423, Lady Bessborough to Granville Leveson Gower, 13 December 1811.

78 Robert Halsband (ed.), *The Complete Letters of Lady Mary Wortley Montagu* (3 vols, Oxford: Oxford University Press, 1965–7), iii. 48, Lady Mary Wortley Montagu to Lady Bute, 1 March 1754.

79 ERO: D/P 94/18/42, E. Stapleton to Mr Langstaff, 2 January 1825.

80 Peter Burke, 'A Civil Tongue: Language and Politeness in Early Modern Europe', in Peter Burke, Brian Harrison, and Paul Slack (eds), *Civil Histories: Essays Presented to Sir Keith Thomas* (Oxford: Oxford University Press, 2000), 31, 41–2.

81 Turner, *Fashioning Adultery*, 36, 38–40.

82 Shoemaker, 'Public Insult', 115, 117, 121.

83 Jonas Hanway, *A Candid Historical Account of the Hospital for the Reception of Exposed and Deserted Young Children* (London, 1759), 33.

84 F.A. Pottle (ed.), *Boswell in Holland, 1763–1764* (London: Heinemann, 1952), 107.

85 Frank Brady and F.A. Pottle (eds), *Boswell in Search of a Wife, 1766–1769* (London: Heinemann, 1956), 87, 93, 109.

86 For kindness towards natural children as a demonstration of charity and virtue, see Gibson, 'Experiences of Illegitimacy', 253–6, 298.

87 *Chronicles of John Cannon*, i. 103; Gibson, 'Experiences of Illegitimacy', 60–63.

88 *Walpole's Correspondence*, x. 59, 62; xxxvi. 150; Gibson, 'Experiences of Illegitimacy', 129–30.

89 Hunt, *The Middling Sort*, 23–5, 35.

90 *Diary of Samuel Pepys*, v. 142, 4 May 1664.

The Language of Exclusion   67

91 *Diary of Samuel Pepys*, v. 113–4, 6 April 1664.
92 *Diary of Samuel Pepys*, v. 115, 6 April 1664; v. 252–3, 25 August 1664; Gibson, 'Experiences of Illegitimacy', 160.
93 *Diary of Thomas Turner*, 244. Tadmor notes that Turner held those he considered as his friends to high moral standards, Tadmor, *Family and Friends*, 205.
94 Thomas Turner, 'Notes on Family History', in Appendix of R.W. Blencowe, M.A. Lower, and G.H. Jennings (eds), *The Diary of a Georgian Shopkeeper* (Oxford: Oxford University Press, 1979), 80.
95 For the Turner family's financial support of Philip see Tadmor, *Family and Friends*, 186.
96 This echoes the dominance of sexual slander cases in multiple courts from this period. Sharpe, *Defamation*, 10; Gowing, *Domestic Dangers*, 61–5; Tim Meldrum, 'A Women's Court in London: Defamation at the Bishop of London's Consistory Court, 1700–1745', *The London Journal*, 19 (1994), 8–11.
97 Shoemaker, 'Public Insult', 99–100.
98 Gowing, *Domestic Dangers*, 64; Sharpe, *Defamation*, 10.
99 Shepard, *Meanings of Manhood*, 155.
100 John March, *March's Actions for Slander and Arbitrements* (London, 1674), 74.
101 Ibid., 65, 68, 70; Henry Consett, *The Practice of the Spiritual or Ecclesiastical Courts* (London, 1685), 18.
102 Sharpe, *Defamation*, 15.
103 BIA: CP.H.4291, Richard Rimer vs George and Hannah Byfield, (1692).
104 BIA: CP.H.3833, Joshua Fenwick vs John Thorp [1684]; CP.H.4619, Dorothy Roberts vs Robert Barraclough, 1663.
105 BIA: CP.H.4775, Timothy Scotson vs Richard Moseley [1665]; CP.H.3107, Christopher Wright vs John Aveyard (1671).
106 BIA: CP.I.1277, John Dalkin vs William Armstrong [1747].
107 Gowing, *Domestic Dangers*, 116–9, 194–7.
108 BIA: CP.H.3833, Joshua Fenwick vs John Thorp [1684].
109 Gowing, *Domestic Dangers*, 60; Shoemaker, 'Public Insult', 114.
110 Shoemaker, 'Public Insult', 114–7; Meldrum, 'A Women's Court', 7.
111 BIA: CP.I.27 [1713–15], George Hippon vs Rowland Winn [1713–15]; CP.I.565, John Murgatroyd vs Sir William Lowther [1715]. In the remaining five cases status was unknown.
112 238 out of 1,249 total defamation cases involved a genteel litigant (nineteen per cent).
113 BIA: CP.I.565, John Murgatroyd vs Sir William Lowther [1715]. The feud between Murgatroyd and Lowther is detailed in 'The Case of Mr John Murgatroyd, Mr Edward Gee, Mr Henry Jacomb and Mr Christopher Barnard, upon the Complaint of Sir William Lowther, Bart.', 'Harper Collection of Private Bills', 1719.
114 Garrioch, 'Verbal Insults', 113, 117.
115 Shoemaker, 'Public Insult', 115–21; Turner, *Fashioning Adultery*, 38–45.

3 Women and Religious Coexistence in Eighteenth-Century England

Carys Brown

Women were considered to be important guardians of community reputation and moderators of polite society in early eighteenth-century England. Despite this, little is known about how their actions affected religious coexistence at the tail end of England's tumultuous long Reformation. Focusing on Presbyterian and Independent women in the aftermath of the 1689 Toleration Act, this chapter highlights that in many instances the faith of these women impeded coexistence by preventing them from conforming to gendered expectations of comely behaviour. However, it also shows that Dissenting women's piety and fulfilment of neighbourly duties opened channels for their inclusion in wider society, and for more positive perceptions of their faith. This study thus emphasises the complex but undoubtedly significant contributions of women to the overall operation of religious coexistence in this period.

Scholarship on the roles of women in both public and private settings has decisively demonstrated that their inclusion within local and national society was contingent on adherence to certain behavioural norms. The ideal woman in eighteenth-century England was submissive to her husband, modest but not prudish, pious but not over-zealous or self-absorbed, and was a member of the Established Church.[1] Outside of the home, women had important roles to play in shaping polite and communal culture, particularly through moderating conversation and cultivating social connections.[2] Women's participation was regulated by a range of gendered expectations, especially in relation to appropriate spaces of participation, modes of speech, and types of consumption; their influence over many aspects of social, economic, and political life was nevertheless significant.[3]

These behavioural norms and expectations are an important consideration for the religious history of the eighteenth century. Until recently, scholarship on religion in this period tended to focus on the role of male preachers, politicians, and polemicists in responding to religious change, but important work has now recognised the centrality of female participation to 'the formation of new practices and discourses'.[4] The degree of women's agency in religious matters appears to have varied significantly between different religious groups. As Naomi Pullin's recent work has demonstrated, the theology of Quakerism allowed women an enhanced role in shaping their church as the movement developed in the eighteenth century.[5] Although other minority and persecuted groups lacked Friends' theological basis for female participation, women also played a significant part in defending and sustaining the faith of persecuted and minority religious communities across the British Isles.[6] Such studies emphasise that the shape of eighteenth-century religion cannot be understood without reference to the varying roles of women in public and private life.

Given that the history of religious coexistence lies at the interface between social and religious history, scholarship that explores the different roles of women in communal and religious life is of undeniable relevance to this field. Yet an increased historiographical sensitivity to the significance of women in shaping religious cultures in eighteenth-century England has not generally been reflected in literature exploring the practical aspects of religious toleration. Over the past thirty years, numerous scholars have conducted valuable work examining the social and economic aspects of religious coexistence, demonstrating its often fragile and apparently pragmatic nature.[7] The role of economic necessity, social status, and neighbourly support in mitigating difference have been underscored as highly significant in helping Europe's populations manage the divisive consequences of religious change.[8] However, this literature's focus on how office-holding, land ownership, and homosocial activities oiled the wheels of coexistence has meant that the specific roles played by women have received relatively little attention.[9]

This case study explores female experiences of religious coexistence, with a specific focus on those who considered themselves to be Presbyterians or Independents, as well as members of mixed congregations who referred to themselves simply as 'Dissenters'.[10] This group are of particular interest in the period after 1689 because of the threat they were perceived to represent to the stability of church and state in the wake of the so-called 'Toleration Act'. This legislation – which brought limited freedom of worship to Protestant Dissenters – was highly ambiguous, causing significant religious and political tension over the precise meaning and implications of the Act.[11] Many contemporaries who were worried about the new freedoms granted to Dissenters argued that, because of their supposed religious enthusiasm, over-zealousness, and history of sedition, Presbyterians and Independents were fundamentally threatening to social stability.[12] Linking them to both the Regicide and a breakdown of social order in the Interregnum, polemicists suggested that these groups were not only politically suspect and potentially seditious, but were also untrustworthy members of society.[13] Their ability to integrate into their local communities in the

70 *Carys Brown*

wake of limited legal toleration thus depended on their ability to overcome this stereotype.

Theologically, Presbyterian and Independent perspectives on the role of women did not diverge significantly from that of the Established Church. Women were not allowed to preach or become ministers, and neither of these groups sought to challenge the patriarchal foundations of society. However, as inheritors of a puritan emphasis on the individual's experience of and relationship to God, female Presbyterians and Independents may have had greater opportunities to exercise authority and autonomy in religious matters than women who remained in the Established Church.[14] Within their religious communities, pious devotion could thus gain these women respect.[15] Yet beyond their religious circles, the responses of others to their religiosity occurred within the framework of expectations about how they should behave within their communities. Dissenting women sometimes found themselves unable to meet these expectations, and this was critical to the operation of interdenominational relations.

This essay uses printed polemics and women's life-writings to examine how the religious and social behaviour of Presbyterian and Independent women could simultaneously inhibit and promote their inclusion within communities outside of their faith. There are problems with both of these types of sources. Ideals and stereotypes as spelt out in print provide a helpful yet clumsy estimation of contemporary views and theoretical expectations about these women. Contemporary life-writing complements these texts by providing detail of community interactions in practice, but, as the latter half of this essay emphasises, the negative tone of spiritual diaries and letters may be misleading. Authors' desire to illustrate piety through their writing somewhat obscures both tacit evidence of neighbourly inclusion, and the degree to which their religiosity may in some instances have in fact bolstered their reputations within their wider communities. Thus, while the essay begins by exploring the violence of the printed word and the social discomfort of Presbyterian and Independent women apparent in their life-writings, the second section suggests that the impression given by these sources of a double exclusion from public life 'on the grounds of gender and religious affiliation' is far from straightforward.[16] It is worth noting that it cannot be assumed that the small selection of diaries and letters used here are necessarily representative. The authors of these sources were mostly of middling status and lived rurally or in small towns. A number of them had family members who were ministers, a fact that undoubtedly influenced their own expectations of piety. Nevertheless, their combined accounts provide crucial suggestions of how gender and religion combined to shape cultures of inclusion and exclusion in eighteenth-century England.

Ideals and Stereotypes

According to contemporary ideals as presented in print, a woman's inclusion within society was contingent on her conformity to certain expectations about moral, social, and sexual behaviour.[17] Her religious faith was an important part of this. As the following discussion shows, conduct guides and printed advice written for female readers made it clear that they could and should exercise their conscience, but that this should be done within a framework of what was appropriate for their sex.

Within the Established Church, women were expected to be active followers of the word, obedient to God's laws, and dutiful in their attendance to prayer and worship, but they were not expected to engage with theology. This ideal was strikingly illustrated in the advice and commentary for women given by the female writer and novelist, Eliza Haywood, who wrote: 'People that enquire too deeply into the mysteries of religion will always find themselves bewildered: – the speculation is above the reach of human reason even in the strongest heads, and when attempted by the more weak is sure to bring on the most fearful distraction of ideas'. She concluded that 'Humbly to believe what we are taught in youth ... is the surest means of enjoying peace of mind in age, and will be our best consolation in the hour of death'.[18] Anecdotes in Haywood's *Female Spectator* repeatedly demonstrated the dire consequences for women not acting modestly in matters of religion. One tale of great woe regarding a woman refusing to conform to her husband's beliefs ended with the woman having her child taken from her, and both husband and wife leading 'a solitary Widowed Life, publicly avowing the Error of their Choice, and in private, it is possible, condemning that of their own Obstinacy'.[19] It was made clear that there could be grave social repercussions when women went beyond the supposed remit of their gender in religious affairs.

Haywood was not alone in her advice that women should not overstretch themselves when it came to religious matters. One guide for the education of daughters, translated from French by the Church of England divine George Hickes, stated:

> As for the Daughters ... there is no need they should be Learned; Curiosity makes them vain and affected; it is enough, they be one day able to govern their Families, and obey their Husbands with submission. This seems confirm'd by the Experience we have of many Women, whom Learning has made ridiculous.

He expressed particular concern about those who 'carry their Curiosity yet much farther, and set themselves to the deciding matters of Religion, tho' they be not at all capable of the Employment'.[20] Although women were understood by some contemporaries to have innately 'a great deal more Religion than *Men*', they were also considered to be 'not very capable' of 'a long abstruse and wearisome Examination' of religious principles.[21]

Women were instead expected to be meek, humble, and cheerful in their religious practice. One conduct guide for young ladies written by dancer and choreographer John Essex in 1722, advised 'a Love for Religion, and decent Behaviour in Divine Worship ... Preciseness is not required, but you may look solemn, yet pleasant, and converse wisely and with a Familiarity becoming Modesty and Meekness'.[22] Numerous guides for young ladies similarly emphasised that they should not be too solemn. The Dublin poet and author Wetenhall Wilkes advised in his *Letter of Genteel and Moral Advice to a Young Lady* (1740), that cheerfulness 'is not only the most Lovely, but the most commendable in a virtuous Person: Whereas sorrowful Faces and gloomy Tempers are owing to mistaken Notions of Piety'.[23]

Printed stereotypes of Presbyterian and Independent women suggested that they wholly failed to live up to this idealised female piety. In a period fraught with disagreement over England's religious settlement, defenders of an Established-Church monopoly feared that Dissenters would 'subvert the Government' and 'ruin the Church'.[24] Aspects of these fears were expressed specifically in relation to Presbyterian and Independent women. The 'Character of a Presbyterian, or a Female Hypocrite', published in a character miscellany in 1703, and reprinted in numerous forms thereafter, is one particularly clear example of this:

> A *Character of a Presbyterian*, or, A *Female Hypocrite*. Is one in whom all good Women suffer, she Censures her whole Sex; yet is herself the most liable to Censure amongst 'em. She hates the *Playhouse* and *Church* alike; the one is an Offence to her pretended Sanctity; the other to her supposed Modesty. The *Surplice* makes her Blush she says; for it looks as if the *Parson* was in his Shirt ... whilst she gives a young Fellow advice against *Wenching*, she slily insinuates a liking for his *Person* ... Nothing angers her so much as that Women are not allow'd to Preach ... but what she can't at the Church, she can at the Table, where she rails against Sense and Antichrist, till a Capon Wing stops her Mouth, and gives the wearied Girl a little Respit.

The author went on to describe how 'Destruction is her Business, Scandal her Devotion, Interest her God, and Dissimulation her Master piece. She's an everlasting Argument'.[25] In spelling out the supposed failure of Presbyterian women to conform to gendered expectations of social, moral, and religious behaviour, the author thus reinforced the argument that religious dissent was, in general, a danger to society.

Women and Religious Coexistence   73

However, the archetypal Dissenting woman was not just described as disruptive; she was also miserable and unattractive. According to one author, 'She wears the best of Silks and Linnen, that ever Prus were put in; but dress so *Odly*, that she spoils her Shape, and the Make of her Face by screwing it into the Model of *Nonconformity*'. This example underlines how religious Dissent could corrupt the feminine beauty of the believer.[26] In 1710, the High-Church Tory polemicist Ned Ward equally emphasised the perceived miserable countenance of Dissenters by commenting in his description of a 'devout lady' of a nonconformist persuasion that 'If you happen to blurt out a merry Jest, she'll cry, *O that the Tongue, which was made to praise the Lord, should so unwarily slide into such Immorality and Prophaneness!*'.[27] The propensity of Presbyterian and Independent women to dedicate time to reading devotional literature was also subject to satirical comment, with one 1708 characterisation of the 'female hypocrite' stating: 'Her Devotion at the *Conventicle* is in turning up the *Eggs* of her *Eyes* to the *Tubsters*, and turning down the Leaves of her *Book*'.[28]

The figure of the sexually deviant and socially disruptive woman was thus central to printed stereotypes of Presbyterians and Independents in England in the first half of the eighteenth century. Refusing to conform to the quiet and obedient behaviour of their female neighbours, these were supposedly women who used their pretended spirituality and religious knowledge to condemn others while they sinned themselves. This stereotype was used not just to cast these women in a negative light but also encapsulated the very essence of Dissent itself. The unruly woman was the perfect metaphor for Protestant Dissent – a danger to state and society. From a comparison of these printed stereotypes with contemporary ideals of female religious behaviour, it would be expected that the exclusion of Presbyterian and Independent women, from all but their religious and family communities, was absolute.

Experiences of Exclusion

Printed ideals and polemical literature might well be expected to give an exaggerated or misleading idea of the everyday experiences of the groups they describe. Yet, in many ways, the impression of exclusion given by these works is confirmed by the records of Presbyterian and Independent women. The behaviour of these women, as reported in their diaries and letters, appears to have gone directly against the ideals presented in advice literature, and in many ways reinforced stereotypes. They were not just religiously provocative but acted contrary to gendered views of appropriate social behaviour. On the surface, therefore, it seems that the interaction of gendered expectations and religious prejudice did lead to the marginalisation of Presbyterian and Independent women within their local communities.

74   *Carys Brown*

One potential barrier to the inclusion of these women within their local communities was that by contemporary standards, they had a strong tendency towards just the sort of serious examination of religious principles that conduct literature advised against. Reading had long had a significant place in the puritan culture from which Presbyterianism and Independency emerged, and reading and exchanging books with others could form an important aspect of a group religious identity.[29] Accordingly, Dissenting women's preference for spending significant amounts of time reading religious texts, and reflecting on their faith rather than engaging in other social activities, could simultaneously bolster a sense of belonging to a religious community and undermine inclusion within wider social communities. This is evident throughout the diary of Rochdale Presbyterian Anne Dawson, who was in her twenties at the time of writing. Following a social visit on 16 February 1722 she wrote: 'I wish that in common conversation our talk might be more of things & less of persons & that our fine Lady's would read & think more & talk less.'[30] In May 1722, again after having spent considerable time in social company, she reflected that 'a book is the most profitable companion', and lamented the time she had wasted on less serious matters.[31]

A similar tone is observable in the diaries of Cheshire Presbyterian, Sarah Savage. Her strong personal association of reading with religiosity led her to comment with regret after a visit to a cousin (who conformed to the Established Church) that 'I discern no footsteps of religion, could not see a book in the house'.[32] In contrast, even when she was offered entertainment in the company of others, she found 'more inward satisfaction with a good Book in my own Closet than with all the Visits, modes, & forms'.[33] Her preference for books over company does appear, as Amanda Herbert has argued, to have isolated her from her local community.[34] Yet, at the same time, as Gillian Wright has shown, it simultaneously fostered a sense of group identity among her family and coreligionists.[35] These were women that contemporary conduct writers would have no doubt suggested, 'Learning has made ridiculous'.[36]

Perhaps more provocatively, some Dissenting women overstepped the boundaries of female authority by disobeying husbands and parents because of their beliefs, and by attempting to proselytise. This could bring them into disrepute with kin and in their communities. An account of the conversion of a Cambridgeshire woman, Mary Churchman, from zealous Anglicanism to Congregationalism, was recorded by her grandson John Churchman in his commonplace book and was subsequently published in 1760. It describes the deeply disruptive effect of her conversion on her relationship with her father.[37] She reportedly tried to conceal that she had been to Congregationalist meetings; according to her grandson's account, she said that:

Women and Religious Coexistence 75

If my Father found it out, that day was spent in nothing but oaths & resolves to murther me, My Mother altho' an Enemy would send a servant to meet me before I could get home to bid me not to appear 'till my Father was gone to bed I have often hid my self upon a Wood stack, & have seen my Father with a Naked knife storming that he would be my death before he slept.[38]

The rage Mary's father felt at his daughter's disobedient Dissent (although he later converted) was devastating, but she remained compelled by her belief to go against his authority.

Religious Dissent more often united families than divided them, but the attempts of women to share their faith could cause considerable tension. Sarah Savage reported the efforts of other Presbyterian women in her community to persuade those around them to attend meetings, including one Mrs Wright, who tried to have her husband 'go along with her to meeting', but received the 'smart reply' that he would '"if I could ... see you any better for going"'.[39] Savage herself also tried to spread her faith. After the aforementioned visit to her cousin in November 1716, she rebuked herself for having been 'so foolish as not to say one serious Word among them, but resolve by Gods grace I will do it, when I have next Opper[tunit]y'.[40] These were women whose dissent went not only against religious norms but also, through their attempts to proselytise, sometimes challenged expectations of submission to male authority. In the context of stereotypes, such as the view that conversation with a Presbyterian woman was an 'everlasting Argument', and wider concerns about the potential for Presbyterians and Independents to undermine the stability of society, these unfeminine presumptions to learning and evangelism would have done little to aid peaceful coexistence.[41]

Furthermore, it appears that the behaviour of these women would have reinforced views that nonconformist women, in general, made miserable and unattractive company. In July 1722, for instance, Anne Dawson found herself in society with a group of ladies playing cards, and rather than participating decided to sit in the room 'imploying my hands much better with my nedle'.[42] The behaviour of Sarah Say, daughter of Suffolk Independent minister Samuel Say, seems to have been similar: her father wrote to her, in about 1740, that 'It has pleas'd me to observe that You can deny Your Self without Pain, or rather if I do not deceive My Self, that it is hardly an Act of Self denial in You to decline the Scenes of various Pleasure which others of Your Age & Sex pursue with such Eagerness'.[43] The refusal of young Presbyterian and Independent women to participate in the social activities of their contemporaries can hardly have aided their ability to integrate across religious boundaries within their communities.

Even when these women did engage in social activity, they did not always employ the pleasantness and innocent cheer expected of them by

76   *Carys Brown*

contemporary conduct writers. Anne Dawson, in particular, gives the impression of a strong aversion to mirth and merriment, chastising herself repeatedly in her diaries for not having been serious enough among social company. On 9 November 1721, she reflected on 'how oft have I indulg'd my self in foolish jesting', while on 19 May 1722, she wrote 'If I take a View of my carrage this Week I must be ashamed of it … I have spent it in trifling and visiting & tho in some company I have been very Chearful & Mery yet I find that true what Soloman says of Laughter it is mad and mirth what doth it; it leaves no true sattisfaction behind it'.[44] Indeed, she seems to have found solemnity much more edifying. For example, after visiting a sick family in July 1722, she concluded that 'it is better to go to the house of mourning than to the house of Feasting for certainly such Melancholy sights if any thing will make me consider my latter end'.[45] Dawson's stated preference for solemnity bears an unfortunate resemblance to Ned Ward's characterisation of the nonconformist woman as unable to hear a merry jest without condemnation.[46] Careful moderation of her social behaviour may have fostered her religious identity, but it is not likely to have encouraged her inclusion within wider social communities.

Such evidence, set against the background of religious stereotypes, suggests that female Presbyterians and Independents lay on the margins of their local communities. Not only did they fail to conform to the established religion, but the demands of their faith meant that in a number of respects, they also failed to meet gender expectations. This was particularly problematic in the context of stereotypes that focused on women as indicators of the general danger that Presbyterians posed to state and society. It also seems to confirm the conclusions of scholars who emphasise the particular social disadvantages faced by female Dissenters.[47] Gendered expectations about social and religious conduct, it appears, made the behaviour of these women a barrier to coexistence rather than its salve.

Inclusion and Neighbourly Women

It is important, however, not to be drawn in by the negative tone of such accounts. When we read the laments of Anne Dawson – that her behaviour among company was too merry, or that the company itself was not pious enough – it becomes apparent that she led a fairly sociable life. The fact that she repeatedly wished she had been less cheerful in company, or used her time more productively, demonstrates that when she was in the midst of social interaction, she did not necessarily adopt the austere countenance that she portrayed as ideal in her self-reflection. In using Dissenting women's life-writing to examine their social behaviour, we should be aware that the deliberately pious tone of much of their writing may not have wholly reflected the actual tenor of their sociability.

Women and Religious Coexistence 77

The sense of isolation and embattlement that many Dissenting women convey in their diaries may have been entirely genuine, but it should also be read within the context of a culture of Protestant Dissent that fostered narratives of suffering.[48] Furthermore, both letters and diaries were written with the edification of others in mind, composed (in part) to promote a set of pious ideals.[49] It is thus unsurprising that it is the social burden of these ideals that comes through most clearly in these sources.

When we read past their very high moral standards, apparent reluctance to waste time on social visits and inability to conform to all the social niceties expected of them, the women discussed here did participate actively in occasions that brought them into sociable contact with those who did not necessarily share their pious expectations. For instance, Cheshire Presbyterian Sarah Savage attended a 'splendid entertainment' at nearby Wrenbury Hall in January 1717, even if she did subsequently claim she would rather have been at home with a good book.[50] Similarly, Worcestershire Independent Abigail Blackmore instructed her fifteen-year-old daughter Sarah that 'if you are asked' to dance or play cards 'you may Refuse', but she evidently assumed that Sarah was likely to be invited to social situations where such activities were happening.[51] Consequently, in spite of all of the ways in which Dissenting women, to varying degrees, represented a challenge to the norms of society, these women were clearly not generally considered by their neighbours and contemporaries to be beyond the social pale.

How then, were Presbyterian and Independent women able to gain a degree of inclusion despite their obvious social and religious nonconformity? One explanation may be that while, on the one hand, the behaviour of these women could be interpreted as representing a fundamental threat to moral and social order, on the other, they were able to gain a degree of inclusion by meeting gendered expectations in sustaining and supporting the moral reputation of the communities in which they lived. Even as they lamented their social behaviour, expressing a desire for solemnity and seeking solace with books, the life-writings of Dissenting women reveal a high level of involvement in sustaining the welfare and reputation of their local communities.

One of the important ways in which women could act to sustain moral standards and develop communal bonds with their neighbours was by visiting others in times of trouble, sickness, and childbirth. This was a means both of caring for individuals and of maintaining the welfare of a community as a whole. Assisting with childbirth could be a means of preserving sexual honesty; helping those troubled by poverty, loneliness, or sickness to remember their duty to God and could prevent them from falling into the temptations of drink or sexual misconduct.[52] Anne Dawson, for instance, was assiduous in fulfilling this aspect of her neighbourly duty. As well as visiting individuals who were unwell, her wider concern with

78   Carys Brown

the moral and physical health of the community brought her into neighbourly contact with those around her.[53] In June 1722, for example, she recorded going with her sisters 'from one house to another through the town to inquire how many had had the small pox since last December & what numbers died & recover'd', which she then proceeded to record in her diary.[54] In this case, the actions of Dawson and her sisters displayed their wider concern for the community and the various individuals they visited, regardless of religious profession. In doing so, the Dawsons plainly stated their place within the local community and its importance to them.

In the seventeenth and eighteenth centuries, visiting the sick was a social expectation, as well as a 'religious exercise'.[55] It is therefore significant that despite religious differences, Presbyterian and Independent women also attended to the sick in their communities. It was common for women to also play prominent roles at moments of birth and death, including acting as midwives. As noted by Bernard Capp, this further offered Dissenting women the opportunity to be included within the wider community.[56] The conversion of Congregationalist Mary Churchman came about following her choice to go to a congregational meeting because of 'the persuasion of a Neighbour that had been usefull to me in my Illness'. This neighbour attended Churchman's sickbed despite the fact that she had no reason to think she would be warmly received. Indeed, Churchman claimed that during this period (before her conversion) she had frequently set her dog on a woman who passed through their family's yard every Sunday in order to go to a meeting.[57] The striking kindness of Churchman's charitable Congregationalist neighbour, who came to her at a time of need, no doubt influenced her later decision to join the faith.

It has long been acknowledged that although not all female relationships were harmonious, the roles women played could serve to ameliorate differences in their communities.[58] In general, those who acted in the interests of the neighbourhood might expect to receive warm treatment, even if they were considered outsiders on the basis of their religion.[59] When Mary Churchman lay dying in 1734, for instance, she was (at least according to her grandson) surrounded by 'her Neighbours who were weeping', as she told them that God saves even 'Sinners to the uttermost'.[60] There are limits to what this account can tell us about attitudes towards Churchman within her community, but the presence of these neighbours does suggest that they held a certain degree of respect towards her. Even those who evidently despised Dissent were sometimes on an individual basis willing to accept their Dissenting neighbours when they behaved in the interests of the wider community. During the mob riots of 1715, for instance, in which the property of many Dissenters was attacked, the High-Church Tory Deputy Registrar of Chester, Henry Prescott, recorded that he had called on one Dissenting woman,

'Mrs. Beech who receives us with Civility and with her fearfull sentiments of the riotous Mobb'.[61] Despite his otherwise declared deep dislike of Dissenters, Prescott at least acknowledged the civil reception he had received and the useful information his female host had provided. Such examples accord with the general stress in histories of coexistence of the role played by principles of neighbourliness in tempering the effect of religious divisions in everyday life.[62] A willingness to fulfil some of the neighbourly roles expected of women undoubtedly would have aided general relations between Presbyterians, Independents, and members of the Established Church on a local level.

Inclusion and Religiosity

Nevertheless, it seems unlikely that a willingness to fulfil the basic practical expectations of neighbourly care was sufficient to ameliorate against widespread and deeply felt ideological impulses to persecute and exclude Dissenters. A focus on the role of the neighbourly actions of Presbyterian and Independent women in smoothing over tensions caused by religious differences can thus only present a partial picture and risks neglecting the fact that their religiosity in itself may have been valued within their wider communities. In fact, these women's religiosity, while a cause of their exclusion, also provided opportunities for their inclusion.

This becomes particularly apparent when we consider the broader contemporary intellectual context. As concerns about libertinism, atheism, and deism increased in the eighteenth century, some members of the Established Church became more willing to accommodate Dissenters in the fight against the greater evil of irreligion.[63] Furthermore, debates about the relative roles of community, conscience, and the courts in regulating individual conduct resulted in an increased discussion of sexual morality and behaviour in the press.[64] In the context of urban growth, increased availability of goods, and higher population mobility, many communities became concerned about 'a wider malaise rooted in luxury, greed and indolence'.[65]

This perceived need to fight against immorality and atheism did in some cases improve relations between Dissenters and members of the Established Church. One well-known initiative that created the conditions for cross-confessional collaboration was the Societies for the Reformation of Manners. Drawing on the idea that the sins of an individual were destructive to the entire community, supporters of the Society were encouraged to be active in regulating vice within their communities.[66] Within this movement, the ideal of Protestant unity against a wider evil and in support of national godliness was prominent; in the battle against vice, divisions between established religion and Dissent might, some hoped, be laid aside.[67] The reality was, admittedly, somewhat different, and for some Anglican clergy, the idea of

80 *Carys Brown*

collaboration with their Presbyterian rivals was unacceptable.[68] Nevertheless, among zealous portions of the laity the creation of such pan-Protestant societies indicates the potential power of shared moral concerns in uniting mainstream religion with Dissenting communities.

While groups such as the Societies for the Reformation of Manners facilitated amity between some pious men across the religious divide, they were male-dominated, and much of their rhetoric promoted an ideal Christian manliness in the face of the perceived creeping influence of commercially driven effeminacy.[69] However, shared moral concerns may have afforded women a point of common interest between those of a different religious profession. In localities concerned about the spread of immorality, and in a society that relied more on the informal self-regulation of communities than on formal means of preventing socially unacceptable behaviour, the actions of female Presbyterians and Independents could easily be construed as being in the interests of their wider community. As we have already seen, despite their professed reluctance to socialise beyond their own religious professions, these women fulfilled the neighbourly duties expected of godly women at the same time as leading exemplary lives. Although much of their motivation in protecting their own reputations was rooted in both an intense sense of their own sinfulness – and a need to protect their religious profession against hostile attack – their self-regulation also resulted in them being upstanding neighbours.

This particular care in guarding and monitoring their own behaviour may have bolstered the reputation of Presbyterian and Independent women within their communities. The fear of neighbourly judgement felt by these women meant that they were often extremely wary of attracting comment through behaviour that might be construed as immoral. Anne Dawson often reflected on how the world might view her and her faith if she failed to live up to high moral standards, commenting in August 1721, that 'we had need to walk cercumspectly [*sic*] because there is many eyes upon us as the eyes of our friends are upon us & will be troubled at our falling & the eyes of our enemies are upon us & wait for our halting'.[70] In March 1722, she was further concerned that 'tho I profess to be bound for a better Country yet I act & car[r]y as if I thought to take up my rest here'.[71] Sarah Savage, too, was acutely aware that her behaviour reflected on her religion as well as her own character, and that she should therefore avoid giving any reason for others to question her morality. In May 1721, she wrote that she 'would so demean my-self as to adorn Religion. that my neighbours may see my Treasure in Heaven is safe'.[72] These women were painfully conscious that their morality had to be impeccable, not just for the sake of their own consciences, but for the protection of the reputation of their religion.

This does not, of course, mean that the pious efforts of these women necessarily resulted in integration within their local communities. Indeed, it is very difficult to find substantial evidence of Anglican women's reactions to the behaviour of individual Presbyterian and Independent women. There are, however, examples of wealthy ladies from within the Established Church maintaining relationships with Dissenting women in their communities, suggesting that they respected one another for their pious behaviour. In the case of Margaret Sheppard, an Independent and acquaintance of Suffolk minister Samuel Say, this extended to employment within the household of one Lady Vane. Writing to Say in the 1730s, Sheppard described how although her employer was not a Dissenter, she was 'a very religious person which is rare in any but more so in her station'.[73] Despite her own conformity, Lady Vane evidently saw an Independent woman as a good choice for a servant in a household of strict religiosity and high moral standards. There is further evidence of the patronage of Dissenting women by wealthy ladies who did not share their religious standpoint. In 1756, for instance, Sarah Savage's daughter-in-law (also named Sarah) was given a pair of tortoiseshell sugar tongs by Lady Willoughby. It is unclear why the gift was given, but this was a fashionable item that suggested that Willoughby felt warmly towards Savage (née Roe), despite their religious differences.[74] In both these instances, the relationship established between the women may have been facilitated by an already moderate attitude of the patrons towards Dissent. Such occurrences nevertheless indicate that the women concerned were well enough respected in their communities that those of higher standing were willing to associate with them.

Given widespread concern about the changing moral shape of society, it seems likely that Presbyterian and Independent women would have been valued in some measure, if not for their religion, then for their moral behaviour. It was surely their moral reputation, as much as their quotidian contributions to practical aspects of community life, which allowed many of these women to circumnavigate prejudices against them. One of the principal means by which women could exercise authority in this period was as guardians of the welfare and reputation of communities and their own families.[75] Women could therefore play a critical part in improving, or indeed worsening, the prospect of those families and networks when they were disadvantaged by religious difference. For all their potential as a focal point for religious conflict, Dissenting women were in a strong position to use the expectations and practices associated not just with their gender but also with their religion to advance their own reputations.

Conclusion

The essay has explored the complex position of Presbyterian and Independent women within local communities in eighteenth-century England. While acknowledging the extent to which their religion disabled them from adhering to gendered norms surrounding religious and polite behaviour, it has stressed the importance of the contributions these women made by adhering to wider gendered expectations about the role of women within their communities. In doing so, it suggests a number of ways in which there may have been a distinctive female contribution to the nature of relations between members of the Established Church and Dissenting congregations in this period. Firstly, it emphasises that the sense of isolation conveyed by Presbyterian and Independent women in their life-writing may belie the extent of their wider sociability. This does not mean that these women felt fully included within social situations, or indeed that they participated in all aspects of polite sociability, but it does highlight that they were often in a position to build social relationships with those around them. Secondly, it reiterates that Presbyterian and Independent women often took great care to fulfil their neighbourly duties. This may have been particularly important for women of these denominations because of the prevalence of the stereotype of Presbyterians and Independents as socially and politically disruptive. Given the existing historiographical emphasis on the role of neighbourliness in facilitating coexistence, these aspects of female involvement, with a particular emphasis on Dissent, deserve more attention. Lastly, it highlights how in the context of concerns about the moral integrity of English society being undermined by luxury, licentiousness, and atheism, the carefully regulated behaviour of Dissenting women may, in the eyes of some, have made them valuable and respected members of their communities. The precise effect of these factors on the long-term acceptance of a more religiously pluralistic landscape in eighteenth-century England demands further exploration.

The power of female Dissenters to use their expected roles as women to facilitate their own and their families' inclusion within their wider communities should not be overstated. It remains that many of their contemporaries were entirely unsympathetic to Presbyterians and Independents, and at times of political crisis Dissenters faced severe and sometimes violent personal attack. For those for whom the principle of liberty of conscience was unacceptable, the religious beliefs and practices of Presbyterians and Independents were fundamentally inimical to the welfare of community and nation, however agreeable their social behaviour.[76] As we have seen, although the pious behaviour of Dissenting women could, on the one hand, be interpreted as making a positive moral contribution, it could also be represented by their opponents in biting satire as a dangerous pretence. The strict adherence of these women to the high standards demanded of them by their religious professions could aid the reputation and survival of Dissent, but it was also potentially highly damaging to it.

It is this paradox that makes the place of women in determining the strength or fragility of religious coexistence so interesting. Moreover, whilst

Women and Religious Coexistence   83

this chapter has focused only on eighteenth-century England, this was not the only context in which arguments about and stereotypes of women were central to disputes between religious communities. Frances Dolan has shown how in the seventeenth century Protestants frequently sought to attack Catholics and Catholicism by associating them with disorderly women.[77] Similarly, in early modern France, gendered categorisations were often used by rival confessions to label the other as dominated by women.[78] Given that women were so central to the discourse that emerged from religious prejudice, the actions of women were surely of pivotal significance to the management and amelioration of those prejudices within communities. If we want to understand religious coexistence, it is perhaps to the actions of women that we must first look.

Acknowledgements

I am grateful to Naomi Pullin and Kathryn Woods for their very helpful editorial attention to this piece. I would also like to thank Harriet Lyon and Tom Smith for their comments on earlier drafts. In quotations from contemporary sources, original spelling and capitalisation have been retained; contractions have been silently expanded.

Notes

1 Alexandra Shepard, *Meanings of Manhood in Early Modern England* (Oxford: Oxford University Press, 2003), 78; Karen Harvey, *The Little Republic. Masculinity and Domestic Authority in Eighteenth-Century Britain* (Oxford: Oxford University Press, 2012), 8; Elaine M. McGurr, *Eighteenth-Century Characters. A Guide to the Literature of the Age* (Basingstoke: Palgrave Macmillan, 2007), 91–2; Emma Major, *Madam Britannia: Women, Church, and Nation, 1712–1812* (Oxford: Oxford University Press, 2012), 127–30.

2 Naomi Tadmor, 'Where was Mrs Turner? Governance and Gender in an Eighteenth-Century Village', in Steve Hindle, Alexandra Shepard, and John Walter (eds), *Remaking English Society: Social Relations and Social Change in Early Modern England* (Woodbridge: The Boydell Press, 2013), 103–4; Amanda Vickery, *The Gentleman's Daughter: Women's Lives in Georgian England* (New Haven and London: Yale University Press, 1998), 9, 206–7.

3 Sara Mendelson and Patricia Crawford, *Women in Early Modern England, 1550–1720* (Oxford: Oxford University Press, 1998), 205–6; Kathryn Gleadle, "Opinions Delivr'd in a Conversation': Conversation, Politics, and Gender in the Late Eighteenth Century', in Jose Harris (ed.), *Civil Society in British History: Ideas, Identities, Institutions* (Oxford: Oxford University Press, 2003), 63–4; Karen Harvey, 'Barbarity in a Teacup? Punch, Domesticity and Gender in the Eighteenth Century', *Journal of Design History*, 21 (2008), 206, 211; Melinda S. Zook, *Protestantism, Politics, and Women in Britain, 1660–1714* (Basingstoke: Palgrave Macmillan, 2013), 9.

4 Sarah Apetrei and Hannah Smith, 'Introduction', in Sarah Apetrei and Hannah Smith (eds), *Religion and Women in Britain, c.1660–1760*

84 Carys Brown

(Farnham: Ashgate, 2014), 2, 16. See also Zook, *Protestantism, Politics, and Women*, 8–10.

5 Naomi Pullin, *Female Friends and the Making of Transatlantic Quakerism* (Cambridge: Cambridge University Press, 2018), 2–3, passim.

6 Rachel Adcock, *Baptist Women's Writings in Revolutionary Culture, 1640–1680* (Farnham: Ashgate, 2015), 118–45; Amanda E. Herbert, *Female Alliances. Gender, Identity and Friendship in Early Modern Britain* (New Haven and London: Yale University Press, 2014), 182–3; Alasdair Raffe, 'Female Authority and Lay Activism in Scottish Presbyterianism, 1660–1740', in Apetrei and Smith (eds), *Religion and Women in Britain*, 63; Cynthia Aalders, '"Your Journal, My Love": Constructing Personal and Religious Bonds in Eighteenth-Century Women's Diaries', *Journal of Religious History*, 39 (2015), 391–2.

7 Benjamin Kaplan, *Divided by Faith: Religious Conflict and the Practice of Toleration in Early Modern Europe* (Cambridge, MA: Belknap Press, 2007), 7–8; William J. Sheils, '"Getting On" and "Getting Along" in Parish and Town: Catholics and their Neighbours in England', in Bob Moore, Henk van Nierop, and Judith Pollman (eds), *Catholic Communities in Protestant states. Britain and the Netherlands, c.1570–1720* (Manchester: Manchester University Press, 2009), 67–83; Nadine Lewycky and Adam Morton, 'Introduction', in Nadine Lewycky and Adam Morton (eds), *Getting Along? Religious Identities and Confessional Relations in Early Modern England – Essays in Honour of Professor W. J. Sheils* (Farnham: Ashgate, 2012), 9.

8 See for example Bill Stevenson, 'The Social and Economic Status of Post-Restoration Dissenters, 1600–1725', in Margaret Spufford (ed.), *The World of Rural Dissenters, 1520–1725* (Cambridge: Cambridge University Press, 1995), 332–59; Bob Scribner, 'Preconditions of Tolerance and Intolerance in Sixteenth-Century Germany', in Ole Peter Grell and Bob Scribner (eds), *Tolerance and Intolerance in the European Reformation* (Cambridge: Cambridge University Press, 1996), 32–47; Adrian Davies, *The Quakers in English Society, 1655–1725* (Oxford: Clarendon Press, 2000); Christie Sample Wilson, *Beyond Belief: Surviving the Revocation of the Edict of Nantes in France* (Bethlehem: Lehigh University Press, 2011); Carys Brown, 'Militant Catholicism, Inter-Confessional Relations, and the Rookwood Family of Stanningfield, Suffolk, c.1689–c.1737', *Historical Journal*, 60 (2017), 21–45.

9 Notable exceptions to this include Pullin, *Female Friends*, 200–51.

10 Ian Moonie, 'Presbyterians and Independents of Congregationalists in Carlisle, 1648–1736', *Transactions of the Cumberland and Westmoreland Antiquarian and Archaeological Society*, 3 (2009), 124; Stephen Orchard, 'Congregationalists', in Andrew C. Thompson, *The Oxford History of Protestant Dissenting Traditions, Volume II: The Long Eighteenth Century, c.1689–c.1828* (Oxford: Oxford University Press, 2018), 30.

11 See Ralph Stevens, *Protestant Pluralism. The Reception of the Toleration Act, 1689–1720* (Woodbridge: The Boydell Press, 2018).

12 Francis Hare, *A Sermon Preached Before the House of Lords, in the Abbey-Church at Westminster, upon Monday, January 31, 1731* (London, 1732), 8, 17.

13 Edmund Gibson, *The Dispute Adjusted, About the Proper Time of Applying for a Repeal of the Corporation and Test Acts by Shewing that No Time is Proper* (Dublin, 1733), 15, 19.

14 Peter Lake, 'Feminine Piety and Personal Potency: The "Emancipation" of Mrs Jane Ratcliffe', *The Seventeenth Century*, 2 (1987), 147, 161; Diane

Willen, 'Godly Women in Early Modern England: Puritanism and Gender', *Journal of Ecclesiastical History*, 43 (1992), 562–3, 578; Ann Hughes, 'Puritanism and Gender', in John Coffey and Paul C.H. Lim (eds), *The Cambridge Companion to Puritanism* (Cambridge: Cambridge University Press, 2008), 298–300.

15 Anne Lawrence, 'Women, Godliness and Personal Appearance in Seventeenth-Century England', *Women's History Review*, 15 (2006), 75; Hughes, 'Puritanism and Gender', 300.

16 Patricia Crawford, 'Anglicans, Catholics, and Nonconformists after the Restoration, 1660–1720', in Susan E. Dinan and Debra Meyers (eds), *Women and Religion in Old and New Worlds* (London and New York: Routledge, 2001), 163; Alison Searle, 'Women, Marriage and Agency in Restoration Dissent', in Apetrei and Smith (eds), *Religion and Women in Britain*, 25.

17 Ingrid H. Tague, *Women of Quality: Accepting and Contesting Ideals of Femininity in England, 1690–1760* (Woodbridge: The Boydell Press, 2002), 30–3, 218–20; Kathryn Woods, 'Skin Colour, Gender and Narratives of Embodied Identity in Eighteenth-Century British Non-Fiction', *Eighteenth-Century Studies*, 40 (2017), 55–6; Elaine Chalus, 'Elite Women, Social Politics, and the Political World of Late Eighteenth-Century England,' *Historical Journal*, 43 (2000), 682, 692.

18 Eliza Haywood, *Epistles for Ladies. By the Authors of The Female Spectator. In Two Volumes* (Dublin, 1757), 33–4.

19 Eliza Haywood, *The Female Spectator* (4 vols, London, 1745–1746), iii. 257.

20 Francois Fénelon, trans. and ed. George Hickes, *Instructions for the Education of a Daughter* (London, 1707), 2–3, 13. This comment in the 1707 translation may have been a response the writings of Mary Astell. Fénelon's text was originally published in French in 1687; Mary Astell's, *A Serious Proposal to the Ladies, for the Advancement of Their True and Greatest Interest by a Lover of Her Sex* (London, 1694) was in part a retort to male writers such as Fénelon who sought to exclude women from education. See Brandy Lain Schillace, '"Reproducing" Custom: Mechanical Habits and Female Machines in Augustan Women's Education', *Feminist Formations*, 25 (2013), 114.

21 Francois Bruys, *The Art of Knowing Women: Or, the Female Sex Dissected, in a Faithful Representation of Their Virtues and Vices* (London, 1730), 36.

22 John Essex, *The Young Ladies Conduct: Or, Rules for Education* (London, 1722), 59–60.

23 Wetenhall Wilkes, *A Letter of Genteel and Moral Advice to a Young Lady: Being a System of Rules and Informations; Digested into a New and Familiar Method* (Dublin, 1740), 16.

24 Hare, *A Sermon Preached Before the House of Lords*, 8.

25 Anon., *Mirth and Wisdom in a Miscellany of Different Characters, Relating to Different Persons and Perswasions* (London, 1703), 3–5.

26 Anon., *The True Characters* (London, 1708), 7.

27 Edward Ward, *The Modern World Disrob'd: Or, Both Sexes Stript of their Pretended Vertue* (London, 1708), 7.

28 Anon., *The True Characters*, 8.

29 Andrew Cambers, *Godly Reading. Print, Manuscript, and Puritanism in England, 1580–1720* (Cambridge: Cambridge University Press, 2011), 6–7, 9.

30 London, British Library, Add MS 71626, Diary of Anne (Dawson) Evans 1721–1722, fol. 18r.

86 *Carys Brown*

31 Ibid., fol. 23r.
32 Oxford, Bodleian Library, MS. Eng. misc. e. 331, Sarah Savage's Diary, 31 May 1714 to 25 December 1723 (C18th copy), 123, entry for 9 November 1716.
33 Ibid., 134, entry for 10 January 1717.
34 Herbert, *Female Alliances*, 170, 184. See also Amanda E. Herbert, 'Queer Intimacy: Speaking with the Dead in Eighteenth-Century Britain', *Gender & History*, 31 (2019), 33–4.
35 Gillian Wright, 'Delight in Good Books: Family, Devotional Practice, and Textual Circulation in Sarah Savage's Diaries', *Book History*, 18 (2005), 56–8.
36 Fénelon, trans. and ed. Hickes, *Instructions for the Education of a Daughter*, 3. There were also a minority of Established Church authors who argued for the intellectual capacity of women. See especially Astell, *A Serious Proposal to the Ladies,* 84–8.
37 The text was published in Samuel James's *An Abstract of the Gracious Dealings of God, With Several Eminent Christians, in Their Conversion and Sufferings* (London, 1760). All quotations here are from John's Churchman's manuscript version – Chelmsford, Essex Record Office, D/DQs 22, 'John Churchman His Book', 1749, fols. 11v–16v.
38 Ibid., fol. 12v.
39 Sarah Savage's Diary, 1714–1723, 105, entry for 18 June 1716.
40 Ibid., 123, entry for 9 November 1716.
41 Anon., *Mirth and Wisdom in a Miscellany of Different Characters*, 5.
42 Diary of Anne Dawson, fol. 38r.
43 London, Dr Williams's Library (hereafter DWL), 12.108(14), Letter from Samuel Say to Sarah Say, c.1738–1745.
44 Diary of Anne Dawson, fols. 4r, 23r.
45 Ibid., fol. 39v.
46 Ward, *The Modern World Disrob'd*, 7.
47 Crawford, 'Anglicans, Catholics, and Nonconformists', 163; Searle, 'Women, Marriage and Agency in Restoration Dissent', 25.
48 James E. Bradley, *Religion, Revolution, and English Radicalism: Nonconformity in Eighteenth-Century Politics and Society* (Cambridge: Cambridge University Press, 1990), 50, 53, 87–8.
49 Wright, 'Delight in Good Books', 55.
50 Sarah Savage's Diary, 1714–1723, 133–4, entry for 10 January 1717.
51 DWL, 12.40/62, Letter from Abigail Blackmore to Sarah Blackmore, 20 November 1725.
52 Mendelson and Crawford, *Women in Early Modern England*, 314; Bernard Capp, *When Gossips Meet: Women, Family, and Neighbourhood in Early Modern England* (Oxford: Oxford University Press, 2003), 361.
53 Diary of Anne Dawson, fol. 39v.
54 Ibid., fol. 31v.
55 Olivia Weisser, *Ill Composed. Sickness, Gender, and Belief in Early Modern England* (New Haven and London: Yale University Press, 2015), 106.
56 Capp, *When Gossips Meet*, 355, 369; Pullin, *Female Friends*, 229–30.
57 'John Churchman His Book', fol. 11v.
58 Capp, *When Gossips Meet*, 272; 381
59 Herbert, *Female Alliances*, 185, 192.
60 'John Churchman his book', fol. 16r.
61 John Addy and Peter McNiven (eds), *The Diary of Henry Prescott. LL. B., Deputy Registrar of Chester Diocese, vol. 2, 25 March 1711–24* (Record Society of Lancashire and Cheshire, vol. CXXII: 1994), 456.

Women and Religious Coexistence   87

62 Sheils, '"Getting On" and "Getting Along"', 67–83; Lewycky and Morton, 'Introduction', 7–9.

63 S.J. Barnett, *The Enlightenment and Religion: The Myths of Modernity* (Manchester: Manchester University Press, 2003), 106; Jeffrey S. Chamberlain, 'The Limits of Moderation in a Latitudinarian Parson: Or, High-Church Zeal in a Low Churchman Discover'd', in Roger D. Lund (ed.), *The Margins of Orthodoxy: Heterodox Writing and Cultural Response 1600–1750* (Cambridge: Cambridge University Press, 1995), 206, 209; W.M. Jacob, *Lay People and Religion in the Early Eighteenth Century* (Cambridge: Cambridge University Press, 1996), 135, 154.

64 David M. Turner, '"Secret and Immodest Curiosities?" Sex, Marriage, and Conscience in Early Modern England', in Harald E. Braun and Edward Vallance (eds), *Contexts of Conscience in Early Modern Europe, 1500–1700* (Basingstoke: Palgrave Macmillan, 2004), 133, 148–9.

65 Steve Poole, '"Bringing Great Shame Upon this City": Sodomy, the Courts and the Civic Idiom in Eighteenth-Century Bristol', *Urban History* 34 (2007), 117.

66 T.C. Curtis and W.A. Speck, 'The Societies for the Reformation of Manners: A Case Study in the Theory and Practice of Moral Reform', *Literature and History*, 3 (1976), 49–50, 60.

67 Craig Rose, 'Providence, Protestant Union and Godly Reformation in the 1690s', *Transactions of the Royal Historical Society*, 3 (1993), 151, 166–7.

68 Jacob, *Lay People and Religion*, 132–3; Stevens, *Protestant Pluralism*, 75.

69 Stephen H. Gregg, '"A Truly Christian Hero": Religion, Effeminacy, and Nation in the Writings of the Societies for Reformation of Manners', *Eighteenth-Century Life*, 25 (2001), 17, 19.

70 Diary of Anne Dawson, fol. 2v.

71 Ibid., fol. 19v.

72 Sarah Savage's Diary, 1714–1723, 283, entry for 28 May 1721.

73 DWL, 12.107(125), Letter from Margaret Sheppard to Samuel Say, 20 March c.1731–2.

74 Chester, Cheshire Archives and Local Studies, CR 147/51, Tortoiseshell Sugar Tongs said to have been given by Lady Willoughby to Sarah Savage [née Roe], c.1756.

75 Mendelson and Crawford, *Women in Early Modern England*, 210, 216–7.

76 See Gordon Rupp, *Religion in England, 1688–1701* (Oxford: Clarendon Press, 1986), 53–70; Donald A. Spaeth, *The Church in an Age of Danger: Parsons and Parishioners, 1660–1740* (Cambridge: Cambridge University Press, 2000), 155–72.

77 Frances E. Dolan, *Whores of Babylon: Catholicism, Gender and Seventeenth-Century Print Culture* (Ithaca, NY: Cornell University Press, 1999), 8, 10.

78 Keith P. Luria, *Sacred Boundaries: Religious Coexistence and Conflict in Early-Modern France* (Washington, DC: Catholic University of America Press, 2005), 194, 205.

4 Failed Friendship and the Negotiation of Exclusion in Eighteenth-Century Polite Society

Naomi Pullin

Friendship was part of the tissue of social relations that bound eighteenth-century elite English society together. Social acquaintances relied on a combination of politeness, good manners, civility, and occasional benevolence, to navigate the complex structures of elite social activity. Underlying cultural discussions about the advantages of friendship was the tacit recognition that the company one chose to keep could be dangerous and had to be navigated with the greatest caution. Concerned about the rise of affectation and declining standards of morality, Richard Steele summed up this paradox in *The Spectator* in March 1711, when he remarked that 'the most polite Age is in danger of being the most vicious'.[1] Indeed, despite their explicit claims for inclusivity, friendship and politeness were also exclusive in their application, operating with an implicit and explicit set of social boundaries, rules, and functions.

This chapter explores the intersection of exclusion and politeness within elite women's sociability through an instance of failed friendship involving Mary Sharpe and her female acquaintances Mary Hamilton and Elizabeth Carter. It is especially concerned with the ambiguity surrounding conceptions of female friendship in eighteenth-century England. The chapter examines two series of letters exchanged between Sharpe and Hamilton, and Carter and Hamilton, over an eleven-year period between March 1779 and January 1790, to argue that politeness was as much a force of division as it was for social unity.[2] Neither Mary Sharpe nor Mary Hamilton are especially well-known figures of eighteenth-century society, but they moved in prominent elite social, political, and intellectual circles. In later life, Mary Sharpe attained a degree of renown as a travel writer, and her 1796 journey through revolutionary France with her husband Andrew Douglas is documented in their jointly published *Notes of a Journey* (1797).[3] Mary Hamilton, who was governess to George III's children, was also a well-connected woman. In addition to a close relationship with Queen Charlotte, she was part of an intimate circle of literary friends that included Margaret Cavendish Bentinck, Hannah More, Fanny Burney, Elizabeth Vesey, Sir Joshua Reynolds, and Horace Walpole.

Failed Friendship in Polite Society 89

Sharpe and Hamilton became close friends through their connection to the bluestocking poet and translator Elizabeth Carter, with whom Sharpe said in 1782 that she 'entered easely into the most enthusiastic attachment'.[4] Their subsequent friendship was characteristic of the rich exchange and intimacy of close friends. But as this chapter will explore, their friendship was fragile. In 1782, Sharpe reported a visible and 'chilling damp' in her relationship with Carter.[5] Sharpe's friendship with Hamilton, moreover, ended dramatically in 1789 when Hamilton assured Sharpe that 'with truth & in charity' she would never 'attempt a renewal of acquaintance'. Hamilton also declared to Sharpe – in a provocation to enmity that was quite unusual among eighteenth-century women of their shared social rank – that she would continue to regard her 'as I have done since the year 1783 as one of the many instances of the imperfection and fickleness of human nature'.[6] This chapter pieces together the circumstances that led to the sudden rupture in this once intimate relationship. In doing so, it demonstrates the fragility of inclusion within women's polite circles.

A great deal of historical work has emphasised the power of politeness in a society based upon personal connections. However, scholars have largely overlooked the consequences of failed friendship. One exception is Soile Ylivuori's recent study of politeness, which has problematised the ideals of polite femininity by drawing attention to the deliberately performative, dissimulative, and hypocritical practices employed by eighteenth-century women in their daily lives.[7] Ylivuori aside, historians have generally failed to acknowledge the importance of exclusion in shaping female identity. In part, this rests on the nature of the surviving sources. Affection, resulting in the exchange of letters, gifts, favours, hospitality, and compliments, often created the conditions for rich archives of documentary evidence, as demonstrated in studies of female sociability by Amanda Herbert and others.[8] The exchange of such favours, of course, ceased once a relationship came to an end or lost its intimacy. Letters or artefacts from intimates that held a sentimental value or emotional attachment were also more likely to be preserved over those that reminded an individual (or their descendants) of negative encounters or broken friendships. For these reasons, it is unusual to find collections of manuscripts or other artefacts that enable examination of the dissolution of friendships through the writings of their central actors.

The correspondence documenting the demise of Sharpe and Hamilton's friendship thus provides rare historical evidence of the nature of exclusion and social ostracism in elite women's sociability. That said, Sharpe, Carter, and Hamilton's correspondence presents some methodological challenges. In the first instance, studying just one archival collection brings the risk of atypicality, since every human connection is unique. Accordingly, the causes of the breakdown in friendship between Carter, Hamilton, and Sharpe cannot be easily mapped onto other failed relationships. Second, we

90 *Naomi Pullin*

cannot read these epistles as straightforward transcripts of the connections between these women, especially because the letters that survive are not representative of a full range of correspondence exchanged between them.[9] Indeed, although all three women are represented in the surviving correspondence that will be examined in this chapter, the majority of letters were either written by Sharpe or Carter.[10]

A third challenge concerns interpreting the feelings and emotions expressed in the letters, and distinguishing 'art and artifice' from 'reality'.[11] In this respect, it is important to remember that politeness required feelings of anger and rage to be concealed by expressions of civility.[12] Equally, utterances that appear 'angry' in the letters might have been offered by their authors with the intention of being humorous in the context of their relationship, which a modern reader may not easily be able to identify.[13] These methodological complexities do not, however, render the ideas and expressions presented in the surviving correspondence meaningless, especially as the language deployed by Sharpe and Carter throughout their exchanges with Hamilton were remarkably candid and open.

Although we cannot use the relationships between Sharpe, Carter, and Hamilton to generalise about the failed friendships of other eighteenth-century women, this chapter aims to draw attention to the limits of what could be considered acceptable within the context of female friendship and sociability. Like many letters of the English aristocracy, Hamilton and Sharpe's letters dealt with every aspect of their lives: ranging from brief messages and compliments, to longer and more substantive epistles addressing subjects such as condolence, gossip, family news, or travel. By employing an approach that focuses on both the theory and practice of failed friendships, this chapter aims to offer some thoughts about the connections between what Phil Withington has aptly termed 'the micro-politics of social practice' and 'the larger structures constituting society'.[14] The discussion will be divided into three sections. The first considers the nature of friendship, sociability, and exclusion at a macro level; exploring the tensions and challenges of polite sociability as conveyed in the didactic and prescriptive literature of the time. The second and third sections focus upon Mary Sharpe and her social circle, using the correspondence she and Elizabeth Carter exchanged with Mary Hamilton to explore why their friendships came to an end. This will enable consideration of the boundaries between acceptable and unacceptable behaviour, and exploration of how the guidance about making and retaining friendships might not always have easily mapped on to the messy reality of women's everyday social interactions.

Friendship and Exclusion in Eighteenth-Century Advice Literature

Friendships were major social relationships in eighteenth-century England, though their meaning and practice varied markedly from how we might understand them today. As Naomi Tadmor has influentially shown, the importance of friendship for men and women of this period rested on the fact that being identified as a 'friend' did not just apply to individually chosen and affective friendship. Instead, it designated a range of relationships, which could denote kin and a wide range of non-related associates, such as patrons, guardians, business partners, religious companions, and prospective lovers.[15] The interconnection between intimate affective friendship, kinship, patronage, and other economic and political relationships makes any reading of the place of friendship in women's lives particularly hard to gauge. This is further complicated by the fact that eighteenth-century definitions of friendship encompassed both older and more modern meanings. For example, in the mid-eighteenth century Samuel Johnson reported that a friend was 'one who supports you and comforts you while others do not', suggesting the importance of warm attachment.[16] On the other hand, older ideas of 'instrumental' friendship, that rested on interest and self-advancement, also persisted. Friends of this sort, writes Allan Silver, were always treated 'as if they might become enemies'.[17]

Shifting conceptions of friendship during the eighteenth century had particular implications for female relationships, since patriarchal inequalities ensured that they were less likely to be economically instrumental than those of their male counterparts. This enabled them to be more emotionally 'interested' and affectionate.[18] Historians of eighteenth-century Britain have generally accepted that women had a central place in the spaces and activities of polite sociability. Many would also argue that female company, and affectionate models of friendship most commonly associated with women, came to encapsulate the ideals of civility and good manners expected of people of quality.[19] In discussions about friendship and politeness, women were generally regarded as more open and sincere in their friendships than men: 'the naturally polite sex'.[20] But the rise of women's participation in polite spaces and conversations brought with it a range of challenges and ideological questions about *who* could be regarded as 'polite' and *what* character traits were to be valorised. It also raised the issue of *how* appropriate behaviour should be regulated and *who* was going to be enforcing it. Defining what constituted exclusive behaviour in eighteenth-century sociability is thus fraught with historical challenges because exclusionary practices could be both physical and conceptual, and depended upon intangible elements such as appearance, personality, good humour, influence, marital status, and age.

Whilst politeness, as Paul Langford has shown, 'had to be attainable' and potentially within the reach of all, deciding who to exclude from a polite circle was just as important as including the right people.[21] At a time when social mobility had the potential to enable those lower down the social ladder to obtain the wealth and polite status enjoyed by the landed elites, it was important for those at the top of society to retain the

92 Naomi Pullin

lifestyle and appropriate manners that traditionally prevailed among their social class. Put another way, there was a need to differentiate between everyday civility, and close and intimate personal bonding. This issue was particularly sensitive in metropolitan centres like London where, from the late seventeenth century onwards, the development of new civic spaces, the rise of associational culture, and the growth of cultural institutions brought greater access to spaces for sociability, while also producing a degree of social confusion and 'masquerade'.[22] 'Politeness was a concept which eased and stabilised the demands of urban living', writes R.H. Sweet, and it was in such spaces that class barriers were less rigid.[23]

Nevertheless, the greater promotion of sociability and civility was problematic because the pursuit of status was deeply embedded in metropolitan life and was complicated by the rise of commercialism. Many scholars draw attention to the individual self-interest and ruthless desire for self-improvement that lay at the heart of eighteenth-century London sociability. Indeed, factionalism, divisions, conflict, and anxiety around strangers all became greater possibilities within a more pluralistic society.[24] In printed conduct books and treatises aimed at female readers, the importance placed on regulating public interaction highlights a contemporary preoccupation with the dangers that too much sociability could bring. The perils of polite company certainly coloured the advice that George Savile, Marquis of Halifax, gave to his daughter.[25] In this text, published in multiple editions in the late seventeenth and eighteenth centuries, he warned of the frequent occasions when women sought to find fault with one another in order to advance their own credit. Above all, it was 'complaisance', or a desire to continually please, that Halifax warned would lead to 'irrecoverable Mistakes'. He wrote to his daughter that it 'hath led your Sex into more blame, than all other things put together'.[26] Thus, too much civility was just as dangerous to a woman's honour as too little.

Life among the metropolitan elite needed constant maintenance. The ever-changing social landscape of the fashionable elite has been explored by Hannah Greig, who draws attention to the 'constant state of flux' among this section of society, who routinely drew in new members and ejected others.[27] Linked to this was anxiety about the wisdom of contracting friendships with strangers whose social backgrounds and credentials were uncertain. Impressionable young women (and men) were singled out by many of the conduct-book writers as particularly susceptible to the dangers of urban politeness, and as needing the most guidance on how best to navigate their sociable encounters. The Scottish physician Alexander Monro warned his daughter in 1753 that a 'dangerous Companion' threatened the very foundations of civil conversation.[28] His private counsel was echoed in other printed advice, such as that provided by the Scottish physician John Gregory in *A Father's Legacy to His*

Daughters (1776). In this, Gregory spoke of the perils of women's 'natural propensity' for friendship. He remarked that it was common for women like his daughters to 'run into intimacies which you soon have sufficient cause to repent of', which had the result of making their 'friendships so very fluctuating'. One of the greatest obstacles, he noted, was a clashing of interests 'in the pursuits of love, ambition, or vanity'. For this reason, Gregory recommended that a close relationship with a man could often be less dangerous than friendship with another woman.[29]

The main reason why so much anxiety surrounded the friendship choices of young women was the potential for dishonour if the relationship broke down. Since women did not have the same legal recourse as men, an elite woman's reputation could be irreparably damaged if her private thoughts and secrets were exposed. 'When a close knit Friendship slips the knot, or is violently broken in sunder', *The Ladies Dictionary* declared, 'Anger and Hatred ensures all the Secrets on either side ... are let fly abroad to become the entertainment and Laughter of the World'.[30] The betrayal of secrets from a broken intimacy was vividly described by one eighteenth-century tract to be like 'Birds let loose from a Cage, and become the Entertainment of the Town'.[31]

The ultimate concern, then, was the potential danger that a former friend might pose to a young woman's reputation, and by extension their family, kin, and other acquaintances. Concern about carefully guarded secrets being divulged was also revealed in answer to a speculative question asked in the *Athenian Mercury* in 1692 about '*why the greatest enmity succeeds the greatest Friendship and Amity?*' The reply from the Athenian Society drew reference to the fact that the 'Freedom and Converse' of close friendship made the parties involved 'more open to one anothers abuses, whereas other Persons that were strangers to their Breasts cou'd have nothing to say against them, or at least not half so much'.[32] Polite ladies were thus to be selective and exclusive when it came to the choice of their closest intimates, but they were also expected to treat their friends with respect and be tolerant of misdemeanours in established friendships to avoid social rupture. As Vickery has argued, women were expected to be 'self-possessed in social encounters, self-controlled in the face of minor provocations, [and] self-sufficient in the midst of ingratitude.'[33]

Although we cannot assume that women (or men) passively absorbed the ideals presented in the didactic literature, the fact that much of the advice was copied between texts and that many of these volumes went through multiple editions suggests that the guidance was accepted as the expected social norm.[34] Moreover, such texts illustrate that polite discourses – largely authored by men – positioned women in a self-policing role, which was presented as essential for women to adopt if they wished to be included in polite society. Accordingly, a woman's inclusion within

94 *Naomi Pullin*

particular social circles could be tenuous and subject to a range of competing factors. In attempting to establish the basis for ideal friendship, prescriptive texts taught women that the ability to present and conduct themselves with respectability was essential. They were also to be cautious about the dissembling outward veneer of others.

Mary Sharpe's Social Circle and the Politics of Politeness

While guidance provided in prescriptive literature relied on cautionary tales to encourage women and men to conform to a set of higher moral standards, it is clear that many of the problems of female friendship that were discussed in such texts were present in the relationships between Mary Sharpe, Mary Hamilton, and Elizabeth Carter. At the same time, their friendships were complicated by the different ways in which they understood and applied meanings of 'friendship', as demonstrated in the correspondence they exchanged. Sharpe's status was noticeably different from her female acquaintances, even though she occupied a similar social rank and participated in the same spaces of sociability. Her fragile footing on the rungs of polite society meant that her behaviour was closely scrutinised and, as her letters reveal, even she regarded herself as an inferior rather than equal to her correspondents. Consequently, Sharpe's experience of failed friendship and social ostracism is useful for understanding how exclusionary practices coexisted with the seemingly inclusive acts of politeness and civility that have so often been characterised as markers of the more universal commercial society that was emerging at this time.

Unlike many of her elite contemporaries, Mary Sharpe's access to polite society was not straightforward. She was born in London in 1753. She was the daughter of the wealthy politician and aristocrat Fane William Sharpe, MP for Callington, Cornwall. Details are scarce, but she may have spent some of her minority in residence with the family of her father's friend Thomas Edwards Freeman, MP for Steyning, West Sussex.[35] In many respects, her lineage should have guaranteed her a place among the London elite, since she inherited her father's large fortune and family estate at Hertfordshire when he died in 1771. Yet the circumstances of her upbringing made her integration into polite society challenging. In a short autobiographical letter that Sharpe wrote to Hamilton in 1782, she recorded how she had been forced to endure a solitary existence in her teenage years. Here she recounted that from the age of twelve she was confined to the family's Hertfordshire estate in Enfield Chase, in a state of 'the severest solitude', under the careful watch of her father and an unnamed inimical governess. Her father's death, when she was eighteen, left her 'with a large fortune and without a Friend', and, four years later, in 1775, she fled to London to begin her

Failed Friendship in Polite Society 95

induction into polite society.[36] By contemporary standards, this was a rather late age to be beginning such an introduction.

Sharpe's confinement at the family estate occurred at the crucial stage when most young elite women began their polite education and integration into the institutions of urban sociability. Urban sociability was generally centred on young unmarried women – in their mid-teens to mid-twenties – who benefitted greatly from the spaces and opportunities for interaction provided by towns and cities.[37] It was through social visits that young women learned about the rituals of sociability with the support of other members of their sex. The absence of this sort of education would have had a serious impact on Sharpe's ability to perform the sociability expected of a woman of her rank. It could also have affected her ability to find a suitor, since the pressure of making a 'good match' forced many young women into frequent public social interactions with members of both sexes.[38]

As a friendless heiress seeking access to the polite spaces occupied by the London elite, Sharpe came to rely on the patronage of her father's former-physician Doctor John Fothergill. Fothergill took pity on this vulnerable young woman, and subsequently came to act, as Sharpe put it, as 'the Guide the Guardian Protector, and Friend of my helpless inexperienced youth'.[39] Sharpe's priority was to establish a close circle of female friends on whom she could rely for support and patronage. Thanks to Dr Fothergill, Sharpe was introduced to the bluestocking Elizabeth Carter, thirty-six years her senior (Figure 4.1). Carter was an unmarried wealthy heiress who was regarded as an important scholar and socialite in London's intellectual circles. Carter was renowned for promoting female education. She also acted as a patroness of aspiring female writers, including Elizabeth Montagu, Catherine Talbot, and Fanny Burney.[40] The close connection Carter fostered with Mary Sharpe was thus not out of character, and there were many reasons for Fothergill to consider it suitable to place Sharpe under Carter's tutelage. This type of relationship, involving a more mature social sponsor taking an active interest in a much younger woman's social education, was not unique to Carter and was characteristic of other older women of a similar status.[41] It also demonstrates that the application of 'friendship' at this time did not have to apply to women who were equals. Sharpe's relationship to Carter instead confirms how unofficial power hierarchies operated among members of the female elite. Indeed, Sharpe's descriptions of their connection are indicative of a curious state of combined friendship and unpaid companionship.

It was through her friendship with Carter that Sharpe became close friends with bluestocking Mary Hamilton (Figure 4.2). In 1777, not long after their first acquaintance, Hamilton began her employment as governess in the court of George III. Despite Hamilton's royal patronage, the connection she shared with Sharpe seems to have been more akin to

Figure 4.1 Elizabeth Carter. Engraving after Sir Thomas Lawrence 1808. Yale Center for British Art. Accession Number: B1977.14.9839.

modern affective friendship than Sharpe's patron-friend relationship with Carter. Early on, Sharpe and Hamilton embraced the intimacy of their relationship and divulged their secrets to one another. Sharpe was particularly grateful to be treated as Hamilton's confidante on matters relating to her position at court and took her responsibility to 'keep to myself what you say in "confidence"' very seriously.[42] Although the nature of these confidences is unclear, it is possible that the trusted secrets to which Sharpe was referring related to a situation that had developed between Hamilton and John Dickenson (Hamilton's future husband) in 1777. As indicated in Hamilton's surviving letters and diaries, she started a correspondence with Dickenson in the hopes of 'advancing ye Intimacy &

Failed Friendship in Polite Society   97

Friendship so long subsisting between or Families'. However, Dickenson clearly had a different impression of her intentions, as Hamilton noted that he began 'to alter [his] manner of *expression*' towards her. In trying to manage this delicate situation, Hamilton determined that she would no longer write to Dickenson, in order to avoid him 'mistaking my meaning'.[43] Unfortunately, little is known about John Dickenson other than the fact that he was a year younger than Hamilton and from a lesser aristocratic family: the only son of John Dickenson of Birch Hall, Manchester. Dickenson first proposed marriage to Hamilton in 1780, but she refused. She nevertheless regretted this decision, and when he proposed again in 1784, she accepted.[44]

Being privy to such intimate information about her friend's thoughts, relationships, and feelings was clearly a great source of pride for Sharpe. In one letter from May 1781, Sharpe acknowledged the 'pleasure' she experienced at being deemed worthy of Hamilton's confidences, despite the fact that Hamilton had 'suffered some painful sensations' in divulging her thoughts and feelings on such matters. The seeming pleasure she took from her friend's misfortunes, Sharpe explained, lay in the fact that sharing them affirmed the special place she held in Hamilton's 'affection'.[45] On leaving court in 1782, Hamilton lived as an independent woman, dedicating much of her time in London to her female friends until her marriage to Dickenson in 1785.

Sharpe's deep emotional investment in her relationships with Carter and Hamilton is continually present in her extant correspondence, where she frequently reflected on the importance of harmonious friendship. By 1782, she had become so intimate with her patron that she claimed to have 'sacrificed every thing to my feelings for her [Carter]'. She also wrote that she viewed her intimate friendship with Hamilton as a 'sacred union, with so much uncommon worth'.[46] Though Sharpe's friendship with Hamilton was of a very different nature to her connection with Carter, various evidence in the surviving correspondence suggests that all three women generally conformed to the ideals of polite sociability expected of eighteenth-century women of quality. They enquired of one another's health, discussed works of literature, undertook social visits, breakfasted together, attended important social gatherings, and accompanied one another to the theatre. They also regularly took the waters at Bath and spent a great deal of time participating in the Spa town's fashionable social life.

In 1779, Sharpe also acted as Carter's travel companion during a tour of western and northern England.[47] Carter suffered from debilitating headaches, and during their travels Sharpe nursed and cared for her during these frequent bouts of illness. The intimacy and emotional investment Sharpe placed in her alliances was reinforced in March 1780, when she requested a piece of Hamilton's hair 'to make a locket for a bracelet, as a companion to one I have of our dear Mrs Carters'.[48] The exchange of hair served as a symbolic

98 *Naomi Pullin*

MARY HAMILTON BY SAUNDERS.
From a miniature in a ring given by her to Mr. John Dickenson after their engagement.

Figure 4.2 Mary Hamilton (later Dickenson). Engraved Frontispiece to *Mary Hamilton: Afterwards Mrs. John Dickenson: At Court and at Home* (1925). Yale Center for British Art. Reference Number: DA483 D5 A4 1925 (LC).

gesture of their close love and affection and suggests that Sharpe viewed her relationship with Carter and Hamilton as inviolable and lasting.[49]

Mary Sharpe and the Consequences of Failed Friendship

The early intimacy of the group's friendship nevertheless faltered over time. The outward displays of intimacy and affection that the women had initially shown to one another became tinged by the challenges of friendship formation, especially when the relationship began to take a more negative turn. A notable turning point came in 1782, when Sharpe agreed to marry the much older Reverend Dr Osmond Beauvoir – twenty-five years her senior – without seeking the consent of her acquaintances. Little is known about Beauvoir or his connection to bluestockings like Sharpe and Carter. All that can be established is that he was Master of the King's School at Canterbury School, which like many institutions of the age would have had links to the Anglican church and thus had connections to London.[50] Although Sharpe defended the reasons for keeping her engagement with Beauvoir secret, which stemmed from the opposition she had encountered from some of her relatives, she failed to follow conventional norms, where it was expected that a young woman's 'friends' would act as intermediaries in arranging courtship and marriage.[51] Undue secrecy in conducting marital arrangements, as David Vincent has argued, was 'mistrusted' because 'it heightened the possibility that inexperienced lovers might make an irrevocable decision unsupervised by their more responsible elders'.[52] This was demonstrated in the trials of Samuel Richardson's protagonist Clarissa, whose failure to heed the advice of her friends and relatives had damaging and destructive consequences.[53] Hamilton had of course disclosed John Dickenson's proposal in 1780, and possibly felt that Sharpe's failure to discuss her marital arrangements showed a lack of friendship reciprocity.

Elizabeth Carter opposed the match, as did many of Sharpe's other acquaintances. Sharpe, like Carter, was an heiress who did not need to marry for financial security and had previously declared that she wished to remain independent and single.[54] The death of her guardian and former-protector Dr Fothergill in December 1780, however, may have altered her views on marriage. For instance, there are hints that without her male protector, she may have felt in need of male guidance, especially in overseeing matters relating to her estate. This was encapsulated in a comment Hester Chapone made to Mary Delaney shortly after the marriage, in which she noted that Sharpe may be happier married to Beauvoir than 'in a single life, for she certainly wanted a protector and guide in the management of her large fortune'.[55] Sharpe also confided to Hamilton that Fothergill's death had made her feel like 'a solitary creature in the midst of this gay world', suggesting that this personal tragedy had altered her views on the need for male companionship.[56] It is nevertheless evident that her acquaintances did not regard the marriage as a 'good match'. In part this may have been because Beauvoir's fortune, as Master of Canterbury School, was no match for Sharpe's. His advanced age may also have been a cause for concern. Chapone, diplomatically remarked that she hoped Beauvoir would be

100   *Naomi Pullin*

'an indulgent *father* to her [Sharpe]', but also noted that the marriage was a 'union none of her friends could have advised'.[57]

Pursuing a life dedicated to intellectual pursuits rather than domestic responsibility was a hallmark of bluestocking culture. Since Sharpe had previously expressed her wish to remain single, her actions seemed to be defying the reason and virtue that lay at the heart of bluestocking sociability.[58] Elizabeth Carter had made a conscious decision not to marry in order to preserve her independence, enabling her to continue her intellectual pursuits. It has also been shown that marriage had a profound effect on women's status and social identities.[59] As Mark Philp has argued in his study of the middling ranks of London society in the 1790s, women's social networks and social lives were strongly dictated by their husbands' professional connections and interests. Few women were able maintain the friendships they had cultivated prior to marriage with the same degree of intensity.[60] There was thus a great deal of potential for marriage to restrict the sociability and intellectual achievements that bluestocking culture tried so hard to foster.

A great deal of ambiguity remained around the issue of marriages driven by love and passion versus those conducted out of economic interest, as was the question of what a socially acceptable courtship might look like. The Scottish physician, John Gregory, for instance, encouraged his female readers to keep 'love matters' a secret from friends because laying 'the heart open to any person … does not appear to me consistent with the perfection of female delicacy'.[61] Yet it is clear that Sharpe's concealment of her intended marriage to Beauvoir was considered beyond the bounds of respectable behaviour by her close female acquaintances. Although there is very little evidence to ascertain why Sharpe's friends objected to the match, the treatment of some of her contemporaries offer hints about how marriage matters could become problematic at all sorts of levels. Hester Thrale's marriage to her daughter's Italian singing master, Gabriel Piozzi, in 1784 was regarded as troubling by her former-bluestocking associates for a variety of reasons, not least because she was a wealthy middle-aged widow marrying a poor professional musician.[62] The response of even Thrale's closest friends was harsh. Aside from the unsuitability of the match, it seems that much of the social ostracism Thrale faced rested on the way in which the courtship was conducted, which involved an open display of passion for Piozzi.[63] Indeed, a mature woman publicising her passionate feelings caused a general outrage across polite society, and, in contrast to Sharpe's secrecy, Thrale's behaviour towards Piozzi directly contravened the 'female delicacy' advocated by conduct writers like Gregory.

The marriage of Thrale's friend and servant Fanny Burney to Alexandre d'Arblay in 1794 was similarly complex and reveals another layer to the tensions that lay at the heart of courtship among the upper echelons of late eighteenth-century society. Burney, like Mary Hamilton, was employed in the royal household, which meant that she wished to avoid public scandal to prevent falling out of favour with Queen Charlotte. Such a fall from grace would have resulted in the loss of her pension, her sole dependable income.[64] D'Arblay was a Roman Catholic liberal French emigre, who not only seemed like an unsuitable match on religious and political grounds, but also because his presence in England posed a serious challenge to the English war effort against France. Although her marriage to d'Arblay came as a great surprise to many of her acquaintances, Burney managed to secure the reluctant consent of her father and used her writings as a means of supporting herself financially as she increasingly distanced herself from metropolitan life.[65] Although Burney avoided the same degree of public scandal as her mentor Hester Thrale, her troubled courtship is revealing of how marriage proved such a problematic issue for well-connected women. It underscores the uncertain grounds upon which an elite woman's social inclusion might be lost and friendships broken.

In this light, it is possible to interpret Sharpe's marriage as being perceived by Carter as a betrayal of female self-advancement and friendship. A glimpse of Carter's views on marriage are evident in a letter from February 1783, when she praised Hamilton for putting an end to a match that would have resulted in 'so disproportionate an alliance'. Carter likened such an act to Hamilton's 'bright silver' being sullied as she became 'manacled by Fetters of old rusty Iron'.[66] It is arguable that alongside the secret courtship, Carter opposed Sharpe's marriage to the elderly Beauvoir on the grounds that interest rather than genuine affection was the prime motivation for the match. Carter's opposition was so strong that Sharpe was forced to confess that 'An unhappy division' had arisen between them since she accepted Beauvoir's offer, which created a 'shadow of a coolness between us'.[67] Although both Carter and Sharpe insisted that their cooling relationship was temporary, their interaction and communication with one another seems to have entirely ceased after this point. In February 1783, for instance, Carter noted to Hamilton that Sharpe's improper behaviour 'has put an end to our Interaction'.[68]

The reasons for Carter objecting to Sharpe's marriage to Beauvoir are unknown. It is evident that she must have had a personal connection to the Beauvoir family, as she was highly invested in the education and living arrangements of Beauvoir's daughter, Betty, which both Sharpe and Carter reference in their letters to Hamilton.[69] Although the details of this dispute remain scant, Carter commented that Betty had gone 'to her Father to say she sh[oul]d be unhappy to live with me'. This suggests that Carter had intended to educate the young woman herself and resented Sharpe's complicity in her removal to another household in Bristol.[70] Carter wrote of these arrangements in July 1782, when she expressed her hopes that Betty's moral and religious principles would prosper under the tutelage of 'this excellent Family as I believe them to be'. The family

102 *Naomi Pullin*

to which Carter is referring is unidentified, but despite her good wishes, this matter was clearly a source of personal consternation. In her letters she said that this had been 'a severe stroke' that she had 'inhumanly been made to suffer'.[71]

Given her own solitary upbringing, as well as her lack of close familial female relationships, it is likely that Sharpe was particularly sensitive to Betty's needs, and respected them, even if they met with disapproval from Carter. Although aware of the context that may have governed Sharpe's actions, Carter viewed the case as one where she had not been shown proper gratitude and respect, and Sharpe's actions as akin to betrayal. Carter regarded Betty's removal to Bristol as evidence that Sharpe viewed her as incapable of providing a suitable education for the young girl. She described the situation as 'a subject which always stabs me to the Heart'.[72] That Carter felt entitled to feel such grievance over Sharpe's choice of education for her stepdaughter suggests that the boundaries of familial relationships and friendship were significantly blurred, for Sharpe – in her position as stepmother to Betty – had no reason to defer to Carter on matters about the girl's education.

Sharpe's marriage also strained her relationship with Hamilton. Since Hamilton's views on the matter do not survive, it is only possible to speculate as to why their relationship also broke down. Their cooling friendship can certainly be observed from the decline in frequency of their communication in the years after the marriage.[73] Hamilton was clearly aggrieved by Sharpe's treatment of their former champion and, although she did not directly intervene, she was unequivocal that Sharpe had been in the wrong and felt it was necessary that she 'made overtures to Mrs Carter for a reconciliation'.[74] Sharpe and Hamilton nevertheless remained in contact after the marriage, and it was to Hamilton that Sharpe divulged the cooling friendship with Carter. Sharpe entreated her friend not to say 'a word … to any one, nor let her perceive you suspect the shadow of a coolness between us'.[75]

Hamilton, however, disclosed this confidential information to Carter, and petitioned her friend for advice on whether she should continue her acquaintance with Sharpe. This suggests that Hamilton too held reservations about the appropriateness of the match, or at least about the manner in which it came about. Carter responded by defending her own behaviour, describing the breach as 'entirely her [Sharpe's] own operation in every particular', but was also clear that she did not want Hamilton's and Sharpe's friendship to suffer as a result. She accordingly encouraged Hamilton to answer Sharpe's letter, acknowledging that 'I will not endeavour to lessen her in your esteem, or to encourage & heighten my own painful Feelings by dwelling on the Injuries I have received'.[76] In February 1783, Carter even berated Hamilton for refusing to accept an invitation by Sharpe. 'Though she has thought proper to act in such a manner with me', Carter wrote, 'I have never endeavoured to

Failed Friendship in Polite Society   103

set any one person against her' and thus 'cannot see why you should not accept of her invitation'.[77]

Carter's active promotion of Sharpe and Hamilton's friendship suggests that she continued to hold her former charge with a degree of affection. Clearly, she was hurt by Sharpe's behaviour and no longer wished to associate with her, but she evidently did not wish ill on her. Hamilton's friendship with Sharpe, on the other hand, seems to have been more superficial. Although it is unclear why Hamilton had begun to withdraw her intimacy from Sharpe, her correspondence with Carter suggests that she may have had her own reservations about being associated with an unruly female acquaintance. In fact, distancing herself from Sharpe may have been a form of self-inflicted punishment for failing to censure Sharpe's behaviour before the affair with Beauvoir had reached the point of no return. After all, the advice literature of this period advised women against making hasty friendships since all parties could be drawn into scandal through the inappropriate behaviour of their acquaintances. The anonymously published *Young Lady's Companion* (1740), a text that was presented as a letter of advice written to a young girl by her father, offered guidance to the fictitious recipient who had entered into friendship with an individual held in contempt by polite society. The authorial father character explained that choosing a friend implied approval of them, and that a woman making a bad choice should expect to be shunned 'and condemned to pay an equal Share with such a Friend of the Reputation she hath lost'.[78] Thus the young woman who had failed to correctly police her relationships and exercise the utmost caution when choosing a friend faced a similar degree of social exclusion as her unruly female companion.

Hamilton married not long after Sharpe, but her marriage to John Dickenson in 1785 seems to have received Carter's approval. The match, however, appears to have been far from equal. As already noted, Dickenson was a year younger than Hamilton and he was an heir to a much smaller estate than Hamilton.[79] Given Carter's praise of Hamilton in February 1783, for ending a match that would have resulted in a 'disproportionate alliance', it is interesting that Hamilton appears to have maintained her status and respectability within their social network.[80] Hamilton had consulted Carter and her other female companions about the courtship, which may have given the relationship an air of decorum. Moreover, since Hamilton had been honest about the relationship and open about her regrets of refusing Dickenson's first marriage proposal in 1780, her conduct may have appeared less dissimulative than Sharpe's.

Adding to the increasing cooling of the friendship, Hamilton failed to heed Sharpe's appeal for secrecy in sharing information with Carter that she wished to keep private. This resulted in a great rupture in their relationship, as revealed in a letter from July 1789, when Sharpe made reference to her former friend's 'impropriety' and intrusion

104 *Naomi Pullin*

'on my distress'.[81] Patricia Meyer Spacks has shown the important place that carefully guarded secrets held in ideas about privacy in the eighteenth century, and it is clear from this exchange that Sharpe viewed this as a significant breach of trust.[82] It was Hamilton's failure to remain 'silent on the subject' that Sharpe later blamed for her inability to reconcile with Carter.[83] Although Hamilton assured Sharpe of her innocence on this matter, the accusation of breaking confidence was enough for Hamilton to end the friendship.

Secrets were regarded in the contemporary advice literature as 'sacred deposits', and disclosing a friend's confidences to others was an act singled out for censure.[84] Although Hamilton's breach of Sharpe's confidence was perhaps a greater betrayal of friendship than Sharpe's secret elopement to Beauvoir, no apology from Hamilton was forthcoming. Instead, she made it clear that Sharpe's accusation of her inability to stay quiet about her friends' cooling relationship was a 'rude' and 'ill bred' indictment not becoming for a gentlewoman.[85] In such a competitive world where social capital was at the centre of a woman's reputation, any accusation of disloyalty could be highly damaging. Charles Allen, for instance, warned in his 1769 work *The Polite Lady* that keeping the secrets of a friend where the relationship had broken would 'procure the love and esteem of every one that knows you'. Those who betrayed their former friend's confidences, on the other hand, would be shunned. Female readers were warned that they would 'incur the hatred of all the world' and create 'a great many enemies'.[86] Hamilton was obviously deeply perturbed at the indictment of being an unreliable confidante even after the friendship had dissolved. She went on to explain that she would continue to regard Sharpe as she had done 'since the year 1783 as one of the many instances of the imperfection and fickleness of human nature'.[87]

Although Sharpe's marriage to Beauvoir precipitated the end of Sharpe and Hamilton's friendship, a number of underlying tensions presaged its demise. Prescriptive literature presented ideal friendship as carefully selected on the basis of equality and mutual satisfaction, but it is clear that this friendship did not match up to this ideal. Sharpe, who had been left a large fortune on the death of her father, was certainly of a similar social rank to her female acquaintances. Yet, her seclusion from polite sociability during those formative teenage years rendered her socially inexperienced, isolated, and lonely. She was forced to acknowledge that the death of her guardian, Dr Fothergill, in 1780 left her in a state of dependence, in which she was forced to 'lean on every creature I meet for support'.[88] This meant that Sharpe never viewed herself as an equal in her friendships with Carter and Hamilton, and was, indeed, never treated as such by her friends.

Connected to this, there were many ways in which hierarchies of power and subordination played out in complicated ways in this web of friendship. Carter, who essentially acted as Sharpe's sponsor and introduced her

Failed Friendship in Polite Society 105

to the polite circles of London, took the place of a maternal figure rather than close confidante. In one letter dated 1781, Sharpe described Carter as her 'dear Mama', and it is clear that it was social education, rather than companionship, that was the primary basis of their connection.[89] Some of Sharpe's comments after the cooling relationship, moreover, are tinged with a slight frustration that she was forced to negotiate her sociability whilst caring for and nursing Carter during frequent bouts of ill-health, to the point where she claimed to have 'sacrificed' her own health and wellbeing 'to my feelings for her'.[90] Carter was sympathetic to the plight of young women in an intellectual male-dominated world. Yet the power she held over Sharpe affirms that exploitation was as characteristic of relationships between women as it was between men and women. As Ylivuori observes, networks of power did not just exist between men and women. 'Instead, women often found themselves dependent on other women in different and complicated ways.'[91]

Carter, a wealthy and unmarried member of the social elite, was clearly a woman who wielded a great deal of power over her female acquaintances. Both Sharpe and Hamilton were ambiguously subordinate to her. Sharpe had much to gain from her association with Carter. Yet, friendship with a young woman whose background was unknown, flouted the very rules of politeness that she herself seems to have advocated. In fact, a criticism Carter made about her acquaintance Mrs Nollekens, who had gained a reputation for not selecting her female acquaintances 'equally well or wisely', suggests that Carter upheld the view of the advice literature that friendship needed to be selective and well-matched.[92] After the friendship between Hamilton and Sharpe eroded, Hamilton explained that she had been 'solicited' by Carter to make an acquaintance with Sharpe and had subsequently 'entered into a friendship'.[93] This level of influence suggests that neither Sharpe or Hamilton were entirely in control of their relationship with one another, or the social acquaintances who surrounded them.

Despite Carter's intervention in Hamilton and Sharpe's friendship, the two women were clearly compatible in terms of their age and social status. Yet, underpinning some of the statements from Sharpe's correspondence to Hamilton is a sense that she felt Hamilton, who was more socially accomplished and experienced, placed lesser value on the friendship than she did. This suggests that there was a whole range of unofficial power hierarchies at play. The deference that Sharpe paid to Hamilton in her letters, where evidence of her sense of social inferiority is most acute, may also have related to Hamilton's position at Court. Indeed, although showing courtesy and respect was a recognised feature of female sociable bonding, Sharpe markedly expressed her thanks for the friendship 'bestowed on me' and 'for permitting me to see you'.[94]

It is possible that Hamilton also viewed the 'friendship' in this way, and deliberately cultivated it as one between a social superior and inferior. We might infer that the uncertain basis on which the relationship was conducted suggests that Hamilton's exchanges with Sharpe were simply displays of civility, deliberately uttered to please Carter. At the same time, it could be argued that following the dissolution of the friendship, Hamilton revised history to suit her personal narrative to lessen her sense of betrayal for herself and her remaining friends by claiming that the friendship had been 'bestowed' on Sharpe rather than mutually entered into. This underscores the tension between the performance of outward courtesy and genuine intimacy between select and exclusive company, as regularly discussed in the conduct literature. In this context, Hamilton's friendship with Sharpe can be seen as a means of enhancing her own friendship with Carter rather than an extension of true friendship to Sharpe.

In a society dependent on credit and small favours, a degree of flattery and dissimulation was necessary to create a sense of bonding and belonging. However, the prescriptive literature made clear that this desire to please was potentially highly dangerous since false flattery and complaisance could easily tip over to hypocrisy. The highest form of dissimulation, as one author declared, occurred when individuals 'not only cloud their real Sentiments and Intentions, but make Profession of, and seem zealously to affect the contrary: This by a more proper and restrain'd Name is call'd Deceit'.[95] This critique highlights the tension between the external performance of polite duties and the naturalness and sincerity expected of women of quality.

Given that the foundation of the friendship was uneasy, it is not surprising that Sharpe felt insecure about her acceptance into Hamilton's circle of acquaintance. There are times when Sharpe apologised for failing to match up to her friend's expectations, particularly when it came to social visits. In May 1779, Sharpe felt obliged to write 'by way of penance' after 'your accusations of neglect, unkindness, unfriendliness & so forth', when she was unable to call on Hamilton the previous Saturday morning. The reason for her inability to fulfil her social obligations, she explained, was because her coach was being repaired. She begged for a prompt reply as proof 'that you are convinced of my innocence'.[96] Sharpe's letter clearly did enough to overcome such accusations, but a similar situation arose the following year when she was forced to write again after failing to visit her friend at Eastbourne. She knew this was a matter about which Hamilton would be 'very much disposed to be angry'. The reason on this occasion was ill health, which made the long coach journey from Deal impossible. Sharpe hoped that her 'justification' would prevent her friend 'harbour[ing] any ideas prejudicial to the sincerity of my wishes to see you'.[97]

In a culture that was conducted through a combination of regular face-to-face interaction and a reliable postal service, it is clear that much anxiety surrounded long-distance friendship. The process of sending and receiving letters, as Vincent has shown, 'added a layer of anxiety to intimate discourse'. It was never clear whether a delayed reply had been caused by the recipient, the method of delivery, or because the writer had offended the recipient, who had then chosen not to reply.[98] Hamilton's epistolary silences were the source of concern for Sharpe, leading to questions about whether her letters had gone missing or if she had done something to offend her acquaintance. Writing from Deal in August 1779, Sharpe requested her friend to write 'but two or three times just to say how you do and whether you have my letter', which she had written six or seven weeks ago. This was a matter, she declared, 'which for a particular reason I very much wish to know'. She playfully threatened that if she were to hear that her friend had received the letter and chosen not to reply, then she would 'call up all my scolding abilities... and use them as seems meet on such occasions'.[99] Although, this threat was entirely in jest, underlying her enquiry was a genuine concern that she had been deliberately ignored by her confidante. This was exacerbated by the fact that she was displaced from the centres of polite sociability in London at the time of writing.

Other components of Sharpe and Hamilton's relationship were also tinged with a concern that their actions might be misjudged by the other. Both women valorised the sincerity of their friendship, but there was clearly unease about whether the words and actions of the other were genuine. Sharpe revealed this tension in a letter dated 24 August 1779, when she expressed her delight at having received a letter from Hamilton. She went on to explain that during her friend's long silence, she had begun to fear that all of her correspondent's previous 'friendly expressions' had merely been 'forms of civility' rather than 'indications of kind regard'.[100] Her anxiety that Hamilton's past expressions of kindness were simply affectation reflects the deep-seated concern present in the conduct literature about the falsity and dissimulation inherent in female sociability. As the sex thought to be more naturally predisposed to politeness, women were taught to deny their own thoughts and inclinations, which meant that some level of dissimulation was constantly present in their practice of politeness.[101] Sharpe's anxiety thus reflected one of the ambiguities raised by contemporary authors about how to discern natural sincerity from affectation or feigned sentiments.

As Sharpe and Hamilton's relationship took a more negative turn, the delicate balance of reputation on the basis of social inclusion raised issues about who had the upper hand in a dispute and how power could be exercised appropriately. Sharpe, for example, felt shunned in public spaces by Hamilton. In one letter, she accused her friend of failing to visit when she came to Bath two years previously, describing how 'I heard nothing of you ... tho' I passed you more than once in the street'. Sharpe attributed this public shaming to her falling out with Carter, and she blamed Hamilton for her fickleness in being unable to treat her with respect, accusing Hamilton of failing 'to permit the civilities of my friendship and acquaintance' now that she ceased to be an 'intimate of Mrs Carter'.[102] She viewed it as unlikely that Hamilton would attempt to renew their friendship when she no longer had Carter as her champion. Hamilton, however, declared that the erosion of their friendship was entirely due to Sharpe's actions. She explained that when she had tried to attract Sharpe's attention from the window of Lady Finch's drawing room, Sharpe had ignored her. She was also agitated by Sharpe's refusal of an invitation to wait on her whilst she was in Bath. Hamilton alleged that her hospitality was continually shunned until 'I never heard anything more from you'.[103]

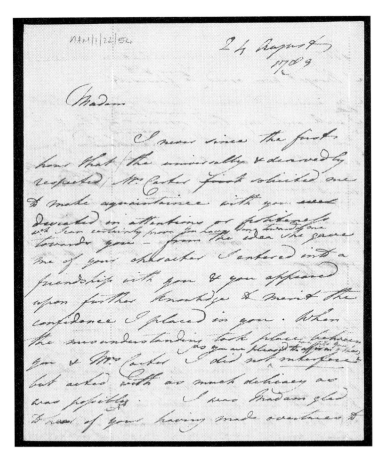

Figure 4.3 Letter from Mary Hamilton (Dickenson) to Mary Sharpe (Beauvoir) Dated 24 August 1789, Where Hamilton Breaks Off the Alliance. John Rylands Library, University of Manchester, Mary Hamilton Papers, HAM/1/22/54.

Failed Friendship in Polite Society 109

As the friendship unravelled, the smallest lapses in politeness shifted the guilt from one party to the other. Shortly after the death of Mr Beauvoir in 1789, Sharpe was perturbed that her former friend (now Mrs Dickenson) had sent her husband to deliver condolences. Sharpe was suspicious about the timing of Hamilton's attempt to renew their friendship and viewed it as 'glaringly insulting to the memory of my beloved husband'. She was also angered that her former friend had not come in person. She explained that had her housekeeper not had the foresight to turn John Dickenson away, she would have given 'pain to a stranger, by confessing my opinion of the impropriety of a person who has behaved to me as Miss Hamilton did, intruding on my distress'. Her discontent with Hamilton led her to resolve that as long as she had 'life and understanding' she would accept no attention from anyone whose 'behaviour ha[d] been disrespectful' of her husband during his lifetime.[104]

Sharpe's decision to address her former friend as 'Miss Hamilton', rather than by her married name, adds an interesting layer to the deepness of their rupture, since it indicates a lack of respect and deference. Indeed, Hamilton was so disturbed by Sharpe's response that she petitioned Carter for information on the matter, to which Carter responded that she knew nothing, explaining that 'there must have been some strange refusal [i]ntended in the delivery of your Civilities to occasion her giving so outrageous a Return to them as you describe'. Hamilton was worried that news of this dispute might have become the talk of the town, yet Carter reassured her that 'I had heard nothing of it till your letter'.[105] Politeness was thus used as the yardstick for both Hamilton and Sharpe to scrutinise and judge the actions of the other. Whether it was in ignoring one another in public or failing to maintain obligations of social visiting and correspondence, both women drew upon notions of exclusion to dismiss the behaviour of the other as impolite and thus to justify the denial of intimacy.

Conclusion

The discourses on politeness and friendship made clear the expectations of correct social deportment by setting down a code of conduct to which genteel women were supposed to subscribe. The dispute between Mary Sharpe and her female acquaintances throws into sharp relief the vulnerability of friendship and the tensions inherent in eighteenth-century ideals of polite sociability. As the didactic literature made clear, women were at once the exemplars of politeness and prone to enter into inappropriate relationships, behaviour, and discourse. Whilst women like Hamilton and Carter saw themselves as having a particular duty to support a young woman lacking a polite education, the relationship they built with Sharpe also reaffirmed her status as a dependent and social inferior. Indeed, Mary Sharpe's change of fortunes from friendless orphan to bluestocking and then to outcast is indicative of the fragility of inclusion

110 *Naomi Pullin*

into polite circles and raises interesting questions about how power was judged and exercised.

Inclusion within polite society could bring women status, honour, and patronage, but it also restricted the agency they could exercise as individuals. Their actions and behaviour were scrutinised by their female acquaintances and, when they were judged to be falling short, they could find themselves subject to gossip, slander, and ridicule. Politeness thus became a mechanism for maintaining norms and served as a benchmark for gauging the failure of female acquaintances in particular contexts. It is clear that marriage and questions surrounding the suitability of the match between Sharpe and Reverend Beauvoir were central to the breakdown of the relationship with Hamilton and Carter, but even before the marriage was proposed, Sharpe's letters are filled with inflections of uncertainty about Hamilton's commitment to their friendship. This insecurity stemmed from her doubts about the authenticity of Hamilton's feelings and is symbolic of the practices of dissimulation spelled out in the prescriptive literature of this period. Though women's experiences could never match up to the ideals set out in such texts, it is nevertheless possible to see the types of activities and behaviours that might disrupt such ideals. The politics and rituals of inclusion and exclusion for eighteenth-century women should thus be seen as a deeply complex and multifaceted phenomenon intimately linked to questions of status, power, and social capital in a highly competitive genteel world.

Acknowledgements

I am grateful to the Leverhulme Trust for providing me with an Early Career Fellowship to pursue this research. Preliminary work on this project was also made possible in 2017 with the support of a Summer Research Fund from the Humanities Research Centre at Warwick. I also wish to thank my co-editor Kathryn Woods for her encouragement, feedback, and support in the writing of this chapter, as well as generously volunteering to access Elizabeth Carter's letters during her holiday in Boston. This chapter would not have been possible without her friendship and investment. I am also grateful to Bernard Capp and Mark Philp for generously reading and providing extensive feedback on drafts of this chapter and to Alexandra Walsham and Mark Knights for their inspiration, support, and collegiality.

Notes

1 Richard Steele, *The Spectator,* no. 6, 7 March 1711, in Donald F. Bond (ed.), *The Spectator* (5 vols, Oxford: Oxford University Press, 2014), i. 30.
2 Manchester, John Rylands Library, University of Manchester, GB 133 HAM/1/22/1-54, Mary Hamilton Papers (1743–1826) (hereafter GB 133 HAM/1/22).

Failed Friendship in Polite Society   111

3 Andrew Douglas, *Notes of a Journey from Berne to England, Through France. Made in the Year 1796*, part 2 (London, 1797).
4 GB 133 HAM/1/22/43, North Parade [Bath], 14 April 1782.
5 Ibid.
6 GB 133 HAM/1/22/54, 24 August 1789.
7 Soile Ylivuori, *Women and Politeness in Eighteenth-Century England: Bodies, Identities, and Power* (London and New York: Routledge, 2019).
8 Amanda Herbert, *Female Alliances: Gender, Identity, and Friendship in Early Modern Britain* (New Haven and London: Yale University Press, 2014); Amanda Vickery, *The Gentleman's Daughter: Women's Lives in Georgian England* (New Haven and London: Yale University Press, 1998), esp. 195–223; and Susan E. Whyman, *Sociability and Power in Late Stuart England: The Cultural Worlds of the Verneys 1660–1720* (Oxford: Oxford University Press, 2002), esp. 87–109.
9 This is something that Vickery observed when comparing the correspondence network of Elizabeth Shackleton with the social encounters she records in her diaries. She concludes that letters from kin are over-represented in the archives, whilst other letters from correspondents with whom Shackleton regularly communicated and socialised do not survive. Vickery, *Gentleman's Daughter*, 29–30.
10 The extensive and understudied records of Mary Hamilton's social encounters are documented in 2,474 pieces of correspondence, 16 diaries, and 6 manuscript volumes housed at the John Rylands Library in Manchester. Sharpe's letters to Hamilton form part of this collection. Around 189 of Elizabeth Carter's letters and notes to Mary Hamilton are housed at the Houghton Library in Boston, MA. I have only found one letter written by Hamilton relating to this dispute: GB 133 HAM/1/22/54, 24 August 1789. This was the letter where she ended the relationship.
11 Whyman, *Sociability and Power*, 11.
12 Vickery, *Gentleman's Daughter*, 8.
13 Similar complexities are discussed by Sally Holloway in '"You know I am all on fire": Writing the Adulterous Affair in England, c.1740–1830', *Historical Research*, 89, no. 244 (2016), 320.
14 Phil Withington, 'Company and Sociability in Early Modern England', *Social History*, 32 (2007), 307.
15 Naomi Tadmor, *Family and Friends in Eighteenth-Century England: Household, Kinship and Patronage* (Cambridge: Cambridge University Press, 2001), 167–72.
16 James Boswell, *Boswell's Life of Johnson, Together with Boswell's Journal of a Tour to the Hebrides and Johnson's Diary of a Journey into North Wales*, ed. by George B. Hill (6 vols, Oxford: Clarendon Press, 1934–1964), iii. 386–91.
17 Allan Silver, 'Friendship in Commercial Society: Eighteenth-Century Social Theory and Modern Sociology', *American Journal of Sociology*, 95 (1990), 1487.
18 Instrumentalism and interested and disinterested friendship are explored by Silver in 'Friendship in Commercial Society', 1474–1504.
19 Lawrence E. Klein, 'Gender, Conversation and the Public Sphere in Early Eighteenth-Century England', in Michael Worton and Judith Still (eds), *Textuality and Sexuality: Reading Theories and Practices* (Manchester: Manchester University Press, 1993), 110–11. See also Whyman, *Sociability and Power*, 4, 93–100.
20 Ylivuori, *Women and Politeness*, 39.

112 *Naomi Pullin*

21 Paul Langford, 'The Uses of Eighteenth-Century Politeness', *Transactions of the Royal Historical Society*, 12 (2002), 314.
22 On the masquerade see Dror Wahrman, *The Making of the Modern Self: Identity and Culture in Eighteenth-Century England* (New Haven and London: Yale University Press, 2004), 157–76.
23 R.H. Sweet, 'Topographies of Politeness', *Transactions of the Royal Historical Society*, 12 (2002), 366.
24 See Peter Borsay, *The English Urban Renaissance: Culture and Society in the Provincial Town, 1660–1770* (Oxford: Clarendon Press, 1989), 278; Elaine Chalus, 'Elite Women, Social Politics, and the Political World of Late Eighteenth-Century England', *The Historical Journal*, 43 (2002), 677.
25 This title was first published in 1688 and new editions were still appearing in print in the 1790s, which included translations in French and Italian. Kathryn Woods has traced 15 editions of this text in print by 1765. Kathryn Woods, 'Dismembering Appearances: The Cultural Meaning of the Body and its Parts in Eighteenth-Century Understanding', unpublished PhD thesis (University of Edinburgh, 2014), 260.
26 George Savile, Marquis of Halifax, *The Lady's New-Years Gift: Or Advice to A Daughter* (London, 1688), 95–125.
27 Hannah Greig, *The Beau Monde: Fashionable Society in Georgian London* (Oxford: Oxford University Press, 2013), 192–228.
28 Alexander Monro (primus), *The Professor's Daughter: An Essay on Female Conduct* (1739), ed. by P.A.G. Monro, M.D. (Cambridge: P.A.G Monro, 1995), 50.
29 John Gregory [Lord Gregory], *A Father's Legacy to His Daughters. By the Late Dr. Gregory, of Edinburgh* (Edinburgh, 1776), 73–4.
30 N.H., *The Ladies Dictionary; Being a General Entertainment for the Fair-Sex* (London, 1694), 223.
31 Anon. [A person of quality], *The Young Lady's Companion; Or, Beauty's Looking-Glass* (London, 1740), 50. This echoed in George Savile's (Marquis of Halifax) view on friendship in *The Lady's New-Years Gift: Or Advice to A Daughter* (London, 1688), 117–8.
32 *The Athenian Mercury, or Casuistical Gazette*, ed. John Dunton, vol. 6, no. 29 (26 March 1692).
33 Vickery, *Gentleman's Daughter*, 8.
34 For a good discussion of the ways in which conduct literature was balanced with the demands of everyday life and social station see Ingrid H. Tague, *Women of Quality: Accepting and Contesting Ideals of Femininity in England, 1690–1760* (Woodbridge: The Boydell Press, 2002), 218–23.
35 Although Sharpe makes no mention of this arrangement in her writings, her father, Fane William Sharpe, made provisions in his will for Mary to reside for the remainder of her minority with Freeman: Sir Lewis Namier and John Brooke (eds), *History of Parliament: The House of Commons, 1745–1790* (London, 1964 and online) https://www.historyofparliamentonline.org/volume/1754-1790/member/sharpe-fane-william-1729-71. Accessed 3 October 2019.
36 GB 133 HAM/1/22/43, North Parade [Bath], 14 April 1782.
37 Robert B. Shoemaker. *Gender in English Society 1650–1850: The Emergence of Separate Spheres?* (London: Longman, 1998), 133.
38 Tague, *Women of Quality*, 72–96.
39 GB 133 HAM/1/22/43, North Parade [Bath], 14 April 1782.
40 For more on Carter see the entry for 'Elizabeth Carter (1717–1805), poet, translator, and writer' in *The Oxford Dictionary of National Biography* (*ODNB*) (Oxford, 2004) https://doi.org/10.1093/ref:odnb/4782.

Failed Friendship in Polite Society 113

41 Chalus, 'Elite Women', 689. Ylivuori also explores this phenomenon in *Women and Politeness*, 57–8.

42 GB 133 HAM/1/22/35, South Lodge [Enfield], 28 June 1781.

43 Elizabeth Anson and Florence Anson, *Mary Hamilton, Afterwards Mrs John Dickenson at Court and at Home from Letters and Diaries* (London, 1925), 53. I am grateful to Mark Philp for this reference.

44 Lisa Crawley, 'A Life Recovered: Mary Hamilton 1756–1816', *Bulletin of the John Rylands Library*, 90 (2014), 30.

45 GB 133 HAM/1/22/34, Bath, 13 May 1781.

46 GB 133 HAM/1/22/43, North Parade [Bath], 14 April 1782.

47 Sharpe's travels with Carter receives passing mention in Montagu Pennington's, *Memoirs of the Life of Mrs Elizabeth Carter*, second edition (London, 1808), 457–8. The journey is also referenced in GB 133 HAM/1/22/9, Henley, 17 May 1779; and GB 133 HAM/1/22/10, 11 June 1779.

48 GB 133 HAM/1/22/20, Stanhope Street [London], 30 March 1780.

49 Sally Holloway, *The Game of Love in Georgian England: Courtship, Emotions, and Material Culture* (Oxford: Oxford University Press, 2019), 81.

50 Augusta Hall (ed.), *Autobiography and Correspondence of Mary Granville, Mrs Delany* (6 vols, Cambridge: Cambridge University Press, 1862), vi. 118. Evidence that he was Master of the King's School is found in the catalogue of the muniments of the hospitals of St Nicholas, Harbledown and St John the Baptist, Northgate, Canterbury. The preface of this was signed by 'the Revd. Mr. Osmond Beauvoir A.M., Master of the King's School at Canterbury A.D. 1765'. Lambeth Palace Library, MS 1132, 1765, 1895.

51 The opposition Sharpe encountered is documented in a letter Hester Chapone wrote to Mary Delaney on 9 November 1782, where she hints that Sharpe's uncle had tried to prevent the marriage by putting delays in their way. Hall (ed.), *Autobiography and Correspondence of Mary Granville*, 119.

52 David Vincent, *Privacy: A Short History* (Cambridge: Polity Press, 2016), 38.

53 Samuel Richardson, *Clarissa: Or, The History of a Young Lady* (London, 1747–1748), 21. See also Tadmor, *Family and Friends*, 261.

54 She makes reference to this and her 'friendship' with Beauvoir in GB 133 HAM/1/22/43, North Parade [Bath], 14 April 1782.

55 Mrs Chapone to Mrs Delany, 9 November 1782, in Hall (ed.), *Autobiography and Correspondence of Mary Granville*, 119.

56 GB 133 HAM/1/22/43, North Parade [Bath], 14 April 1782.

57 Mrs Chapone to Mrs Delany, 9 November 1782, in Hall (ed.), *Autobiography and Correspondence of Mary Granville*, 119.

58 GB 133 HAM/1/22/43, North Parade [Bath], 14 April 1782.

59 See for example Tague, *Women of Quality*, 72–96.

60 Mark Philp, *Radical Conduct: Politics, Sociability and Equality in London 1789–1815* (Cambridge: Cambridge University Press: forthcoming, 2020), 93–122, esp. 100–101.

61 Gregory, *A Father's Legacy*, 66–7.

62 For more on Thrale's marriage to Piozzi see James L. Clifford, *Hester Lynch Piozzi (Mrs. Thrale)* (New York: Columbia University Press, 1987), 203–32.

63 Clifford, *Hester Lynch Piozzi*, 218–20; and Claire Harman, *Fanny Burney: A Biography* (London: Harper Collins, 2000), 168–99.

64 Harman, *Fanny Burney*, 236.

114 *Naomi Pullin*

65 Ibid., 226–46.
66 The prospective suitor remains unnamed in their correspondence. Boston, MA, Houghton Library, University of Harvard, bMS Eng 1778, Elizabeth Carer and Hannah More letters to Mary Hamilton, Box 2, fol. 50, Deal [Kent], 6 June 1784 (hereafter bMS Eng 1778).
67 GB 133 HAM/1/22/43, North Parade [Bath], 14 April 1782.
68 bMS Eng 1778, fol. 31, 16 February 1783.
69 GB 133 HAM/1/22/43, North Parade [Bath], 14 April 1782; bMS Eng 1778, fols. 17 and 23, Deal [Kent], 1 July 1782 and 21 September 1782.
70 bMS Eng 1778, fol. 16, Deal [Kent], 31 May 1782.
71 Ibid., fol.18, Deal 29 July 1782.
72 Ibid., fol. 23, Deal 21 September 1782.
73 Only 9 letters and notes survive in the period between Sharpe's marriage in 1782 and Hamilton and Sharpe's dispute in 1778, none of which is more than a few lines in length.
74 GB 133 HAM/1/22/54, 25 August 1789.
75 GB 133 HAM/1/22/43, North Parade [Bath], 14 April 1782.
76 bMS Eng 1778, fol. 23, Deal [Kent], 21 September 1782.
77 bMS Eng 1778, fol. 31, 16 February 1783.
78 Anon., *The Young Lady's Companion*, 50–52.
79 Crawley, 'A Life Recovered', 30.
80 bMS Eng 1778, fol. 50, Deal [Kent], 6 June 1784.
81 GB 133 HAM/1/22/52, Bath, 31 July 1789.
82 Patricia Meyer Spacks, *Privacy: Concealing the Eighteenth-Century Self* (Chicago: University of Chicago Press, 2003), 15.
83 GB 133 HAM/1/22/52, Bath, 31 July 1789.
84 Gregory, *A Father's Legacy*, 66.
85 GB 133 HAM/1/22/54, 25 August 1789.
86 Charles Allen, *The Polite Lady: Or a Course of Female Education. In a series of Letters, From a Mother to Her Daughter* (London, 1769), 72.
87 GB 133 HAM/1/22/54, 25 August 1789.
88 GB 133 HAM/1/22/37, Stanhope Street [London], 27 January 1782.
89 GB 133 HAM/1/22/9, Henley, 17 May 1779.
90 GB 133 HAM/1/22/43, North Parade [Bath], 14 April 1782.
91 Ylivuori, *Women and Politeness*, 57.
92 Quoted in Philp, *Radical Conduct*, 19.
93 GB 133 HAM/1/22/54, 24 August 1789.
94 GB 133 HAM/1/22/12, Tunbridge Wells, 24 August 1779; GB 133 HAM/1/22/37, Stanhope Street [London], 27 January 1782.
95 Anon., *An Essay in Defence of the Female Sex. In a Letter to a Lady. Written by a Lady,* fourth edition (London, 1721), 102.
96 GB 133 HAM/1/22/9, Henley, 17 May 1779.
97 GB 133 HAM/1/22/29, Deal [Kent], 20 September 1780.
98 Vincent, *Privacy*, 19.
99 GB 133 HAM/1/22/11, Deal [Kent], 6 August 1779.
100 GB 133 HAM/1/22/12, Tunbridge Wells, 24 August 1779.
101 See for example Monro, *The Professor's Daughter*, 21.
102 GB 133 HAM/1/22/52, Bath, 31 July 1789.
103 GB 133 HAM/1/22/54, 25 August 1789.
104 GB 133 HAM/1/22/52, Bath, 31 July 1789.
105 bMS Eng 1778, fol. 87, Chapel Street [London], 8 January 1790.

Part II
The Boundaries of Community

5 The Negotiation of Inclusion and Exclusion in the Westminster Infirmary, 1716–1750

Kathryn Woods

On 14 January 1716, a small group of eminent Anglican gentlemen met in St Dunstan's Coffee House, Fleet Street, to discuss the establishment of a 'Charitable Society for Relieving the Sick Poor and Needy'. The aim of this newly formed charity – to be funded through subscriptions and donations from elite donors – was to provide food, medical assistance, respite care, and religious instruction to the sick poor through outdoor relief. Among those that the charity said it would assist were sick poor from within and outside the parish of St Margaret's Westminster who were unable to pay for medical care or maintain accommodation. They also agreed to care for homeless, abandoned pregnant women nearing delivery, and sick prisoners.[1] With grand ambitions to help so many, but with a limited initial fund of £10, the charity's pockets were empty by April 1716.[2] Within the year the charity had ceased activity.[3]

In 1719, the society reassembled. At this time, the charity agreed to exclude pregnant women and prisoners from accessing assistance and moved away from their outdoor model of medical relief (where financial charity, food, or services were given without the recipient needing to enter an institution). Instead, they were to focus their efforts on establishing a small hospital at a private house in Petty France, Pimlico. These decisions appear to have been strategic; made in relation to the charity's earlier financial difficulties. It seems that, in the view of the Society, its previous failure was because elite donors were reluctant to support pregnant women and prisoners. They also appear to have viewed a hospital-based model of medical charity as more appealing to potential donors. This can only be inferred, due to lack of surviving evidence, but the historians Jonathan Barry and Colin Jones do note that hospitals were popular recipients of charity during this period because they were 'subject to rigorous and highly public rules of admission and methods of administration'. This enabled donors to 'sleep peacefully abed at night, assured that their money was being properly spent'.[4] In a poster advertising the establishment of the Westminster Infirmary from 1719, it was stated that the hospital would relieve 'the SICK and NEEDY, by providing them with lodging, with proper Food and Physick, and Nurses to

118 *Kathryn Woods*

attend to them during their Sickness, and by procuring them Advice and Assistance of Physicians or Surgeons'. 'Upon this Understanding', it was explained that 'such sums of money have been advanced and subscribed by several of this charity'.[5] The charity's early turbulent period seems to have taught trustees a lesson: that to ensure a steady stream of donations they needed to be reflexive to the sensibilities of the London elite, and negotiate with them to determine how their charity was delivered and who was included or excluded as its beneficiaries.[6] Debates concerning inclusion and exclusion were thus woven into the cultural foundations of the Westminster Infirmary.

This chapter explores exclusion as it was defined and implemented in the structures and processes of the Westminster Infirmary and how exclusion was experienced and negotiated by various hospital stakeholders. The Westminster Infirmary is a fitting case study because it was the world's first voluntary hospital entirely funded by donations and subscriptions. This chapter is especially interested in how the institutional culture of the Westminster Infirmary, as a new sort of 'Enlightened' medical institution that relied 'largely on the enthusiasm of the local community', evolved between 1719 and 1750.[7] There is a particular focus on the period 1735–1740; an especially turbulent time in the hospital's history when a dispute occurred between the Board of Governors and the physicians about the site of the hospital's relocation (which was necessary due to expanding patient numbers). While the governors preferred a location at Buckingham Gate (where the Westminster Infirmary eventually moved in 1735), another property in at Hyde Park Corner was considered as more favourable by the physicians. The physicians who lost the argument subsequently resigned their posts at the Westminster Infirmary and went on to establish St George's Hospital at their preferred site at Hyde Park Corner. For the Westminster Infirmary, this ushered in a period of new managerial methods and approaches. It also brought with it the *en masse* enlistment of a new staff of physicians and the creation of a new set of conditions for inclusion and exclusion. Alongside the hospital's management and daily activities, this chapter is also interested in how the hospital's cultures of exclusion were shaped by broader changes occurring in London during this period. These developments included increasing urbanisation and migration; shifting hierarchies of social order and status; changing gender norms; new cultures of charity and associational culture; rising rates of poverty, crime, and alcoholism; and tensions surrounding religion.

In an effort to examine these big themes, this chapter does not aim to tell a detailed or comprehensive history of the Infirmary's early history; this has already been thoroughly documented elsewhere.[8] Nor is this a history of the changing relationship between state, religious, and charitable healthcare provision, although these issues form a backdrop

Exclusion in the Westminster Infirmary 119

to the analysis.[9] Instead, this chapter offers a social history of the Westminster Infirmary. Specifically, it explores how socio-economic developments of the period were reflected in the activities of the institution, and the experiences of people who worked for and were treated by the hospital. It shows how various people involved with the hospital – trustees, medical and auxiliary staff, patients, and patient visitors – shaped the institution and its approaches to inclusion and exclusion. Of specific interest is how the institution responded to behaviours by trustees, staff, and patients that implicitly or explicitly ran counter to both its own norms and to those of eighteenth-century society more widely. In summary, the chapter aims to detail how the Westminster Infirmary, an institution where power and authority were nebulously located in its early years, created structures, processes, and norms to deal with behaviour that it judged 'unruly' and, in so doing, created an institutional identity for itself.

Sources for this chapter include the trustees of the Westminster Infirmary meeting minutes and print material that advertised the hospital's activities intending to encourage financial donations. Detailed in these sources is information about the patients admitted to and released from the hospital, the hiring and firing of staff, debates over the creation of new orders and resolutions, and changes to the hospital's governance. Print materials produced by the Westminster Infirmary, like its proposals and reports, played an important role in engaging the eighteenth-century urban elite in the hospital's activities and assisted in the creation of its institutional identity. These materials also culturally communicated ideas about social inclusion and exclusion that were born in the context of the hospital and provided a blueprint for the operation of voluntary medical charity more broadly.

In its approach to this wide range of sources, the chapter focuses on moments of disagreement and cases involving unruly behaviour. These instances were largely outside the usual realms of operation for the hospital but created moments for the institution to reflect on its identity and its approaches to inclusion and exclusion. One challenge with these sources is that they only provide information about the hospital and its patients from the perspective of the hospital's trustees and senior management. There is thus a limit on the extent to which we can access actual patient experience through such records. Another problem is that several issues around patient-hospital relations are excluded. For example, these sources provide little information about the events preceding the patients' admittance to the hospital or the experiences of patients who were turned away. To get at some of these stories, this chapter also makes selective use of cases from the Old Bailey and contemporary writing about urban life.

The first part of the chapter examines how the foundation and structures of the Westminster Infirmary reflected broader socio-economic

120 *Kathryn Woods*

developments and contemporary social, gender, and religious norms. Section two focuses on issues of inclusion and exclusion concerning staff. Part three looks at patient experiences and the hospital's reactions to moments of unruliness, with a focus on the hospital's criteria and processes of admission, and how hospital stakeholders negotiated them. The final section examines the hospital's policies and practices concerning discharge and how and why they evolved between 1719 and 1750. Collectively, this analysis will show that issues concerning inclusion and exclusion were central to the creation of the Westminster Infirmary's habitus and identity.[10] At the same time, the chapter will demonstrate that in this early period of the hospital's history, its idioms, structures, and processes of inclusion and exclusion were both explicitly and implicitly open to negotiation by hospital stakeholders.

The Westminster Infirmary and Social Order

In the first half of the eighteenth century, England was undergoing significant political and socio-economic transformations. Nowhere was this change felt more keenly than in London. In 1600, London's population was around 200,000, but by 1750 it had grown to an estimated 675,000.[11] Death rates in the city outranked birth rates for most of this period, largely caused by high rates of infectious disease.[12] London's overcrowded and unsanitary living conditions, malnutrition, and food adulteration also caused susceptibility to chronic disease among the working population.[13] Among the first group of thirty patients treated by the Westminster Infirmary between 10 February 1720 and 13 July 1720, four were cited as suffering from 'consumption' (tuberculosis or other wasting diseases), two scurvy, two rheumatism, two fever, and three menstrual diseases. Other cited causes of disease among admitted patients included leprosy, scrophula (also known as the 'Kings Evil'), strains, joint problems, and asthma.

The main factor in London's eighteenth-century population increase was rising in-migration.[14] Although London's commercial and industrial growth relied on such migration, it also provoked widespread social anxiety. A particular concern was that London was becoming a magnet for poor migrants who preyed on London's residents for financial support. For example, in 1729, the Quaker merchant Joshua Gee – in a surprisingly un-Quakerly manner – complained:

> If any person is born with any defect or deformity, or maimed by fire or any other casualty, or by any inveterate distemper, which renders them miserable objects, their way is open to London, where they have the free liberty of shewing their nauseous sights to terrify people, and force them to give money to get of them.[15]

Exclusion in the Westminster Infirmary   121

Equally, many Londoners objected to seeing the ugliness of disease and poverty on London's streets. In February 1731, a correspondent to the *London Journal* complained that the people of London should not have to suffer the sight of deformed beggars wandering 'the streets exposing their distorted limbs and filthy sores'.[16]

Several factors compounded Londoners' anxieties about migration, poverty, and disease. First was a recognition that the parish system of poor relief was unable to cater sufficiently for migrants or provide adequate support to London's sick poor.[17] Secondly, hospital provision was insufficient in the capital. As early as 1676, the English philosopher, economist, and physician William Petty complained that one 'cause of defect in the art of medicine is that there have not been Hospitalls for the Accomodation of sick people. Rich as well as Poor'.[18] Indeed, until the establishment of the Westminster Infirmary, London only had two hospitals that explicitly catered for the sick poor: the religious and state-funded hospitals of St Bartholomew's in Smithfield, and St Thomas's in Southwark. Both of these hospitals also required a nominal fee from patients, thereby excluding the truly destitute from access. Thirdly, high rates of migration, poverty, and disease in the city were regarded as indicators of a failure in the social order. This ideological correlation, as Lynn Hollen Lees suggests, resulted from a tendency, on the part of the contemporary elite, to transfer 'their hostility to the dirt, disease, and decay of early industrial society on to the figures of the dependant poor'.[19]

By the early eighteenth century, the London elite were becoming increasingly frustrated by lack of state action in response to London's poverty problems. They were also more articulate about what they perceived as the key issues. In the Charitable Proposal drawn up by the Charitable Society for Relieving the Sick Poor and Needy in 1716, it was stated:

> amongst those who do receive Relief from their respective Parishes, many suffer extremely, and are sometimes lost, partly for want of Accommodations and proper Medicines in their own Houses or Lodgings, (the Closeness and Unwholesomeness of which is too often one great Cause of their Sickness) partly by the imprudent laying out of what is so allowed, and by the Ignorance and Carelessness or Ill Management of those about them.[20]

In this sense, the establishment of the Charitable Society for the Sick Poor and Needy, and later the Westminster Infirmary, can be seen as an effort by London's elite to solve poverty issues for themselves. The shift in charitable focus, from merely providing relief for the sick poor towards correcting perceived social problems, was new to the eighteenth century. Among other things, this change was connected to evolving

122   *Kathryn Woods*

ideas of Protestant civic responsibility and the rise of new 'enlightened' sensibilities among the emergent middle classes and elites, which together created a greater social commitment to philanthropy.[21] The establishment of the voluntary hospital was thus part of the evolution of new 'enlightened' approaches to medical charity.

The trustees of the Westminster Infirmary used Londoners' fears about the sick poor to promote support for their charity. In a published statement of the hospital's aims after 1719, it was remarked that it was 'obvious to any one that walks the Streets' that existing frameworks of charity were 'not sufficient to preserve great Numbers ... from Beggary, to the Grief of all good Men, and the no small Reproach of our Religion and Country'.[22] Correspondingly, the establishment of the Westminster Infirmary was presented as a means of restoring social order in the city, in part by physically removing the sick poor from London's streets. Writing about the establishment of the Royal Hospital at Greenwich in 1728, a similar sort of institution, the building's architect Nicholas Hawksmoor proposed that such hospitals were a necessary means of 'rectifying the irregular and ill management of the polices of great cities'.[23] In this way, the establishment of the Westminster Infirmary and other voluntary hospitals were aligned with national concerns. This was made explicit in a printed report advertising the charity's activities from 1723, where the Westminster Infirmary described its charity as a 'Blessing upon the whole Nation', ensuring:

> the Hungry being fed, the Naked cloathed, the Stranger taken in, the Ignorant instructed, the Sick visited and relieved, and many Poor industrious People, who have nothing but the Labour of their Hands to subsist upon, preserv'd from perishing miserably, or becoming a Burden to their Country, and render'd useful Members of it.[24]

The Westminster Infirmary was an Anglican institution and, as such, sought to solve contemporary problems by ministering the souls, as well as the bodies, of the sick poor. It achieved this by providing patients with daily visits from Anglican clergymen during their hospital stay, as well as access to religious and conduct texts like Henry Hammond's edition of *The Whole Duty of Man* (1658). This dual approach was considered the best means of resolving complex social problems in a period when social ills, including disease, were interpreted as the result of moral failings on the part of individuals and society more broadly.[25] Through the hospital, the trustees also sought to stifle the threat of religious Dissent in the city. For example, Paul Slack has traced the roots of London's voluntary hospital movement to charitable societies such as the Society for Promoting Christian Knowledge (1699), which was set up by the Anglican Clergy in West London to address contemporary social problems and perceived 'competition from Dissent and Popery'.[26]

Donors and Staff

The establishment of the Westminster Infirmary was part of the rise of associational culture in Enlightenment London. Historians such as Peter Clark and Ileana Baird note that clubs and societies were significant in the creation of elite social networks during the eighteenth century. As Peter Borsay suggests, this was at a time when London experienced difficulties 'integrating a large and sometimes heterogeneous body of people into a viable community'.[27] The Westminster Infirmary adopted a range of approaches to engage donors and socially reward them for their charitable activity, including newspaper adverts that listed donors by name, and social events like yearly charitable sermons.[28] Initially, donor numbers were quite small but numbers expanded after the Prince of Wales, future George II, donated to the charity in 1721. Although many donors were motivated by genuinely charitable intentions, sometimes the elite's involvement was viewed cynically as a means of them vainly and publicly displaying their moral and religious 'virtue', consolidating connections, and demonstrating their wealth, power, and influence. In characteristically scathing style, the physician and social commentator Bernard Mandeville wrote in 1723 that 'Pride and Vanity have built more Hospitals than all other Virtues together'.[29]

Evidence from donor lists shows that subscribers to the Westminster Infirmary were primarily from the aristocratic and gentry elite, and the 'polite' professional and commercial classes.[30] Indeed, the four founding members of the Charitable Society for Relieving the Sick Poor and Needy were the banker Henry Hoare (who provided the first financial donation of £10), the wine merchant Robert Witham, the religious author William Wogan, and Reverend Patrick Cockburn. Donor lists also illustrate that a high number of women from similar sorts of backgrounds subscribed to the charity. The active engagement of female subscribers was particularly important to the Westminster Infirmary's success. Its inclusion of women – unmarried, married, and widowed – as charitable donors, reflected women's increasingly prominent role in the organisation of sociable activities within polite society at this time.[31] The charity also seems to have been proud of elite women's participation in their activities. In the letter the Westminster Infirmary sent to King George I in 1721, thanking him for his endorsement of the charity, it was stated that 'the voluntary contributions of several of the Nobility and Gentry of both the sexes' had enabled the hospital to preserve 'the lives of some hundreds of your Majesty's poor subjects'.[32]

Female subscribers had views that were distinct to male subscribers, governors, and physicians on how the hospital should operate and who should be admitted. These women voiced their opinions through dialogue with members of the all-male trustee board and, on occasion, by sending letters to express their views. For example, in 1738, the hospital

124   *Kathryn Woods*

considered at length whether to admit patients known to be suffering a venereal disease. Among the evidence considered by the trustees, and recorded in the trustees meeting minutes, was a letter sent by thirty female donors opposing the proposal to admit such patients. Their objection was that this move undermined the hospital's original aim to provide care to the 'deserving' sick poor. The letter stated:

> Gentlemen,
>
> We who are subscribers to the Infirmary at St James Street Westminster having been well informed that several of the Trustees do Endeavour to introduce venereal patients into that place for cure; contrary to what we apprehended and Believed would be the practice of the Infirmary. Therefore we do think it requisite to show our great Dislike of admitting such patients, hindering the Industrious sick poor being Admitted. We therefore hope that you gentlemen, who have the liberty of attending the Gen. Board will come to such a Resolution, as will Effectually prevent the admission of all such patients.[33]

This letter evidences how far donor stakeholders considered some forms of exclusion as essential to the hospital's successful functioning. It also shows how the voluntary hospital's model of charity empowered its subscribers to have a say over the hospital's activities, some of whom – such as women – were excluded from similar sorts of decision making in other contexts. Moreover, it reveals that elite female donors had particular perceptions of the types of poor to be included and excluded from access to the hospital, and how they made their opinions known in distinct ways, largely through negotiating with male governors through bureaucratic and social means.

In terms of medical staff, the Westminster Infirmary was a highly 'enlightened' institution in providing care to the sick poor that was administered by physicians who held a medical degree, in addition to trained surgeons, apothecaries, and nurses. It is important to note that at this time most of the population, outside of the polite commercial classes, would have been unable to afford the medical care of accredited physicians or even expert surgeons. Instead, the majority of the population would have relied on domestic medicine, and treatment or care from medically experienced neighbours, midwives, barbers, and 'quacks'.[34] Essentially, the Westminster Infirmary could have just offered care to the sick poor from barber-surgeons and nurses – without the involvement physicians – and this would have still constituted a far better level of medical care than they could financially or socially procure for themselves.

While the surgeons and apothecaries who worked for the hospital were paid a salary, the physicians offered their services for free.

Exclusion in the Westminster Infirmary   125

Physicians were attracted to these roles because they brought social prestige and networking opportunities to mingle with elite donors as potential clients. Such work also supplied them with interesting and challenging medical cases.[35] The hospital's physicians, in a position of power due to their professional training and provision of free services, had considerable autonomy over patient admittance and discharge. For example, on 3 January 1721, contrary to the hospital's standard processes, it was reported that one of the hospital's physicians, Mr Aldis, 'gave notice to the board that a poor man being found perishing ... with hunger and cold', had been given by him some 'victual's' and money 'to carry him to his habitation in the country'.[36] This shows how physicians involved with the Westminster Infirmary felt able to bend the rules because the charity largely depended on their voluntary support to function. That said, after 1735, when many of the original attending physicians at the Westminster Infirmary left following the dispute regarding the hospital's relocation to Buckingham Gate, such instances of rule-bending became less common. This suggests that the mass resignation of the original attending physicians from the Infirmary may have been, at least in part, to do with shifting contours of power between the established physicians and the Infirmary's governors, alongside a more general refusal to comply with changes that would have publicly suggested that their power was lesser than that of the governors.

The hospital also employed a female matron, female nurses, and other mixed-gender auxiliary staff, such as cooks (mainly women) and orderlies (mainly men). The matron's main responsibilities included the daily running of the hospital and ensuring that the hospital's rules were adhered to.[37] After the physicians, the matron had the most power in determining patient admittance or removal. The matron was also responsible for reporting any issues with the hospital's management to the board before trustee meetings, and it is through the matrons' reports that we learn of most of the instances of unruly behaviour in the hospital. The positioning of a woman in this considerable position of power is in some ways surprising, but nevertheless consistent with contemporary gender norms that placed women in charge of orderly household management, including management of servants and care of the sick.[38] Like most female heads of households, the hospital's matron also guarded and managed the hospital's keys.[39]

Another of the matron's responsibilities was ensuring the employment of 'appropriate' nurses and auxiliaries at the Westminster Infirmary. In the hospital's early years there were no specific criteria for any of these positions and instead, appointments were left to the matron's discretion. However, over time rules were introduced by the governors regarding nurses' behaviour and conduct. These would have guided decisions over who the matron employed and how she vetted applicants. The first explicit rule regarding the employment of nurses was implemented at the

126   *Kathryn Woods*

Westminster Infirmary in 1742 after it was discovered that a nurse, Ann Martin, and a cook, Margaret Humphreys, were Catholics. This was a problem because the Westminster Infirmary was an explicitly Anglican institution, but also because Catholics were seen to be a dangerous threat to the social order and Protestantism more broadly.[40] The presence of these women in the hospital was thus, in many ways, seen as a Catholic plot to undermine the activities of the Infirmary, which wished to promote Protestant values. Both Martin and Humphreys were soon dismissed after these discoveries about their religion were made public. The hospital also subsequently ordered that:

> none but true Protestants shall at any time hereafter be admitted to any services or employ in or about the Infirmary, and that all servants or wages who are not or shall be suspected to be Papists or Profess the Romish Religion, shall give full satisfaction and proof to the Society of their being Protestants.[41]

This example shows how the balances of power shifted in the period under consideration from individuals to the institution via the implementation of rules. It also demonstrates how contemporary socio-economic and political issues informed the identity, structures, processes, and practices of the hospital in its early years.

Admission

Hospital admission, or refusal of admission, represents the most explicit cultural enactment of social inclusion and exclusion in a medical context. The medical historian Guenter B. Risse suggests that the exclusion of the sick from the healthy was among the earliest aims of hospitals. Explaining the social and medical functions of hospital admission practices from the classical age through to modern times, Risse suggests that these rites symbolise 'the transition to patienthood', and help social actors understand – and give social meaning to – the passage across the liminal threshold between health and sickness, and social and medical space.[42] In this sense, hospital admission practices are meaningful to both the sick and the healthy and facilitate the demarcation of the different social roles and expectations that are attached to individuals judged healthy or diseased.[43]

Hospitals' admission criteria are not historically fixed. Instead, they vary according to shifting social and institutional values, changing conceptions of disease, and alterations in attitudes towards patients' social worthiness.[44] Historians of early modern England have noted that from the mid-seventeenth century authorities increasingly distinguished between the 'deserving' and 'undeserving' poor, and sought to 'clarify institutional responses in the form of institutional support'.[45] Recently,

Exclusion in the Westminster Infirmary   127

however, Kevin Siena has argued that evidence from treatises penned by eighteenth-century doctors, especially those published before 1750, suggest more 'ambiguous' medical attitudes towards the poor, 'with some overtly condemning the poor but others resisting that urge'.[46] As we will see, this ambiguity characterises the Westminster Infirmary's attitudes towards the sick poor in the period between 1716 and 1750. Indeed, whether people were categorised as 'deserving' or 'undeserving' was largely determined on an individual basis, albeit with some exceptions, such as in the case of people with venereal diseases.

At the time of its establishment, the Westminster Infirmary deliberately styled itself as a more open and accessible institution than London's other charitable hospitals. This was because it did not require any sort of fee and offered treatment to patients from any English parish, as well as 'foreigners'. The Westminster Infirmary held true to many of its original inclusive aims throughout the period considered in this chapter. In the first year of the hospital's operation, 17 per cent of the total number of patients admitted were described as 'strangers' from outside London, with a further 16.6 per cent being from parishes outside of St Margaret's Westminster.[47] Some migrants came from much further afield. For example, in 1719 the hospital treated a Dutch 'foreigner', Adrien van Reyney, for consumption. Likewise, in 1721 it was recorded that the hospital had provided assistance to Ann Lolbech, 'a stranger of Lancarts Forfshire', in Scotland, who had been blinded by a lightning strike.[48] The Westminster Infirmary's focus on treating patients regardless of their parish origins was one of its most distinctive and enlightened characteristics. This was because this approach recognised, and provided a solution for, the failings of parish-based systems of charity at a time when people were increasingly mobile. This approach provided a blueprint for other London voluntary hospitals, such as St George's Hospital (1735) and the London Hospital (1740).

Although in some respects the Westminster Infirmary was inclusive in its approach to patient admission, in others it was highly exclusionary and selective. Among the patient groups who were usually denied access to the hospital on application were non-Anglicans, people with mental illnesses, those suffering from long-term infirmity, and the dying. Indeed, from the start, the Westminster Infirmary explicitly excluded anyone who the hospital's physicians did not believe they could treat within two months of admission. Two months of admission was also denoted as the maximum length of stay for any patient. As they were employed in practice, these criteria probably meant that, for the most part, the hospital excluded elderly patients who would have been considered likely to die during their hospital stay. Instead, preference was shown to the sick poor who were young or middle-aged with 'treatable diseases' like scurvy, rheumatism, colds or flu, menstrual abnormality, or injury.

128 *Kathryn Woods*

The Westminster Infirmary also routinely excluded patients with contagious diseases, such as typhoid and smallpox, from admission. This was, in part, due to the infectious nature of these diseases, but also because such cases were difficult to treat. Lessons about the contagious nature of smallpox were only learned by the Westminster Infirmary over time, resulting in changing practices of admission and treatment of patients with these diseases. For example, on the 25 April 1738, it was stated in the governors' board minutes that:

> Having been represented to the Board that great Dangers and Inconveniences have attended the keeping of persons in the House that are sick of the smallpox ... for the future every person sick of the smallpox be immediately sent out of the House to a Nurse, to be provided by the Apothecary and Matron till such a time as a proper place may be found for them.[49]

This shows that there were occasions when the Westminster Infirmary's governors made efforts to mitigate the exclusion of patients who were denied hospital admission on the basis of general policy, by offering other forms of support, namely through outdoor relief.

Although the Westminster Infirmary's records enable us to establish instances when the Board of Governors bent their rules to facilitate treatment for patients that might usually be excluded from the hospital, it is impossible to substantiate how many applicants were directly turned away. This is because the Westminster Infirmary did not keep records – at least that survive – that documented cases of patients who were denied admission. It is therefore difficult to establish, either quantitatively or qualitatively, how the hospital's rules were applied to individual patients and the reasons given for their exclusion from admission. Our best evidence to this effect comes from the admission data from the St Margaret's Workhouse Infirmary, established in 1725, that was in close proximity to the Westminster Infirmary. In his analysis, Siena suggests that thirty-eight per cent of St Margaret's workhouse inmates were admitted because of illness or sickness due to their inability to pay for health care or prove their charitable case elsewhere.[50] Siena also notes that in 1734, seventy-nine per cent of the patients in the workhouse infirmary were suffering from the pox (whether it was smallpox or venereal disease is difficult to establish, partly due to the confusion surrounding its diagnosis), itch (infectious skin diseases), and fever. The St Margaret's Workhouse Infirmary data suggests that people with these diseases were routinely excluded from London's other hospitals, including the Westminster Infirmary.[51]

In practice, the Westminster Infirmary's processes of admission were socially and culturally complex. Siena suggests that '[g]etting into a voluntary hospital was fraught with uncertainty, and it was particularly

Exclusion in the Westminster Infirmary   129

hard for those with dubious reputations or no connections or those suffering from aliments ... that called their character into question'.[52] To be granted admission to the Westminster Infirmary, patients required a letter of recommendation. It was stated in the hospital's policies that patients could be recommended to the hospital by a trustee, a physician, or a donor. An order of 1721 stated that the hospital would admit 'poor sick persons inhabiting the parishes of St Margaret's or others may be recommended by any of the subscribers or benefactors'.[53] This clause meant that a sick and poor Scot, for example, who had been previously working with or for someone who was a charity benefactor – and willing to recommend them – would be able to obtain treatment from the Westminster Infirmary. A parishioner of St Margaret's, by contrast, who had the same socio-economic and health circumstances as the Scot, but who had no connections to a donor, could be denied access.

Recommendations from subscribers and donors came in the form of letters, which were used to show that the proposed patient was deserving of medical care by the hospital and was also morally sound.[54] The ability to recommend patients suggests that one of the potential reasons for donor's involvement with the charity was that it enabled them to provide their servants with a very basic form of workplace insurance. To aid the administration of this 'recommendation' system, the hospital provided printed copies of forms which could be filled out by subscribers and benefactors to facilitate the admittance of patients.[55] The only stipulation that was put upon donors who were recommending patients from outside the parish was that they should 'oblige' themselves 'to take care of the said person upon his Recovery' and cover burial costs if the patient died.[56] On admission, the orders also stated that patients from parishes outside of St Margaret's were required to provide certified letters from their home parish which stated that following the patient's discharge from the Westminster Infirmary they would receive necessary care and charitable support from that parish. It is ambiguous as to whether this letter was to be acquired by the hospital, on the patient's behalf, or the patient themselves.[57] Whether the hospital required such letters ahead of a patient's admission to the Infirmary is also unclear.

How patients obtained letters of recommendation from benefactors is equally unclear and not documented in hospital records.[58] All patients required this sort of letter for admission. In most cases, recommended patients were likely the past or present employees of charitable benefactors, or family or friends of employees who had petitioned their employers, as subscribers of the charity, to support their claims for relief.[59] For example, in an Old Bailey case from 1742, a witness, who described himself as a Goldsmith, testified to the character of the daughter of one of his employees, Jane Wood, who was accused of stealing. Prior to the crime being investigated, and as a way of providing a good account of her character, he explained that she had been

130   Kathryn Woods

'frightened into Fits some Years ago, by some Soldiers coming into the House, which took away her Senses'. Following this episode, he recounted that he had 'got her into the Infirmary at Westminster, and she was sometime there before she was cured'.[60] This shows how people of standing were able to use their position and connections to support the admission of patients to the Westminster Infirmary.

Before admission, all patients had to be examined by a hospital physician. This examination was used to confirm the nature of the patient's disease and establish whether they met the criteria for treatment. Risse suggests that these 'encounters could be frustrating and deceptive, as prospective patients tried hard to tell doctors the "right" stories about their sufferings to ensure admission', while doctors looked out for 'symptoms or signs that clearly marked particular diseases'.[61] Following this examination, applicants who were not considered to meet the hospital's criteria for treatment were turned away directly. No reports were created, as far as is evident from the records, in relation to these turned-away applicants. On the other hand, in the case of patients recommended for admittance, the hospital's doctors submitted reports, often no longer than a few lines, to be verified by the hospital's board. These reports included the patient's name and the nature of their disease and were used for official record-keeping. Sometimes, although rare, the physician's decisions could be trumped by subscribers and donors, especially if they were particularly generous or influential supporters. For example, on 3 January 1721, Cath Stevens, who had been recommended by one of the charity's major patrons, Lady Dodsley, the Royal governess, was said to have been 'examined by the physicians and pronounced incurable, having the Gout'. This was initially judged as grounds to exclude her from admission. However, the trustee board's meetings minutes noted that it was 'ordered nevertheless upon consideration of my Lady's recommendation that she be admitted for a fortnight'.[62]

Nonetheless, when it came to recommending patients, doctors tended to have more influence than subscribers and donors. When the Westminster Infirmary first opened, neither donors nor physicians had any limit on how many patients they could recommend. Yet, in 1729, due to the rising success of the hospital and growing patient numbers, the hospital governors decreed that physicians and surgeons 'may each have two in and two outpatients'. The donors, by comparison, could only have two inpatients and one outpatient at any one time.[63] In this respect, the role of doctors in the admission process enabled the Infirmary to function like a proto-accident and emergency hospital. For example, in 1750 one of the physicians was brought to the Old Bailey to testify in the case of William Riley who was accused of murdering Samuel Sutton with a clothes hanger. Soon after the crime had been committed, the mortally wounded victim had been brought by his friends to the hospital in an

Exclusion in the Westminster Infirmary 131

effort to save him and was admitted by one of the attending physicians, John Pile. Pile testified:

> I am surgeon to the Westminster Infirmary. The deceas'd was brought there on Saturday was seen in the evening. I found he had a wound on the left side of the belly, near the navel, where the intestine came out; he languish'd till Monday morning, and then died. It was about an inch long. The gut was not cut, but there was a large quantity of it out; and all that was out mortified. That was the occasion of his death.[64]

Alongside failure to produce a letter of support or meet the requirements of admission, there were numerous other factors that could cause patients to be turned away by the Westminster Infirmary. Quite frequently the hospital was full, especially in the early years when the hospital resided in the locations of, firstly, Pretty France, Pimilco (which accommodated ten beds), and secondly, St Bartholomew's, Smithfield between 1720 and 1724 (accommodating eighteen beds). On 6 September 1724, both Jane Farrant and Jane Belcher were given out-patient care until the hospital had space for admission.[65] Financial difficulties and the poor state of the rented buildings used to house the hospital at different stages in its early history also caused challenges. For example, on the 19 November 1729, it was decreed that 'in consideration of the present low state of this Infirmary', no patients should be admitted 'till a General Board is called'.[66] The hospital moved again in 1735 to a new residence at Buckingham Gate which accommodated ninety-eight beds. Debates over this relocation caused an irreconcilable split between the managing trustees of the Westminster Infirmary and its attending physicians, causing the physicians to separate themselves from the charity and establish their own hospital, St George's Hospital, at their preferred site at Hyde Park Corner.[67]

The inclusion or exclusion of particular patient groups, especially venereal patients, was a subject of debate between hospital governors, benefactors, physicians, and patients throughout the period 1716 to 1750. It involved all these key stakeholders because it was perceived by some to fundamentally alter the institution's essential charitable mission, and the overall ability of the Westminster Infirmary to support the sick and deserving poor. Before the 1730s, there is little mention of the issue of venereal disease in the Westminster Infirmary's records. This suggests the sick poor with these diseases were not deliberately excluded. Interestingly, however, there is also no record of patients with this type of illness being admitted for treatment. Yet, after 1735, the new hospital administration and doctors seem to have regarded the issue of whether to admit venereal patients as a particular challenge. This might have been because of increasing numbers of applications from patients with such diseases, maybe as a result of

132 *Kathryn Woods*

overcrowding in London's other hospitals. But it also might suggest that the earlier staff body of physicians for the Westminster Infirmary, who left in 1735, may have been more willing to overlook these issues and/or deceive the board about the nature of the complaints of the patients they admitted. Either way, in 1738 the Westminster Infirmary trustees ordered the establishment of a committee to consider:

> what persons are properly objects of this charity, to enquire into the methods hitherto followed both amongst us and at other hospitals on the choice of patients to be Admitted, and to draw up a report of what method shall appear to them the most satisfactory to the subscribers, most for the Good and Safety of patients, and most for the peace and prosperity of the society.[68]

Upon considering the issue, the committee recommended that venereal patients should not be admitted to the hospital for treatment in the future. The stated reasons for this decision were manifold, including the previously mentioned objections of the female donors and the apparent lack of precedent for the admission of such patients, as evidenced in the Infirmary's patient records. Yet, the main reason for their exclusion, according to the committee, was that venereal patients could not be considered eligible for admission because: 'persons infected with venereal disease do generally bring it upon themselves by their own lewd and vicious habits'. It was also proposed that by allowing these patients access, the hospital would be causing 'the exclusion of many more deserving objects'.[69]

Discharge

In comparison to admittance, described in detail by historians such as Risse, the history of patient discharge has received limited historical attention. The reasons for this are unclear, but it is likely because the structures, processes, and practices of patient discharge are more nebulous than admission and tend to be more deeply intertwined with individual patient treatment and case histories. Indeed, at least in relation to the Westminster Infirmary, practices of patient discharge tended to be reactive to individual cases rather than planned processes, meaning that they are less well documented in formal institutional records. The standard evidence of discharge we have from the surviving records is a few lines stating the name of the patient and when they were discharged, whether or not they had been cured, or if they had died. In a few more exceptional cases, there is evidence of potentially controversial reasons why a patient was discharged without a cure.

Practices of discharge are worth studying because they are highly revealing of institutional cultures, shifting pressures within and outside

Exclusion in the Westminster Infirmary 133

institutions, and because of their symbiotic relationship with rules of admittance. In terms of the Westminster Infirmary in the period considered, practices of discharge reveal how the 'rules' were negotiated between various hospital stakeholders. They also indicate some of the methods used to maintain social order in the hospital, and ways in which the hospital responded to challenges caused by London's social problems. There was also a close relationship between instances of patient discharge and structures of admission. For example, after dealing with particular cases of unruly behaviour, it was common practice for the hospital to pass new rules of admission to prevent similar instances arising in the future. This approach to the development of admission rules was significant because it increasingly made the hospital a more exclusive space.

Numerous factors could lead patients to be discharged from the Westminster Infirmary after admission. The most common cause of patient discharge, it is important to note, was cure. For example, in a public account of 1734, it was reported that in the period December 1719 to March 1734, 228 patients had left the hospital 'cured', in comparison to 10 discharged for irregularity, and 24 discharged incurable.[70] To be discharged, patients had to have their leave of the hospital agreed by the physicians and trustees. Successful cure of patients was something that the hospital celebrated as evidence of its social value and impact, and to encourage ongoing and increased support for the institution. This explains why the hospital regularly published figures on the numbers of successfully treated patients. After 1721 it was also ordered that 'everyone discharged cured from this infirmary be enjoined by the chairman to give publick thanks in their parish churches'.[71] This was a further means of promoting the charity and publicising its good deeds across London, England, and beyond. In addition, this practice served to reaffirm the hierarchical distinctions between the givers and receivers of charity. Records of who had, and who had not, given thanks to the charity were recorded in the trustees' meeting minutes, with those who failed to provide thanks being denied future access to care by the hospital.

Patients could also be discharged prematurely from the Westminster Infirmary following discoveries about the nature of their disease during treatment. For example, on 30 March 1721, Robert Pight was discharged due to mental illness. The physician attending his case noted: 'this House is not the proper for the care of Robert Pight him being a lunatic. Ordered to be discharged'.[72] The Infirmary's exclusion of patients with mental diseases was consistent with London's other medical hospitals in the same period. The mentally ill were routinely shunned from such institutions because of their behavioural unpredictability, and difficulties relating to their treatment. At the same time, they problematised clear patient categorisation, which was challenging in

134 *Kathryn Woods*

institutions like the Westminster Infirmary where such categorisation was central to the hospital's effective operation. On a deeper level, mental illnesses often provoked concern in medical institutions and society more broadly because there was a recognition that 'its definitions, its boundaries, its meanings' were 'a distorted mirror of shifting social order'.[73] The founding ethos of the Westminster Infirmary was to restore order, and in this sense, it is easy to see how the treatment of the mentally ill was problematic within this context. The only institutional treatment option for the mentally ill in London in this period was Bethlem Hospital, described by Allan Ingram as 'where madness went to hide its face'.[74]

Another cause of early patient discharge was a failure on the part of patients to uphold decent behaviour. The hospital's rules were generally policed and reported to the board of trustees by the hospital's matron. In the hospital's early years, the trustees were confronted with a difficult case which seems to have taken them by surprise, as evidenced by the extensive discussion that was devoted to it in their meeting minutes. On 17 August 1720, it was reported that Rob Winnington, a patient, had 'behaved himself in a very rude and scandalous manner'. Among his crimes were 'motioning quickly' – a euphemism for masturbation – 'cursing and swearing', and 'having abused Matron and servants at this Infirmary with cursings and threatings of every language'. Mr Winnington was subsequently brought before the board to explain himself, where he stated that his behaviour was caused by drunkenness. The board declared that Mr Winnington should immediately be discharged.[75] No rules were put in place following this case, but this was the beginning of the hospital's long-standing and complicated challenge in dealing with patients' alcohol consumption.

From the 1720s, there were escalating problems with gin consumption within the hospital and in society at large. Gin drinking was on the rise during this period due to its lack of licensing, ease of distillation, cheapness, and its popularity among London's poor and working classes on account of its alcoholic strength. Roy Porter notes that gin was widely 'sold in workhouses, prisons, brothels and barbers' shops'. Evidence in the Westminster Infirmary's records suggests that it was also sold in hospitals.[76] For example, on 21 March 1721, Dr Wasey reported to the board that a patient, Sam Moor, was cured and should be immediately discharged, but on discharge should be reprimanded by the chairman of the trustees for 'attempting to introduce a scandalous custom of extorting money from fellow-patients upon admission to the house for ... drinking money'.[77] While this money might have been for beer, it was more likely to have been collected for gin, as the hospital provided a weekly allowance of beer for each patient. On 21 February 1721, it was ordered that 'the matron take a strict care that no strong liquor be brought into this infirmary from any publick house'.[78] As the poor were

Exclusion in the Westminster Infirmary 135

unlikely to have been able to afford any strong liquor other than gin, it seems that this was another reference to London's gin issue as encountered by the hospital. Indeed, this rule appeared around the same time that the authorities were considering legal steps to curb the consumption of gin. In 1721, the Middlesex magistrates complained that gin was 'the principal cause of all the vice and debauchery committed among the inferior sort of people'.[79]

Issues with gin consumption among patients continued throughout the period between 1720 and 1760. In the 1730s, the Westminster Infirmary sought to collaborate with other local hospitals to address the social and moral challenge presented by gin. On 22 July 1735, the trustees established a committee to look into developing a coordinated response with the 'Governors and Trustees of Bartholomew's, St Thomas', Guy's Hospital and the Hospital of Hide-Park Corner'. The aim of this collaboration, the Westminster Infirmary's trustees wrote, was 'to prevent the Entertaining of any patients that have contracted their Distempers by drinking Gin or other spiritous Liqueurs, and if so desire them to cooperate with this society in discountenancing that most pernicious practice'.[80] At this stage it was also ordered that 'whatever patient or patients be discovered to drink gin or any other spirituous liquors that they be forthwith expelled from this house'. The new rule also stated that 'any nurse or servant' who was 'found guilty of suffering or knowingly to permit any patients of this infirmary to drink the said liquors' would 'immediately be discharged'. This stands as a testament to the ubiquity of gin consumption among the working classes in London at this time.[81]

Theft was another problem for the Westminster Infirmary and a cause of early patient discharge in several cases. Incredibly, it was only after fifteen years of operation that the hospital introduced a specific rule about what to do in cases of theft by patients. This came about due to an incident involving one of the hospital's in-patients, Mary Pearce, who in 1735 was spotted by one of the hospital's religious visitors entering a 'genever shop' (small premises where gin was sold and consumed). After following Pearce into the shop, the anonymous hospital visitor searched Pearce to find that she was carrying a cap and apron belonging to the Infirmary. On questioning by the board, Pearce revealed that she intended to sell these items, and had already sold another apron belonging to the house, to buy gin. Perhaps surprisingly, the hospital chose not to prosecute her, whether out of genuine sympathy for Pearce's situation or to avoid bringing ill-repute on the institution. They may also have been concerned about the severity of her punishment if the case was taken to the Old Bailey, which would have most likely been hanging. Pearce's ability to show contrition seems to have been a deciding factor. The minutes recorded: 'upon her humble subscription and begging pardon, no further punishment be inflicted on her but only that she is expelled from the house'.[82] For future cases, however, it was determined that any

136   Kathryn Woods

theft would result in both expulsion of the patient and their prosecution, thereby preventing the trustees to show the same level of leniency as they had to Mary Pearce.

Conclusion

The historian David Sabean suggests: 'What is common in community is not shared values or common understanding so much as the fact that members of a community are engaged in the same argument, in which alternative strategies, misunderstandings, conflicting goals and values are threshed out'.[83] This chapter has argued that for the Westminster Infirmary, debates, and negotiations between the hospital's various stakeholders – centring around particular moments of inclusion and exclusion, and instances of unruly behaviour – served to create a distinct identity and sense of community for the hospital; albeit one where stakeholders' values and goals remained distinct.

This chapter has shown that in its establishment, the Westminster Infirmary deliberately styled itself as an inclusionary institution; offering medical care and support to the sick poor who were unable to access treatment by other means. Yet, despite these aims, the establishment of the hospital was largely connected to a perception among the social elite about the need to remove the sick poor from the streets and to restore a sense of social order in the city. Social changes such as urbanisation, migration, changing patterns of social organisation, shifting gender norms, the rise of associational culture, religious conflict, as well as rising poverty, crime, and alcoholism, all played roles in shaping the Westminster Infirmary's culture.

The chapter has also evidenced numerous ways in which the hospital's stakeholders were touched and impacted by the socio-economic changes taking place in London during this period, and how they used the hospital to achieve their own ends in relation to these developments. The collective dialogue around poverty and disease, and the structures, processes, and practices produced by the Westminster Infirmary – information about which was spread through the hospital's print materials and the social networks of benefactors and recipients of charity – produced new discussions and alternative strategies for resolving the challenges of social organisation, poverty, and disease management. As evidenced by the subsequent rise of the voluntary hospital movement across Britain in the eighteenth century, many seem to have viewed the Westminster Infirmary's voluntary model of medical charity as an effective method of solving some of the issues wrought by socio-economic change that created benefits for the elites, emergent middle classes, and the poor alike.[84]

What has also been illustrated by this chapter is that in its first thirty years, the activities of the Westminster Infirmary were open to

Exclusion in the Westminster Infirmary 137

negotiation by various stakeholders. Various examples have been provided of how donors, trustees, physicians, and patients negotiated the structures, rules, and processes of the hospital for their own purposes. Nevertheless, access to involvement in the hospital was always denied to excluded groups, like Catholics, as well as some of the most vulnerable members of society, including patients who were labelled infectious, mad, or sexually deviant. Equally, over time new structures and rules were introduced in response to specific instances of unruly behaviour. This created a more firmly established habitus of inclusion and exclusion across different levels of the hospital's administration. Ultimately this served to curtail the stakeholders' powers of negotiation and created a more bureaucratically focused approach to the delivery of voluntary charitable relief as it evolved over the eighteenth century.

Notes

1 London Metropolitan Archives, City of London (hereafter LMA), H02/WH/A/01/001, *Minutes of the Trustees*, vol. 1 (1716 January–1724 June), 3–4.
2 John Woodward, *To Do the Sick No Harm* (London: Routledge, 1974), 11.
3 For further discussion of the Charity's early financial difficulties see Joseph Graeme Humble, 'Westminster Hospital: First 250 Years', *British Medical Journal*, 15 (1966), 156.
4 Jonathan Barry and Colin Jones (eds), *Medicine and Charity Before the Welfare State* (London and New York: Routledge, 1994), 7.
5 LMA, H02/WH/A/01/065, Poster Advertising the Purpose and Activities of the Westminster Infirmary (July 1720).
6 Woodward, *To Do the Sick No Harm*, 17.
7 Ibid., 17.
8 Joseph Graeme Humble, *Westminster Hospital 1716–1974*, second edition (London: Pitman Medical Publishing Company, 1974); Walter George Spencer, *Westminster Hospital. An Outline of its History* (London: H. J. Glaisher, 1924); John Langdon-Davies, *Westminster Hospital. Two Centuries of Voluntary Service, 1719–1948* (London: John Murray, 1952).
9 For further discussion on this historiography see Jonathan Andrews, 'History of Medicine: Health, Medicine and Disease in the Eighteenth Century', *British Journal for Eighteenth Century Studies*, 34 (2011), 503–15; Guenter B. Risse, *Mending Bodies, Saving Souls: A History of Hospitals* (Oxford: Oxford University Press, 1999), 8.
10 Pierre Bourdieu defines habitus as the mental frameworks that inform how individuals perceive the world in which they live. Pierre Bourdieu, *Outline of The Theory of Practice* (Cambridge: Cambridge University Press, 1977), 72–3.
11 Roy Porter, *London: A Social History* (London: Penguin Books, 1994), 98.
12 Edward Anthony Wrigley, *Population and History* (London: Weidenfield and Nicolson, 1969), 70–4.
13 Leonard Schwarz, *London in the Age of Industrialisation: Entrepreneurs, Labour Force and Living Conditions, 1700–1850* (Cambridge: Cambridge University Press, 1992), 133–5 and 141; John Landers, *Death in the Metropolis: Studies in the Demographic History of London, 1670–1830* (Cambridge: Cambridge University Press, 1993), 353–5.

138　*Kathryn Woods*

14 Schwarz, *London*, 127–8; Edward Anthony Wrigley, *English Population History from Family to Reconstitution, 1580–1837* (Cambridge: Cambridge University Press, 1997), 204; Wrigley, *Population and History*, 70–4.

15 Joshua Gee, *The Trade and Navigation of Great Britain Considered* (London, 1729), 38–9.

16 *London Journal* (13 February 1731), quoted in Tim Hitchcock, *Down and Out in Eighteenth-Century London* (London and New York: Hambledon, 2004), 114.

17 Woodward, *To Do the Sick No Harm*, 4, 8.

18 Marquis of Lansdowne (ed.), *The Petty Papers: Some Unpublished Writings of Sir William* Petty (2 vols, New York: A. M. Kelley, 1967) ii. 176.

19 Lynn Holden Lees, *The Solidarities of Strangers: The English Poor Laws and the People, 1700–1948* (Cambridge: Cambridge University Press, 1998), 23.

20 Westminster Infirmary, *Annual Report*, 3 January 1721–2 to 16 January 177–3, 'An Account of the Proceedings of the Charitable Society for Relieving the Sick and Needy at the Infirmary in Petty-France, Westminster'. Quoted in Woodward, *To Do the Sick No Harm*, 11–2.

21 Donna Andrew, 'Two Charities in Eighteenth-Century London', in Jonathan Barry and Colin Jones (eds), *Medicine and Charity*, 82.

22 Quoted in Anon., 'The Origin and Evolution of the 18th Century Hospital Movement', *Hospital* (17 January 1914), 429.

23 Paul Slack, 'Hospitals, Workhouses and the Relief of the Poor in Early Modern England', in Ole Peter Grell and Andrew Cunningham (eds), *Health Care and Poor Relief in Protestant Europe 1500–1700* (London and New York: Routledge, 1997), 229.

24 Westminster Infirmary, *An Account of the Proceedings of the Charitable Society for Relieving the Sick and Needy at the Infirmary in Petty-France Westminster* (London, 1723), 3–4.

25 Penny Roberts and William Naphy (eds), *Fear in Early Modern Society* (Manchester: Manchester University Press, 1997), 3.

26 Slack, 'Hospitals, Workhouses and the Relief of the Poor', 239.

27 Peter Clark, *British Clubs and Societies 1580–1800: The Origins of an Associational World* (Oxford, 2000); Richard J. Morris, 'Voluntary Societies and British Urban Elites, 1780–1850', *The Historical Journal*, 26 (1983), 95–118; Ileana Baird (ed.), *Social Networks in the Long Eighteenth Century: Clubs, Literary Salons, Textual Coteries* (Newcastle upon Tyne: Cambridge Scholars Publishing, 2014); Peter Borsay (ed.), *The Eighteenth-Century Town: A Reader in English Urban History* (London, 1990), 12.

28 Andrew, 'Two Charities in Eighteenth-Century London', 83.

29 Bernard Mandeville, *The Fable of the Bees: Or Private Vices, Publick Benefits*, second edition (London, 1723), 269.

30 Paul Langford, *A Polite and Commercial People: England 1727–1783* (Oxford and London: Clarendon Press, 1998), 61–5.

31 Sylvana Tomaselli, 'The Enlightenment Debate on Women', *History Workshop Journal*, 20 (1985), 101–24; Katharine Glover, *Elite Women and Polite Society in Eighteenth-Century Scotland* (Woodbridge: The Boydell Press, 2011), 4.

32 LMA, H02/WH/A/01/001, *Minutes of the Trustees*, vol. 1 (January 1716–June 1724), 218.

33 LMA, H02/WH/A/01/005, *Minutes of the Trustees*, vol. 5 (April 1738–June 1740), 180.

Exclusion in the Westminster Infirmary 139

34 Michael Stolberg, *Experiencing Illness and the Sick Body in Early Modern Europe*, translated by Leonard Unglaub & Logan Kennedy (Basingstoke: Palgrave Macmillan, 2011), 58–64.
35 Woodward, *To Do the Sick No Harm*, 23.
36 LMA, H02/WH/A/01/001, *Minutes of the Trustees*, vol. 1 (January 1716–June 1724), 160.
37 Woodward, *To Do the Sick No Harm*, 29–30.
38 Amanda Vickery, *The Gentleman's Daughter: Women's Lives in Georgian England* (New Haven and London: Yale University Press, 1998), 127–60.
39 Ibid., 133.
40 Gabriel Glickman, *The English Catholic Community, 1688–1745* (Woodbridge: The Boydell Press, 2009), 2.
41 LMA, H02/WH/A/01/007, *Minutes of the Trustees*, vol. 7 (April 1742–November 1743), 33.
42 Risse, *Mending Bodies*, 8.
43 Talcott Parsons, *The Social System* (London: Routledge, 1951), 428–33.
44 Woodward, *To Do the Sick No Harm*, 41.
45 Andrew Spicer and Jane L. Stevens Crawshaw (eds), *The Place of the Social Margins, 1350–1750* (London and New York: Routledge, 2016), 4.
46 Kevin Sienna, *Rotten Bodies: Class and Contagion in Eighteenth-Century Britain* (New Haven and London: Yale University Press, 2019), 13.
47 LMA, H02/WH/A/01/065, 'The First Proceedings of the Trustees', July 1720.
48 LMA, H02/WH/A/01/001, *Minutes of the Trustees*, vol. 1 (January 1716–June 1724), 149.
49 LMA, H02/WH/A/01/005, *Minutes of the Trustees*, vol. 5 (April 1738– June 1740), 14.
50 Kevin Siena, 'Contagion, Exclusion and the Unique Medical World of the Eighteenth-Century Workhouse', in Jonathan Reniarz and Leonard Schwarz (eds), *Medicine and the Workhouse* (Woodbridge: The Boydell Press, 2013), 20.
51 Ibid., 24.
52 Ibid., 22.
53 LMA, H02/WH/A/01/001, 'Orders Relating to the Recommending of Patients' in *Minutes of the Trustees*, vol. 1 (January 1716–June 1724), 424.
54 For further discussion of this process see Risse, *Mending Bodies*, 232–5.
55 H.W. Hart 'Some Notes on the Sponsoring of Patients for Hospital Treatment under the Voluntary System', *Medical History*, 24 (1980), 446–60; H.W. Hart, 'The Conveyance of Patients to and from the Hospital, 1720–1850', *Medical History*, 22 (1978), 397–407.
56 LMA, H02/WH/A/01/001, 'Orders Relating to the Recommending of Patients', 424.
57 Ibid., 425.
58 Siena, 'Contagion, Exclusion and the Unique Medical World of the Eighteenth-Century Workhouse', 22–3.
59 Risse, *Mending Bodies*, 232–3; Siena, 'Contagion, Exclusion and the Unique Medical World of the Eighteenth-Century Workhouse', 22.
60 *The Proceedings of the Old Bailey – London's Central Criminal Court, 1674–1913: Old Bailey Proceedings Online* (www.oldbaileyonline.org, version 8.0) (hereafter *OBP*), 21 October 1742, trial of Jane Wood (t17420909-38).
61 Risse, *Mending Bodies*, 235.
62 LMA, H02/WH/A/01/001, *Minutes of the Trustees*, vol. 1 (January 1716–June 1724), 157.

140   *Kathryn Woods*

63 LMA, H02/WH/A/01/002, *Minutes of the Trustees*, vol. 2 (June 1724–November 1729), 489.
64 *OBP*, 12 October 1750, trial of William Riley (t17500912-61).
65 LMA, H02/WH/A/01/002, *Minutes of the Trustees*, vol. 2 (June 1724–November 1729), 23.
66 Ibid., 1008.
67 Humble, 'Westminster Hospital', 57.
68 LMA, H02/WH/A/01/005, *Minutes of the Trustees*, vol. 5 (April 1738–June 1740), 120.
69 Ibid.
70 Westminster Hospital, *An Account of the Proceedings of the Charitable Society for Relieving the Sick and Needy* (London, 1734), 3.
71 LMA, H02/WH/A/01/001, *Minutes of the Trustees*, vol. 1 (January 1716–June 1724), 149.
72 Ibid., 172.
73 Andrew Scull, *Anglo-American Psychiatry in Hospital Perspective* (Berkeley, CA: University of California Press, 1989), 8.
74 Allan Ingram with Michelle Faubert, *Cultural Constructions of Madness in Eighteenth-Century Writing* (Basingstoke: Palgrave McMillan, 2005), 7.
75 LMA, H02/WH/A/01/001, *Minutes of the Trustees*, vol. 1 (January 1716–June 1724), 116–7.
76 Porter, *London*, 181.
77 LMA, H02/WH/A/01/001, *Minutes of the Trustees*, vol. 1 (January 1716–June 1724), 256.
78 Ibid.
79 Quoted in Porter, *London*, 181.
80 LMA, H02/WH/A/01/004, *Minutes of the Trustees*, vol. 4 (November 1734–March 1738), 231.
81 Ibid.
82 Ibid.
83 David Sabean, *Power in the Blood: Popular Culture and Village Discourse in Early Modern Germany* (Cambridge: Cambridge University Press, 1987), 29.
84 Woodward, *To Do the Sick No Harm*, 36.

6 Defining the Boundaries of Community?

Experiences of Parochial Inclusion and Pregnancy Outside Wedlock in Early Modern England

Charmian Mansell

In 1587, parish constable Roger Chardon was cited to appear before the Exeter church court, accused of fathering the illegitimate child of his servant, Joanne Hull. The court heard from witnesses of his failed attempt to conceal her pregnancy. Their testimonies revealed that Chardon had paid five shillings to a poor woman named Avice Friar, who was instructed to secretly convey Hull from Exeter to Taunton, around forty kilometres away. Chardon had issued them with passports so they would not be apprehended for vagrancy upon their arrival in Taunton. But his carefully laid plan was foiled. Richard Hitchens, a suspicious neighbour, followed the two women on their journey. According to Hitchen's testimony, when he arrived in the city at nightfall, Friar mistook him in the dark for Chardon's brother-in-law and inadvertently betrayed Chardon's plot. She told him confidently that when he returned to Exeter, he could report to Mr and Mrs Chardon that: 'Joane is well and that they doe sett their harts at rest and feare nothing of the matter for [they] shall never [hear] a feather springe of it and … I will warrant that Roger Chardon shall never hear sounde of the matter into Exeter.'[1]

Emerging from the pages of court records documenting cases like this is a narrative of the exclusion of single pregnant women from the early modern parish (and sometimes county). Church court depositions in which parishioners reported on the immoral behaviour of men and women, like Roger Chardon and Joanne Hull, are littered with instances of unmarried pregnant women being shunted from the parishes in which they lived. For example, in 1625, Susan Ford of Wotton-under-Edge, Gloucestershire, was sent to Wiltshire, where she delivered her illegitimate child.[2] In 1572, William Jackson of Staunton, in the same county, transported his pregnant servant, Elizabeth Godwin, 'away to Morton in Worstershir to one of his cozens Henry Rogers'. The perceived economic burden of this woman was explicitly laid out in this case: despite being bribed with wheat in exchange for Godwin's keep, Rogers refused to keep her in his house for long (and quickly sold the wheat).[3]

142   *Charmian Mansell*

As a married man and parish constable of Exeter, the social and economic cost of fathering an illegitimate child must surely have weighed heavily on Roger Chardon's mind. By sending Joanne Hull away, he sought to avoid detection and loss of reputation among his neighbours. This was a practice in which the early modern community has also been seen as complicit, and the idea that there was a growing culture of parochial exclusion of pregnant, unmarried women is firmly entrenched within the scholarship of early modern society. In *When Gossips Meet*, Bernard Capp explores the role that other women could play in shunning unmarried mothers from communities.[4] Similarly, in her work on perceptions of early modern illegitimate pregnancy, Laura Gowing characterises pregnant single women as a potential 'threat to the survival of individuals, households and parishes', particularly in times of dearth.[5] The 1598 Elizabethan Poor Laws – and the piecemeal legislation that pre-dated them – addressed the issue of vagrancy and relief of the poor by placing economic responsibility for those unable to work on the parish itself through taxation.[6] The guiding principle was that everyone had a parish of settlement, usually claimed through birth, marriage or apprenticeship, to which they should be 'returned' if they became vagrant or reliant on parish relief.[7] Migrant unmarried mothers (often servants) were prime targets of this legislation.[8] If the paternity of an illegitimate child could not be attributed to a settled parishioner, the cost of maintaining mother and child fell upon the community. Economic motivations frequently drove parishioners to ensure that women without a claim of settlement did not remain in the parish once their pregnancy was discovered. Studies of settlement and bastardy examinations therefore suggest the zealous defence of parish boundaries and the forcible return of pregnant single women to their parish of origin. Right to poor relief, Keith Wrightson argues, defined the 'boundaries of community by the recognition of settlement and entitlement'.[9] Keith Snell pinpoints the origins of an eighteenth-century 'culture of xenophobia' in this Elizabethan formalization of parochial welfare provision.[10]

Over the last thirty years, work on sociability and neighbourhood has expanded to consider communities and networks that existed across place and space.[11] However, it is still assumed that women who conceived outside wedlock were routinely excluded from their communities, as a result of the spatial relocation described above. While entitlement to poor relief defined the boundaries of the administrative unit of the parish, as this chapter will demonstrate, unmarried pregnant women were not indiscriminately shut out from the social and economic networks they had established. Nor did their participation in these communities simply cease after an illegitimate child had been born. As the question mark in the title indicates, this chapter reassesses the presumption that the expulsion of a pregnant, unmarried woman from the parish in which she lived automatically barred her from community life.

Parochial Inclusion and Pregnancy 143

It suggests that the motivations – particularly economic anxieties – behind spatial relocation or physical ejection from the parish must be separated from our conceptual understanding of how neighbourhood and community operated.

In conceiving a child out of wedlock, a woman was seen to have behaved outside the norms of her gender. This was because female reputation, credit, and honour were built upon sexual morality. Defamation cases in the church courts highlight the destructive power that the words 'whore' or 'jade' could have upon a woman's social and economic standing.[12] Often, it was the case that an unmarried woman with an illegitimate child faced the prospect of a lifetime without a husband. Indeed, single mothers were generally considered unattractive prospects by potential suitors due to the economic burden of maintaining and caring for another man's child. For some of these women, then, marriage – the most desirable state of respectability – was never to be achieved. What were the experiences of these women living in early modern England? How were they treated by their neighbours? To what extent were they excluded from the social and economic practices of the communities in which they lived? How far did their actions bar them from inclusion?

This chapter addresses these questions using evidence of women's experiences of pregnancy outside wedlock recorded in the church court depositions of the dioceses of Bath and Wells, Exeter, Gloucester, and Winchester between 1550 and 1650. It considers experiences of both illegitimate pregnancy and single motherhood. The chapter is divided into three parts. The first section demonstrates how these women could 'make amends' for their actions in the eyes of the law and their neighbours. The second part considers the nature of support and charity offered within the early modern community. The final part explores the parochial acceptance of single mothers through evidence of their inclusion in legal processes as court witnesses. It is not my intention to argue that unmarried mothers were never excluded from early modern communities. Indeed, as the case of Joanne Hull demonstrates, this was a very real experience for some women. However, what this chapter aims to do is shift attention to the informal forms of support some unmarried mothers received from their neighbours, alongside underscoring the experiences of those who continued to remain within the social and economic communities to which they belonged. This raises questions about defining the parish by its economic concerns, rather than its social mores and values. The micro-politics of *inclusion* rather than exclusion that unmarried mothers experienced have received little sustained attention in the historiographies of pregnancy and parish relief.[13] This chapter goes some way to redress this oversight and contributes to the development of a better understanding of the processes of inclusion and exclusion that defined and sustained local communities.

144   *Charmian Mansell*

Church Court Depositions

This is by no means the first time that experiences of unmarried pregnant women have been studied using court records. Studies of infanticide, bastardy, and harbouring single pregnant women have, in particular, relied on this type of evidence.[14] Laura Gowing's work on infanticide from the records of the Northern Circuit Assizes highlights the social and economic vulnerability of women who conceived out of wedlock. Often with little wealth or social standing, these women felt they had few options but to end their child's life.[15] The evidence from the church court depositions discussed here displays a broader spectrum of experiences of unmarried mothers. It also presents a range of parochial views on these women and their place within the community.

Diocesan courts were charged with enforcing morality and discipline in early modern society. Cases could be heard in court via one of two routes. Firstly, the courts arbitrated conflicts between individuals (*instance* suits), including defamation and matrimonial disputes. The court also acted as a plaintiff in its own right in office (*ex officio*) cases, acting upon reports of wrongdoing. Churchwardens were responsible for identifying and reporting miscreants, and bishops and their deputies periodically visited parishes to ensure that offenders were brought to justice. Witnesses were produced and asked to outline their knowledge of their neighbours' transgressions. Their testimonies were, of course, subjective, and we have no way of knowing the veracity of the events given in the reports. Thus, while care must be taken in analysing church court depositions, it is also important to note that those who provided testimonies in such cases hoped that the court would accept these testimonies as the truth. These narratives can therefore be taken as evidence of plausible and conceivable attitudes towards single pregnant women.[16]

Tales of illicit sex resulting in illegitimate children were most frequently recorded in court cases relating to adultery and extra-marital affairs. The experiences of pregnant single women were also recorded in matrimonial suits; these women often pursued action against male sexual partners who they claimed had promised to marry them prior to their liaison. In these cases, unmarried mothers sought to ensure that such promises of marriage were upheld to protect their own reputations, as well as their children's. Although pre-marital sex was certainly frowned upon, a child born prior to marriage was nonetheless upheld as legitimate, as demonstrated in Kate Gibson's chapter in this volume.[17] Across all types of cases, details of illegitimacy and single motherhood are also found in witnesses' responses to cross-examination questions (known as interrogatories). These questions, often relating to witnesses' wealth and social standing, sought to discredit their testimonies. The defendant frequently dredged up revelations of extra-marital affairs and children born out of wedlock from decades past. This evidence was then used to

Parochial Inclusion and Pregnancy 145

mount a case against the veracity and integrity of a witness's deposition. In this chapter, experiences of illegitimate pregnancy are thus drawn from a variety of contexts, and some of the evidence that will be examined was recorded incidentally to the case itself. These sources not only shed light on the experiences of illegitimacy but also indicate how a discussion of pregnancy outside wedlock was part of an ongoing community dialogue about inclusion and exclusion, sometimes over the course of an individual's life or across generations.

Making Amends with the Church

Church court officials brought both men and women before the court who they suspected to have engaged in sex outside marriage. Extramarital sex was referred to in the records by a variety of terms including 'having the carnal knowledge of', 'incontinence', 'fornication', and 'adultery'. The courts were particularly active when an illegitimate child was born, or when their birth was soon anticipated. Although conception outside wedlock was considered a sin by the ecclesiastical authorities, structures were in place to allow one to make amends. Moreover, the legal framework of the courts helped to shape attitudes towards those who conceived outside wedlock.

Severity of punishment often depended on the gravity of the offence, but the typical sentence for pre- or extra-marital sex was penance. Penance for sexual deviancy usually involved wearing a white sheet in church – often on several occasions – and sometimes in other communal spaces, such as the marketplace, and asking for forgiveness.[18] Such sentences were not always carried out. To avoid humiliation, wealthier parishioners often negotiated the conversion of the penance to a monetary fine.[19] Despite the element of shame involved in the performance of penance, it was not intended simply as a punishment, nor was it designed to exclude the transgressor from the spiritual community. It was an opportunity for repentance.[20] In 1576, Elizabeth Hawkins and Walter Bennett of Northleach, Gloucestershire, were discovered to have had a child out of wedlock. Elizabeth was ordered to perform penance in the parish church the very next Sunday wearing a sheet, and then again in Northleach market the following Wednesday. There is no record of Walter's punishment, although this may be due to incomplete records rather than varying gendered patterns of penance for this offence.[21] Hawkins presumably did not comply since both she and Bennett were subsequently recorded in the calendar of the Gloucester court as having been excommunicated.[22]

For women who conceived outside wedlock, performing penance was part of the process of being accepted and re-welcomed into the spiritual community. In Somerset in 1609, Elizabeth Lerry, the wife of a shoemaker, was called to appear as a witness in a defamation case.

146 *Charmian Mansell*

However, in an attempt to dismantle her testimony and undermine the case, the defendant asked other witnesses to testify what they recalled of Lerry's pregnancy before she was married. According to one witness, Lerry had given birth to 'a base child by a young man named John Seelye'. But Lerry's neighbour, Francis Culliford, contended that this should not be to her discredit, as she had *'satisfied the lawe for this crime* 8 or 9 yeeres since'.[23] Culliford's statement suggests that Lerry had been subject to punishment by the church court and it was therefore understood that she had atoned for her sin. Furthermore, she had subsequently married a shoemaker, who must have been fully aware of her past. Accordingly, despite having had a child out of wedlock, Elizabeth Lerry was seemingly able to achieve the respectability of a married woman, and gain access to the social capital that marriage brought with it.

Similarly, in 1611, the defendant in a Gloucestershire defamation case attempted to discredit the plaintiff, Martha Higgens, by asking witnesses what they knew of Martha's bridal pregnancy. Margaret Sadler, a married woman, acknowledged Higgens's offence, but added that 'she was punished in this court for the same'. Another witness, a butcher named Richard Meddall, agreed that Higgens had previously made amends as 'she was questioned for the same'. These cases show that sex outside marriage was clearly not forgotten by the community. Yet, they also suggest that lay people believed that the punishments meted out by the church courts were not intended to further stoke rumours and gossip, but to bring the matter to a close. Once penance had been performed, the offence was no longer regarded as a blot or stain on one's character or reputation.[24] The legal framework of the courts thus helped to shape attitudes towards those who conceived outside wedlock. Generally speaking, parishioners appear to have been able to move beyond the moral transgressions of their neighbours. This suggests that if a woman did experience exclusion from the community at the time of the offence, it was not forever. Genuine remorse, alongside a public display of contrition, were key mechanisms that allowed them to be welcomed back into the fold.

There were, of course, other consequences of illicit sexual liaisons resulting in the birth of illegitimate children. Submitting to correction might cleanse men and women of their sins, but for the single mother there were always further challenges of meeting the economic and care needs of a new-born child while also combatting the difficulties that resulted from a diminished reputation. Marriage clearly presented a route by which single mothers and their illegitimate children might escape social and economic stigmatisation. Alan Macfarlane notes that bastardy was treated with more leniency when the marriage expectations of their parents and others were fulfilled.[25] Family members were often involved in negotiating marriages for their pregnant daughters. In 1567,

Parochial Inclusion and Pregnancy 147

for example, Alice Paw of Dowland, Devon, found support from her brother and brother-in-law in her matrimonial suit against John Brennelcombe. They helped bear the financial costs of the suit, and also testified on her behalf that Brennelcombe had promised marriage and was responsible for her pregnancy.[26]

However, as Diana O'Hara found in her investigation of matrimonial suits, it was not just family who were involved in brokering marriages for unmarried women. A surrogate family of what she terms 'fictive kin' including masters, mistresses, bedfellows, fellow servants, and neighbours were also instrumental in marriage formation.[27] It is perhaps unsurprising that masters responsible for the pregnancies of their female servants were particularly keen to see these women married. In 1627, Peter Lane of Englishcombe, Somerset, left the service of Morgan Creese after three years. During this period, Creese persistently attempted to coerce Lane to marry Joanne Pickering, another servant employed in the household. Pickering identified her employer, Creese, as the father of her child. Lane described to the court the promises Creese had made upon his discovery of the pregnancy: he was offered twenty pounds to marry Pickering and was invited to live in a property Creese owned in the nearby parish of Berkley.[28] In other cases, unsuspecting suitors became fathers to other men's children. In 1609, Joanne Webb of Oldbury, Gloucestershire, confessed that while working as a servant in Thomas Pearce's house, he had forced himself upon her and she had become pregnant. A hasty marriage was then arranged between Webb and the unwitting Benjamin Walker of Hewelsfield, which enabled the child's true paternity to be concealed and relocated Webb to the opposite bank of the River Severn. The truth was only revealed upon the death of the child. According to the testimony of Richard Tucker, a churchwarden of Oldbury, Webb confessed to her husband that:

> Mr Thomas Pearce had the carnall knowledge of her bodye divers tymes when she dwelt with him: once on certen strawe when she was heating of a kettle on the fyer and att dyvers other tymes when she was goeinge to make upp the beds in his house.

While Webb's deception was outlined to the court, an underlying sense of empathy can be detected in the witnesses' words. Gentleman Henry Townsend deposed that Webb's confession to her husband was made 'uppon her knees with greate repentance'. By contrast, witnesses noted that Pearce, a married man with five or six children, offered Walker 40 shillings 'to conceale his sayde wieves speeches and speake noe more of it'. Walker clearly refused his offer, and it was Pearce, not Webb, who faced punishment in the church court for adultery.[29] Perhaps the court sympathised with Joanne Webb because the child had died, and thus deemed her repentance in words sufficient for her reconciliation with the

148 *Charmian Mansell*

community, even if reconciliation with her husband was surely to be a lengthier process.

Yet, finding a match for a pregnant woman was not only the concern of men anxious to avoid the shame and economic culpability of fathering an illegitimate child. Other members of the community also sought partnerships for unmarried pregnant women. For example, the master and mistress of Jane Powell of Charlton Kings, Gloucestershire, sought to 'make maryadge' in 1590 between Powell and their male servant, Nicholas Lewes, who was allegedly the father of her child.[30] Although the match was ultimately not possible, this case demonstrates the couple's role in community-building and their attempt to establish a new household within the parish. Macfarlane famously claimed that there was little sense of community to be found in early modern English villages.[31] However, such evidence from church court depositions demonstrates the contrary. The involvement of the parish in negotiations of marriage on behalf of single expectant women exposes a different narrative of belonging and inclusion. It indicates that many in the parish desired these women, who faced the prospect of economic vulnerability and social stigmatisation, to remain part of their communities. *Inclusion* rather than *exclusion* was often the intention.

Likewise, neighbours could be instrumental in the process of securing marriages for unmarried pregnant women. In many matrimonial disputes, men and women were called upon by pregnant single women and unmarried mothers to confirm that they were, or had been, pregnant brides-to-be. The testimonies of these neighbours hinged on proving that the child's father refused to uphold a legally binding betrothal, and that both marriage and baby were accordingly legitimate in the eyes of God and the law. In 1602, widow Catherine Jones of Millbrook, Hampshire, testified in a marriage suit on behalf of her servant, Marie Dore, that she was betrothed to Richard Parrett, who was a frequent visitor to the house in courtship. Jones deposed that the child Dore carried was not illegitimate, but the product of their legally binding betrothal. Her testimony was accompanied by depositions from two neighbours: a husbandman named Howell Jones, and a married woman named Maria Sliden. Although the latter witness was Marie Dore's cousin, neither Dore nor Jones had any connection of kinship to her.[32] Likewise, in 1613, husbandman Tanner of Swainswick, Somerset, deposed that he had witnessed the betrothal of Elizabeth Hopkins and John Webb. Hopkins was pregnant, and Tanner noted that 'untill this matter fell out [occurred] the said Hopkins was accompted for an honest and grave young woman'. Yeoman Thomas Smith similarly agreed that she 'was held for a verye civill & honest young woman'.[33] In some instances, pregnant unmarried women thus received their neighbour's support. Rather than being callously turned away, such cases show that they were instead steered towards the respectable path of womanhood.

Parochial Inclusion and Pregnancy   149

Their neighbours brokered marriages to secure more favourable futures for them within their communities as respectable married women. This inclusion was not automatic. Indeed, like exclusion, it was clearly the product of individual circumstances, and thus negotiated between individual women and their wider community.

Support and Charity

Where a match was not possible – especially in cases where the social and economic distance between a pregnant unmarried woman and the father of her child was too great – the neighbourhood offered other forms of assistance. Within church court depositions, single pregnant women who had been ejected from their place of residence can be found sojourning in the homes, barns, and outbuildings of others. Marjorie McIntosh and Richard Helmholz both identified a significant (and increasing) number of individuals charged with unlawfully hosting (or 'harbouring') such women in their homes in the sixteenth century.[34] This prompts further investigation into what this tells us about early modern communities. In 1602, yeoman Thomas Quarman of Ditcheat in Somerset, 'for charityes sake', placed his former servant Mary Loxton in his barn to give birth, 'being greate with a bastard', to offer her some small comfort. In this case, Quarman did not expect his servant to remain in the parish, as he defined the period of her stay as 'untill shee should bee delivered of her childe' and had regained 'her strength to go abroade againe'.[35] In a similar vein, Gowing notes that in infanticide cases, those closest to the pregnant woman, such as other members of the household in which she lived, were often complicit, helping to conceal her pregnancy and in some cases, the dead child. 'Those outside the household', she suggests, 'were readier to confront, challenge and search those they suspected of illegitimate pregnancy'.[36]

Evidence suggests that other members of the community were also willing to offer help to single pregnant women. This is perhaps not wholly surprising for, as Lena Cowen Orlin, Gowing, and others have shown, the early modern household was porous and open to those beyond the immediate family.[37] Sound travelled between thin partition walls. Chinks and holes in doors and windows exposed household affairs to the neighbourhood. Fundamentally, neighbours, and sometimes strangers, moved frequently in and out of one another's domestic spaces on errands and social visits. The household could therefore be an inclusive space in which a sense of community was deeply rooted. While some single pregnant women were expelled from the homes of their employers, other doors could be open to them. It is noteworthy that women played an important role in facilitating this culture of inclusion and exclusion. Indeed, as Gowing notes, women often found

150 *Charmian Mansell*

themselves in a bind where they had to negotiate between a series of contradictory expectations. On the one hand, by offering hospitality to their neighbours, they were fulfilling a key duty of womanhood. On the other, they were forced to decide whether harbouring unmarried pregnant women in their homes was beyond the pale given that it was against ecclesiastical law.[38]

Men, too, struggled with these conflicting concerns. In 1590, Edmund Everesse of Charlton Kings, Gloucestershire, was examined by the church court for harbouring an unmarried pregnant woman in his home and failing to turn her in to the ecclesiastical authorities for punishment. Everesse does not appear to have been related to this woman and outlined no motivation for offering her shelter other than for charity's sake.[39] In 1606, William Shepherd of Pitcombe, Somerset, was similarly charged for harbouring a single pregnant woman named Dorothy Sims in his house. Witnesses described his behaviour as the 'offencive and scandalous keeping and harbouring of the said woeman'. It was noted that upon the complaint of parishioners to the Justice of the Peace, the woman was forcibly removed from the parish. However, Shepherd's actions suggest he held a different view on the principles of inclusion and exclusion than that of the community. The testimony of husbandman John Berryman offers an insight into Shepherd's motivations: he deposed that 'within these dozen yeeres last past, a sister of the said Sheppards came to his house at Pitcomb and there was delivered of a childe, being a bastard by report'.[40] This experience had surely affected Shepherd's perception of illegitimacy and encouraged him to challenge the politics of parochial exclusion. These cases show that a spectrum of experiences and perceptions of illegitimate pregnancy and childbirth existed in early modern England. Lack of access to the 'civilising rituals of birth in private' forced some unmarried pregnant women to give birth in fields and other open spaces.[41] However, other women found support, assistance, and shelter from their neighbours and other individuals in the parishes in which they lived.

In deciding how to treat these women, early modern society had to weigh the implications of ecclesiastical law against their own consciences. As the evidence indicates, many individuals did not withhold compassion for pregnant single women. Despite the economic burden that a fatherless child and its mother could place on the parish, ideas of morality and charity could prevent the unscrupulous shunting of the single migrant woman to her parish of settlement to receive relief for her illegitimate child. This 'solution' certainly conflicted with traditional parochial charity on behalf of the less fortunate. Early modern homilies reinforced the idea that the more fortunate had a social and religious duty towards the needy: one homily, first published in 1547 and reissued throughout the sixteenth and seventeenth centuries, stressed the importance of showing mercy and pity 'upon the poor

Parochial Inclusion and Pregnancy 151

which be afflicted with any kind of misery'.[42] Felicity Heal notes that early modern definitions of hospitality proposed that the neighbour and stranger, whether rich or poor, should have equal access to a host's generosity.[43] Still, as Steve Hindle notes, although charity was undoubtedly regarded as a Christian obligation, the real question was on whom it should be bestowed.[44] Within scholarship on charity and alms-giving, the deservedness of the single pregnant woman, whose economic fortune was immediately diminished upon the birth of her child, has received less attention.

A case heard in the church court of Bath and Wells in 1574 sums up the complexity of this issue. In her testimony, Alice Davies, the unmarried servant of Thomas Walker, deposed that she was entreated on a number of occasions to have sex with her master. She had lived in the parish of Combe Martin for nearly two years, originating from Axminster, around eighty-five kilometres away. Finding she was pregnant, Alice was sent back to Axminster, but on arrival reported to the constable there that Thomas Walker was the father of her child. She was consequently returned to Combe Martin with the expectation that Walker should pay towards the child's maintenance. However, he denied the allegation and was, as she deposed, 'displeased with her'. This was clearly a fraught situation for the parishioners of Combe Martin. William Fry, a husbandman of the parish, explained his concerns:

> He hopeth that the parishe shall be discharged of fynding Alice davie her child. And if Thomas Walker clare [clear] hym self then he thinketh the parishe shalbe charged with the fyndinge the same child.

Returning Davies once again to Axminster appears to have no longer been a possibility. Despite Walker's denial, Davies had nonetheless named the father as an inhabitant there. There was thus a clear economic motive for the parishioners there to ensure that the paternity of the child was pressed upon Walker. Yet the actions and behaviours of the parishioners were not purely driven by money. Indeed, in her deposition, Davies acknowledged the kindness of the people of Combe Martin, recollecting that 'while she did lie in child bedd the parisshners of Combe did fynde and of charitie relieve her ... and her child'. Gowing notes the difficulties that single pregnant women could face in planning for childbirth, and here we see the community coming to Davies's aid.[45] Twelve months after giving birth, she no longer worked in Walker's service but remained in the parish and got 'her lyvinge by spyyning and carding'. The inhabitants of Combe Martin continued to dole out maintenance payments for her child, but Davies also worked to support herself and her baby. This 1574 case illustrates the extent to which a local community might take the word of an unmarried pregnant woman over that of her master. But it also reveals their tolerance and

152 *Charmian Mansell*

inclusion of this young woman within the community during and following her pregnancy. Indeed, she described their actions as charitable and was ultimately not excluded from the parish, nor from its economic activities.[46]

Charity towards single pregnant women also took other forms. In 1568, Isott Riches of Rockbeare, Devon, was sent fifteen kilometres away to Kilmington to give birth to her illegitimate child. In this case, the reputed father was a gentleman named Frances Yard, who denied the allegation. The couple were not likely to marry due to the difference in social status and, as Yard denied paternity, Riches would receive no contribution towards the child's maintenance. Unable to work during the final stages of her pregnancy, and facing limited prospects once the child was born, Riches's position was undoubtedly precarious. Her former mistress, Katherine Brooke, deposed that 'she craved of her brother [who had also formerly been Riche's master] xii d [12d] for charitie sake that she mought [might] send her. And dyd send it to her'.[47] Society was thus aware of the economic strain that a child placed on a single woman. It is noteworthy that Riches was not close to her former mistress; in fact, she claimed Katherine had beaten her and treated her poorly in the past. Twelve pence was not a large sum of money to receive – in 1609, Eleanor Boult of Trull in Somerset demanded the same sum *per week* from Robert Somers, the alleged father of her illegitimate child – and Brooke's gift was likely to have been a one-off payment. However, it was a gesture of support and an indication of Brooke's sympathy for her former servant's predicament.[48] It shows that a mistress might maintain a connection with her pregnant servant, even upon her exclusion from the parish. This relationship might also be negotiated over great distances.

The charity that early modern society showed to single pregnant women is not only found in the shelter they provided or the money they doled out. It can also be glimpsed in their participation in legal challenges. Across a range of cases, they often stepped in as witnesses to testify in support of unmarried mothers and single pregnant women. The testimonies found in the church courts of men and women who upheld the claims and reputations of unmarried mothers demonstrates support that existed within communities. While the economic security of the parish, as outlined above, accounts in some part for the willingness of parishioners to set out their knowledge of the extra-marital affair, their testimonies also indicate a sense of compassion and moral responsibility for single mothers. Of the 319 deposition-producing cases of adultery and incontinence promoted between 1555 and 1634 by the church court of the diocese of Bath and Wells alone, only 42 defendants were women. A total of 277 male offenders were produced by the courts and their neighbours freely testified against them. In 1618, for example, two married women of Somerset deposed against Gilbert Roe. Agnes Noel

Parochial Inclusion and Pregnancy 153

told the court that Christian Cook had told her three years before that he was:

> a naughtye man: for he allured me up into the bed, and did playe with me. And sayeth that this deponent having at that tyme a daughter in lawe that wrought [worked] at his the saide Gilberts house she willed this deponent to have her awaye.

According to the testimony, Cook found herself pregnant and was later sent away to her aunt's house. Not only does this case demonstrate Noel's commitment to seeking recompense for Roe's actions, it also highlights the close relationship that existed between the two women. Cook confided in this female acquaintance and sought to protect the morality of her daughter-in-law.[49] An oral culture of confiding, sharing stories, and issuing warnings about sexually depraved men existed amongst women. It thus seems that in many early modern parishes, single women who fell prey to men's advances were listened to, and that their cautionary advice was heeded by other women within the community.

Even when several years had passed, former neighbours recalled and recounted the difficult experiences that unmarried mothers in their communities had faced. In a 1607 case against Jane Drew of Newent in Gloucestershire, who was suspected to run a bawdy house, Anna Clark, a thirty-year-old single woman deposed that her neighbour Jane Hooper:

> had a base childe begotten of her bodye aboute some twoe yeares agoe & either a litle before or somewhat after Midsomer last past she this examinate beinge with the saide Jane hooper in her house att Newent ... she the said Jane hooper did theare weepe & lament to this examinate her heard [hard] fortune in haveinge the said childe.

Clark recalled that Hooper's misery was at the hands of Jane Drew, her neighbour. Drew had allegedly asked Hooper to deliver some shirts to her house. According to Clark's testimony, this was a trap. When Jane Hooper arrived at the house, she was locked in a room with a stranger lodging there named Thomas Dun and there 'receaved her trouble'. Clark's testimony was one of three that recounted the same series of events. Elizabeth Nurberry, the wife of a broad weaver, deposed that Jane Hooper had 'wept & lamented' over the deception and the resulting pregnancy. At the time of her deposition, Nurberry was hosting Hooper in her house, another illustration of how early modern people were willing to accept women who had children out of wedlock into their homes.[50] Furthermore, the willingness of members of the community to become embroiled in legal disputes as witnesses on the behalf of single mothers demonstrates that retribution could be sought collectively.

154 *Charmian Mansell*

Although vulnerable, single pregnant women could, in many instances, expect to find continued support from their neighbours and friends.

Acceptance and Inclusion

Across the corpus of church court depositions, numerous examples of single mothers like Jane Hooper who were not expelled from the parish are to be found. Many were recorded as witnesses in disputes brought to court by others. These women were trusted, tasked with the responsibility of providing evidence on behalf of their neighbours and friends. They were part of the complex social fabric of the communities in which they continued to live. Often selected by their neighbours to give evidence, rather than being requested by law to testify, these women were well-placed to do so as they were not only familiar with the quotidian rhythms, routines, and experiences of their fellow parishioners, but were also part of the same community. The presence in court of single mothers as witnesses, who offered support to their (typically female) neighbours, situates them within the important female support networks described by Capp in his study of early modern gossip.[51] In 1616, witnesses in a defamation case told the Bath and Wells court that Marie Plumbley had given birth to 'two base children, the last [one] three years ago'. Plumbley's own deposition on the behalf of the plaintiff records that she was still living as an unmarried woman in the parish of Wedmore (even though this was not her place of birth) and had done so for the past six years. The father of Plumbley's illegitimate child may have agreed to pay towards its maintenance, thereby releasing the parish from any sense of obligation to pay parish relief to the mother and children. Whatever the story of settlement and relief is here, the depositions nonetheless reveal that Plumbley's immorality was forgiven, albeit not forgotten, as she was called upon by her neighbour to testify in court on her behalf.[52]

It is possible that in some cases few alternative witnesses were available. Only those who were present when defamatory words were spoken or at the betrothal of a couple, for example, could act as legitimate witnesses. In 1609, Katherine Knight of Ditcheat, Somerset, produced just two witnesses to testify in support of her charge of defamation against Alice Cooper: a young girl named Joanna Gould, and a thirty-year-old single woman named Elizabeth Sherwood. If Katherine's claim of defamation is assumed to be true, Joanna and Elizabeth may have been the only two individuals present at the time the offending words were spoken. Gould was Knight's sister, and her close affinity made her a less reliable or plausible witness. Sherwood was not related but had had a child out of wedlock. In the interrogatory questioning designed by Alice Cooper's proctor to discredit the witnesses, Sherwood was asked about this pregnancy. She deposed that she 'had a base child by one

Parochial Inclusion and Pregnancy 155

whoe should have byn her husband', thereby admitting to the offence but providing an explanation that seemingly conformed to social expectations. Gould, her fellow witness, also asserted that it was true that 'about 8 yeres sithence [since] Elizabeth Sherwood had a base childe', but added that she 'hath ever sithence byn of good name and fame'.[53] While the politics of inclusion continued to be contested, time could nonetheless allow those who had been sexually deviant to atone and earn a place within the community of court witnesses.

As mentioned earlier, sexual misdemeanours were clearly not forgotten by those furthering a cause in the ecclesiastical court. In many cases, countersuits and interrogatory questions, designed by the opposing party to undermine the testimonies of the plaintiff's witnesses, targeted those who had parented children out of wedlock. This was not gender specific. In 1564, for example, witness John Ryde of Chudleigh, Devon, deposed that Nicholas Hamlyn, another witness 'had a power [poor] mans wyffe, one Rolstons wyff, with hem [him] to spynyng and begote her with child and the basterd is at home with hem'.[54] It seems illogical that plaintiffs continued to draw their witnesses from a pool of men and women with miscreant pasts. Relatively few church court cases came to a verdict because most suits were settled out of court. It is thus accordingly difficult to determine whether tales of the ill repute of a witness had any real consequence on court proceedings. Importantly, neighbours frequently testified not only to an unmarried mother's good character but also to her credit and inclusion within the economic practices of the community. In a 1625 defamation dispute, married witness Elizabeth Batchley of Bathampton, Somerset, responded to allegations that Edith Harrold was not a credible fellow witness as she had given birth before she was married. Batchley recalled that forty-year-old Edith had brought the child into the parish of Bathampton many years before. She was born in Wingfield in Wiltshire and had lived there for roughly thirty years of her life, before moving to Bathampton. Around five years before her own examination in this case, Harrold had married a husbandman named Roger. Elizabeth deposed that ever since she had moved to the parish, 'she hath lived very honestly by her honest labor in spynninge and carding and is well liked of all the parishioners of Bathampton'. Her pregnancy as an unmarried woman was considered unimportant in this case because she had married and was commended for her 'honest labour'.[55] Both these attributes, her marriage and labour, were clear indications of her respectability in the parish.

The example of Elizabeth Batchley shows that despite the challenges they may have faced when unmarried and pregnant, women – who had the good fortune to find a route to respectability – continued about their lives and engaged in social and economic activities befitting their status and gender. Macfarlane offers similar evidence that the plight of

156 *Charmian Mansell*

the unmarried mother was generally overlooked in terms of working relations as long as the child was maintained.[56] In some cases, those who remained unmarried took up service. For example, Elizabeth Sherwood (discussed in the 1609 Dicheat defamation case above) had an illegitimate child and remained single. However, she was not barred from finding work in the parish and was employed as a domestic servant in the house of William Addams.[57] While single women surely navigated and negotiated community attitudes towards their motherhood outside wedlock, it is clear that exclusion was not a default reaction. These women continued to be included within community practices of life and work.

Conclusion

The story of Joanne Hull, outlined at the beginning of this chapter, has no happy ending but nevertheless ends on a hopeful note. Following her expulsion to Taunton, she returned to Exeter one year later. Her child was dead, but she demanded thirty shillings from her former master as reimbursement for her costs as she now wished to marry and required a dowry. On her journey into Exeter, she stopped and told those who had once been her neighbours of her plight. She lamented:

> I have lackt a yere and more to save one mans honesty … and he did begett me with child and sent me awaye and I canne staye away no longer for I have nether hose nor shoes and I will complayn of him to the Justices.

Joanne received the support of these former neighbours, who appeared as witnesses before the court to testify against Roger Chardon. The economic motivations behind the removal of an unmarried pregnant woman from the parish are only part of the story of how inclusion in and exclusion from the early modern community was negotiated.

The depositions of the church courts function as a repository of evidence of friendships, connections, and associations built by women who had children out of wedlock. Their testimonies are full of details of the economic and social networks to which they continued to belong. Historians have tended to see pregnant, unmarried women as passive and vulnerable. Indeed, they were frequently described as being 'carried away' in the records, suggesting that their ties with the parish and its inhabitants were cut.[58] Certainly, some of these women found themselves in positions of vulnerability or isolation. Yet, while actions were rarely forgotten in the early modern parish, and could be unearthed years later in the church courts, this chapter has shown that the neighbours of these women were seldom indiscriminately hostile towards those with a miscreant past and resulting illegitimate children. In exploring this evidence, it has been shown here that when historians consider how the boundaries were drawn around early modern communities and parishes, it is important to think beyond purely economic factors. While the system of poor relief ring-fenced parish resources for settled inhabitants, even this system operated with some flexibility. Collectively and individually, parishioners acted charitably. Many supported single women during pregnancy and continued to do so years later. Depositions of the church courts serve as a reminder that single women who found themselves pregnant were integral members of the communities in which they lived and, in many cases, remained as such as they navigated their lives as mothers.

Notes

1 Devon Heritage Centre (hereafter DHC), Chanter 862, Office v Richard Chardon (1587).
2 Gloucestershire Archives (hereafter GA), GDR/148, Dorothy Greene v Richard Greene (1625).
3 GA, GDR/25, Elizabeth Godwin v William Jackson (1572).
4 Bernard Capp, *When Gossips Meet: Women, Family, and Neighbourhood in Early Modern England* (Oxford: Oxford University Press, 2003), 147–8.
5 Laura Gowing, *Common Bodies: Women, Sex, and Reproduction in Seventeenth-Century England* (New Haven and London: Yale University Press, 2003), 118.
6 'The Relief of the Poor (39 Eliz I c.3) (1598)' and 'For the Punishment of Rogues, Vagabonds and Sturdy Beggars' (39 Eliz I c.4) (1598) summarised in Paul Slack, *The English Poor Law, 1531–1782* (Basingstoke: Macmillan, 1990), 52–3.
7 This idea was later consolidated in the 1662 Act of Settlement. See Steve Hindle, *On the Parish?: The Micro-Politics of Poor Relief in Rural England c.1550–1750* (Oxford: Oxford University Press, 2004), 301–2.
8 Slack, *The English Poor Law*, 28.
9 Keith Wrightson, 'The Politics of the Parish in Early Modern England', in Paul Griffiths, Adam Fox, and Steve Hindle (eds), *The Experience of Authority in Early Modern England* (Basingstoke: Palgrave Macmillan, 1996), 21.
10 K.D.M. Snell, *Parish and Belonging: Community, Identity and Welfare in England and Wales, 1700–1950* (Cambridge: Cambridge University Press, 2006), 39, 81–161.
11 This approach has yielded important results in studying criminal communities, news exchange, and religious groups. Examples include Paul Griffiths, 'Overlapping Circles: Imagining Criminal Communities in London, 1545–1645', in Alexandra Shepard and Phil Withington (eds), *Communities in Early Modern England: Networks, Place, Rhetoric, Politics, Culture and Society in Early Modern Britain* (Manchester: Manchester University Press, 2000), 115–33; Ruth Ahnert, 'Maps Versus Networks', in Noah Moxham and Joad Raymond (eds), *News Networks in Early Modern Europe* (Leiden: Brill, 2016), 130–57; Liesbeth Corens, *Confessional Mobility and English Catholics in Counter-Reformation Europe* (Oxford: Oxford University Press, 2018).

158 *Charmian Mansell*

12 Alexandra Shepard has demonstrated that this too could be true for men (the words 'rogue' and 'knave' could convey meanings of sexual deviance) and that women's honour could equally be bound up in other types of deviance, such as inability to manage finances. However, Laura Gowing's conclusion that 'sexual honour was overwhelmingly a female concern' continues to ring true in the evidence. See Alexandra Shepard, *Meanings of Manhood in Early Modern England* (Oxford: Oxford University Press, 2003), chapters 6–7; Laura Gowing, *Domestic Dangers: Women, Words and Sex in Early Modern London* (Oxford: Oxford University Press, 1996), 109.

13 Notable exceptions to this include scholarship on the crime of harbouring unmarried pregnant women and infanticide. See, for example, Marjorie K. McIntosh, *Controlling Misbehavior in England, 1370–1600* (Cambridge: Cambridge University Press, 1998), 83–4; R.H. Helmholz, 'Harboring Sexual Offenders: Ecclesiastical Courts and Controlling Misbehavior', *Journal of British Studies*, 37 (1998), 258–68; Laura Gowing, 'Secret Births and Infanticide in Seventeenth-Century England', *Past Present*, 156 (1997), 87–115. However, these works focus on specific crimes related to illegitimate pregnancy rather than considering the experiences of single pregnant women as a whole. Dave Postles has examined some of the dynamics of social and parochial exclusion; however, his focus is largely upon the migration or forced ejection of unmarried mothers from the parish. See Dave Postles, 'Surviving Lone Motherhood Early Modern England', *The Seventeenth Century*, 21 (2006), 160–83.

14 The study of illegitimacy has often relied on a combination of baptism records and settlement examinations. See, for example, Keith Wrightson and David Levine, *Poverty and Piety in an English Village: Terling, 1525–1700* (Oxford: Oxford University Press, 1995), 126–33, Peter Laslett, 'The Bastardy Prone Sub-Society', in Peter Laslett, Karla Oosterveen, and Ricard Michael Smith (eds), *Bastardy and its Comparative History: Studies in the History of Illegitimacy and Nonconformism in Britain, France, Germany, Sweden, North Amerca, Jamaica, and Japan* (Boston, MA: Harvard University Press, 1980), 217–46. On harbouring unmarried pregnant women, see McIntosh, *Controlling Misbehavior*, 83–4; Helmholz, 'Harboring Sexual Offenders', 258–68.

15 Gowing, 'Secret Births', 92.

16 For a fuller discussion of the construction of narratives by early modern witnesses in court, see Natalie Zemon Davis, *Fiction in the Archives: Pardon Tales and their Tellers in Sixteenth-Century France* (Cambridge: Cambridge University Press, 1987).

17 Kate Gibson, 'The Language of Exclusion: "Bastard" in Early Modern England', 47, 50, 52.

18 Martin Ingram, *Carnal Knowledge: Regulating Sex in England, 1470–1600* (Cambridge: Cambridge University Press, 2017), 108–15.

19 F.D. Price, 'The Administration of the Diocese of Gloucester, 1547–1579', unpublished PhD thesis (University of Oxford, 1939); F.S. Hockaday, 'The Consistory Court of the Diocese of Gloucester', *Transactions of the Bristol and Gloucestershire Archaeological Society*, 46 (1924), 219.

20 Suzannah Lipscomb's work on the consistories of early modern Nîmes indicates that some unmarried mothers or women who had engaged in sex

Parochial Inclusion and Pregnancy 159

outside marriage were active in seeking forgiveness, approaching the courts themselves to purge themselves of sin. See Suzannah Lipscomb, *The Voices of Nîmes: Women, Sex, and Marriage in Reformation Languedoc* (Oxford: Oxford University Press, 2019), 219.

21 Martin Ingram, for example, also notes evidence of male culprits performing penance. See Martin Ingram, *Church Courts, Sex and Marriage in England, 1570–1640* (Cambridge, 1988), 256–7.

22 GA, GDR/40 (1576).

23 Somerset Heritage Centre (hereafter SHC), DDCd41, Joanne Culliford v John Stokes (1609). Italics my own.

24 GA, GDR/122, Martha Higgens v Joan Chettle (1615).

25 Alan Macfarlane, 'Illegitimacy and Illegitimates in English History', in Laslett, Oosterveen, and Smith (eds), *Bastardy and its Comparative History*, 75.

26 DHC, Chanter 856, Alice Pawe v John Brennelcombe (1567).

27 Diana O'Hara, *Courtship and Constraint: Rethinking the Making of Marriage in Tudor England* (Manchester: Manchester University Press, 2002), 38, 99–121.

28 SHC, DDCd61, Office v Morgan Creese (1627).

29 GA, GDR/100, GDR/106, George Smith v Thomas Pearce (1609).

30 GA, GDR/65, Office v Edmund Everesse (1590).

31 Alan Macfarlane, *The Origins of English Individualism: the Family, Property and Social Transition* (Oxford: Blackwell, 1978), 5.

32 Hampshire Record Office, 21M65-C3-11, Mary Dore v Richard Parrett (1602).

33 SHC, DDCd45, Elizabeth Hopkins v John Webb (1613).

34 McIntosh, *Controlling Misbehavior*, 83–4; Helmholz, 'Harboring Sexual Offenders', 262.

35 SHC, DDCd34, Office v Thomas Hellier (1602).

36 Gowing, *Common Bodies*, 140.

37 Lena Cowen Orlin, *Locating Privacy in Tudor London* (Oxford: Oxford University Press, 2007), 177–83; Gowing, *Domestic Dangers*, 190.

38 Gowing, *Common Bodies*, 140, 151–7.

39 GA, GDR/65, Office v Edmund Everesse (1590).

40 SHC, DDCd30, Office v William Shepherd (1606).

41 Gowing, *Common Bodies*, 151.

42 'Homily of Alms Deeds, and Mercifulness Towards the Poor and Needy', in Ronald B. Bond (ed.), *Certain Sermons Or Homilies (1547): And, a Homily Against Disobedience and Wilful Rebellion (1570): A Critical Edition* (Toronto: University of Toronto Press, 1987), 1–25.

43 Felicity Heal, *Hospitality in Early Modern England* (Oxford: Oxford University Press, 1990), 3–4.

44 Hindle, *On the Parish?*, 96.

45 Gowing, *Common Bodies*, 156.

46 SHC, DDCd15, John Cox v Thomas Walker (1574).

47 DHC, Chanter 858, John Roo v Frances Yard (1568).

48 SHC, DDCd41, Robert Somers v Eleanor Boult (1609).

49 SHC, DDCd49, Office v Gilbert Roe (1618).

50 GA, GDR/100, Ann Francombe v Jane Drewe (1607).

51 Capp, *When Gossips Meet*, 55–68.

52 SHC, DDCd51, Jane Oaklie v Elizabeth Gorway (1616).

53 SHC, GGCd41, Katherine Knight v Alice Cooper (1609).

160   *Charmian Mansell*

54 DHC, Chanter 855a, Office v Richard Rawe (1564).
55 SHC, DDCd59, Sara Chamberie v Joanna Cottell (1625).
56 Macfarlane, 'Illegitimacy and Illegitimates in English History', 75–6.
57 SHC, GGCd41, Katherine Knight v Alice Cooper (1609).
58 For example, in 1567 Isott Riches of Rockbeare in Devon was 'carried' to and left 'at one Clapham's howse' in Kilmington in the same county, when her pregnancy was discovered. DHC, Chanter 858, John Roo v Frances Yarde (1568).

7 Hunting, Sociability, and the Politics of Inclusion and Exclusion in Early Seventeenth-Century England

Tom Rose

In his 1575 hunting manual, *The Noble Arte of Venerie or Hunting*, George Gascoigne wrote that hunting was 'a sport for Noble peeres, a sport for gentle bloods'.[1] Similarly, Nicholas Cox began his book on field sports by telling the reader that 'Hunting is a Game and Recreation commendable not onely for Kings, Princes, and the Nobility, but likewise for private Gentlemen'.[2] Notably excluded from these statements were men below gentry status and women. Hunting was a performance of elite manhood and part of what Anthony Fletcher has called 'the working of patriarchy' in early modern England.[3] The contemporary legal framework was complicit in placing the right to hunt in the hands of a few landed male elites. In a Star Chamber case during the reign of James I, Sir Francis Bacon said that hunting helped 'to keep a difference between the gentry and the common sort'.[4] The 1604 Game Law also made hunting the exclusive right of the greater gentry and nobility, requiring those below the rank of esquire to meet strict wealth qualifications.[5] At a time when traditional hierarchies were increasingly blurred, the values of landed income stated in the Game Laws have been argued by Alexandra Shepard to have had 'connotations of gentility' due to the way they were used to demarcate people of higher gentry status from those of the lower gentry and so-called 'middling sort'.[6]

Legal policies and practices of exclusion relating to land ownership and hunting have captured the attention of historians of early modern England. There has been a particular focus on poaching as an illegal form of hunting that produced various forms of social and political conflict. Gender historians have also noted the sport's incredible androcentrism.[7] What has received less attention, however, is the social politics of legitimate hunting. In their seminal study of the gentry in early modern England, Felicity Heal and Clive Holmes simply maintain that 'the hunting party ... was a strongly established feature of elite sociability', and that 'the obligations of status, sociability and reciprocity that [hunting] entailed, made it exceedingly difficult for a rural gentleman to eschew hunting'.[8] This chapter takes a more critical look at the politics of social participation in early seventeenth-century English hunting culture.

162   Tom Rose

It will use the conceptual framework of analysis used by Phil Withington in his research on company and sociability, where he suggests that social participation was political and involved 'inclusions, exclusions, and the construction of boundaries (both visible and invisible to the historical eye)'.[9] In the case of seventeenth-century hunting parties, boundaries existed between those of different social status, with most of the English population unable to hunt (or only able to do so as servants). At the same time, differentiation existed between individual members of the gentry and nobility. It is important to note, however, that the boundaries of participation that centred upon gender were also permeable, perhaps more so than traditional scholarship has suggested. Each hunting party consequently had several inclusions and exclusions dependent on the individual context in which these acts of sociability were performed.

Hunting sociability can be traced through various sources, including letters, diaries, household accounts, and court depositions. These sources each have their own emphases (both implicit and explicit) on who was and was not involved in the constant rounds of hunting that characterised elite lifestyles during this period. The first section of this chapter will look at conscious acts of inclusion and exclusion among those who wielded political power, and the fluidity of these boundaries in the ever-changing world of factional disputes and contests over power. It will focus on the strategies of patronage used by the Secretary of State Sir Robert Cecil (later Earl of Salisbury), as well as the exclusion of Sir John Savile from hunting parties in Yorkshire in the 1620s. The second section will explore how religion affected hunting sociability in the years following the English Reformation. The famous case of the Catholic hunting party that arrived at the house of the Puritan Sir Thomas Hoby in August 1600 will be examined as a particularly illustrative example of the often complex intersection of inclusion and exclusion in the religious politics of this period. The third section will analyse the anomalous position of women in hunting culture, where they were not entirely excluded but participated within carefully defined limits. Despite restrictions, it will be suggested that hunting practices provided women with the opportunity to be politically active and engage in the political life and customs of the time.

Hunting and Factional Politics

Susan Whyman has argued that 'sociability was a fundamental element of power in a society based upon personal connections'.[10] Across early seventeenth-century England, those wielding power constantly hunted with one another. In 1610, Norfolk Justices of the Peace went hawking together after they had completed their work administering the Oath of Allegiance among the county's Catholic population and just before they were supposed to meet for the next quarter sessions.[11] Likewise, in 1617,

Hunting and the Politics of Exclusion 163

the Earl of Dorset travelled into Sussex, where he was Lord Lieutenant, and 'all Country Gentlemen met him with their Grayhounds' at his county residence at Buckhurst. He was also reported to have 'hunted in many Gentleman's Parks'.[12] That same year, the Chancellor of the Duchy of Lancaster, along with the Duchy's Attorney-General auditor, and Receiver-General, hunted with 'divers other countree gentlemen' when they travelled up to Lancashire on Duchy business.[13] These convivial occasions were undoubtedly important at a time when face-to-face contact was vital to how politics was conducted.[14]

If personal friendships or animosity were central to the exercise of power, the conscious decision to involve certain figures within the sociability of the hunt meant that the sport could be used to facilitate a pathway from exclusion to inclusion. In February 1601, the second Earl of Essex attempted to remove his rival, the Secretary of State Sir Robert Cecil, from office. The failed rebellion resulted in Essex's execution and the arrest and punishment of many of his co-conspirators, among whom was the Earl of Bedford.[15] In 1607, however, Bedford was begging Cecil, now the Earl of Salisbury, for permission to kill two or three braces of bucks in one of the Secretary of State's parks, 'havinge not manny grownds of my owne.'[16] This request was granted, and the next summer Bedford put in a similar request 'for so great a kindeness … with promisse upon my honor, moderatly to exercise my pleasures, where you shall appoint, not offending the Game willingly in any respect whatsoever'.[17] By this time, Cecil had become an important patron for Bedford and his wife. This grant of sporting access was beneficial to both parties. On the one hand, it allowed Bedford to return into the fold of the Jacobean regime and, in so doing, gain a powerful patron at court. On the other, it allowed Cecil to consolidate his own power and to stymie potential opposition to his dominant position at court.

Of more significance for Cecil, was dealing with the potentially complicated issue of Essex's son. Following his father's execution, the ten-year-old Robert Devereux was stripped of his titles and wealth. However, upon the succession of James VI of Scotland to the English throne in 1603, Devereux's fortunes were reversed, returning him to the status of Earl of Essex. Subsequently, in January 1606, he married the Earl of Suffolk's daughter, Frances Howard.[18] Her family posed a significant challenge to Cecil's dominance at the Jacobean court. In response, that summer, Cecil used hunting to counteract the alliance by encouraging his own son, Viscount Cranborne, to befriend Essex. Cecil sent Cranborne on a hunting progress through Staffordshire, Cheshire, and Lancashire, where he was joined by Essex and Essex's cousin, Henry Rich. In Staffordshire, the three teenage boys stayed at Drayton, the seat of the Earl of Devonshire, Rich's stepfather. His mother, the Countess Dowager of Devonshire, reported in a letter to Salisbury that 'your sonn is a perfett horse man, and can nether be out ridden, nor matched any

164   *Tom Rose*

waye'. She also wrote of the 'extreame melincolye' that had overcome the three boys after Cranborne announced his intentions to leave them and journey further north into Lancashire and stay with Salisbury's cousin, the Countess of Derby.[19] In the end, Essex and Rich journeyed with Cranborne. When they arrived at the Earl of Derby's residence, despite spending all of the previous night travelling, they 'were so far from wearines as [they] spent all the day in hunting'.[20] As seen in this case, seemingly innocuous offers of sport, including between kin, were pragmatic acts of realpolitik to noblemen.

The fluidity of hunting sociability meant that gentlemen who were once included in rounds of hunting could be purposefully marginalised and excluded because of political antagonisms and rivalries. This is evidenced in the case of the changing relationship and hunting activities, over more than three decades, between the fourth Earl of Cumberland and his one-time friend, and later opponent, Sir John Savile. Cumberland and Savile were two of the most powerful figures in early seventeenth-century Yorkshire. Both were elected to the Commons as knights of the shire in 1604, and this close political relationship was reinforced and expressed through regular hunts.[21] In 1607, Savile hosted Cumberland at Howley before travelling to a park owned by Cumberland to hunt together. Similarly, in 1614, upon returning to Yorkshire following the dissolution of the Addled Parliament, they hunted together in parks in Huntingdonshire and Nottinghamshire.[22] Yet a marriage alliance between Cumberland and Sir Thomas Wentworth, who married the Earl's daughter in 1611, would eventually make Cumberland and Savile enemies, and there was consequently a decline in hunting sociability between the two.

Over 1616 and 1617, Wentworth and Savile first fought over the office of *Custos Rotolorum*. Then, in all but one of the parliamentary elections in the 1620s, Wentworth (supported by Cumberland and the other principal gentry landowners of Yorkshire) found himself running against Savile. Historians have paid a great deal of attention to the formal politics of office-holding and parliamentary elections.[23] The political consequences of elite sociability at all other times, by contrast, has largely been ignored. The principal landowners who allied with Wentworth were gentlemen for whom the Earl of Cumberland and his son, Henry Lord Clifford, regularly provided hunting at their residences of Londesborough Hall and Skipton Castle.[24] The extant papers of the politician Sir Arthur Ingram show that these rounds of sporting sociability were regularly reciprocated.[25] In contrast, from 1615 until his death in 1630, Savile was not present at either Londesborough or Skipton. He was even absent when they hosted the Council in the North, of which Savile was vice-president from 1626 until 1628.[26] These acts of marginalisation directed against Savile were therefore simply another

Hunting and the Politics of Exclusion 165

space in which political rivalries were being practised in the everyday lives of noble and gentry elites.

The final act of this socio-political rivalry was a charivari hunt against Savile in October 1628, which sought to challenge and undermine the power and standing that Savile had gained from his recent ennoblement in July 1628. As a Lord, Savile now had parliamentary patronage of the borough of Pontefract and was made steward of all lands there. Yet a few months before his ennoblement, Pontefract had elected Sir John Jackson and Sir John Ramsden to the Commons, two close friends and political allies of Wentworth. In October, they returned from the capital to Pontefract, 'to know what service the Townsemen would commaund them'. While there, they wished to take part in some hare hunting on the grounds of Thomas Vavasour, who claimed a franchise of free warren on land now under the stewardship of Savile. The contested hunting rights made the sport a perfect opportunity for making a mockery of Savile to the wider local community of which he was now the head. Following the first day's hunting, Jackson and Ramsden 'came into the Towne ... and there vaunted at their feasts that they had hunted and would hunt, and that [Savile] should know it, and in a taverne read [Savile's] letter [which called for a restraint in killing hares in the honour of Pontefract] in scorne'. As a steward, Savile was gamekeeper of the grounds and, at the sight of the hunting party the next day, he 'with manie other his freinds and servants, came with their weapons into the feilds, and in ryotous manner assaulted Sir John Jackson'. Savile struck at Jackson with his sword and told him 'that a pott of ale were fitter for him then a sword'. Savile then retreated, perhaps because his company – of around thirty – were outnumbered by the forty to fifty accompanying Jackson and Rafmsden, who with their 'companie continued the hunting tenne dayes'.[27] Savile's ostracism from elite society was thus displayed to the rest of the community.

Hunting and Religion

Religious politics could similarly lead to a series of inclusions and exclusions within hunting sociability. The sport was important to gentlemen and noblemen of all religious backgrounds, whether Puritan, conforming Protestant, or Catholic. For Catholics, the cultural and legal connotations of the hunt meant that participation in the sport was a way of proclaiming their leading status in society, despite their political and legal marginalisation by the Elizabethan and early Stuart state. Furthermore, the sociability of the hunt was a means of navigating the tumultuous religious landscape wrought by the English Reformation. Including and excluding Protestants in their sport was an important coping strategy for Catholic elites. Moreover, a notorious case of Catholic hunting, from August 1600, further reveals how, through an act

166   *Tom Rose*

of intrusion under the guise of friendly sociability, the boundaries of inclusion and exclusion were porous within even a single sociable space.

In the seventeenth century, it was common for Catholic elites to hunt with Protestants, including those responsible for administering recusancy laws or the Oath of Allegiance.[28] This was emblematic of the 'everyday ecumenism', or the processes of 'getting on' and 'getting along' as described by the historian Bill Sheils, which is now seen as widespread in early seventeenth-century communities.[29] For instance, the Earl of Kingston was included in a list of Nottinghamshire recusants presented to the Commons in 1628 but hunted with his Protestant friend, neighbour, and deputy lieutenant of the county, Sir Gervase Clifton.[30] Hunting was the bedrock of their friendship, and Kingston's letters to Clifton are full of details of hunting trips, gifts of venison, and requests to go hunting together.[31] But on other occasions, hunting was a mode of intra-confessional sociability. In August 1607, the Earls of Northampton and Worcester went hunting at Wardour, the seat of Baron Arundell in Wiltshire, 'and so kill[ed] a brace or two of stags'.[32] The sport followed the marriage of Arundell to Worcester's daughter and helped to cement a kinship connection between these aristocratic families who both had Jesuit sympathies that transcended county boundaries. The arrangements for the hunt were overseen by Northampton, who was, at the time, the most powerful Catholic in the realm.[33] In this case, the socialising that occurred was fairly private, allowing potentially dangerous and sensitive conversations to occur in relative safety. Similar examples can be observed with the hunting activities of John Gerard, a Jesuit priest active in England from 1588 until 1606, who regularly went out hunting with Catholic gentlemen, and would use those secluded moments out in the field to persuade them to support the Jesuit cause.[34]

This dichotomy between religious inclusion and exclusion was not always so clear-cut. In August 1600, a Catholic hunting party, having purposefully chased deer a considerable distance from their starting point through Pickering Forest in North Yorkshire, sought hospitality at Hackness, the seat of the Puritan magistrate, Sir Thomas Posthumous Hoby. Over the past ten years, Hoby had orchestrated a campaign of 'practical antipapistry' against North Riding Catholics, harassing and persecuting them at every opportunity.[35] Despite this virulent anti-Catholicism and warnings within godly writings and instruction texts making clear the dangers of engaging in anything more than 'necessary' sociability with Catholics, Hoby adhered to the traditional codes of hospitality and invited the hunting party into his home.[36] William Eure, the leader of the hunting party and the recusant son of the vice-president of the Council in the North, would later describe Hoby's hospitality as 'not answerable to our northern entertainmentes'.[37] In reality, Hoby was superficially included in the hospitable practices surrounding hunting culture whilst simultaneously being excluded from the actual company

Hunting and the Politics of Exclusion 167

of the hunting party. Indeed, immediately after being invited in, the hunting party began playing cards; these were brought by one of the huntsmen, since gambling was not permitted at Hackness. The hunting party's attempts to include Hoby in such sociable practices, which they knew were unacceptable to their godly host, was therefore a political act of intrusion against a long-time religious enemy.

Hoby entertained the 'guests' alone – his wife was ill – and Sir William Eure (the uncle of William Eure, the group's leader) commenced drinking healths to the hosts. Hoby 'answered that if drinking wolld make my ladie well he colld finde in his harte to drinke himselfe drunke but otherwise since it wolld doe her no good, and he himself hurte he desired them to pardon him for he wolld drinke his ordinarie'.[38] They talked 'of horses and dogs, sports whereunto Sir Thomas never applied himself'.[39] This was the first act of exclusion, for they knew that Hoby's religious sensibilities restricted his ability to partake in their company. Eventually, Hoby bid his guests goodnight, but the revelries continued, and the 'singinge of strange tunes' purposefully interrupted the nightly prayers of Hoby's servants.[40] From then on, social niceties and the guise of inclusive sociability were dropped, as the hunting party sought to humiliate and dishonour their host.

The next morning, the hunting party drank more alcohol at breakfast. Early in the proceedings, Richard Cholmley spilt his drink, and the mood quickly soured. Before breakfast had been finished, William Hilliard 'rose from the table & swore he wolld drinke no more healthes' to his hosts. The huntsmen made more noise, and Sir Thomas sent word for them to be quiet, as his wife was ill and resting in bed. In reply, Eure said that 'I came not for his meate & his drinke but to see my Ladye.' He then denigrated Hoby's hospitality, proclaiming that he would pay for the provisions they had consumed, but would then 'sett up hornes at his gate & be gone.'[41] In similarity to the cases discussed by Susan D. Amussen in this volume, this slanderous comment, which directly attacked Hoby's control over his household and dependents, rendered him a failed patriarch.[42] The parallels in the mindsets of early modern Englishmen between the family and the state meant that such defamatory language undercut Hoby's role as a governor in the body politic, and thereby delegitimised the anti-Catholic persecution that he was overseeing. Indeed, in the aftermath of the event, Hoby was further humiliated by Baron Eure, the father of the group's leader, who asked him why he had failed to defend his wife's reputation that morning with his sword.[43]

The threat of cuckoldry was the tipping point for Hoby, and he told William Eure and his company to leave immediately. Eure remained resolute: he would only leave once he had seen Lady Hoby. Moreover, Eure now threatened to hold the household hostage, even 'if there came [twenty] or [forty] against them', for at that moment a commission had arrived in Hackness on some local government matter. With these

168   *Tom Rose*

threats, Lady Hoby agreed to meet with Eure. A servant tried to lock the door after he went into her chamber to stop the rest of the hunting party from entering but was thrown against a table as the group forced their way in. Before leaving, one member of the party saw a pair of stag's horns that were hung as decorations. He proclaimed, 'by gods harte, I wolld the stages hornes were as hard nailed or as hard fastned upon Sir Thomas his head, as they were there'.[44] With that, the party left the house and, on horseback, trampled across the newly raked forecourt and broke some windows with stones. With the Hobys' honour ruined, the group of unruly Catholics went off for another day's hunting.[45] William Eure was later fined £100 in the Court of Star Chamber, but the political shaming of his enemy, enacted through the superficial desire to socialise with him, had been successfully achieved.

Women and Hunting

Analysis of female involvement in the hunt further demonstrates how the distinctions between inclusion and exclusion were frequently blurred and negotiated. Hunting was imagined as a specifically male activity. For instance, hunting was characterised in Sir Thomas Cockaine's *Short Treatise of Hunting* (1591) as serving as preparation for war. Meanwhile, no mention of hunting or hawking was made in Richard Braithwaite's *The English Gentlewoman* (1641), in stark contrast to its companion volume published the same year, *The English Gentleman*, where hunting and hawking were the first recreations listed as suitable entertainments for men of leisure.[46] This conduct literature imagined women to have a private role in the household while their husbands engaged in the more public and visible acts of hunting. The dynamics of individual marriages and family relations, as well as the relative independence of widows, meant that the reality was less binary than this clear presentation of hunting as an expression of elite, masculine identity.

Given the sustained rejection of hunting as a suitable leisure activity for women in printed literature, it is not surprising that their role in hunting culture has been overlooked and underplayed by historians. For example, Jane Whittle and Elizabeth Griffiths in their work on the household account books of the Norfolk gentlewoman Alice Le Strange have recently argued that 'the display of gentry status through exclusive pastimes and spending patterns was largely a male preserve'. They maintain that while some women did go hunting and hawking, these sports were activities predominantly for gentlemen.[47] Sara Mendelson and Patricia Crawford have similarly contended, although not in relation to hunting, that 'the higher a woman's social position, the less likely she was to share or invade male physical or psychological space'.[48] Yet, such interpretations overemphasise the boundaries between the male and

Hunting and the Politics of Exclusion   169

female realms of early modern English social life, which research by Amanda Flather and others has shown were frequently blurred. Indeed, Flather suggests that 'social space in early modern England was not organised towards the rigid patterns of segregation prescribed by popular culture and writers of prescriptive texts'. Instead, she proposes that 'patriarchal norms shaped perceptions and experience but they did not wholly determine them'.[49] The following discussion will show that women engaged in hunting culture, albeit not necessarily in the style of the sport associated with men, and typically in the company of their husbands. It will also show that by engaging in hunting, both in its exercise and its culture in the broadest social sense, women could carve out a significant role for themselves in support of family strategies and the political machinations of their husbands.

Women typically did not participate in the chase, although this was not always the case. Paintings of Queen Anne of Denmark by Paul Van Somer (1617) (Figure 7.1) and of Charles I and Queen Henrietta Maria by Daniel Mytens (c. 1631-2) (Figure 7.2) show both consorts participating in the chase. Both queens in these images wear dresses, and their horses are equipped with side saddles.[50] What women were expected to wear and how they were expected to ride were physical constraints, placed upon them by patriarchal norms, that deliberately disabled them from performing at the same level as men by hindering their ability to ride quickly. In June 1607, Emanuel Scrope and his wife, Lady Elizabeth, had permission to hunt a stag in Sherwood Forest, with a forest officer in attendance. After a while, their attention was diverted to chasing (but only catching, not killing) a hind calf – a far slower animal than a fully-grown stag. Why they did so is not entirely clear. It can be inferred, however, that it was because Elizabeth, riding side-saddle, would have been unable to keep up with a stag chase. Even with this adjustment, Elizabeth seems to have fallen behind because when an argument broke out during the chase between the forest officer who had accompanied them, and another official who did not know of Scrope's warrant to hunt, Elizabeth 'was not in view' of the argument.[51]

It is also possible that women deliberately let the men in their parties outperform them out of fear of upsetting the patriarchal order and thereby losing their chance to participate. Those who did challenge gendered codes were ridiculed. Sir Nicholas Le Strange, for example, reported in his jestbook a story he had heard from his cousin Dorothy Gurney, in which she and other gentlewomen living around Bury went hunting and hawking. During these sporting trips, they wore breeches so they could ride astride. Sometime later, the ladies went to dinner at the house of Sir Edward Lewknor, where they were rebuked by a Puritan minister, who 'declaim'd much against' the practice. A young, sporting gentleman defended them, Robert Heigham, who responded to the minister that 'if an Horse throwes them, or by mischaunce they get a fall,

Figure 7.1 *Anne of Denmark* (1574–1619) by Paul Van Somer (1617). Royal Collection Trust / © Her Majesty Queen Elizabeth II 2020. RCIN 405887.

had you not better see them in their Breeches then Naked?' Although Heigham appeared to win the argument (the minister struggled to respond), Le Strange described what the ladies did as 'vaine'.[52] Although Le Strange's jestbook, which remained in manuscript form, was primarily designed for private entertainment, this evidence shows that men were clearly disturbed when women challenged patriarchal norms in order to hunt, such as donning breeches instead of dresses. Women, then, could only participate if they agreed to adhere to the rules laid out by those wielding patriarchal authority.

Rather than the chase, early seventeenth-century Englishwomen engaged in either slower pursuits, like hawking and falconry, or entirely sedentary sports, such as bow and stable hunting (the shooting of deer driven towards the hunting party). Sir John Oglander, a keen sportsman, wrote that an ideal wife would, 'in the afternoon … ride abroad a-hawking and stay forth till night'.[53] This sporting culture was so ingrained that participants reacted to events according to their gender and

Hunting and the Politics of Exclusion 171

Figure 7.2 Charles I and Henrietta Maria Departing for the Chase by Daniel Mytens (c. 1630–1632). Royal Collection Trust / © Her Majesty Queen Elizabeth II 2020. RCIN 404771.

social expectations. In August 1619, John Chamberlain was invited by his friend Lady Winwood to a hunt at Ware Park. They were joined by Winwood's niece and her husband, Sir John Trevor, and four others, including Capell Bedell, who had married the daughter of the park's owner, Lady Fanshawe, two months earlier. The hunting party were shooting at bucks when Lady Winwood struck one but did not bring it down. Bedell chased after it, and 'following hard … his horse caried him against a tree, so that with blowe and fall he was sore battered and bruised'.[54] Although ending in injury, it is clear that Bedell sought the masculine honour that would be gained from successfully chasing and killing the buck. The women, meanwhile, seemed to think it improper to engage in anything more than the shooting of game.

As widows, Winwood and Fanshawe had a relatively high degree of independence and hence wielded considerable power. Thus, through inviting their guests to hunt at their parks they were able to take a leading role in the hunt and oversee matters typically reserved for the male head of the household.[55] In 1624, a year after her husband died, Lady Grace Manners of Haddon Hall wrote to her cousin Sir George Manners, of Fulbeck in Lincolnshire, stating that: 'I trust you and my Lady will hold to your purpose of coming here this summer, and if you appoint the time I hope Sir Francis Leek and his lady will meet you and

172   *Tom Rose*

kill a dozen bucks at the least.'[56] Lady Grace was not only proactive in inviting one of her kin and a close neighbour to hunt with her but was also able to demonstrate her heightened sense of status, as the invitation was sent to the heads of the household, who would then bring along their wives. With their unique access to land ownership and the social privileges that came with it, widows could take on a more active role in hunting culture than those whose husbands were still living.

Yet, even if subordinate, wives still played a key role in hunting sociability, especially in furnishing friendships that contributed to a family's political and social standing.[57] Such responsibilities, Barbara Harris has argued, allowed women to 'accept, even flourish in, their subordinated positions'.[58] In late August or early September 1601, the gentleman servant to the newly-married Elizabeth Grey wrote back to her mother, the Countess of Shrewsbury, reporting that her husband's uncle, the Earl of Kent, had taken her on a hunting trip lasting multiple days across Bedfordshire, where the Earl was Lord Lieutenant. Nearly every day they hunted with other Bedfordshire elites as part of the Earl's informal exercise of power and authority; enabling him to form and maintain friendships and political alliances. On 24 August, after visiting and feasting with the Countess of Bedford at Woburn, the Earl of Kent did 'desyer' Elizabeth to visit Baroness Cheyne's park where they 'weare entertained with the Lord Delaware and his Lady and Sir John Croftes and his Lady and ther was kylled a lease [two] of buckes and ther was provided a very good diner'. The next day, Elizabeth was at the baptism of Mr Golding's child, a kinsman of her new husband. They then went to Woodstock where the Earl of Kent 'did entertayne my Lady Elyzabeth excedinge kyndelye as his Lordship ever doth'. On 25 August, Kent 'did furnyshe her Ladyship with all nesisary attendance fytte for a hunting Jurneye be sydes the atendaunce of divers gentilemen of bedfordesheyre'. They hunted with bows and greyhounds in a park owned by the Earl of Bedford before going to the royal park of Higham to hunt. The following day, they went to Bletso park, where Baron St John, Sir Edward Radcliffe (the newly-appointed deputy lieutenant of the county), and other un-named gentlemen, met Elizabeth. St John as host 'did take excedinge paynes to make my Ladies sporte and comaunded a [banquet] to be provided at the logge and after the kyllinge of a brace of Buckes did accompany my Ladye towards Bedforde'. On 27 August, Elizabeth hunted with Baron Compton at the park owned by the Catholic Baron Mordaunt and killed 'an excedinge greate' number of deer. On the final day of the trip, it was reported that she was also there 'againe wheare we had vere greate sporte'.[59]

The trip was clearly undertaken under the Earl of Kent's prerogative: it was he who did 'desyer' Elizabeth to go on this trip, he who 'did entertayne' her, and he who 'did furnyshe her' for the hunting trips. It also shows that from an early stage, Elizabeth was incorporated into the

Hunting and the Politics of Exclusion 173

informal exercise of family power, as Grey clearly viewed the hunt as essential to exercising his influence and maintaining their standing. Moreover, Elizabeth's involvement in such political networking was not unusual since three other women, Baroness Cheyne, Baroness De La Warr, and Lady Crofts, also engaged in these rounds of sporting sociability. Indeed, across early seventeenth-century England we find women involving themselves in the social politics of the hunt in a range of ways. One way was through giving gifts of venison. Elizabeth Grey's mother, the Countess of Shrewsbury, in 1602 gave a 'very fatt stagg' to the President of the Council in the North. Five years later, she gifted 'a verie greatte and fatt Stagge' to the deputy lieutenant of Derbyshire, Sir Francis Leake. She expressed her hopes that 'it shalbe merrily eaten att the assises wher your Lordeshypp and my Ladie shall be often remmembred'. In return, Leake offered Shrewsbury and his wife the chance to hunt at his park.[60] The Earl of Shrewsbury was Lord Lieutenant of Derbyshire and so, even through private sporting acts, his wife was able to partake in his political world.

Perhaps most striking were the actions of Barbara Gammage Sidney, the wife of Viscount Lisle (later Earl of Leicester), of Penshurst in Kent. Her husband was absent every summer because, as Lord Chamberlain of Queen Anne's household, he was always attending the Queen consort on her royal progress. Thus, in the place of her husband, Viscountess Lisle was responsible for the hunting-based entertainments and venison gifting provided at Penshurst. On a number of occasions, she hosted family members who were important courtiers at the Jacobean court, including two favourites of the King, Baron Hay and the Earl of Montgomery, Kentish knights, and Sir John Throckmorton, the deputy governor of the Cautionary Town of Flushing in the Low Countries, where Lisle was governor.[61] Viscount Lisle clearly entrusted his wife to act as his proxy to maintain various friendships and political alliances. Such demonstrations of hospitality centred around sports show how women like Viscountess Lisle and the Countess of Shrewsbury could gain a significant degree of independence and achieve political agency.

It is worth remembering, however, that female involvement in these practices of sociability was nonetheless restricted, since women typically needed the permission or acquiescence of the male head of the household to host such events. This can be observed in the surviving evidence of one hunting occasion on 4 August 1618, when the Countess of Dorset, Lady Anne Clifford, recorded in her diary that her husband 'went to Penshurst but would not suffer me to go with him although My Lord & Lady Lisle sent a man on purpose to desire me to come'. She further described how Dorset 'hunted, & lay there all night, there being my Lord of Montgomery, my Lord Hay, my Lady Lucy & a great deal of other Company'. Despite going on to say that 'my Lord & I part reasonable good friends, he leaving me his Grandmother's ring', there is a clear

174   *Tom Rose*

undercurrent of anger at her exclusion from this type of sociability which had involved many other women whose husbands had permitted them to attend.[62] The actions of the Earl of Dorset contrast starkly with Viscount Lisle. One explanation for this is that the Dorsets' marriage was notoriously unhappy, especially after the death of Lady Anne's mother in 1616 when she entered into a dispute with her uncle, the Earl of Cumberland, over the inheritance of her estates at Skipton. She publicly opposed Cumberland in law, despite the combined pressure of her husband, courtiers, and even the King, to give up her birthright.[63] Prohibiting her from hunting was, therefore, one way in which the Earl of Dorset could exercise control over his wife, even as she challenged his authority through other means. Thus, not only were women excluded from certain styles of hunting, their inclusion – or exclusion – from more acceptable sporting occasions was still very much determined by patriarchal authority.

Conclusion

Hunting enabled those who wielded power in early seventeenth-century England to socialise with their fellow political elites and consolidate their social standing and political influence. It also facilitated cross-confessional cooperation by enabling Catholics to befriend their Protestant gentry neighbours, who might even have been responsible for their persecution. It could be used as a mechanism for marginalising or ostracising political rivals, and in promoting solidarity among co-religionists at the exclusion of those of different faiths. In some instances, the social politics of the hunt also provided women with an opportunity to carve out a role for themselves in both the management of their households and in wider political machinations.

Still, in maintaining a monopoly over the sport, there were many ways in which men limited how far women could be involved and they retained a central role in determining the activities in which women could legitimately partake. Hunting sociability was thus part of what Michael J. Braddick and John Walter have called the 'grids of power' in early modern England: how politics were exercised, negotiated, and contested among the ruling elites.[64] Above all, this chapter has shown that each act of hunting involved several inclusions and exclusions which gave political significance to the socialising that occurred. This complicates the traditional picture of hunting culture by showing that those who were excluded were not a homogenous bloc of people below a certain social status or a certain gender. Instead, the politics of inclusion and exclusion within hunting sociability were fluid, modulating over time, or even within a single social space, and were entirely dependent on a variety of factors including personal relationships, political affiliation, religion, and gender.

Notes

1 George Gascoigne, *The Noble Arte of Venerie or Hunting* (London, 1575), sig. B5r.
2 Nicholas Cox, *The Gentleman's Recreation* (London, 1674), 1.
3 Anthony Fletcher, *Gender, Sex, and Subordination in England 1500–1800* (New Haven and London: Yale University Press, 1995), 131–5. For further work on manhood, see Elizabeth A. Foyster, *Manhood in Early Modern England: Honour, Sex and Marriage* (London: Longman, 1999); Alexandra Shepard, *Meanings of Manhood in Early Modern England* (Oxford: Oxford University Press, 2003); and Alexandra Shepard, 'From Anxious Patriarchs to Refined Gentlemen? Manhood in Britain, circa 1500–1700', *Journal of British Studies*, 44 (2005), 281–95.
4 James Spedding et al. (eds), *The Works of Francis Bacon* (15 vols, London: Houghton Mifflin, 1857–1874), v. 88.
5 The 1604 Game Law required freeholders to possess an income of £40 per annum to hunt on their own land, while those with life estates required an income of £80 per annum. All others were required to have £400 of personal property. 1 Jac. I, c. 27, in Alexander Luders et al. (eds), *The Statutes of the Realm* (11 vols, London: Dawsons, 1810), iv. 1055–6.
6 Alexandra Shepard, *Accounting for Oneself: Worth, Status, and the Social Order in Early Modern England* (Oxford: Oxford University Press, 2015), 107–9. John Morrill likewise argues that ownership of £40 of freehold land was an important way to distinguish between the greater and lesser gentry. John Morrill 'The Northern Gentry and the Great Rebellion', in *The Nature of the English Revolution* (London and New York: Routledge, 1993), 196. See also Henry R. French, 'The Search for the "Middle Sort of People" in England, 1600–1800', *The Historical Journal*, 43 (2000), 278.
7 On poaching, see Roger B. Manning, *Hunters and Poachers: A Cultural and Social History of Unlawful Hunting in England, 1485–1640* (Oxford: Oxford University Press, 1993); and Daniel C. Beaver, *Hunting and the Politics of Violence before the English Civil War* (Cambridge: Cambridge University Press, 2008). See also Edward Berry, *Shakespeare and the Hunt: A Cultural and Social Study* (Cambridge: Cambridge University Press, 2001), esp. chapters 1, 3 and 5; and Andrew Hopper, 'The Wortley Park Poachers and the Outbreak of the English Civil War', *Northern History*, 44 (2007), 93–114. On women, see Fletcher, *Gender, Sex, and Subordination*, 131–5; and Jane Whittle and Elizabeth Griffiths, *Consumption and Gender in the Early Seventeenth-Century Household: The World of Alice Le Strange* (Oxford: Oxford University Press, 2012), 184–209.
8 Felicity Heal and Clive Holmes, *The Gentry in England and Wales, 1500–1700* (Basingstoke: Palgrave Macmillan, 1994), 289, 292.
9 Phil Withington, 'Company and Sociability in Early Modern England', *Social History*, 32 (2007), 301.
10 Susan Whyman, *Sociability and Power in Late-Stuart England: The Cultural Worlds of the Verneys 1660–1720* (Oxford: Oxford University Press, 1999), 4.
11 John Richers to Sir Nathaniel Bacon, 31 August 1610, in Alfred Hassell Smith et al. (eds), *The Papers of Nathaniel Bacon of Stiffkey* (6 vols, Norwich: Norfolk Record Society, 1978–2017), vi. 195.
12 David J.H. Clifford (ed.), *The Diaries of Lady Anne Clifford* (Stroud: Sutton, 1990), 61–2, 65.
13 Francis R. Raines (ed.), *The Journal of Nicholas Assheton of Downham* (Manchester: The Chetham Society, 1848), 54, 57, 60.

176   Tom Rose

14 Keith Wrightson, *English Society, 1580–1680*, second edition (London: Routledge, 2003), 69–72.
15 See the entry for 'Lucy Russell [née Harington], Countess of Bedford (bap. 1581, d. 1627), Courtier and Patron of the Arts', in *The Oxford Dictionary of National Biography (ODNB)* (Oxford, 2004) https://doi.org/10.1093/ref:odnb/24330.
16 Hatfield House, Hertfordshire, Cecil Papers 193/123 (hereafter cited as CP), Bedford to Salisbury, 3 July 1607.
17 CP 125/168, Bedford to Salisbury, 14 June 1608.
18 Vernon F. Snow, *Essex the Rebel: The Life of Robert Devereux, the Third Earl of Essex, 1591–1646* (Lincoln, NE: University of Nebraska Press, 1970), 21–2, 27–9.
19 CP 193/15, Devonshire to Salisbury, August 1606.
20 CP 193/17, Derby to Salisbury, August 1606.
21 Simon Healy, 'Yorkshire', in Andrew Thrush and John P. Ferris (eds), *The History of Parliament: The House of Commons 1604–1629* (hereafter *HP: 1604–1629*) (London, 2010 and online) https://www.historyofparliamentonline.org. Accessed 5 August 2019.
22 Chatsworth House Archives (hereafter CHA), Bolton Abbey Accounts 73, and 95, f. 207v.
23 See esp. Fiona Pogson, 'Wentworth, the Saviles and the Office of *Custos Rotulorum* of the West Riding', *Northern History*, 34 (1998), 205–10; Richard Cust, 'Wentworth's "Change of Sides" in the 1620s', in Julia Merritt (ed.), *The Political World of Thomas Wentworth, Earl of Strafford, 1621–1641* (Cambridge: Cambridge University Press, 1996), esp. 66–7; Richard Cust, 'Politics and the Electorate in the 1620s', in Richard Cust and Anne Hughes (eds), *Conflict in Early Stuart England: Studies in Religion and Politics 1603–1642* (London: Longman, 1989), 143–46; and Peter Salt, 'Sir Thomas Wentworth and the Parliamentary Representation of Yorkshire, 1614–1628', *Northern History*, 16 (1980), 130–68.
24 These included Sir Richard Cholmley and Sir Thomas Fairfax of the North Riding; Sir Matthew Boynton, Sir William Constable, and Sir John Hotham of the East Riding; and Sir Thomas Fairfax, Sir Arthur Ingram, Sir Peter Middleton, Sir Henry Savile, and Sir Henry Slingsby of the West Riding. John T. Cliffe, *The Yorkshire Gentry from the Reformation to the Civil War* (London: Athlone Press, 1969), 283. For their appearance at Londesborough, see CHA, BA/73–86.
25 For the sports provided by Ingram see Jack Nolson to John Mattinson, 18 August 1621, and John Mattinson to Ingram, 2 July 1632, in Royal Commission on Historical Manuscripts, *Reports on Manuscripts in Various Collections* (8 vols, London, 1901–1914), viii. 20, 33.
26 For Savile's absence during this decade-and-a-half see, CHA, BA/79–84. For his absence during the entertainments provided by the Council in the North see CHA, BA/80, 83. Evidence for hunting-based sociability involving the council members can be seen in the Clifford accounts, with the Earl and his son frequently ordering hounds and huntsmen to be brought up to York when they were in the city on official business. CHA, BA/168, ff. 21v–23; BA/174, f. 138; and BA/175, f. 148v.
27 Samuel R. Gardiner (ed.), *Report of Cases in the Courts of Star Chamber and High Commission* (Westminster: Camden Society, 1886), 145–8.
28 For further examples of this practice, see Tom Rose, 'Hunting in Early Stuart England: Status, Sociability, and Politics', unpublished PhD thesis (University of Nottingham, 2020), 178–80.

29 William J. Sheils, '"Getting On" and "Getting Along" in Parish and Town: Catholics and their Neighbours in England,' in Benjamin Kaplan, Bob Moore, Henk van Nierop, and Judith Pollman (eds), *Catholic Communities in Protestant States: Britain and the Netherlands c. 1570–1720* (Manchester: Manchester University Press, 2009), 67–83; Alexandra Walsham, 'Supping with Satan's Disciples: Spiritual and Secular Sociability in Post-Reformation England', in Nadine Lewycky and Adam Morton (eds), *Getting Along? Religious Identities and Confessional Relations in Early Modern England – Essays in Honour of Professor W.J. Sheils* (Farnham: Ashgate, 2012), esp. 50–51; and Anthony Milton, 'A Qualified Intolerance: The Limits and Ambiguities of Early Stuart Anti-Catholicism', in Arthur F. Marotti (ed.), *Catholicism and Anti-Catholicism in Early Modern English Texts* (Basingstoke: Palgrave Macmillan, 1999), esp. 99–103.

30 See the entry for 'Robert Pierrepont, First Earl of Kingston upon Hull (1584–1643), Landowner and Royalist Army Officer', in *ODNB* https://doi.org/10.1093/ref:odnb/22230.

31 Nottingham University Manuscripts, Cl C 283, 648, 289, 677, 683, Kingston to Clifton, 27 July 1631, 25 August 1631, 22 December 1632, 21 February 1639, and 6 November 1639.

32 James Marvin to Maria Thynne, 19 August 1607, in Alison D. Wall (ed.), *Two Elizabethan Women: Correspondence of Joan and Maria Thynne, 1575–1611* (Stoke-on-Trent: Wiltshire Record Society, 1983), 40.

33 See James E. Kelly, 'Counties Without Borders? Religious Politics, Kingship Networks and the Formation of Catholic Communities', *Historical Research*, 91 (2018), 22–38.

34 John Morris (ed.), *The Condition of Catholics under James I: Father Gerard's Narrative of the Gunpowder Plot* (London: Longmans, Green, 1872), xxiii–xiv, xxxv–xxxvi.

35 Michael Questier, 'Practical Antipapistry During the Reign of Elizabeth I', *Journal of British Studies*, 36 (1997), 371–96. This event is also discussed in Felicity Heal, 'Hospitality and Honor in Early Modern England', *Food and Foodways*, 1 (1987), 321–3; and Heal and Holmes, *Gentry*, 3–6.

36 Walsham, 'Supping with Satan's Disciple's', 45–46.

37 CP 180/3, William Eure, enclosed in a letter sent by his father to Sir Robert Cecil, 16 January 1601.

38 The following is mostly taken from the testament of one of Sir Thomas Hoby's servants, Robert Nettleton, in the subsequent Star Chamber case made by Hoby against Eure. The National Archives, Star Chamber 5/H22/21, ff. 8–9 (hereafter Star Chamber).

39 CP 88/17, Hoby to the Privy Council, 5 September 1600.

40 Star Chamber 5/H22/21, ff. 8–9.

41 Ibid.

42 Susan D. Amussen, 'Failing at Patriarchy: Gender, Exclusion and Violence, 1560–1640', 187–92.

43 Simon Healy, 'Hoby, Sir Thomas Posthumous (1566–1640), of Hackness, nr. Scarborough, Yorks. and Blackfriars, London; later of Twickenham, Mdx.', in *HP: 1604–1629*.

44 Star Chamber 5/H22/21, ff. 8–9.

45 CP 180/3, William Eure enclosed in a letter sent by his father, Baron Eure, to Cecil, 16 January 1601.

46 Sir Thomas Cockaine, *A Short Treatise of Hunting* (1591); Richard Braithwaite, *The English Gentleman* (1641); and Richard Braithwaite, *The English Gentlewoman* (1641), 93.

178   *Tom Rose*

47 Whittle and Griffiths, *Consumption and Gender*, 185.
48 Sara Mendelson and Patricia Crawford, *Women in Early Modern England: 1550–1720* (Oxford: Oxford University Press, 1998), 210.
49 Amanda Flather, *Gender and Space in Early Modern England* (Woodbridge: The Boydell Press, 2007), 133.
50 See Richard Almond, 'The Way the Ladies Ride', *History Today*, 62, no. 2 (2012), 36–39.
51 Lambeth Palace Library (hereafter LPL), MS 3203, f. 419, Thomas Woodward to Shrewsbury, 11 June 1607.
52 Henry F. Lippincott (ed.), *'Merry Passages and Jeasts': A Manuscript Jestbook of Sir Nicholas Le Strange (1603–1655)* (Salzburg: Institut für Englische Sprache und Literatur, Universität Salzburg, 1974), 102.
53 Francis Bamford (ed.), *A Royalist's Notebook: The Commonplace Book of Sir John Oglander* (London: Constable, 1936), 131.
54 Norbert E. McClure (ed.), *The Letters of John Chamberlain* (2 vols, Philadelphia, PA: The American Philosophical Society, 1939), ii. 259.
55 Mendelson and Crawford, *Women in Early Modern England*, 176–8.
56 Lady Grace Manners to Sir George Manners, 10 July 1624, Royal Commission on Historical Manuscripts, *The Manuscripts of His Grace the Duke of Rutland, G.C.B., Preserved at Belvoir Castle* (4 vols, London, 1888–1905), i. 470–1.
57 Barbara J. Harris, 'Women and Politics in Early Tudor England', *The Historical Journal*, 33 (1990), 259–81; and Elaine Chalus, 'Elite Women, Social Politics, and the Political World of Late Eighteenth-Century England', *The Historical Journal*, 43 (2000), 669–97.
58 Barbara J. Harris, 'Sisterhood, Friendship and the Power of English Aristocratic Women, 1450–1550', in James Daybell (ed.), *Women and Politics in Early Modern England, 1450–1700* (Aldershot: Ashgate, 2004), 22.
59 LPL MS 3203, f. 393, Piggott to Shrewsbury, late August/early September 1602.
60 LPL MS 3202, f. 52, Burghley to Shrewsbury, 12 September 1602; and LPL MS 3203, f. 300, Leake to Shrewsbury, 6 July 1605.
61 Viscount Lisle to Viscountess Lisle, 2 September 1610, 15 June, 21 July 1615, and 28 July 1617, in Margaret P. Hannay et al. (eds), *Domestic Politics and Family Absence: The Correspondence (1588–1621) of Robert, First Earl of Leicester, and Barbara Gammage Sidney, Countess of Leicester* (Aldershot: Ashgate, 2005), 154, 191, 205.
62 David J.H. Clifford (ed.), *The Diaries of Lady Anne Clifford* (Stroud: Sutton, 1990), 60.
63 Richard T. Spence, *Lady Anne Clifford: Countess of Pembroke, Dorset and Montgomery (1590–1676)* (Stroud: Sutton, 1997), ch. 3.
64 Michael J. Braddick and John Walter, 'Introduction. Grids of Power: Order, Hierarchy and Subordination in Early Modern Society', in Michael J. Braddick and John Walter (eds), *Negotiating Power in Early Modern Society: Order, Hierarchy and Subordination in Britain and Ireland* (Cambridge: Cambridge University Press, 2001), 1–42.

Part III
Exclusions in Ritual, Law, and Bureaucracy

8 Failing at Patriarchy

Gender, Exclusion, and Violence, 1560–1640

Susan D. Amussen

Early modern patriarchy had a problem. While the broad contours of patriarchal order were widely accepted, the tensions within it made it almost impossible to be a successful patriarch. Men were expected to govern their households, and particularly their wives. That required both that men exercised their responsibilities in governing their families, and that women acknowledged and acted on their subordination to husbands and fathers. Patriarchy was demanding and controlling on both men and women. While a considerable effort was made to ensure that people's behaviour conformed to what was expected, the challenge of policing patriarchy was that it was not entirely coherent: patriarchal ideas were constituted in different ways in theology, economics, medicine, law, and science.[1] The authorities were concerned both with simple misbehaviour, such as adultery and disorder, as well as gendered transgressions that incorporated violence: domestic violence, scolding, and witchcraft. Scholars have, over the last thirty years, identified many of the ways that patriarchy was enforced for women; from scolding and witchcraft to accusations of adultery. While historians have explored the nature of masculinity, and models of manhood, they have paid less attention to how men's performance of patriarchy was policed. How were the boundaries of patriarchy defined in early modern communities? What were the consequences of disruptions and failures of patriarchy? And what role did violence play both in disrupting patriarchy and enforcing it? In this essay, I will focus on how men's performance of patriarchy was observed and responded to, with emphasis on the role of violence and the threat of violence in that process.

One challenge, both in enforcing patriarchy and analysing its enforcement, was that the same actions that disrupted the patriarchal order were also used to control it. Indeed, the same acts and behaviours could be perceived by different observers to both support and undermine patriarchy.[2] This presents issues for assessing the role of violence in the policing of the patriarchal order. The idea of correction – ensuring that people behaved as expected – shaped not just formal processes of social control and punishment, but informal ones as well. For example,

182 Susan D. Amussen

narratives around brawls in alehouses were as likely to claim the need to discipline unruly neighbours as discussions of legal punishment. Forms of violence that were defined as disorderly – scolding, alehouse brawls, wife beating, and murder – were often understood by participants as creating order. Violence used by authorities to enforce patriarchy, including ducking scolds, whipping, and execution, was also copied in informal contexts.[3] Within the household, 'correction' was commonly used, and while some domestic manuals opposed husbands using violence to correct their wives, not all did. The discipline of children and servants was also considered necessary, and they were regularly given physical 'correction'.[4] Some behaviours, like skimmingtons to punish disorderly households, were seen by their organisers as enforcing order, and by their victims as a source of disorder. Violence was both a cause of patriarchal disorder, and a tool for enforcing order.

In policing gender norms, people not only paid attention to specific transgressions, but the whole way people carried themselves. The process of enforcement almost always began (and often ended) outside formal legal processes. Both informal and official mechanisms were used to define those who transgressed as disreputable and untrustworthy, resulting in their exclusion from respectability. This process, accomplished through admonition, insults, verse libels, charivari, presentations to the church courts, and sometimes presentations to royal courts, has left traces across the court records and pamphlet literature of early modern England. These sources defined some people as having 'good credit and reputation', and others not. While credit was largely based on economic worth, moral character was also important, as is reflected in the defamation suits brought to defend reputation. Such definitions were often contested, and records of conflict over behaviour are testament to competing values and expectations. While those whose behaviour transgressed gender norms were rarely imprisoned, they were subject to shaming rituals as well as formal punishments, especially the stocks and the ducking stool. Such rituals, even those that were informal, were remembered for many years, and shaped reputations and relationships within communities. Although their targets were not physically removed from communities, those subject to such ritual humiliation often chose to move. Some violations of gender norms led to more serious consequences. Rape, for instance, was a felony that could lead to execution. Execution was the ultimate exclusion, as it removed someone from the community of the living.[5]

Some causes of gendered disorder are better documented than others. The more significant the impact outside the household, the more likely we are to know about it through surviving source evidence. Men's failures in governing their wives (whether through abuse or neglect) was more often recorded than their parallel failures with children and servants. As I will show, this discrepancy can be explained by the greater impact that violence against wives had on local order. Offences based on speech, like scolding and defamation, are also well documented, and have been studied extensively.[6] Furthermore, while there has been considerable work on verse libels, there has been less focus on their gendered dimensions.[7] Speech was explicitly linked to violence in witchcraft, the gendered nature of which has been widely recognised, since witches were believed to act against others through harmful speech.[8] Yet insults, libels, scolding, and even cursing, could not only disrupt gender norms but reimpose them by articulating boundaries of exclusion. Insults – the source of many conflicts recorded in defamation cases – depended on implicit expectations that had been (allegedly) violated. The implicit expectations are even more evident in the admonitions that were often the first response to misconduct. Such admonitions articulated norms and could even challenge the authority of the head of household. In a separation case before the Norfolk Consistory Court in 1696, Mrs Cooke testified that when her neighbour John Robinson beat his wife she intervened and told him that 'he was a very ill man to beat his wife at that rate'. Her action was ultimately ineffective but was nevertheless symbolically important.[9] The policing of men and women repeatedly involved informally reprimanding behaviours that might be seen as undermining gender order.

My analysis of the control of gender depends on a central characteristic of the mental world of early modern England: the habit of analogical thinking, with a particular emphasis on the parallels between the family and the state. Gender relations, both in context of the family and society more broadly, had political consequences. Most violations of the gender order represented one of two types: the disorderly or unruly woman, or the failed patriarch who was unable to govern his household.[10] Both were omnipresent in social practice and the social imaginary of early modern England, and similarly linked the social realm to the political. Unruly women were thought to be exceptionally common. Indeed, assumptions about women's nature meant that they were expected to be unruly. But women's natural disposition for disorder did not imply that men had no responsibilities. Instead, it made it more important that men governed their wives, and ensured that wives, children, and other members of their households behaved. The failed patriarchs, who form the focus of this essay, were often unable to control their wives and also other household dependents. The most visible cultural stereotype of the failed patriarch was the cuckold: the man who failed so much as a husband that his wife was unfaithful. As this suggests, patriarchy could be undermined through sins of both omission and commission. Disorderly women and failed patriarchs were two sides of the same coin; while women were held accountable for their own behaviour, men were held accountable both for their behaviour and, at times, that of their wives.

184 *Susan D. Amussen*

The records that have allowed historians to trace disorder, and responses to it, including the defamation in the church courts, Star Chamber cases, and cases brought before the quarter sessions, are rarely direct. Testimony in church courts and quarter sessions was recorded by scribes. Witnesses were always responding to questions that framed the narrative, and only certain issues could be the subject of litigation. Yet within those constraints, we can see social and community concerns, even if they are shoehorned into legal categories. Furthermore, the stories told frequently provide details irrelevant in law that illuminate the informal modes of enforcement that preceded or accompanied legal action. These allow us to see the behaviours that people perceived as necessary to police. By making the violent potential of speech part of the analysis of violence, we can gain a fuller understanding of the social dimensions of exclusion within early modern communities.

The Spectacle of Elite Failures

Patriarchy's policing of men has been less fully examined for the period before 1640 than later in the century. The early Stuart debate on women, as well as the prominence of witchcraft and scolding, have drawn more attention.[11] Yet in many ways, failed patriarchs were a greater source of anxiety than disorderly women. Analysis of cases of failed patriarchs demonstrate a wide range of ways in which gender order was enforced through violence: from execution to rape, festive violence, and domestic violence. Men most often failed as patriarchs by not conforming to what Alexandra Shepard has called the hegemonic model of 'patriarchal masculinity', where men exhibited self-control and financial independence, and governed their households to ensure that their wives, children, and servants were god-fearing and obedient. The failure to conform could stem from deliberate participation in disorder and violence but might also come down to the simple fact that they were unable to govern their households effectively.[12] Meeting these expectations was particularly important for propertied men whose position created an expectation of patriarchal leadership.

One of the best-known failed patriarchs of early modern England was the Earl of Castlehaven. As an Earl, he would have been expected to govern both his household and the surrounding community. Yet his failures as a patriarch and the resultant disorder in his household – some of it violent – led to his execution. The competing narratives in this case help demonstrate the tensions of patriarchy. In late 1630, Castlehaven's son wrote to Charles I. As the sources show, he told his father that he was appealing to the King as the father of his country to remedy his natural father's abuses.[13] At Castlehaven's subsequent trial by his peers, the prosecution produced evidence that he had encouraged servants to have sex with his wife, and, on at least one occasion, participated in her rape by holding her down. He had also encouraged his son's wife to sleep with servants. On top of this, he was alleged to have had homosexual relations with some of his servants, and to have imported a local prostitute into the household. Castlehaven's defence was that his sexually voracious wife had intentionally cuckolded him and had conspired with his son to bring him to ruin so that they could share his estates between them. Even by this account, however, Castlehaven had failed in his patriarchal duty: a successful patriarch would not allow or enable such behaviour by his wife and his heir. His was a household in which both the social and moral order had been turned upside down through violence and sex. In the end, the Earl was found guilty of rape and buggery. At the outset of the trial, Attorney General Heath struggled to understand how a gentleman could do such terrible things, and his conclusion was stark: 'He believed not God, he had not the fear of God before his eyes; he left God, and God left him to his own wickedness.' After a trial that had repeatedly emphasised the ways his behaviour placed him outside the community of both Christians and peers, Castlehaven was executed by beheading on Tower Hill on 14 May 1631.[14]

Execution, the most extreme form of exclusion, was rarely used to ensure patriarchal conformity. Castlehaven's execution, as well as the lurid details of the charges against him, may have been unusual, but his failures to govern his household were not. Sir Pexall Brocas (1563–1630), heir to his wealthy grandfather, Sir Richard Pexall, lived a life of disorder that combined general rowdiness with sexual misconduct and physical violence that is documented by at least eighteen Star Chamber cases and six Chancery cases between 1584 and 1625. Patriarchal responsibilities extended far beyond sexual conduct, since his financial recklessness, unruly behaviour, and sexual offences all contributed to his inability to maintain an orderly household.[15] In his youth, Brocas was part of a group of rowdy young men and was in debt at the time of his marriage to Margaret Shirley in 1584. If his marriage had been intended to encourage him to settle down and take on the responsibilities of a head of household, it failed: Brocas was unable to shed the antipatriarchal behaviour of his youth, which took new forms as he gained access to his property. Notwithstanding being described in a Star Chamber case in 1602 as 'a man of very lewde behaviour and disordered course of liffe', he was among a large group of men knighted by James I on his arrival in London in 1603. In early 1604 he was pardoned for all 'ryotts and unlawfull assemblies'. He was also pardoned both for forging a deed as well as the consequent forfeitures, and from any suits in any royal court.[16]

In later years, Brocas was best known for his sexual exploits, having reputedly fathered over seventy illegitimate children, some in London, others at his estates in Hampshire and Buckinghamshire. In 1605, a Hampshire farmer alleged that he had 'forsaken the company of his own wife',

186 *Susan D. Amussen*

and 'lived lewdly with other women'. In the Star Chamber cases brought against him, it was revealed that he had bastards by at least two of the maidservants, and also 'kept three or four other lewd women in his house', marrying two of them off (bigamously in one case) to other servants. One of the maidservants deposed that she had often seen another maid in bed with him. Several of his menservants were also reputed to be 'of very bad life'. In February 1612, just a few months before a Star Chamber hearing, a London letter-writer reported that one of Brocas's 'young mignons' had recently done penance at St Paul's Cross. It was said that Brocas had 'entertained and abused [her] since she was twelve years old' (the age at which a girl could consent to marriage). When Brocas himself did penance in 1614, after repeatedly defying his conviction by the Court of High Commission for 'notorious adulteries with divers women', he turned up with thirty men in scarlet livery. They afterwards accompanied him when he went to demand free dinner from the Lord Mayor.[17]

Violence was never far from the surface in Brocas's activities and he apparently never aspired to respectability. As with Castlehaven, his status and wealth made his violation of expected behaviour especially egregious. As a gentleman, his patriarchal responsibilities extended to his community. But in 1610, Brocas was accused of murdering his steward in particularly violent fashion. It was reported that Brocas's steward had his 'skin flayed and taken away from his head and face, his eyes put out and his hands cut off besides diverse other cuts and wounds'. Brocas then allegedly had the Sheriff stack a coroner's jury to blame the death on suicide rather than murder.[18] Within his household, Brocas was on bad terms with his own son, who he accused, in a twist that seems taken from the revenge tragedies so popular at the time, of trying to poison him to gain possession of his estates. Besides this, he was a bad neighbour, quarrelling with Hampshire residents over tithes, and allegedly trying to intimidate 'honest men' with vexatious lawsuits.[19] The requirement from the courts that Brocas perform public penance, and the multiple lawsuits against him, demonstrate the wide range of ways that authorities and neighbours sought to enforce patriarchal responsibilities.

Brocas's career shows that the Earl of Castlehaven was not an anomaly. Equally, as disorderly as Brocas was, there were others whose behaviour was even more disturbing by contemporary standards. In a Star Chamber suit Brocas brought against William Norton, recorded by Lord Chancellor Ellesmere in 1612, it was Norton's behaviour and unruly household that concerned Ellesmere. During the summer of 1611, Norton had allegedly taken the lead in a succession of drunken orgies, many of them occurring on Sundays during service time. 'Pails of drink' were consumed; healths were drunk to the devil (kneeling), the Pope, and Romish priests; there were mock 'knightings' of some of Norton's companions to reward them for their drinking prowess; and there was open contempt for both church and government. If the Lord Chief

Justice came, Norton declared, he would kill him. On at least one of these occasions, Norton was reportedly 'stark naked'. The behaviour described was not only disorderly but challenged the fundamental hierarchy of both church and state. Ellesmere was outraged by the way that Norton, as a gentleman, had actively encouraged his companions to reject social, political, religious, and gender expectations. Furthermore, like Brocas and Castlehaven, Norton was overfamiliar with his servants, undermining his patriarchal authority and the expectation that he should keep his household in good order.[20] To provide context, William Gouge in his influential conduct book *Of Domesticall Duties* (1622), offered extensive guidance for husbands and heads of household, which stated that to 'suffer their servants to be their companions, playing, drinking, reveling with them', was a core failing and mistake of many masters.[21] The misconduct of men like Norton and Brocas demonstrates that although patriarchal expectations determined the behaviour of wives, children, and servants, men were, above all, expected to govern their households.

As we have seen, the career of Sir Pexall Brocas was certainly violent and dramatic. Yet, like that of Castlehaven, his behaviour was threatening precisely because it represented an exaggerated version of familiar rejections of patriarchal norms. Pexall Brocas was not the first young gentleman to get into debt, nor the first (or last) one to be accused of sexual misconduct, even if the seventy illegitimate children are an exaggeration. Tensions between fathers and sons, visible in both the Castlehaven and Brocas cases, were inherent in a system where young men's access to property depended on the death of the father. Castlehaven and Brocas may have been spectacular failures as patriarchs, but they were dangerous because the difference between them and other men was of degree, not kind. The volume of litigation in early modern England suggests that informal responses to conflict and disorder were frequently ineffective, leading to men (and women) using the courts to define, and reassert, boundaries of family and accountability.[22]

Cuckolds and Violence

Castlehaven's case can be understood as one of marital breakdown; one where, as was often the case, there was no possibility of legal separation. At the time, marital breakdown represented a failure of manly government over the household. The usual community response to this form of conflict was to try to reconcile the spouses, and thus reconstitute the patriarchal family unit. In cases of irretrievable marital breakdown, there were two legal options: separation or annulment. Both were rare. For women to sue for a separation, they had to demonstrate violence that was more than 'that any woman might well beare at hir husbands hands'.[23] Legal separations, like annulments, were also expensive. As a

188   *Susan D. Amussen*

result, informal separations were far more common, often governed by privately negotiated written agreements.[24]

The best evidence of the process of exclusion and policing of patriarchy is evident in responses to accusations of adultery. This is because informal reactions – from insults to charivari – often generated a response within the legal systems. Such accusations were frequent sources of litigation. Some of this was straightforward: people accused of sexual offences were presented to the church courts, and, if found guilty, were required to do penance. Such was the case with Sir Pexall Brocas.[25] Yet, perhaps more revealing, are the more complex cases of libels and insults examined below. These cases appeared primarily in Star Chamber cases. They demonstrate the multiple ways gendered misconduct was identified and policed.

The process of monitoring and chastising failed patriarchs is evidenced through instances involving cuckolds: men whose wives had been unfaithful. Cuckolds were a familiar part of the social and imaginative landscape of early modern England. Jokes and insults around cuckoldry were key to regulating gender boundaries and frequently depended on the violence of language. Any suspicion of adultery on the part of a wife was a problem, but the most striking examples were those wittols who, like Castlehaven, apparently did not just accept adultery (which was bad enough) but promoted it. And yet, in the catch-22 so common with patriarchy, adultery on the part of women was almost expected, owing to the negative characterisations of women created by patriarchy itself. In jest, at least, the assumption was that all men were cuckolds and, therefore, on some level were not responsible for failures in their wives' behaviour. Still, in practice, men were held responsible by their communities for failing to govern their wives. A London landmark in the period was Cuckold's Haven, or Cuckold's Point, a location a little east of the City on the Surrey shore. John Taylor, the Water Poet, wrote, 'Unto that Tree are plaintiffs or defendants ... some cuckolds, some cuckold makers'. Taylor played for some time in this piece with the assumption that to be married was to be a cuckold.[26] The symbol of the cuckold was the horn, and horn jokes are omnipresent in comedies of the period because being a cuckold was believed to be the inheritance of a married man. The horns were based on the mythological classical figure Actaeon who was turned into a stag after seeing the naked Diana. While Actaeon was punished for what he saw (a naked goddess), the early modern cuckold was mocked for what he did not see.[27] The anxiety in cuckold jokes, key to their operation, thus stemmed from the fact that an ability to see the cuckold horns meant that any man – in theory – could be a cuckold. The laughter was fuelled both by men's vulnerability to being branded a cuckold, and the social consequences of being one. In a society where personal reputation was key, the accusation of being a cuckold had material consequences.

Jokes about cuckolds served to define the boundaries of patriarchy. While they were a subject of jest, there is extensive evidence to show that the targets of these jokes (unsurprisingly) were not amused. After all, whether you thought the horns were funny depended on your position. Examination of cuckold jokes of the period allow us to follow a trajectory from words to shame to violence. Their survival in court records is a reminder of their impact. They emphasise the sharp edge of ritual humour. Indeed, the mere act of using a horn as decoration identified a putative cuckold and those who should be excluded from the ranks of 'good' patriarchs. In 1591, when Norfolk villagers decorated their church at midsummer, they used two branches, 'the one bowed one way, the other another way', to create a set of horns at the seat belonging to Joan Holmes and her husband. In Dorset in 1609, ram's horns were hung up outside the church during a wedding, while the following year in Somerset, horns were hung outside the window of a newlywed couple. More aggressively, in the late 1580s, Richard Lamberd of Helions Bumpstead, Essex, defamed the minister by placing horns in the chancel of the church.[28]

The violent and exclusionary implications of cuckoldry could be even more explicit. In Norwich in 1609, a man threw a pair of ox horns into a shop, saying: 'Take that for the key to your bedchamber door'.[29] In the midst of a conflict over church seats and other issues in Cornwall, the minister William Robinson brought 'a great and huge pair of goat hornes' and threw them against Edward Fosse's window, and followed it by 'bragging what he had done'.[30] Even insults which depended on the image of horns often had connotations of force. When Alice Phesey of London told William Dynes that 'thy hornes are so great that thow canst scarce get in at thine own doores, take heede thou dost not breake a hole with thy hornes through thy neighbours wall', the vivid image obviated the need for actual horns.[31] Horns could be deployed in political or religious conflict as well. As Tom Rose explores in his chapter in this volume, a Catholic hunting party that sought hospitality at the home of the Puritan Sir Thomas Hoby deliberately offended him by drinking and playing cards. The next morning, when Hoby asked them to be quiet as his wife was ill, they threatened to hang horns at the gate if they did not see her.[32]

If insults and jokes about cuckolds demonstrate the informal mechanisms of policing and exclusion, these processes became more elaborate–and the violence often more explicit–in verse libels. Libels, which were highly satirical and often lengthy poems that were recited or sung, were written on subjects from politics to domestic behaviour. We know about many of them because of Star Chamber cases brought against their authors, whose targets articulated the damage they had caused to their reputations. In many cases, written copies were circulated more broadly, often beyond the immediate locale where they were written. Many of the

190   *Susan D. Amussen*

poems, and the attendant circulation of them, included implicit violence.[33] When in the early 1620s John Gordon, Gentleman of Melbury Osmond, Dorset, was suspected of adultery with Elizabeth, the wife of the Dorset gentleman Edward Frances, a malicious libel attacking the honour of both men began to circulate. The first verse of the libel against them read:

> Francis Nedd/with Acteon's head/doth square up and down/his head being high/he doth stye[stay]/to maister all the town/and Bes the bear/doth swell and swear/she will maister be/of all the wives for hye degree/and well she may I tell you trues,/be maistres in London of the Stews./For pompe and pride she bears the be/ll, She is as proud as the devil of hell/, But her husband I might be/I would make her leave her venerie.

The insult was created by the juxtaposition of the mythological reference to Actaeon, followed by the description of Elizabeth as a 'bear' and the mistress of 'the stews', a reference to brothels in Southwark. The reference to a bear, whether as a threat or as the subject of baiting, suggests both violence and danger. But the most important line was the last: a good patriarch would ensure a wife's fidelity. The libel was copied, repeated, and sung in 'divers places in the county of Dorset'. John Gordon and Edward Frances, the two subjects satirised in the libel, joined together in a Star Chamber suit against the authors.[34]

Similarly, the Leicestershire gentleman John Gobert brought two different cases against Thomas Brewster in Star Chamber in 1605 and 1606. In the first, he complained of a libel designed to look like a list of articles presented to a court, which alleged that a local curate had slept with a number of women, including Gobert's wife Luce, to whom he had been married for twenty-one years. While the libel was primarily directed at Edward Astill, the Vicar, Gobert thought it sufficiently important to bring a suit. The following year, the authors of the first libel, presumably annoyed by the Star Chamber suit, circulated another libel near Gobert's London home, which called him 'cuckoldly clown' and accused him of giving his wife to Astill. Verse libels directed at Gobert soon circulated, ridiculing him as a 'cuckoldy clown', and accusing him of being a 'promoter and common cuckold'. The libel included the verse: 'if I be a cuckold it is no matter/for that it is horned luck/because others my wife do fuck'. Gobert, in his complaint, noted that he and his wife had a 'commendable and a good reputation', and that Brewster had 'causeless malice and hatred' towards them. Furthermore, Gobert proposed that the goal of the 'faulse and fayned invencions, reports, and slanderous libels' was to 'make them infamous' among their neighbours.[35] Gobert's complaint emphasises the ways that verse libels and the court cases used to defend their honour constituted efforts to define boundaries of acceptable masculine behaviour. For his part, Gobert suggested that his response was

Failing at Patriarchy 191

necessary to protect his reputation. The lack of explicit references to violence in these cases does not mean these were not understood as violent. In a period where the oral tradition was stronger than the written in most communities, words were actions, and violent words and violent actions were considered parallel because they both had a significant impact on people's lives. The reputations and credit that men defended were also of material value. For example, for years after Robert Reede of Tiverton had a libel and horns attached to his door, people in the street would laugh and make the sign of horns when they saw him.[36]

The link between insults and violence becomes more evident in instances of the skimmington ride. This was the English version of the charivari, common in many countries across early modern Europe, which was usually directed at households where the wife was unfaithful, a scold, or beat her husband, which were often assumed to coincide. An engraving from the 1628 work *English Customs,* shows these dual elements of the skimmington ride in action (Figure 8.1). As the image shows, the ritual of the skimmington represented an effort on the part of the community to reinstate patriarchal order. At the same time, it illustrates the violence that both prompted and enforced exclusion in English communities during this period. The ritual was focused on condemning unruly wives, but also sought to shame the husbands who had failed to govern them. For example, in Quemerford, outside of Calne, Wiltshire in 1618, the skimmington procession that was directed at Thomas Mills and his wife Agnes planned to 'wash her [Agnes] in the cucking stool' at Calne (the usual punishment for scolds). At the same time, however, the man riding the horse had 'two shoeing horns hanging by his ears' that were used to suggest that Thomas was a cuckold.[37]

Such rituals were often festive events for communities but had militant elements. For example, in the previously mentioned case, 'three or four hundred men, some like soldiers, armed with pieces and other weapons' were present. The leaders rushed into the house and dragged Agnes Mills from it, and 'beat her black and blue'.[38] The violence here was not imagined or implicit: it was explicit, targeting the household for its departure from patriarchal norms. A similar scenario is evidenced in 1653, when a crowd of people came to the house of John Day in Ditcheat, Somerset, 'hooping and hallowing'. One man was 'ryding upon a cowle staffe', while another carried 'a great payre of hornes'. They called Day a 'cuckold, and threatened to throw his wife into the Poole'. Once again, the cuckolded husband was shamed, but his (allegedly) unfaithful wife was threatened with being ducked like a scold. Those who were part of this procession planned 'to make merry with Skimmington', and were promised a 'barrel of beer'. Whatever pleasure the participants took in the event was not shared by John Day and his wife.[39] Nicholas Rosyer, who alleged his family had lived in Wetherden, Suffolk, for two hundred years, moved to the neighbouring village of Haughley after being a target

192 Susan D. Amussen

Figure 8.1 A Woman Beats Her Husband with Her Household Keys, Whilst a Skimmington Takes Place in the Background with the Husband Depicted as a Cuckold with Horns on His Head. STC 10408.6, Anon., *English Customs. 12 Engravings of English Couples with Verses* (London, 1628), Image 9, 'Well Worth to Scurge, So Weake A Patch'. Used by Permission of the Folger Shakespeare Library.

of a skimmington.[40] In all these cases, men were held responsible (and punished) for their wives' behaviour. Skimmingtons, combining festive license with mob justice, often aimed to punish offenders directly. In so doing, they emphasised the communal importance of properly governed households. The folk punishments imposed by skimmingtons repeat the insults contained in libels and make violence explicit.

Violent Husbands

While cuckolds could plausibly blame their failure as patriarchs on their wives, men accused of domestic violence could not. Domestic violence was one of the most frequent causes of marital breakdown during this period and is an example of how violence disrupted the gender order.[41] In most instances, the first response to patriarchal violence against women and children were efforts on the part of family and neighbours to effect changes in the man's behaviour to enable a reconciliation, demonstrating the centrality of the household to early modern English social organisation. These responses generally aimed to avoid exclusion. In 1596, Anne Felmingham's daughter called her mother's neighbour for assistance in the middle of the night to 'rescue'

Failing at Patriarchy 193

Anne from her husband Thomas. On another occasion, a neighbour had found Anne weeping, 'her head cloathes, face, and breast cloathes' all bloody. The neighbour recounted that while his wife 'pacified' Anne, he had admonished Thomas to 'live quietly with his said wife or else to put her away'. While Thomas described his actions as a justifiable method of correcting his wife's faults, neighbours were clear it had gone too far.[42] A century later, Hannah Robinson alleged that her husband John had both beaten and starved her, with a servant testifying that he 'often beat, kick and abuse[d]' his wife. When the neighbour admonished the servant for not interfering, she replied 'that her Master had threatened in case she stird to open the doore which was then shut he would either cut her throat or run his knife into her'. Furthermore, she reported that while John Robinson ate wheat bread regularly, his wife and servant only ate barley bread. Robinson thus treated his wife and servant equally. This in itself could have been seen as a form of abuse, but also demonstrates Robinson's authoritarian and abusive approach to his patriarchal role as head of household.[43] Even the gentry, whose homes provided a degree of privacy that protected them from inquisitive neighbours, sought reconciliations first. When Clement Walker stabbed his wife 'with full intention to kill her', his knife pierced her bodice and stomacher, but she was protected by her whalebone stays. While her brothers and father sought advice on separation from a lawyer, her cousin Christopher Pitt helped effect a reconciliation. The impulse here was to prevent the need for legal action. Pitt was present at his cousin's deathbed two years later, when Walker promised his dying wife that Pitt would ensure the proper education of their children.[44]

We saw with Castlehaven and Brocas how too much intimacy with servants undermined patriarchal order. When such forms of over-familiarity involved sexual relationships with servants and violence against a wife, the problem was even more severe. These situations challenged both the social and gender order. In 1629, several residents of Beeston, Norfolk, presented a petition complaining about the gentleman, Thomas Vyolett, who was violent and abusive to his wife, Susan. The complaint appears to have been in support of an action brought by Susan, where she enlisted community support to define his behaviour as unacceptable. The substance of the complaint makes the links between speech and violence clear. Susan reported that Thomas threatened her and his servants with a knife at various times, and several servants left his service to protect their lives. But even worse, in recent months before the complaint, Vyolett had introduced Elizabeth Hewes into his household as a servant. Hewes was described as 'a roaringe, swearing, debeise and swaggeringe woman', but Vyolett took all the keys from his wife – including those for trunks and coffers containing his money – and gave them to Hewes, so that she could 'rule over his sayd wyef and children and household'. In turn, Elizabeth had mistreated both Vyolett's wife

194   *Susan D. Amussen*

and children, ordering them about 'more like doggs than Christians'. When one of his relatives reminded him of his duty to love his wife, Vyolett responded that he cared no more for her 'then I doe for a fart that falles from my breeches'. Susan Vyolett's neighbours were not surprised that she had left her husband's house and while the precise implications of the widespread support for her complaint are not clear, local notables henceforth decided that the household was sufficiently disorderly to marginalise this particular gentleman.

In the context of a patriarchal society, men's failure to govern their families, whether through their own disorderly behaviour or their inability to control the behaviour of wives and servants, was a source of disorder. That disorder was policed in multiple ways. Insults and chastisement were generally the first response, but those who were recalcitrant might have also been subject, like Thomas Vyolett, to legal action. Thus, the violence associated with failed patriarchs could be destructive of order or, as in the case of skimmingtons, be an attempt to reassert order. Petitions like the one brought against Thomas Vyolett showed how far a man's failure to govern his household properly could override the usual grant of 'credit and reputation' afforded to a gentleman.[45]

Conclusion

What does examination of the processes by which failed patriarchs were identified and monitored tell us about the mechanisms of exclusion in early modern England? Historians have long acknowledged that the boundaries of gender were regularly policed in early modern England. The structure of patriarchy and its contradictions meant that failure on the part of patriarchs was inevitable and, indeed, the rules of patriarchal masculinity and virtuous womanhood were regularly breached. This chapter has demonstrated that the failures that mattered were ones where the patriarchal disorder significantly undermined social or political order.

This chapter has also demonstrated that the policing of patriarchy was a central feature of social and political life across a range of early modern contexts; one that began with admonition or insults and extended through informal and formal processes. The importance of reputation meant that the 'credit' given to men was a crucial tool of control, through which communities and those under patriarchal household rule might hold them to account. Neighbours who criticised men whose behaviour, or that of their households, failed to maintain the patriarchal ideal were able to act because they defined their actions as transcending the boundaries of respectability. Responses to insults, charges of cuckoldry, and verse libels demonstrate the implicit violence that actions and words carried for early modern English people. Moreover, just as the regulation of failures of patriarchy varied according to context, so too did processes of exclusion where the level of threat to the social order determined the community's response. In some cases, this action might result in the re-integration of men who had failed as patriarchs into their households and communities, whilst more extreme behaviour could result in an execution. Regardless of its, scale, however, exclusion was a critical tool in ensuring that men played their role in the patriarchal order.

Acknowledgement

A previous version of this essay was written for the workshop 'Framing Violence', organised by Adriane Lentz-Smith and Jehangir Malegam and held at the Duke University History Department in 2015. It has benefited from comments there, and at the 'Cultures of Exclusion' conference in 2017, particularly from Naomi Pullin and Kathryn Woods.

Notes

1 I discuss this in greater detail in my essay 'The Contradictions of Patriarchy in Early Modern England', *Gender & History*, 30 (2018), 1–11; also see Susan Amussen and David Underdown, *Gender, Culture and Politics in England, 1560–1640: Turning the World Upside Down* (London: Bloomsbury, 2017), esp. 5–7, 27–31, 36–49, 51–3.

2 See discussion of the visit of the Eure hunting party to the home of Sir Thomas Hoby in Tom Rose, 'Hunting, Sociability, and the Politics of Inclusion and Exclusion in Early Seventeenth-Century England,' 166–8.

3 Susan D. Amussen, 'Punishment, Discipline, and Power: The Social Meanings of Violence in Early Modern England', *Journal of British Studies*, 34 (1995), 1–34.

4 See Susan D. Amussen, *An Ordered Society: Gender and Class in Early Modern England* (Oxford: Basil Blackwell, 1988), 42–3.

5 See Alexandra Shepard, *Accounting for Oneself: Worth, Status and the Social Order in Early Modern England* (Oxford: Oxford University Press, 2015); and Amussen, *Ordered Society,* 98–101, 152–5; Laura Gowing, *Domestic Dangers: Women, Words and Sex in Early Modern London* (Oxford: Oxford University Press, 1996), 112–38.

6 For scolds, see David Underdown, 'The Taming of the Scold', in Anthony Fletcher and John Stevenson (eds), *Order and Disorder in Early Modern England* (Cambridge: Cambridge University Press, 1985), 116–36. For updated discussions, which assess the critiques of Underdown by Martin Ingram, see Rachel Weil, 'Politics and Gender in Crisis in David Underdown's "The Taming of the Scold"', *History Compass*, 11 (2013), 381–8; and Susan D. Amussen, 'Turning the World Upside Down: Gender and Inversion in the Work of David Underdown', *History Compass*, 11 (2013), 394–404. For defamation, Gowing, *Domestic Dangers*, passim; J.A. Sharpe, *Defamation and Sexual Slander in Early Modern England: The Church Courts at York* (York: University of York, Borthwick Institute of Historical Research, 1980).

196 *Susan D. Amussen*

7 For libels, see Adam Fox, 'Ballads, Libels, and Popular Ridicule in Jacobean England', *Past and Present*, 145 (1994), 47–83; Alastair Bellany and Andrew McRae (eds), 'Introduction', *Early Stuart Libels: An Edition of Poetry from Manuscript Sources*, Early Modern Literary Studies Text Series I (2005), http://www.earlystuartlibels.net/htdocs/index.html. Accessed 23 January 2014; Laura Gowing, 'Women, Status and the Popular Culture of Dishonour', *Transactions of the Royal Historical Society*, Sixth Series, 6 (1996), 225–34.

8 For an overview of the voluminous literature on witchcraft, see the essays in Brian Levack (ed.), *Oxford Handbook of Witchcraft in Early Modern Europe and Colonial America* (Oxford: Oxford University Press, 2014). See also Kirilka Stavreva, *Words Like Daggers: Violent Female Speech in Early Modern England* (Lincoln, NE: University of Nebraska Press, 2015), esp. 76–83.

9 Norfolk Record Office (hereafter Norf. R.O.) DEP/53, Robinson mul. con Robinson vir.

10 This argument is developed in Amussen and Underdown, *Gender, Culture and Politics*, esp. 21–50, 51–76.

11 For an overview of the debate on women, see, Amussen and Underdown, *Gender, Culture and Politics*, 21–2, 24–7, 43–9; I have also explored these issues in 'Cuckold's Haven: Gender and Inversion in Popular Culture', in Malcolm Smuts (ed.), *The Oxford Companion to the Age of Shakespeare* (Oxford: Oxford University Press, 2016), 528–42. For other discussions of manhood that include the policing of men's behaviour, see Elizabeth A. Foyster, *Manhood in Early Modern England: Manhood, Sex and Marriage* (London: Longman, 1999); Alexandra Shepard, *Meanings of Manhood in Early Modern England* (Oxford: Oxford University Press, 2003); for a recent overview, see Tim Reinke-Williams, 'Manhood and Masculinity in Early Modern England' in *History Compass*, 12 (2014), 685–93.

12 Alexandra Shepard, 'From Anxious Patriarchs to Refined Gentlemen? Manhood in Britain, circa 1500–1700', *Journal of British Studies*, 44 (2005), 281–95, esp. 291.

13 J. Bruce et al., *Calendar of State Papers Domestic for the Reign of Charles I* (23 vols, London, 1858–97), iv. (1629–1631), 371; the most recent overview of the case is Cynthia B. Herrup, *A House in Gross Disorder: Sex, Law, and the 2nd Earl of Castlehaven* (Oxford: Oxford University Press, 1999).

14 London, British Library (hereafter BL), Harl. MS 390, fol. 529: Mead to Stuteville, 19 December 1630; Thomas B. Howell, *Cobbett's Complete Collection of State Trials and Proceedings for High Treason and Other Crimes and Misdemeanors* (33 vols, London, 1809–1826), iii. (1627–1640), 410; for the ways the prosecution defined him, see Herrup, *A House in Gross Disorder*, 64–79; for his defence, 83–7.

15 Montague Burrows, *The Family of Brocas of Beaurepaire and Roche Court, Hereditary Masters of the Royal Buckhounds, with Some Account of the English Rule in Aquitaine* (London, 1886), 208–14: Brocas reached his majority in 1584, and litigation regarding the estate continued at least until 1617; the last lawsuit in which he is recorded is 1625, Kew, London, The National Archives (hereafter TNA), C/3/353/47, John Gill v. Pexall Brocas and others (1625). Amussen and Underdown, *Gender, Culture and Politics*, 61–3.

16 For debt, see Burrows, *The Family of Brocas*, 215–6. Debts, and whether they have been properly paid, is at issue in a number of cases in which Pexall

was involved late in Elizabeth's reign: TNA, C 3/233/71 Brocas v Worsopp (1593); and TNA, C 3/223/22, Sir Pexall Brocas vs Sir John Danvers kt and another. The cases regarding land purchase and possible forgery include TNA, STAC 5/N17/11; STAC 5/B106/39; STAC 5/B17/19; and STAC 5/A48/ 32: there are references within testimony in these Star Chamber cases to cases in Chancery and Exchequer. For the quote, see TNA, STAC 5/A57/21, Bill of Complaint; for the pardon, see SP 38/7, f. 58v. Brocas (listed as Brockhurst) was one of a large group knighted by James on his arrival in London: John Nichols, *The Progresses, Processions, and Magnificent Festivities, of King James the First* (4 vols, London, 1828), i. 118.

17 TNA, STAC 5/A57/21, Attorney General v. Brocas & West; STAC 8/8/11: Attorney-General v. Brocas (1605); STAC 8/82/3: Sir Pexall Brocas v Thomas Brocas (1613); and SP 38/7, f. 58 v, 18 January 1604. For the allegations of 70 or more children, Burrows, *The Family of Brocas*, 221; John Chamberlain, *The Letters of John Chamberlain*, ed. Norman McClure (2 vols, Philadelphia: American Philosophical Society, 1939), i. 334.

18 TNA, STAC 8/20/10, Attorney-General v. Scullard, Hasker, Crooke, and others; this is related to the conflicts in STAC 8/67/16, Brocas v. Wilkinson, Wadloue, Morralle, and others: the case is in Star Chamber as a miscarriage of justice.

19 TNA, STAC 8/8/11 (Att.-Gen. v. Brocas); STAC 8/8/8 (Att.-Gen. v. [Edwardes] et al.); STAC 8/82/3 (Sir Pexall v. Thomas Brocas, 1613); and STAC 8/260/11 (Savage v. Lambert et al., 1621).

20 The cause of this case is unclear: we know of it only from Lord Chancellor Ellesmere's notes on the case, San Marino, California, Henry Huntington Library, EL 2786. He describes the suit as 'Sir Pexall Brocas v William Norton Ar., Robert Hyett, William Mistlebrook, John Arlatt, Richard Osborne, Luke Lessame, Mathewe Watts, Robert Wexton, John Philipps, John Crooke, William Mitten, Anthonie Denbigh, Richard Denbigh, Thomas Bloes, George Godwyne'. The hearing was held in May 1612 and refers to events that had occurred a previous summer. The notes appear to be based largely on depositions and interrogatories, for a missing Star Chamber case (or at least one that has escaped cataloguing). There is an earlier case between Brocas and Norton in TNA, STAC 8/75/20, Brocas v. Ward, Norton, Smart, Newman alias Newcombe (1607), in which Brocas alleged that Norton and his allies broke down hedges and pastured their cattle on his land.

21 William Gouge, *Of Domesticall Duties* (London, 1622), 651–2.

22 Christopher Brooks, 'Litigation, Participation, and Agency in Seventeenth and Eighteenth Century England', in David Lemmings (ed.), *The British and their Laws in the Eighteenth Century* (Woodbridge: The Boydell Press, 2005), 155–81; and Christopher W. Brooks, 'The Longitudinal Study of Civil Litigation in England, 1200–1996', in Wilfred Prest and Sharyn Roach Anleu (eds), *Litigation Past and Present* (Sydney: University of New South Wales Press, 2004), 24–43, esp. 27–34.

23 For the legal context, see Tim Stretton, 'Marriage, Separation and the Common Law in England, 1540–1660', in Helen Berry and Elizabeth Foyster (eds), *The Family in Early Modern England.* (Cambridge: Cambridge University Press, 2007), 18–39; Norf. R.O. Marie Beck con William Beck, DEP/10, Bk 10, June 1565, testimony of Margaret Goodwyn: Goodwyn continued to say William Beck was not 'so cruell or to hate hir so much that she should require further securitie of her life ... than other honest wifes have'.

198   *Susan D. Amussen*

24 For this process, see Amussen, *Ordered Society*, 123–9; Lawrence Stone, *The Road to Divorce: England, 1530–1987* (Oxford: Oxford University Press, 1990), 190–4; Foyster, *Manhood in Early Modern England*, 164–77; Tim Stretton, 'Contract and Conjugality in Early Modern England' in Lorna Hutson (ed.), *The Oxford Handbook of English Law and Literature 1500–1700* (Oxford: Oxford University Press, 2017), 410–30, esp. 414–6.

25 For an overview, see Martin Ingram, *Church Courts, Sex and Marriage in England, 1570–1640* (Cambridge: Cambridge University Press, 1988), 43–58.

26 John Taylor, *A New Discovery by Sea, With a Wherry from London to Salisbury* (London, 1623, STC 23778), sig. A3–A4. See also Amussen, 'Cuckold's Haven', 528–42; Douglas Bruster, 'The Horn of Plenty: Cuckoldry and Capital in the Drama of the Age of Shakespeare,' *Studies in English Literature*, 30 (1990), 195–216, esp. 195–7; Henry Machyn, *The Diary of Henry Machyn, Citizen and Merchant Taylor of London, From A.D. 1550–A.D. 1563*, edited by John Gough Nichols (London: Camden Society, 1848, reprinted New York: AMS Press, 1968), 283 (25 May 1562); and Edward Sugden, *A Topographical Dictionary to the Works of Shakespeare and His Fellow Dramatists* (Manchester: Manchester University Press, 1925), 140.

27 Claire McEachern, 'Why Do Cuckolds Have Horns', *Huntington Library Quarterly*, 71 (2008), 607–31, esp. 616–7.

28 Norf R.O. DEP/26, Holmes con Elmar, f. 315v; Wiltshire Record Office, Deans Peculiar, Presentments, 1609, no 18; TNA, STAC 8/152/7. Glovier con Warren et al.; F.G. Emmison, *Elizabethan Life: Morals and the Church Courts* (Chelmsford: Essex County Council, 1973), 127.

29 Norf. R.O. DEP 35, William Gray con Robert Nash, f. 21v.

30 TNA, STAC 8 140/29, Complaint of Edward Fosse, Yeoman.

31 Quoted in Laura Gowing, 'Gender and the Language of Insult in Early Modern London', *History Workshop Journal*, 35 (1993), 17.

32 Rose, 'Hunting, Sociability, and the Politics of Inclusion and Exclusion', 166–8.

33 Fox, 'Ballads, Libels, and Popular Ridicule', 47–83; Bellany and McRae (eds), 'Introduction', *Early Stuart Libels:* several of these libels, most of which are political, directed particularly at courtiers, include references to horns and cuckolds. See for example L10, Nv11, Oi5, Oii5, R8.

34 TNA, STAC 8/153/29, Gordon, Frances v. Auncell, Owen, and others, 1622/23.

35 TNA, STAC 8/150/5, Gobert alias Goborne v. Brewster (1605); STAC 8/150/4: Gobert v. Brewster, 1606. The quotations are taken from the bill of complaint in STAC 8/150/5.

36 Fox, 'Ballads, Libels, and Popular Ridicule', 47–83, esp. 74–5.

37 The text of the complaint in this case is quoted in Martin Ingram, 'Charivari and Shame Punishments: Folk Justice and State Justice in Early Modern England', in Herman Roodenburg, Petrus Cornelis Spierenburg, Clive Emsley, and Eric A Johnson (eds), *Social Control in Europe, 1500–1800* (Columbus, OH: Ohio State University Press, 2004), 297–8. See also Underdown, 'The Taming of the Scold', 130–1.

38 Ingram, 'Charivari and Shame Punishments', 297–8.

39 Somerset Record Office, CQ 3 1/86 (2), fol. 154.

40 TNA, STAC 8/240/19, Rosyer v. Quarrye, Hamont, and Horne, 1604.

41 Susan D. Amussen, '"Being Stirred to Much Unquietness": Violence and Domestic Violence in Early Modern England', *Journal of Women's History*, 6

(1994), 70–89. For a recent overview, see Joanne Bailey and Loreen Giese, 'Marital Cruelty: Reconsidering Lay Attitudes in England, c.1580 to 1850', *History of the Family*, 18 (2013), 289–305.

42 Norf. R.O., DEP 28, Anne Felmingham con Thomas Felmingham, ff. 401–3.

43 Norf. R.O., DEP 53, Robinson con. Robinson, 28 January 1696/7.

44 BL, Add MS 29974, Pitt Family Correspondence, ff. 168, 169v, 170, 172–3.

45 Norf. R.O., C/S3/27, 'Articles of misdemeanours against Thomas Vyolett, Gent and one Elizabeth Hewes his woman servant'.

9 They 'Know as Much at Thirteen as If They Had Been Mid-Wives of Twenty Years Standing'

Girls and Sexual Knowledge in Early Modern England

Sarah Toulalan

The title of this chapter references an assertion made in the late seventeenth-century satire *The Parliament of Women* (1684), about how girls acquired sexual knowledge by talking among themselves or reading popular printed books on the body and reproduction.[1] This, and other similar snippets, prompt questions about how young people acquired sexual knowledge in the past. They also have wider implications for considering how possession of such knowledge may have affected perceptions of a girl's modesty and chastity. The fictional comment that girls 'know as much at Thirteen as if they had been Mid-wives of twenty years standing,' was, of course, an exaggeration made for a literary effect to underscore the potential dangers of female literacy. It is nevertheless indicative of how print literature concerning sexual matters – whether in books of midwifery that described the generative organs and their role in conception, or erotic and pornographic literature – could be regarded as dangerous because it incited immoral thoughts and behaviour. For example, Nicholas Culpeper's work on midwifery was judged obscene by some commentators and was listed, among other well-known books of midwifery, by the author of *The Practical Part of Love* (1660), as reading kept in a brothel for perusal by its customers. This was presumably because it was believed to arouse sexual desire as well as provide information about sex and bodies.[2] The identification of girls aged thirteen as having the knowledge expected of experienced midwives was significant because it raised the possibility that sexual knowledge could corrupt girls reaching sexual maturity, making them vulnerable to seduction, affecting not only their moral state but also their future prospects.

Reports of trials for sexual assault and rape of girls that were held at the Old Bailey in London during the late seventeenth and eighteenth centuries provide evidence for what girls knew – or did not know – about sex and bodies. They also show that knowledge of these matters varied according to age.[3] This evidence suggests that once girls were over the

Girls and Sexual Knowledge 201

age of ten, when consent became an issue in trials for rape, the extent and nature of their sexual knowledge could matter in securing guilty verdicts. Informing these legal proceedings were gender norms that created expectations that girls should be modest and chaste. A girl's reputation for immodesty or sexual immorality could undermine an accusation of rape in a legal case by potentially influencing how she, and her testimony, was perceived by the court. In these trials, evidence about the personal reputation of both the victim and the accused was considered relevant, and witnesses for both parties could be called to provide testimony about the character of the individuals involved in order to influence a jury's verdict.[4] Although for an accused man his prior sexual behaviour was only one component of his reputation, for a woman the most important factor affecting her character was whether she was regarded as modest and chaste by her community. Such classifications were largely based on perceptions rather than fact. Yet, as Faramerz Dabhoiwala has noted, in the early modern mind 'unchastity always betrayed itself in every aspect of a woman's behaviour'.[5]

This chapter investigates how far we can establish the extent of young girls' exclusion from the knowledge of sex by examining their testimonies as reported in trials for rape and sexual assault held at the Old Bailey in London between 1674 and 1799. It analyses the reported testimony of girls aged under ten up to the age of fourteen to establish the changing nature and extent of their sexual knowledge. It also compares their testimonies with those of girls and women aged over fourteen to draw conclusions about differences in their sexual knowledge. Particular attention is paid to differences in the words and phrases to describe sexual parts of the body used in such accounts according to age. Of three hundred and six trials for rape held at the Old Bailey between 1674 and 1799, around two-thirds mention the age of the complainant. When age was mentioned, it usually indicated that the complainant was young or, in one case, very old.[6] Girls aged fourteen or under comprise just over half of the total number of complainants, yet they account for more than eighty per cent of those for whom ages are noted. The remaining twenty per cent, except for three women aged twenty-seven, thirty-two, and eighty, were aged between fifteen and twenty.

Although in her study of early modern English rape trials Garthine Walker suggests that 'depositions were likely to have been transcribed by clerks more or less verbatim', analysis of these reports is complicated by the fact that what girls may have said in a pre-trial deposition, or in the courtroom itself, was filtered through those who recorded their testimonies.[7] Short, summary reports of trials often reproduced testimony as a linear narrative. However, evidence was not given in this way in court, as it was elicited through questioning. As stated in a 1754 rape trial report: 'This was the substance of her many broken answers to many questions put to her, as to the fact.'[8] Although this is the only

202 Sarah Toulalan

report to explain that the child's testimony had been compressed – with the questions omitted, and the answers running together as if they were a coherent narrative – it is not the only one to have been crafted in this fashion. It is also clear that in some testimonies words and phrases have been substituted for the child's own, especially legal phrases that were unlikely to be known to children, such as 'had carnal knowledge of her body'. However, those reporting the trials for rape and sexual assault at the Old Bailey did not always substitute such standard terminology for sex when reporting the words of these girls during a trial. We can thus surmise that when the language attributed to the young deponents deviated from the usual legal formulations, and from the descriptions used by girls and women aged over fourteen, they are likely to be those that were actually used by the girls when giving their evidence. Accordingly, although they may have been mediated, these words and phrases tell us something about the nature and extent of the sexual knowledge of younger girls, just as the language used by counsel in their questions can tell us what they expected girls of these ages to know and understand. The chapter first discusses contemporary cultures of sexual knowledge and knowledge exchange before moving on to explore how sexual knowledge and sexual consent were revealed in court testimony.

Sexual Knowledge Cultures and Exchange

Knowledge of sex was a deeply problematic subject for early modern people, especially medical authors who wished to include the latest thinking about issues to do with sex and reproduction in books of anatomy, medicine, health, and midwifery.[9] These authors risked accusations of obscenity and violation of contemporary moral and social boundaries, albeit with the stated intention of educating readers rather than of arousing them sexually. Their anticipated audience were primarily other educated 'sober minded' men, like themselves, who would benefit from such knowledge.[10] Midwifery books, such as Jane Sharp's *Midwives Book* (1671) and Martha Mears's *The Pupil of Nature* (1797), might also be aimed at midwives and married women who needed to understand the sexual body to deliver infants in the birthing chamber successfully, or to treat reproductive, venereal, and gynaecological disorders with home-made remedies produced from medicinal recipes.[11] Such knowledge was usually acquired through experience and practice – artisanal training methods – rather than through formal education and reading. Midwives were expected to be married women or widows who learned their trade through apprenticeship to another experienced practising midwife.[12] Women married to surgeons may have also provided medical assistance to their husbands when treating female patients with venereal disease, or, in some cases, continued this practice as widows.

Girls and Sexual Knowledge 203

The promise of examination by another woman would likely have been appealing to female clients as it would have enabled them to preserve their modesty.[13] Some midwifery books were aimed at female midwives and married women because they were not expected to possess the theoretical and anatomical knowledge that came with a medical education, which was increasingly thought to be essential for ensuring successful deliveries. Edward Chapman noted in the preface to his *Treatise on the Improvement of Midwifery* (1735), that many of the fatal mistakes he had seen committed by midwives during the twenty-seven years of his practice might have been avoided 'had they ever read a Treatise so well adapted to their capacities, and at the same time so full and plain'.[14] The reference in *The Parliament of Women* to girls of thirteen being as knowledgeable as midwives worked as satire precisely because such girls did not belong to the category of legitimate, sexually knowledgeable women.

Young and unmarried women were not expected to engage in sexual behaviour before marriage and were thus excluded from sexual knowledge. A group of women who defied this expectation were prostitutes and bawds, who were extremely sexually knowledgeable and were considered morally suspect as a result.[15] Their understanding of sex was understood to be experiential rather than theoretical in origin. Pornographic and erotic texts played on this conceit by deploying characters or narrators who were either prostitutes or older, experienced, married women, who taught younger women about sex. For example, in Nicolas Chorier's *Aloisiæ Sigæae Toletanæ Satyra Sotadica de arcanis Amoris, et Veneris*, first published in Latin in c.1659/60, and translated into vernacular languages to reach a wider European audience, the pornographic dialogues take place in a domestic setting among women from the upper social ranks rather than between prostitutes. In this book, a young married woman, Tullia, teaches her about-to-be married fifteen-year-old cousin Ottavia about sex by verbal and practical instruction about the sexual parts of the body and the nature of coitus, including through recounting stories about her own sexual experiences.[16]

There has recently been much scholarly interest in the production and exchange of knowledge in the early modern period and eighteenth century. The Enlightenment, in particular, has been identified as 'the dawn of that great epoch of knowledge making'.[17] The ways in which knowledge was made, and made known, have been studied concerning both material culture and the social networks through which theories, ideas, and facts were exchanged and debated, gradually passing into wider acceptance.[18] Some scholars have also paid attention to the spread of literacy and learning, and the institutions that supported their growth. Others have studied the oral cultures through which knowledge circulated among those whose literacy was limited.[19] Despite women's generally lower rates of literacy, recent scholarship has demonstrated that they actively participated in knowledge creation and exchange through social networks, both hetero- and homo-social. It has also shown how female spheres of activity shaped women's knowledge.[20] This could have negative consequences. As Mario DiGangi has remarked, 'the premise that common intimacy and common speech among women could promote unchaste sexuality understandably generated patriarchal anxiety'.[21]

Young girls and other unmarried single women were generally excluded from the socially and culturally sanctioned female-dominated spheres in which sexual matters were discussed, and knowledge disseminated, such as the birthing chamber, juries of matrons, and midwifery. Despite the implication in *The Parliament of Women* that young girls might gain sexual knowledge through reading books of midwifery, or other popular works that addressed sexual issues, the published Old Bailey trial reports discussed in this chapter do not indicate that girls, when demonstrating knowledge of sex or sexual language, gained it through their reading. This may have been because the courts were simply not concerned with the origins of a girl's knowledge or because an absence of literacy and learning was assumed for the girls who made these complaints of rape since they were overwhelmingly from the servant, labouring, trade, and artisanal ranks of society.[22]

Given the social background of girls whose accusations of rape and sexual assault resulted in a prosecution, it is likely that most did not read or have the wherewithal to purchase the reading matter that might provide them with such knowledge. That said, it cannot be ruled out altogether as many were domestic servants who could have had access to printed matter through their domestic arrangements or working lives.[23] Traditional histories of literacy during this period suggest that the majority of the population did not possess basic literacy (the ability to read, if not to write), that those lower down the social scale and living in rural areas were less likely to possess such skills, and that women had much lower rates of literacy than men.[24] However, more recent work on women's literacy in early modern London indicates that more girls were likely to have learned to read than previously estimated.[25] Moreover, some evidence of reading and the circulation of pornographic or erotic texts among younger female readers has provided hints that a few girls from higher social ranks may have obtained reading matter about sex.[26] It has been noted that those lower down the social scale could have acquired this knowledge from observation of animals or overhearing a ribald conversation between adults.[27] Some reports, both from the Old Bailey and provincial newspapers, show that some girls were raped and sexually assaulted by schoolmasters while at school, or by someone they encountered while making their way to or from a school. This suggests that these girls may have been literate or in the process of acquiring literacy.[28] Nevertheless, there are very few indications in the Old Bailey

Sessions Papers of the origins of girls' sexual knowledge, nor from where they learned the words and phrases they used in their testimonies.

Young women's sexual knowledge has most commonly been investigated through their experiences of courtship, seduction, and as victims of male sexual predation.[29] Some scholars have looked at the literature of advice that was aimed at young people. However, the sexual advice contained therein, while acknowledging young people's sexual desires, simply urged chastity, avoidance of bad company, and the exercise of self-restraint.[30] Yet, very little has been surmised about how and when girls acquired knowledge of sex in terms of their use and understanding of sexual language, what they may have known about the functions and uses of the sexual parts of the body, and how far they may have understood the social and moral significance of such knowledge. The discussion below addresses this lacuna through a detailed exploration of these issues as revealed in girls' court testimonies.

Sexual Knowledge and Sexual Consent

The extent of girl's exclusion from knowledge about sex and sexual parts of the body was a key issue in many trials concerning rape and sexual assault from the Old Bailey during the period under discussion. If a girl was under the age of ten, her understanding of what had been done to her did not matter for the purposes of the prosecution. This was because consent was not an issue for the court in achieving a conviction. The second statute of Westminster of 1576 set the age of consent for prosecuting rape as a felony at ten, reducing it from the age of twelve, which had previously corresponded with the age of consent for a girl to marry.[31] There seems to have been an assumption that before the age of ten a girl was not only likely to be ignorant of sexual matters, but would also have no understanding of them. The *Ordinary's Account* of the trial of Steven Arrowsmith in December 1678 made precisely this point. It noted: 'it being Death by the Law to have Carnal knowledge of any Female childe under Ten years of age, even although with her consent: which from those so young is reasonably presum'd to proceed from an innocent Indiscretion and Ignorance of what they are tempted to.'[32]

Similar interpretations were offered throughout the eighteenth century, and the legal guidance published in 1794 stated that consent was 'immaterial' for a girl under the age of ten 'by reason of her tender years she is incapable of judgment and discretion'.[33] However, once a girl was over the age of ten, the question of whether or not she had consented to sexual activity was very important to the outcome of a trial. This can be seen in the trial of John Hunter for the rape of ten-year-old Grace Pitts in 1747. In this case, Hunter was acquitted because there was neither evidence of violence nor proof that Grace had resisted: her testimony showed that she went with him willingly into the room where she sat

206 *Sarah Toulalan*

upon his lap and acquiesced in exchange for an orange.[34] It is clear from the trial report that the jury were unhappy that they had to consider the question of her consent. They had to be reminded by the judge that the age of consent was set at ten – whether or not they thought this was appropriate – even if they believed that Grace's consent had been obtained by 'delusion and deceit'.[35]

Indications of a girl's sexual awareness included the ability to use the correct words for sexual body parts. This was believed to indicate knowledge of sex and thus implied that she might understand the activities to which she was being asked to consent. Indeed, demonstrating sexual knowledge could make a difference in how a girl's behaviour was interpreted and could influence the court's decision in judging whether she had consented. The cultural exclusion of girls from sexual knowledge meant that if a girl revealed that she had knowledge of sex there might be some doubt raised about the extent of her modesty and chastity. In turn, girls' demonstration of sexual knowledge, presumably learned through reading or prior sexual experience, could call into question the legitimacy of their testimony and thus their denial of consent. As Walker has observed, consciously spoken sexual language revealed sexual knowledge that might further imply complicity.[36] Such knowledge was problematic as it should have been restricted to married women and learned within the marriage bed.

A girl's admission of sexual knowledge, or an indication that she was knowledgeable about such matters, could suggest a potential lack of modesty or chastity. If not raising suspicions of previous sexual activity, her knowledge might, at the very least, suggest that she engaged in immodest discourse in which sexual matters were discussed or bawdy talk and jokes were exchanged. This was in a context where women's loose talk aroused suspicions of correspondingly loose behaviour. It can be surmised from at least one case – for deception and perjury following a trial for rape – that girls became familiar with specific words to do with sex from talking among themselves, especially from conversations with older girls. Elizabeth Broadben and Rachel Hannet, both aged fourteen, accused John Baynham of rape and Sarah Clifton of acting as his accessory in 1755, but after the accused were acquitted, the two girls confessed that they had been coerced by their master, Charles Wiesenthall (or Wirsanthall), into giving false evidence. It was stated that they 'denied all they had sworn, and said, Their master had debauched them, and put them upon swearing as they did'.[37] Broadben and Hannet were two of nine girls aged between ten and sixteen employed as apprentices and living in Wirsanthall's house. The girls who were called to give evidence at Wirsanthall's trial for deception and perjury all used the same word to refer to sex: 'impudence'.[38]

The words 'impudent' or 'impudence' were particularly associated with sex because they described shameless and immodest behaviour.

These terms were also used to refer to sexual behaviour directed towards a girl, or as another word for penis.[39] Two of the other girls who gave evidence at Wirsanthall's trial, one aged ten and the other thirteen, both used the word 'impudence' to refer to sex. They both said that this was what Rachel Hannet, aged fourteen, had told them had been done to her. Ann Forbes, aged nearly eleven testified, 'She said he had done impudence with her'. Esther Crosier, aged thirteen, likewise confirmed that 'She said he did impudence to her'. Only Esther was asked to clarify what she meant by this and so explained that she had understood that 'He lay with her'. Esther's clarification suggests that, at the age of thirteen, she was aware that 'impudence' was a term that referred to sex, and she also knew that there were other perhaps more commonly used terms to describe such an act.[40] The court's request for clarification of what they meant by 'impudence' also implies that it could be interpreted in other ways, perhaps as behaviour that was sexual but that did not necessarily go as far as intercourse. The repeated use of the word 'impudence' for sex among this small group of girls nevertheless suggests that conversations were at least one way through which girls learned a vocabulary of sex and came to understand what sexual acts involved. They gained this sort of understanding around the ages associated with physical sexual development.

Sexual Knowledge and Court Testimony

The discussion in this section argues that young girls' testimonies, recorded during prosecutions for their rape and sexual assault, demonstrate that girls acquired sexual knowledge in stages, as their vocabulary for sex and the sexual parts varied according to age. There were often – although not always – differences in the level of detail that children and girls in their early teens gave in their testimony in court about what had happened to them sexually. This was in comparison to what was asked of married women or widows, who might tell the court only that another man had done to her what her husband did. This difference can be explained by expectations of female modesty when speaking about sexual matters in a public space. Indeed, Walker argues that it doubly compromised a woman's chastity if she spoke openly about sex. So, when giving testimony, women emphasised issues other than the sexual act itself: the violence, the struggle, the inability to keep resisting.[41]

Reports of rape trials held at the Old Bailey show that modesty constrained some girls and women from going into detail about what had happened to them. This was a problem because, without evidence of exactly what had been done, the accused could not be convicted. In the report of the trial of Philip Roberts for the rape of Jane Harris, aged twelve, in December 1683, it was recorded that: 'The Girl her self, also her Mother, and a Midwife gave some Evidence against him; but either their

208 *Sarah Toulalan*

over-much modesty, or for some other reason, it was so favourable, that no positive Proof being thereof, he was Acquitted.'[42] But, as Laura Gowing has noted, 'modesty had to be learned', and younger girls may not have been so reticent because they did not yet fully comprehend that they should not speak openly about sexual matters.[43] Expectations about different levels of sexual knowledge also account for this difference in the nature of the testimony, for when younger girls did not know or understand sexual terms or acts they were often asked to describe them in more detail in order to make it clear to the court exactly what had been done to them. The earlier discussion of the use of the word 'impudence' shows how the court sought clarification of a term or phrase that might have had more than one meaning or inference. They thus needed to be certain that those giving testimony both understood that it was referring to sexual intercourse *and* were using it with that meaning. Walker notes that 'the lack of attention to a graphic description of the details of sexual intercourse was a consequence of what was perceived to be unproblematic', but the opposite was also true in cases concerning sexual violence against girls, since attention was paid to what *was* seen as problematic.[44]

It was expected that older girls and women would understand what was meant by phrases such as 'lay with you' or 'had carnal knowledge', while younger ones would not. Thus, an older married woman could be asked to clarify her statement that 'the Prisoner lay with me' in quite general terms in the expectation that she would know exactly what it meant, placing it specifically in the context of marital sex. For example, in 1746, Mary Irish was asked: 'I find you are a marry'd Woman, you understand what is meant by lying with you. Had he Knowledge of your Body, as your Husband had?'[45] However, the court expected that much younger, especially prepubescent, girls would have no knowledge of either the language used to talk about sexual intercourse or of what such language might actually mean. As we shall see, younger girls were questioned more closely about the details of exactly what a man had done to their bodies so that it could be clearly established to the court that full sexual intercourse – penetrative sex with ejaculation – had taken place.

Younger girls often did not have a term for sexual intercourse, suggesting that they had no knowledge of the sexual act that had occurred. They also often referred to genitalia only in relation to the excretory function of urination, indicating that they were unaware that they had another – sexual – purpose. However, it is not always possible to relate testimony to a trial verdict. This is because in some cases, reports are not complete verbatim transcripts of what was said in court, especially for those that took place in the late seventeenth and early eighteenth centuries. The verdict is also not always explained.

The age of consent for the purpose of prosecuting rape in seventeenth- and eighteenth-century England did not align neatly with contemporary ideas about the boundaries of childhood, particularly as marked by sexual development at puberty. Although the 1576 Westminster statute set the age of consent for prosecuting rape as a felony at ten, girls' sexual development was generally believed to happen around fourteen, or later. Girls aged between ten and fourteen were still considered unready for sex because they were not menstruating regularly and were thus believed to lack the lubrication necessary to enable penetrative sex. Consequently, they would also be thought to lack sexual awareness, as sexual feelings and desire were understood to be prompted by puberty. This meant that there was a 'grey area' between the ages of ten and fourteen when a young girl was legally able to consent to sexual intercourse but was unlikely to have undergone the sexual development of puberty or to understand fully what sex was.[46]

In contrast to prepubescent girls who did not yet have a vocabulary of sex, phrases used by older girls and married women to describe rape usually tended to designate it in terms that were commonly used for sexual intercourse. Sarah, wife of Charles Denman, and a mother of four children, for example, testified that he 'got his ends of me; that is, he was concerned with me', and then later that 'He had carnal knowledge of my body to all intents and purposes'.[47] Similarly, Elizabeth Worsley, wife of Joseph Worsley, who accused Christopher Pearson of raping her in June 1766, said that at first he 'did not get his end on me', but the following week 'he had his will'.[48] The youngest girl who testified using these phrases was twelve, suggesting that she had acquired an understanding of what such acts meant. Elizabeth Upington described as 'an infant of twelve years and upwards', told the court that Elizabeth Crew put William Page to lie with her but 'he could not have his will of me that way, and he put his finger up my body'.[49] This phrasing suggests that Elizabeth had some understanding of what sex involved, and how it might be spoken about.

Girls under the age of twelve (and some above) do not seem to have had this sexual vocabulary. They therefore often gave more detailed accounts of what was done to them, which indicated that penetration had taken place, despite not being able to name the act. Girls may have said that 'something' was put into them, but they did not know what it was. Mary Faucet, aged nine, testified that John Cannon 'threw me on the Bed, took up my Coats and unbutton'd his Breeches, and put something into me, – I don't know what it was'.[50] She was asked to clarify where exactly this 'something' was put into her, but she either did not know the right words or did not want to use the words she knew, because she appears to have pointed to her body, saying, 'He put it in here'.[51] Similarly, in 1747, ten-year-old Grace Pitts seemed not to understand what John Hunter had done to her. She told the court under questioning from counsel that Hunter 'shut the Door and used me ill; he set himself down in the Chair, and pulled something out of his Breeches, and pulled me to him'.[52] After further questioning about whether she

210 *Sarah Toulalan*

had been hurt by it and why she did not cry out, Grace was asked again, more directly, if she knew what had been done to her: 'Was you sensible all this Time what he did to you? if you was not sensible, how could you tell that it hurt you?', to which she replied, 'I was sensible it hurt me, but was not sensible what it was'. Her sexual ignorance, and hence her sexual innocence and prior chastity, were thus established for the court. This evidence of her lack of knowledge also explains why the jury in this particular trial appeared to find it difficult to accept that she was able to consent to intercourse with Hunter, which allowed his acquittal. Her testimony indicated ignorance of sex and sexual consent, but as she was just over the age of ten, the absence of evidence of force, combined with her implicit consent – she willingly went with him and sat in his lap because he promised her an orange – had to be accepted by the court.[53]

The same word – 'something' – was also used by a slightly older girl, Hepzibah Dover, aged thirteen. Hepzibah's mother testified that her daughter had told her that William Garner, a carpenter to whom she had been sent to fetch some shavings, 'bid me come up stairs, and he laid me down upon my back, and pulled up my petticoats, and put something into my body'.[54] We cannot know if she would have used the same word herself in court because the trial report indicates that she was asked directly: 'What did he do when he laid down upon you? Did he put his private parts into your body?'; Hepzibah merely responded 'Yes'. However, this does indicate that by the time she came to testify in court, three months after her rape, she knew that the 'something' he put into her body was 'his private parts', even if she may not have understood this at the time of the crime. However, the direct question indicates an expectation that, at the age of thirteen, she would know whether or not he had used this part of his body. An older girl or woman might use a very similar word – 'thing' – but, if they did, they were using it specifically as another word for penis, in line with common usage at this time.[55] In 1768, nineteen-year-old Mary Brickinshaw told the court that John Sheridan 'lay with me', and then, when asked to be more specific, said that 'He put his thing into me'.[56] The term 'his thing' was understood as referring specifically to the penis, whereas the more general term 'something' indicated a young girl's ignorance of what exactly it was that a man used to enter her body.

The descriptions that some girls gave of their injured body parts demonstrate that they only associated this part of the body with urination. This suggests that they may not have known that they had other functions – sexual and reproductive – nor that there were other specific terms for the parts that performed these functions. In January 1721, seven-year-old Mary Tabor told her mother that William Robbins 'put his Finger into the Place where she made Water, and also put the thing with which he made Water, into the Place where she made Water'.[57] Such lack of knowledge about the sexual use of body parts

Girls and Sexual Knowledge   211

was indicative of a broader ignorance about sex: what it was and what it might be for. This formulation is likely to be the child's own words because other, more formulaic language was not included in the trial report, as it clearly had been on other occasions. The report of the trial of William Stringer for the rape of Jane Field aged seven, for example, summarises Field's evidence and uses the words 'private parts' to refer to the man's genitals: 'The child was examined, but not upon oath, who said she carried a pot down into the cellar, the prisoner there took her and set her on a box and kissed her, and put his private parts to her's, but did not put it into her.'[58]

By the age of twelve, some girls seem to have had words for sexual parts and an awareness that there was something shameful and wrong about what had been done to them. Martha Chalkley, aged twelve, at first answered the question about what Richard Knibb put into her body by saying, 'It was his nastiness'. When asked what she meant 'by that word', she said that she meant his 'y[ar]d'.[59] Martha's use of these two words – 'nastiness' and 'yard' – shows that she *did* know the correct word for a man's penis, even if she used another more colloquial and childish word first. Her initial use of the euphemism 'nastiness' also indicates some awareness that it was not acceptable to name the male sexual organ in public as she at first avoided using the correct term. The euphemism itself further implies that she was aware that there was something distasteful about this body part and the sexual use to which it had been put. Martha does seem to have had some understanding that sexual activity was not acceptable because, when asked why she did not tell her mother of the alleged rape, she said that it was 'Because I was asham'd to speak of it'.[60] At the age of twelve, Martha understood that sexual body parts, and the behaviours associated with them, were shameful and that it was not acceptable for her to speak of sexual matters, whether privately to her mother or publicly in a court of law. The shame associated with actions involving these parts of the body might also be indicated by other euphemistic terms used by girls in their early teens. A witness at the trial in July 1772 of John Coates for the rape of twelve-year-old Anna Dixon, said that Anna had told her that her master had 'got on me while I was asleep' and that 'he came again, and did you know what'.[61] Anna seems to have been aware that this behaviour was wrong and might harm her reputation as she also told a witness that 'she was ruined'.[62]

By the age of fourteen girls seem to have had some knowledge of bodies and sex, even if it does not appear to be fully complete. When fourteen-year-old Elizabeth Broadben was asked, 'What did the man do?', she answered, 'He put his private parts upon me at first'. When pressed further about what more he did, she responded, 'Then he put his hands upon my private parts; he put his fingers into my private parts'.[63] Whether or not Elizabeth herself used the term 'private parts' or if it was

212   *Sarah Toulalan*

substituted by the author of the trial report for her actual words cannot be established. It nevertheless indicates that she had used a specific term rather than a more generalised reference to 'something'. She had knowledge that these were particular body parts which she might name, but her knowledge appeared to be limited to only being able to name the parts. Indeed, she did not seem to be aware that the male 'private parts' had another function in addition to the non-sexual one of urination. When asked 'Did you observe any thing come from him?', she seemed not to understand that she was being asked about emission as her response was at first negative. But on being pressed further as to whether she found 'any thing particular' she replied, 'He made water upon me'. This answer again suggests that, like much younger girls, the only thing wet that she knew came from a man's private parts was urine or 'water'. She did not yet know that men ejaculated during sex, which might lead to pregnancy if she had begun to menstruate.

The question of seminal emission is thus another way of assessing the extent of a girl's sexual knowledge. During trials, girls were pressed to clarify whether or not emission, as well as penetration, had taken place. When married women, midwives, surgeons, or other medical practitioners were asked to give their opinion about whether, in their view, ejaculation had occurred or was necessary to communicate a venereal infection, the court was explicit, asking either about 'Emissio Seminis' or 'whether there was an Emission of Seed'.[64] At the trial of Joseph York, for the rape of nine-year-old Elizabeth Long in 1732, the Apothecary, John Smith, who was called to give evidence about her venereal disease was asked directly if emission was needed to cause such an infection: 'Could it be contracted without an Emissio Seminis on the Part of the Boy? You understand me?'; Smith responded, 'I believe – it might'. It was important to establish this information, as it would constitute further evidence of rape. However, medical evidence was frequently elicited to show that the contrary was in fact the case: neither penetration nor emission were needed to transmit a venereal disease. Such an infection was evidence of sexual contact of some kind, but not necessarily of rape. This is because medical practitioners asserted that an infection could be transmitted by 'impure cohesion' alone, that is, by 'foul' matter coming into contact with the genitals through external contact only.[65] A surgeon, William Barrel, in 1768 testified at the trial of William Allam for the rape of eight-year-old Elizabeth Hall that 'the disorder is communicable, if the two parts touch one another'.[66] However, when younger girls were asked about emission, the court seemed to anticipate that they would not understand the terms used for this aspect of the sexual act. Girls were instead asked whether they felt anything come from the man that was wet, or whether they perceived 'any Thing else'.[67]

Questioning about emission was intended to establish whether the sexual act had been completed because the man had ejaculated.

Girls and Sexual Knowledge 213

Although not always specified in discussions of rape law, William Hawkins's *Treatise of the Pleas of the Crown* (1739), defined rape as including 'some Degree of penetration, and also of Emission'.[68] Similarly, medical writing understood sex, for the purposes of procreation, as completed by the ejaculation of male seed. Medical authors who subscribed to both Aristotelian and Galenic-Hippocratic models of conception understood the male ejaculate as the principal generative material that acted upon the female matter to form and shape the foetus.[69] These classical models of reproduction persisted into the eighteenth century alongside new theories about egg-producing ovaries in women, and the observation of 'animalcules' in sperm, that continued to emphasise the primacy of the male ejaculate.[70] Male emission was thus understood in law and medicine, as well as more widely in society, as signifying the completion of sexual intercourse.

The difference in the nature of the questions asked to establish emission implies an expectation that an older woman, especially one who was married, or who had been married, would be able to confirm to the court precisely what had taken place. Betteridge May, the wife of John May, was asked, 'Did he do all that was necessary on his part towards getting a Child?' This question implied that she would know that he would have had to ejaculate to complete the act and for pregnancy to result.[71] Similarly, in 1755, a widow, Sarah Robertson, who told the court that she was certain that she was not pregnant after being raped by Benjamin Jones, was asked: 'Then he did not lay with you in so complete a manner as your husband did?' It was expected that a widow, sexually knowledgeable from her married life, would know and understand what was involved in sexual intercourse and for conception to occur. This questioning stands in contrast to that of twelve-year-old Anna Dixon who was pressed several times on the issue of emission. She was first asked: 'Did you perceive any thing besides something hard?' Then, after she said no, was asked, 'You did not perceive any thing after he got off you?' Anna clearly did not understand what counsel was seeking to find out with this line of questioning, as she replied that she was 'sore two or three days'. Finally, she was asked again, more explicitly: 'Was nothing left behind when he got off?' It is possible that her master, John Coates, who she had accused of rape, did not climax, but it is equally plausible that Anna simply had no idea what she was being asked. Seventeen-year-old Mary Warnett, though, seems to have understood the question of whether she felt anything come from Thomas Meller when she testified against him at his trial in June 1769, as she answered directly, albeit to say that she was not sure: 'With the horror and fright I was in. I do not know whether I felt any thing come from him or no'.[72] When further pressed on this issue, her response again directly addressed the question, suggesting that she understood what was being asked of her: 'I believe I felt something come from him then; but I was in such horror, I thought

214 *Sarah Toulalan*

he would have killed me; with the fright, I am not certain.'[73] The absence of a request for further clarification likely indicates that the court found this response unproblematic and was satisfied that she had understood the nature of the question.

As I have shown elsewhere, there were a handful of trials in which testimony was elicited from witnesses about young girls' chastity and modesty. This indicates the possibility that girls, even as young as ten or eleven, were believed to have some sexual understanding.[74] The testimony of a witness in one of these trials, that of Julian Brown accused of raping Susan Marshall, aged eleven, in 1735, suggests that Susan knew how babies were made and that she may have engaged in sexual play. This testimony undermined perceptions of her as the innocent victim of an older man who had left her 'torn' and infected with venereal disease from a forcible penetration. The witness testified that she had heard Susan talking and laughing with another girl about 'how they had served two Boys, and this Girl said, I paid his Shins with the Fire-shovel, I love to play at Man and Wife, but I do not like him'. Another witness testified that Susan had told her that Brown 'had had to do with her' and, when asked why she had not cried out, replied: 'Because, says she, he gave me a Dram of Anniseed, and I shall have a pretty Baby of my own to nurse, and that will be better than crying out.'[75] This evidence clearly indicated that Susan had some idea about what it was that married men and women did together and that what they did would produce a child. But the evidence about what Susan had said may also have been even more damaging to perceptions of her character because it appeared to show her shamelessly declaring that she would have a baby without being married. It is not possible to ascertain how far this evidence influenced the jury's decision to acquit Brown, especially as there was other evidence that undermined the accusation of rape. Other likely influential evidence included the testimony of a surgeon that Brown did not have a venereal infection. The indication of sexual knowledge allegedly displayed by Susan Marshall, however, seems to have been unusual for a girl of that age.

Conclusion

This chapter has established the nature and extent of girls' knowledge about sex as revealed through their testimonies in court during trials for rape and sexual assault. It has been argued that between the ages of ten and fourteen there was a gradual shift from a lack of sexual awareness or understanding about what sex was, including the sexual function of the 'private parts', to some knowledge of terms for sex and what these might mean. Without understanding the terms for sexual intercourse, younger girls often had to provide more detailed descriptions of what was done to them than older girls and women. This evidence was necessary for the

Girls and Sexual Knowledge 215

court to establish to its satisfaction whether penetration and emission had taken place so that a charge of rape might be substantiated. Girls, some even up to the age of fourteen, did not always know that the 'private parts' had a function other than for urination. Therefore, they continued to describe seminal emission as 'making water', indicating that their knowledge was still limited, even if they knew the correct terms to use for these body parts and had words or phrases for sexual intercourse. The knowledge supposedly demonstrated by eleven-year-old Susan Marshall, that 'to play at Man and Wife' could produce a child, seems to have been unusual, and potentially negatively influenced perceptions of her in court. Women were understood to acquire sexual knowledge through experience rather than formal education. Accordingly, signs of sexual knowledge could be interpreted as potential indicators of prior sexual experience. The cultural exclusion of girls from the spaces and networks in which sexual knowledge was exchanged meant that possession of such knowledge could negatively affect perceptions of their chastity, potentially influencing the outcome of a trial. However, a demonstrable lack of sexual knowledge did not mean that younger girls were excluded from the courtroom and the prosecution of sexual crime because they did not have the 'correct' terminology. Instead, their ignorance of a formal vocabulary of sex facilitated a more explicit picture of what had happened to be painted for the court, whilst also confirming their status as innocent children without sexual awareness or understanding.

Notes

1 Anon., *The Parliament of Women: Or, a Compleat History of the Proceedings and Debates, Of a particular Junto, of Ladies and Gentlewomen, With a design to alter the Government of the World. By way of Satyr* (n.p., 1684), 29.

2 Sarah Toulalan, 'Pornography, Procreation and Pleasure in Early Modern England', in Bradford K. Mudge (ed.), *The Cambridge Companion to Erotic Literature* (Cambridge: Cambridge University Press, 2017), 105–22, 110. On the dangers of erotic literature see Karen Harvey, *Reading Sex in the Eighteenth Century: Bodies and Gender in English Erotic Culture* (Cambridge: Cambridge University Press, 2005), 46–50; Sarah Toulalan, *Imagining Sex: Pornography and Bodies in Seventeenth-Century England* (Oxford: Oxford University Press, 2007), 52–6; James Grantham Turner, *Schooling Sex: Libertine Literature and Erotic Education in Italy, France, and England 1534–1685* (Oxford: Oxford University Press, 2003). On women's reading more generally see, for example, Jacqueline Pearson, 'Women Reading, Reading Women', in Helen Wilcox (ed.), *Women and Literature in Britain 1500–1700* (Cambridge: Cambridge University Press, 1996), 80–99.

3 The Old Bailey Sessions Papers are pamphlets that give an account of trials from each session held at the Old Bailey surviving from 1674 and published regularly until April 1913, available online as *The Proceedings of the*

216 *Sarah Toulalan*

Old Bailey – London's Central Criminal Court, 1674–1913: Old Bailey Proceedings Online (www.oldbaileyonline.org, version 8.0) (hereafter OBP).

4 On the importance of male reputation in defence of an accusation of rape see, for example, my discussion of George Tennant's prosecution for the rape of Mary Craggs, aged 9, in Sarah Toulalan, '"Is He a Licentious Lewd Sort of a Person?" Constructing the Child Rapist in Early Modern England', *Journal of the History of Sexuality*, 23 (2014), 21–52, 36, 47–51.

5 Laura Gowing, *Domestic Dangers: Women, Words, and Sex in Early Modern London* (Oxford: Oxford University Press, 1996), 2–4, 61–2; Faramerz Dabhoiwala, 'The Construction of Honour, Reputation and Status in Late Seventeenth- and Early Eighteenth-century England', *Transactions of the Royal Historical Society*, 6 (1996), 201–13, 207.

6 The victim, Sibila May, was aged 'about eighty years old'. OBP, October 1683, trial of William Williams (t16831010a-11).

7 On the proceedings and their problems see John H. Langbein, 'The Criminal Trial before the Lawyers', *University of Chicago Law Review*, 45 (1978), 263–316; Clive Emsley, Tim Hitchcock and Robert Shoemaker, 'Publishing History of the Proceedings', OBP; Robert B. Shoemaker, 'The Old Bailey Proceedings and the Representation of Crime and Criminal Justice in Eighteenth-Century London', *Journal of British Studies*, 47 (2008), 559–80; Garthine Walker, 'Rereading Rape and Sexual Violence in Early modern England', *Gender & History*, 10 (1998), 1–25, 8.

8 OBP, February 1754, trial of Stephen Hope (t17540227-56).

9 See my discussion in 'Pornography, Procreation and Pleasure', 107–11.

10 Helkiah Crooke, *ΜΙΚΡΟΚΟΣΜΟΓΡΑΦΙΑ [Microcosmographia]: A Description of the Body of Man. Together with the Controversies Thereto Belonging* (London, 1615), 197.

11 Jane Sharp, *The Midwives Book, Or the whole Art of Midwifry Discovered* (London, 1671); Martha Mears, *The Pupil of Nature; or Candid Advice to the Fair Sex, on the Subjects of Pregnancy; Childbirth; the Diseases Incident to Both etc.* (London, 1797). See also Eve Keller, 'The Subject of Touch: Medical Authority in Early Modern Midwifery', in Elizabeth D. Harvey (ed.), *Sensible Flesh: On Touch in Early Modern Culture* (Philadelphia: University of Pennsylvania Press, 2003), 62–80, 64–5.

12 Doreen Evenden, *The Midwives of Seventeenth-Century London* (Cambridge: Cambridge University Press, 2000); Hilary Marland (ed.), *The Art of Midwifery: Early Modern Midwives in Europe* (London and New York: Routledge, 1993); Pamela Smith, Amy Meyers, and Harold Cook (eds), *Ways of Making and Knowing: The Material Culture of Empirical Knowledge* (Michigan: University of Michigan Press, 2014).

13 On examination of female patients by wives of practitioners see Michael Stolberg, 'Examining the Body, c.1500–1750' in Sarah Toulalan and Kate Fisher (eds), *The Routledge History of Sex and the Body 1500 to the Present* (London and New York: Routledge, 2013), 91–105, 97–99. For diagnosis and treatment of venereal disease by the widow of a surgeon-apothecary in practice, see OBP, January 1749, trial of George Tennant (t17490113-15).

14 Edmund Chapman, *A Treatise on the Improvement of Midwifery, Chiefly with Regard to the Operation*, second edition (London, 1735), ii.

15 There is much literature on prostitution in the early modern period. See my discussion of prostitutes and sexual knowledge in Toulalan, *Imagining Sex*, esp. 21–2, 27–31; on bawds, see, for example, Mario DiGangi, *Sexual Types: Embodiment, Agency, and Dramatic Character from Shakespeare to Shirley* (Philadelphia: University of Pennsylvania Press, 2011), 159–61.

16 Nicolas Chorier's book was translated into French as *L'Académie des Dames*, and was also referred to in English as *The Schoole of Women*. A very abbreviated version of the book was also published in English as *A Dialogue Between a Married Lady and a Maid, Tullia and Octavia* by around 1684; the earliest extant version held by the British Library is dated 1740. The earliest extant English translation of the original book is from the late nineteenth century: *The Dialogues of Luisa Sigea (Aloisiæ Sigeæ Satyra Sotadica de Arcanis Amoris et Veneris) Literally Translated From the Latin of Nicolas Chorier* (Paris: Isidore Liseux, 1890). See my discussion of the text in *Imagining Sex*, 148–9. David Foxon provides a bibliographic history in *Libertine Literature in England 1660–1745* (New York: University Books, 1965), 38–43.

17 Pamela H. Smith and Benjamin Schmidt, 'Knowledge and its Making in Early Modern Europe', in Pamela H. Smith and Benjamin Schmidt (eds), *Making Knowledge in Early Modern Europe: Practices, Objects, and Texts, 1400–1800* (Chicago and London: Chicago University Press, 2007), 1–18, 1.

18 Peter Burke, *A Social History of Knowledge: From Gutenberg to Diderot* (Cambridge: Polity, 2000) and *What is Knowledge?* (Cambridge: Polity, 2016); Adrian Johns, *The Nature of the Book: Print and Knowledge in the Making* (Chicago and London: Chicago University Press, 1998); Barbara J. Shapiro, *A Culture of Fact: England, 1550–1720* (Ithaca: Cornell University Press, 2003); Smith and Schmidt (eds), *Making Knowledge in Early Modern Europe*; Smith, Meyers, and Cook (eds), *Ways of Making and Knowing*.

19 Adam Fox, *Oral and Literate Culture in England 1500–1700* (Oxford: Clarendon Press, 2000), 12–15; Roger Chartier, *The Order of Books: Readers, Authors, and Libraries in Europe between the Fourteenth and Eighteenth Centuries*, trans. Lydia G. Cochrane (Cambridge: Polity, 1994), 3.

20 Chandra Mukerji, 'Women Engineers and the Culture of the Pyrenees: Indigenous Knowledge and Engineering in Seventeenth-Century France', in Smith and Schmidt (eds), *Making Knowledge*, 19–44. See scholarship on women's scientific and medical knowledge and its exchange: Elaine Leong, *Recipes and Everyday Knowledge: Medicine, Science, and the Household in Early Modern England* (Chicago: University of Chicago Press, 2018); Elaine Leong and Alisha Rankin (eds), *Secrets and Knowledge in Medicine and Science, 1500–1800* (Farnham: Ashgate, 2011), 1–20; Anne Stobart, *Household Medicine in Seventeenth-Century England* (London: Bloomsbury, 2016).

21 DiGangi, *Sexual Types*, 160.

22 See my discussion in Sarah Toulalan, 'Child Sexual Abuse in Late Seventeenth- and Eighteenth-Century London: Rape, Sexual Assault and the Denial of Agency', in Nigel Goose and Katrina Honeyman (eds), *Childhood and Child Labour in Industrial England: Diversity and Agency, 1750–1914* (Farnham: Ashgate, 2013), 23–43, 31–3.

23 For an example of books provided for a household see John Barnard and Maureen Bell, 'The English Provinces', in John Barnard and D.F. McKenzie (eds), *The Cambridge History of the Book in Britain: Volume 4, 1557–1695* (Cambridge: Cambridge University Press, 2002), 665–86, 685.

24 David Cressy, *Literacy and the Social Order: Reading and Writing in Tudor and Stuart England* (Cambridge: Cambridge University Press, 1980), 13, 41, 176–7.

25 Eleanor Hubbard, 'Reading, Writing, and Initialling: Female Literacy in Early Modern London', *Journal of British Studies*, 54 (2015), 553–77.

218 *Sarah Toulalan*

26 For example, the giving of a copy of *L'Escole des Filles* to a maid of honour at the court of Louis XIV: Turner, *Schooling Sex*, 112.

27 Laura Gowing, 'Knowledge and Experience, c.1500–1750', in Toulalan and Fisher (eds), *Routledge History of Sex and the Body*, 239–55, 241.

28 See, for example, *OBP*, May 1676, trial of Schoolmaster (t16760510-7); May 1754, trial of William Kirk (t17540530-36); and October 1777, trial of Benjamin Russen (t17771015-1). It was reported in 1796 that: 'On Saturday last EDWARD FREEMAN, a schoolmaster, was executed at Ely for a rape on one of his own scholars, only ten years of age': 'News', *Oracle*, 1 September, 1796, *Seventeenth and Eighteenth Century Burney Newspapers Collection* https://www.gale.com/intl/c/17th-and-18th-century-burney-newspapers-collection. Accessed 30 March 2020.

29 Elizabeth S. Cohen, 'Straying and Led Astray: Roman Maids Become Young Women c.1600', in Elizabeth S. Cohen and Margaret Reeves (eds), *The Youth of Early Modern Women* (Amsterdam: University of Amsterdam Press, 2018), 277–96; Eleanor Hubbard, 'A Room of their Own: Young Women, Courtship and the Night in Early Modern England', in Cohen and Reeves (eds), *The Youth of Early Modern Women*, 297–313.

30 Benjamin B. Roberts and Leendert F. Groenendijk, '"Wearing Out a Pair of Fool's Shoes": Sexual Advice for Youth in Holland's Golden Age', *Journal of the History of Sexuality*, 13 (2004), 139–56; Marja van Tilberg, 'Becoming a Woman in the Dutch Republic: Advice Literature for Young Adult Women of the Seventeenth and Eighteenth Centuries', in Cohen and Reeves (eds), *The Youth of Early Modern Women*, 255–74.

31 For a discussion of the change in law and its purpose see Antony E. Simpson, 'Vulnerability and the Age of Female Consent: Legal Innovation and its Effects on Prosecutions for Rape in Eighteenth-Century London', in G.S. Rousseau and Roy Porter (eds), *Sexual Underworlds of the Enlightenment* (Manchester: Manchester University Press, 1987), 183–7.

32 Anon., *The Confession and Execution of the Two Prisoners that Suffered at TyBurn on Munday the 16th of Decemb. 1678. Viz. Nathaniel Russel, a Bayley's Follower, for Murdering a Young Man in Whites-Alley. And Steven Arrowsmith, for a Rape Committed on a Girl between Eight and Nine years of Age* (London, 1678), 4; see online at *OBP*, *Ordinary of Newgate's Account*, December 1678 (OA16781216).

33 Sir William Blackstone, *Commentaries on the Laws of England*, twelfth edition (London, 1794), 212.

34 See my discussion in 'Child Sexual Abuse', 36–7.

35 *OBP*, trial of John Hunter (t17470428-28).

36 Walker, 'Rereading Rape', 6–7. Langbein has observed that '*Most* of what was said at an Old Bailey sessions must have been omitted', although later reports become much more substantial: Langbein, 'The Criminal Trial before the Lawyers', 271.

37 *OBP*, December 1755, trial of John Baynham Sarah Clifton (t17551204-29).

38 *OBP*, May 1756, trial of Charles Frederick Wirsanthall (t17560528-45).

39 The *Oxford English Dictionary (OED)* defines 'impudent' as meaning shameless and 'impudence' as shamelessness, from at least 1386, deriving from the Latin 'pudere' meaning to make or feel ashamed: 'impudent, adj. and n.'. September 2019. Oxford University Press www.oed.com/view/Entry/92902. Accessed 22 October 2019.

40 *OBP*, May 1756, trial of Charles Frederick Wirsanthall (t17560528-45).

41 Walker, 'Rereading Rape', 5–11.

42 *OBP*, December 1683, trial of Philip Roberts (t16831212-24). See also September 1717, trial of Robert Lee (t17170911-39).

43 Gowing, 'Knowledge and Experience', 241.

44 Walker, 'Rereading Rape', 8.

45 *OBP*, February 1746, trial of James Raven (t17460226-32).

46 See my discussion in Sarah Toulalan, '"Unripe" Bodies: Children and Sex in Early Modern England', in Fisher and Toulalan (eds), *Bodies, Sex, and Desire*, 131–50.

47 *OBP*, April 1762, trial of John Clark (t17620421-4).

48 *OBP*, September 1766, trial of Christopher Pearson (t17660903-70).

49 *OBP*, January 1748, trial of William Page (t17480115-4).

50 *OBP*, September 1723, trial of John Cannon (t17330912-55).

51 Ibid.

52 *OBP*, April 1747, trial of John Hunter (t17470429-28).

53 See my discussion of her consent in Toulalan, '"Is He a Licentious Lewd Sort of a Person?"', 31.

54 *OBP*, September 1748, trial of William Garner (t17480907-50).

55 Eric Partridge, *Shakespeare's Bawdy* (London and New York: Routledge, 2002 [1947]), 259–60; 'thing, n.1', *OED*. March 2019. Oxford University Press, www.oed.com/view/Entry/200786. Accessed 25 April 2019.

56 *OBP*, April 1768, trial of John Sheridan (t17680413-30).

57 *OBP*, January 1721, trial of William Robbins (t17210113-28).

58 *OBP*, April 1768, trial of William Stringer (t17680413-47).

59 *OBP*, December 1750, trial of Richard Knibb (t17501205-40).

60 Ibid.

61 *OBP*, July 1772, trial of John Coates (t17720715-52).

62 See my discussion of the language of ruination in Sarah Toulalan, 'Child Victims of Rape and Sexual Assault: Compromised Chastity, Marginalized Lives?', in Andrew Spicer and Jane Stevens Crawshaw (eds), *The Place of the Social Margins, 1350–1750* (London and New York: Routledge, 2016), 181–202, 186–8.

63 *OBP*, December 1755, trial of John Baynham, Sarah Clifton (t17551204-29).

64 For questioning about emission and infection see *OBP*, December 1732, trial of Joseph Pearson, alias York (t17321206-69); for emission of seed to complete the act see *OBP*, September 1723, trial of John Cannon (t17330912-55).

65 *OBP*, July 1751, trial of Christopher Larkin (tl7510703-21). See my discussion of this issue in Toulalan, '"Is He a Licentious Lewd Sort of a Person?"', 38–40.

66 *OBP*, September 1768, trial of William Allam (tl7680907-40).

67 *OBP*, April 1747, trial of John Hunter (t17470429-28).

68 William Hawkins, *A Treatise of the Pleas of the Crown: Or, A System of the Principal Matters Relating to that Subject, Digested under their Proper Heads*, third edition (London, 1739), 108.

69 In the Aristotelian model of generation only men contributed seed for conception to occur, while the Galenic-Hippocratic model allowed that women also contributed seed (albeit a weaker, thinner and hence 'a more imperfect seed'). Crooke, *Microcosmographia*, 162.

70 Matthew Cobb, *The Egg and Sperm Race: The Seventeenth-Century Scientists Who Unravelled the Secrets of Sex, Life and Growth* (London: Pocket Books, 2007 [2006]), 243–6; Maryanne Cline Horowitz, 'The "Science" of Embryology Before the Discovery of the Ovum', in

220 *Sarah Toulalan*

Marilyn J. Boxer and Jean H. Quataert (eds), *Connecting Spheres: European Women in a Globalizing World 1500 to the Present* (Oxford: Oxford University Press, 2000), 104–12.
71 *OBP*, July 1734, trial of [no name] (t17340710-33).
72 *OBP*, June 1769, trial of Thomas Meller, otherwise Brooks (t17690628-8).
73 Ibid.
74 Toulalan, 'Child Victims of Rape and Sexual Assault', 189–92.
75 *OBP*, October 1735, trial of Julian Brown (t17351015-28).

10 Inscription and Political Exclusion in Early Modern England

Nicholas Popper

The following chapter uses the activity of the Tower of London Record Office to explore the complex dynamics of inclusion and exclusion that were produced by the intensifying early modern dependence on written records. The records in the Tower, like those in other state archives, anchored highly exclusionary visions of politics through the texts that they housed and the forms of inscription that they enshrined. By providing a case study of women's activities in the Tower of London Record Office and their representation in its holdings, this chapter explores the artificial nature of the prescriptive and legal past the archive constructed.

Consultation of the records emerged as a widespread political tool in early modern England, as the written word assumed greater importance and as such documents came to be used as ballast for political authority and expertise.[1] The circulation of the Tower records among the political elite was one iteration of the heightened value assigned to the textual recording of political activity in enduring material form. Beginning in the late sixteenth century, European statesmen and administrators increasingly depended on the copying, collection, and mobilisation of manuscript political records and a range of other documents in the performance of their duties.[2] Familiarity with such writings was perceived as conveying several benefits. For example, transcribing letters exchanged between statesmen might enhance a collector's understanding of causation in political life, while the copying of official records might provide formulas for writing new documents. Copied documents also served as evidence for policy proposals, with those striving to secure power intently seeking to acquire this sort of political paperwork.

Elizabeth I's reign saw a combination of forces that initiated the explosion of inscription and collection in England.[3] This increasing suffusion of paper followed a series of political crises that escalated the urgency for the provision of counsel and created a climate of increased competition for preferment. In addition, changing intellectual currents created a culture where political actors relied more heavily on empirical evidence and written records. These developments resulted in the proliferation of copies of official documents as well as unofficial writings

222 *Nicholas Popper*

such as letters, policy papers, drafts, memoranda, and transcriptions of official records, often retrospectively grouped and referred to as 'state papers'. The formulation of political expertise, the practice of statecraft, and the material conditions of political engagement were structured by sharing, circulating, and reading such inscriptions. Over time, copying government documents and records – the originals of which were housed in archives, offices, studies, cartularies, and treasure rooms throughout the realm – became critical in the arsenal of political and legal action.[4]

Historians have long been sensitive to the ways in which early modern Britons were denied active participation in the political sphere on account of their status, gender, age, property, and other qualities. This chapter enhances such work by positing that such exclusions were also perpetuated through the regime of inscription.[5] This was in large measure because the inheritance of paperwork and records reflected the official monopoly exercised by landowning adult men who occupied the web of crown, church, and local offices that formed England's political system.[6] As scholarship by Judith Bennett, Sara Mendelson and Patricia Crawford, and others has emphasised, women and other politically marginalised individuals were sometimes able to influence formal authority or exercise their own power through informal means, but the voluminous paperwork produced by medieval and early modern governments occluded or minimised their acts and spaces of power.[7] The increased reliance on archival records thus replicated and perpetuated an embedded exclusionary vision of political and legal activity.[8]

Preserving and circulating the records required labour. Yet, much of this activity was performed by individuals who were marginalised by, or absent from, the texts of the records, especially women. The juxtaposition between women's central roles in caring for the Tower of London archives and their underrepresentation in the material evidence it stored makes the women of the Tower an ideal case study for exploring the exclusionary dimensions of regimes of inscription. The physical presence of women in the Tower of London repository – the case at the heart of this chapter – can be glimpsed only through brief references captured in the two surviving account books of the Tower from the early 1670s.[9] Nevertheless, these documents reveal women's essential contribution in the preservation and usage of Britain's material past for political and legal ends. Excavating women's roles in the Tower's archives suggests that the power of these records, which lay at the heart of the regime of inscription, depended on the work of individuals whose historical presence the records themselves concealed.[10]

In what follows, I begin by providing a brief study of early modern England's archive-driven political practice. I will then use three prisms to illuminate women's engagements with the Tower records. First, I provide an overview of women's presence within the Tower records. Secondly, I explore the contradictions that surfaced when women tried to mobilise

Inscription and Political Exclusion 223

the archival regime for their own benefit. Finally, I investigate how women's involvement in the archive facilitated the use and authority of the records. The emphasis on text, mediation, and labour in this chapter does not aim to neaten a messy story, but rather seeks to envelop the complexity and tensions of the archive's inclusions and exclusions. Women's place within this early modern English archive, as this chapter will detail, confirms what colonial historians have forcefully revealed in relation to indigenous and enslaved populations: archives can enable glimpses at the otherwise hidden lives of those systematically excluded from the exercise of power, but such glimpses emerge from an archive that inescapably articulated, generated, and reproduced relations of power. Interrogating the past through such evidence requires scholars to see the archive as a multifaceted historical tool and historical actor in its own right, one which in different lights can both illuminate and obscure.[11]

Paperwork and the Practice of Early Modern Politics

Most studies focusing on the political ramifications of developments in seventeenth-century communication and technology have concentrated on the expansion of printed material. This scholarship maintains that print's production, proliferation, and consumption created new opportunities for the participation of individuals traditionally excluded from politics.[12] The circulation of the manuscript records held at the Tower of London reveals that the expansion of print was accompanied by a growth in the dissemination of handwritten political writings. In contrast to print, these writings reinforced the boundaries between those who did and did not belong within this world of governance. The intensifying reliance on inscriptions also initially fostered the collection of older materials rather than the production of new writings, resulting in the increased circulation of pre-existing materials and the multiplication of textual forms that adhered to longstanding conventions.

The Tower Record Office was foundational to this regime. This was because the transcriptions produced by and for its visitors helped spur a dramatic increase in the scale of the archives amassed by Elizabethan and early Stuart counsellors and administrators.[13] Massive programmes of transcription enabled figures like the Lord Treasurer William Cecil, Lord Burghley (1520–1598) and his son Robert (1563–1612); Secretary of State Francis Walsingham (1532–1590); Clerk of the Council Robert Beale (1541–1601); Lord Chancellor Thomas Egerton (1540–1617); George Carew, Earl of Totnes (1555–1629); and Privy Counsellor Sir Julius Caesar (1557/8–1636), to accumulate collections that dwarfed all but the most exceptional repositories of previous generations.

The inscription practices of Thomas Egerton are representative of the value that these political officials placed on archives. Beginning in

224 *Nicholas Popper*

1581, Egerton progressed from being Elizabeth's Solicitor General to Attorney General. Subsequently, in 1596, Egerton was appointed Lord Chancellor and Keeper of the Great Seal. He would maintain these positions through James VI and I's reign until his death in 1617. Over his lengthy career, Egerton built an archive of thousands of items, which contained enormous quantities of copies alongside original letters and government instruments, and his own drafts, memoranda, and notes.[14] Egerton's interest in collecting such records was well-established among his contemporaries. For example, the English antiquarian and lawyer William Lambarde was one of many who gave Egerton lavish presentation copies of medieval records as gifts.[15] Despite the importance of such artefacts, they were rarities within Egerton's archive. For the most part, it consisted of purely functional transcriptions, such as a volume of extracts transcribed from Kings Bench and Common Pleas rolls from the reign of Edward I, collected by Deputy Chamberlain of the Exchequer Arthur Agarde, who supplemented them with paratextual notes taken from other official records.[16] Similarly, much of Egerton's parliamentary collection consisted of copies from parliamentary rolls, contemporary journals, as well as of acts, bills, petitions, and speeches.[17] His archive also contained large numbers of drafts of patents and grants that were produced through adapting precedent copies to new political instruments.[18]

Egerton's archive served as a fundamental resource for developing his political action and knowledge. The deployment of such materials also structured Egerton's political horizons. Indeed, when he wished to compose documents for government use, Egerton often relied on past examples that he accessed through copies (which perhaps themselves were copies of copies). For example, he used his collection of patents and charters relating to the creation of nobility from Edward III's reign to provide himself with possible blueprints for those moments when his chancery composed similar grants. Likewise, when Egerton wished to build his expertise about an institution, office, or court, he often made notes or copies of reports, instructions, and other materials to establish its functions, responsibilities, and privileges.

Tracking the notes Egerton made from archival research illuminates how the archive fuelled his political practice and shaped his understanding of political thought and action. In the early years of James I's reign, when seeking to staunch the haemorrhaging of money from the King's coffers, he compiled a list of 'The Propositions I have made for relieveinge the king upon state as it now stands, as warranted by lawe, reason, and example'. Egerton cited evidence from the close rolls of the reigns of Edward III and Henry IV to show that there was a historical precedent for stopping and delaying payments, noting that: 'there was a proclamation to staye the payment of all annuities.'[19] Similarly, during the height of debates over the union of Scotland and England following James's accession to the English throne in 1603, Egerton consulted records in the Tower to find evidence to demonstrate that even under the height of English dominion in France under the Lancastrians, the Crowns had remained separate: a point that was likely intended to reassure various parties fearful of the consequences of union.[20] Finally, in roughly the same years, when Egerton composed a note concerning the 'liberties of his subiects' which the king could 're-streyne' by prerogative because they were 'agaynst the commen weale' – a list that included, 'glasses, woade, tobacco, dyce, cardes, players, beare-wards, paynters of pure complexion, fencers' – he again scoured Tower records for precedents.[21]

While the function of Egerton's archive was novel, its contents primarily consisted of copies, imitations, or notes of past records. The vast scale of his collection did not reflect the increased recording of communications previously conducted orally or the generation of new political forms or genres. Rather, as the product of an accumulation of materials generated according to longstanding governmental order, his archive was shaped by what had already been written and what he deemed significant from the records of the past. The Elizabethan and early Stuart emphasis on copying thus multiplied the volume of written materials throughout James I's reign, but it did not loosen the bounds of political inscription to include individuals, communities, or practices that had been previously absent. Instead, the archive provided a tool that allowed those who controlled it, and were able to access it, to use England's past to stipulate its present.

Exclusionary Texts and Inscriptional Patriarchy

Figures like Thomas Egerton exalted documents produced in the administration of public authority. These writings were not socially or politically neutral, and instead carried a tacit set of priorities, hierarchies, presumptions, and absences. By the sixteenth century, paperwork had long been an instrument for the consolidation of power. As Michael Clanchy has demonstrated, the medieval English state relied on formal written records to articulate and legitimise its authority, and its dependence stimulated a remarkable textual output.[22] After the reign of Edward I, the Crown increasingly governed through writs, charters, patents, warrants, deeds, and other inscriptions. Combined with the testimonies of church governance, these bureaucratic documents constituted the majority of written materials produced in England before the sixteenth century. Correspondingly, the copying, collecting, and circulation practices of Egerton, and others like him in early modern Europe, amplified the embedded exclusions of such documents. This served to perpetuate the formal patterns of exclusion vested in the authority of official records, further eliding the complex of oral and gestural communication at the heart of informal negotiations of power.[23]

226 *Nicholas Popper*

The Tower Record Office was a bustling place from the late sixteenth century and continued to be so throughout the seventeenth.[24] Because the materials it held testified to vast swathes of England's political and legal past, the Record Office drew a steady stream of visitors propelled by distinct motivations: landowners seeking to establish disputed property titles; representatives of towns and corporations searching for their original charters and confirmations; recent appointees to crown offices investigating the scope of their duties; antiquarians hoping to excavate arcana of the medieval past; and MPs seeking ballast for their positions in political debates. Exploring the Tower's holdings – mostly chancery items preceding the reign of Henry VIII, such as charter rolls, patent rolls, escheat rolls, inquisitions post-mortem, and perambulations – required paying a 10-shilling fee, for which a clerk would consult the archive's catalogues and pull desired materials to be examined in Caesar's Chapel. Some visitors also requested exemplifications or copies, which could be obtained for additional fees depending on the amount of paper required. Thus, for a price, the Record Office offered visitors the material evidence embodying England's prescriptive past that they could then use for their own ends.

Though women featured in the inscriptions archived in the Tower and elsewhere, the discriminatory structure of English politics and contemporary gender norms ensured that they were significantly underrepresented. The relative absence of women in the records held in the Tower of London, and the instances when they did appear, underscore how the clerks who composed these records operated with a clear sense of what warranted recording and what did not. The choices they made memorialised a homocentric world of political and legal business where access to power, authority, and inheritance was conditioned not only by gender, but also by a range of other considerations including wealth and age. This patriarchal political system both sustained and was sustained by the activities of clerks and statesmen like Egerton. Indeed, these writings were principally circulated for, and by, a restricted group of elite men exercising power within church, parliament, courts, and other government institutions, as a means of solidifying and legitimising their claims to authority. It is also worth noting that many people interacted with England's numerous local courts rather than with the institutions that deposited records in the Tower. Local courts' production of records were similarly directed towards the formal exercise of power dominated by elite men.

The marginalisation of women in the extant records reflects their deprivation from formal power. When they appeared in the records – within grants and deeds listed in the charter rolls, patent rolls, close rolls, and escheat rolls – they did so as wives, widows, sisters, and daughters: female roles that were defined by relationships with men. That women were not treated as legal actors in their own right indicates their subjection within a legal and political system that severely restricted their access and participation. In all of these iterations, women were subject to subordinating institutions and laws. The best-known example is the doctrine of coverture, which deprived women of the ability to serve as agents in a vast range of legal and political business. Egerton was particularly active in proposing measures to exclude women's direct participation in litigation, especially in cases where they were attacking others rather than defending their own honour or reputations.[25]

Scholars have demonstrated that women, especially those of high status, possessed strategies to exert some degree of agency in the marginalising spaces of England's law courts and public political spheres.[26] In particular, high ranking widows possessed unusual legal standing to secure their own future, for example by acting as creditors or as land or property holders. However, this autonomy was unavailable to many lower status women, and lack of patriarchal protection came with its own cultural and social disadvantages. Women could also assert some control by exerting informal pressure behind the scenes as financial or legal contracts were being negotiated. For example, the dynamics of the Goodwin family, as detailed in Bernard Capp's chapter in this volume, constitutes an extreme version of more ordinary cases where women pressured male relatives to bequeath them inheritances in order to promote their own financial security.[27] The records solemnifying formal agreements from the Tower Office archives, discussed below, provide further tantalising glimpses of background conversations, negotiations, gossip, and more. Furthermore, women could exercise agency by invoking 'scripts' that emphasised their own conformity with the cultural values of adjudicating authorities. For example, women would often protect their modesty by having male lawyers or relatives speak on their behalf in courts of law.[28] In both approaches, women typically emphasised their own subordination, creating a paradoxical situation where their actions reinforced the frameworks from which they were excluded.[29]

Cultural hierarchies were thus deeply embedded in the material texts preserved in the Tower, for women's appearances in the records – regardless of their effective agency outside the realm of inscriptions – confirmed the homocentric depiction of England's spaces of political and legal power. The world of inscription mediated political business and legal proceedings in ways that enshrined cultural hierarchies and exclusions. This was because the authority invested in inscribed instruments of governance was an essential means by which those in authority asserted, remediated, and legitimised their power. When Egerton or the myriad of other individuals like him consulted such sources, they engaged in the construction of a deliberately masculinised version of England's past.

228 Nicholas Popper

Gendered Mediations

The exclusions embedded in early modern archives mean they provide an incomplete representation of contemporary experiences. Whilst political records perpetuated only a filtered testimony of the practices and social relations that underlay their production, women's place in the political culture of early modern England can nonetheless be glimpsed in the records held by the Tower. Ledgers of the Tower of London records, most notably from the 1670s, show how visits were occasionally made by women or by agents representing their interests. In August 1670 Lady Alice Lisle paid ten shillings 'for a search of the Mannor of Burgate and Ibsley abs Bere' in Southampton, which her agent 'Mr Hooke of the Subpoena Office in Chancery' retrieved the following month.[30] Similarly, Henry Champion was a frequent visitor to the Tower as solicitor for Elizabeth Percy, Countess of Northumberland.[31] It is important to note that both of these women were widows at the time, which granted them economic independence that, along with their status, likely encouraged them to initiate searches of the lands that had come into their possession.[32]

More strikingly, women could also serve as agents representing the interests of men. Indeed, the ledgers contain references to other women visiting the office as agents for others. For example, entries for 1670 record two visits by a 'Mrs Morley' on behalf of 'Mr Bernard of ye Treasurer's Remembrancers Office'.[33] Mrs Morley may have been granted this access because she was married to an 'Esqr Morley', who visited the Tower in October of that year and was noted as a friend of future Keeper William Petyt, who was another regular visitor to the Tower Records Office at this time.[34] Her visits to the Record Office, where she was actively engaging with the records, testify to the fact that the archive was not a purely homosocial space. It also reveals how women, in certain cases, might perform archival labour.

These examples show that those traditionally excluded from the archive could thus participate in the regime of inscription by mobilising its resources to their benefit. Yet, participation in archival regimes by such individuals and groups often entailed reinforcing exclusionary hierarchies. One particularly illustrative example of the ways in which women might become involved in the activities of the Tower Record Office without resisting wider patriarchal ideals is the case of Elizabeth Ryley Jr, wife of the Tower's clerk William Ryley Jr. He had inherited the Deputy Keepership in 1667, after three decades of apprenticeship to his father.[35] The continuity of the Ryley family in these offices was remarkable but also fraught; they had been accused of Royalist sympathies during the Interregnum and then were distrusted for their Parliamentarian employment after the Restoration. Shortly after William's death in 1675, Elizabeth petitioned King and council for

Inscription and Political Exclusion   229

'some present reward for the reall and hearty services (of her late deceased husband) to your Majestie in the greate want and necessitie she and her poore familye now undergoe'.[36] Elizabeth's earlier life had not prepared her for such dire conditions. She was the daughter of Sir Anthony Chester, second baronet, of Chicheley, and her brother the third baronet was long-time JP in Buckinghamshire and MP for Bedford in 1685. The meagre income from Ryley's position had placed the family on the edge of penury, a position compounded by raising the two children of Ryley's brother Phillip following his death in the Second Anglo-Dutch War.

It is likely that Ryley Sr would have given vital support to the family while he was still alive, for his death in 1667 revealed how tenuous their security was. Almost immediately after the elder Ryley's death, Ryley Jr wrote to Secretary of State Joseph Williamson requesting more profitable employment, while elaborating the many services he and his father had provided to the crown. He would repeatedly petition for aid in subsequent years.[37] To strengthen his pleas, Ryley Jr compiled what he saw as an exemplary list of the services that he and his father had performed. In this he recounted how the two had found the original Solemn League and Covenant and the Concessions at Breda signed by Charles II and then declined an offer from the Scots of £2000 for them. They had also recovered the 'Originall memorable Recognition' of James I's title to empire; transcribed a massive collection of treaties for Secretary of State Arlington; supervised the 1661 printing of the *Placita Parliamentaria* which 'did vindicate the Militia for the king'; and had overseen many other weighty state services.[38] Beyond these exceptional acts, Ryley Jr noted that they had eased the restoration of the House of Lords by fulfilling the body's ceaseless demands for records of its past practices. Moreover, since his father's death, Ryley Jr had been engaged in a massive program of restoring and preserving 'the Rolls in the Raigne of King John, Hen 3 and severall other kings raignes'.[39]

Ryley either never delivered this list or kept a copy and, after his death, Elizabeth uncovered it within his papers. Like many of her female contemporaries, who were often tasked with oversight of household papers, especially after their husband's deaths, Elizabeth seized on this opportunity. She subsequently revised elements of her husband's documents for inclusion in her petition to the King, although it is unclear whether she did this herself or employed someone else to do so.[40] The edits were subtle but revealing. The revisions did not transform the substance of her husband's claims, but strikingly switched the voice from first to third person, recognising the diminished power of her voice. For example, she changed the beginning from 'My deceased father and my selfe' to 'The Petitioners deceased father and late husband'. In addition, when explaining why Ryley had not accepted the Scottish bribe, the document was altered from 'I resolved, I would never betray my king and country'

230 Nicholas Popper

to 'he resolved, he would never betray his king & country'.[41] As Frances Dolan has shown in her study of word choice in seventeenth-century depositions, this was a strategy widely employed by women in legal testimonies and witness statements to present their viewpoints without overtly subverting patriarchal conventions.[42] In this way, Elizabeth deliberately conformed to wider gendered expectations of deference and passivity. Her edits were then later incorporated into a fair copy, which was included with a formal petition. This was similarly written in the third person.[43]

It could be argued that this petition illuminates Elizabeth's troubled later life, deprived of any income while seeking to support so many children.[44] Indeed, it does, but it is also important to note such a limited view of her life wholly depends on the inclusions and exclusions of the archival culture in which her husband laboured. The extant evidence of her early widowhood consists solely of a formal petition with enclosure, which survives because it made it into Joseph Williamson's hands, along with the revised draft of her husband's labours. This latter document likely survives because it remained amongst Ryley's household papers, which were then acquired by Williamson from Elizabeth. These papers are testimony to Elizabeth's experience, to be sure, but they reduce the totality of her life to its limited interaction with the clerical world that generated and preserved such paperwork.

The petition did clearly represent Elizabeth Ryley's interest. But there are limitations as to how much we can regard this document and episode as representative of her voice, for, as Dolan notes, these petitions were mediated by the archive's materiality and politics of organisation.[45] For one, Elizabeth's statement was already founded on her husband's earlier version, which he had kept and preserved. Moreover, it is highly probable that the petition was physically penned by someone else. This can be evidenced in the re-writing of her husband's list of services, where the transcriber had made the decision to place the statement in the third person rather than in Elizabeth's own voice. Above all, the fair copy elided the basic fact that the document was revised at her instigation. The labour and work Elizabeth exerted towards the production of the petition was thus excluded from the material object of the formal petition itself.

The remaining archival evidence in this episode, taken literally, reduces Elizabeth's life to the subordination and helplessness underlying her petition. But situating the document in its context of creation tells a slightly different story. The production of this document minimised and hid a collaborative exercise of preserving, composing, and circulating inscriptions, which was dependent on Elizabeth's activity and motivation, and relied on her searching for and capitalising on the written materials of her husband. On the one hand, the petition outlines Elizabeth's assured poverty and supplicatory helplessness. But, on the

Inscription and Political Exclusion   231

other, the very existence of the petition and the process of its construction reveals how women such as Elizabeth were immersed within a textual cosmos that could be purposefully mobilised to their benefit if they possessed an understanding of its workings. It also shows how they were able to strategically work within its framework of gender and power expectations.

Labour Within the Tower Record Office

The practice of revivifying past inscriptions to facilitate political knowledge and action required more than just the labour of reading them. Indeed, alternative forms of labour were performed by individuals whose tacit and informal participation was written out of the official records. As the ledgers of the Tower Record Office from the 1670s show, the preservation, mobilisation, and circulation of the material records was a fundamentally social activity that depended on collaboration and a range of custodial practices, many of which were performed by women. In fact, the operations of the Tower suggest the likelihood of women's broader participation in the regime of inscription, even if it left only bare material traces.

Maintaining the archive and fulfilling its responsibilities were demanding endeavours requiring collective effort. Basic maintenance of the records necessitated constant attention, requiring everything from confirming that they were re-filed in the correct spaces, to monitoring calendars of the papers that might grow unusable through overuse, to ensuring that paper, parchment, pen, ink, tape, thread, and needles were in ready supply. Clerks also struggled to stave off the records' traditional enemies of vermin, water, and fire, as well as ensure that the vaulted stone space was heated and clean. This last issue constituted a particular problem, for dust literally leached off the parchment skins on which most original records were recorded. Further cleanliness problems were also caused by the soot rising from warming fires and the moisture seeping through the stone walls to create a thick and corrosive grime that imperilled the integrity of the records lying on the bookshelves between the arches.

Preserving England's material past was thus, in part, a task of sanitation. The regulations that hung in the Tower accordingly dictated 'that ye roomes in ye office shall be kept cleane & swept once or more every weeke and the writtes & records therin preserved from cobwebbs dust filth & putrefaction'.[46] Fulfilling this charge fell to women employed by the Tower, in particular 'Goody Walsh', 'Mother Walsh', or 'Mrs Walsh', who appeared in the Tower's ledgers in the 1670s.[47] Though engaged in stereotypical 'women's work', she was a permanent salaried employee.[48] Walsh typically appeared in the ledgers between 1670 and 1675, when receiving advances on her annual salary of £2.[49]

232 Nicholas Popper

Her position must have been sufficiently stable as she was willing to lay out her own money in support of her work. This was evidenced in late 1670, when she was reimbursed four pence for purchasing a broom.[50] Walsh may have also been 'the woman' repeatedly referred to in the records as taking advances on a comparable salary during this period. Other unnamed women were occasionally paid extra for additional sweeping of the Office and were similarly reimbursed for purchases of cleaning supplies like brooms, baskets, mops, and cobweb brushes.

The items used by such women were part of the rich material culture of the Tower Office, along with the several types of paper, ink, parchment, sand, tape, clasps, pins, locks, keys, and waters 'to refresh the blind and imperfect records'.[51] Their tools were needed to keep the spaces clear for clerks to pull requested materials. They also staved off the relentless sedimentation of dust and filth that imperilled the legibility and durability of records, and no less importantly, to keep food detritus from attracting the rats, mice, and weasels whose appetites might – as was so often the case in other archives – lead them to feed on the records. These women may also have been the intended users of 'a hand brush to brush the records', suggesting that their responsibilities may have extended to the upkeep of the rolls themselves.[52]

The Tower Record Office's female employees were the most constant presence in the office aside from the clerks, who would have spent much of their time fulfilling the inquiries of visitors, ensuring supply of essential items, and keeping accounts. For these men, the office resembled one of the learned households common across early modern Europe: it paid for their lodging and was where they often took meals.[53] The labour of the Tower Record Office's female employees thus extended beyond maintaining the physical space of the archive to caring for the clerks as well. For instance, in January 1671, Goody Walsh was paid a shilling 'for Washing Mr Jenyngs cloathes', and the following month she received three shillings 'for her attendance on him while he was sicke'.[54] After Jennings fell ill and died, the office paid for his funeral services and assumed his debts. Jennings's death reveals how much the Tower's operations were supported by the invisible labour of women both inside and outside of this space. His nurse received eight shillings after his death, and his remaining rent was paid – as it had been previously – to his landlady 'Mrs Carter'.[55]

The Tower Record Office, in short, depended on women's labour to preserve and circulate its records. The ability of the Tower's male employees to perform their duties was contingent upon their contributions. Preserving these records from obscurity and ruin entailed collaborations and shows the importance of female labour in keeping the space from declining into disrepair. This reveals that the archive was not solely a masculine space but, like early modern households, was one in which women were both central to its operations and could access and use it.

Inscription and Political Exclusion   233

Although it has not previously been acknowledged by historians, women performed a vital role in preserving and circulating the public testimonies of past political and legal actions for use by statesmen, antiquaries, property owners, and historians.

Conclusion

Through its focus on the archives of the Tower of London Record Office, this chapter has explored a number of dimensions relating to the cultural practice of politics in early modern England. Above all, it has shown that the structure of politics reinforced the exclusion of certain groups of people from formal political participation. This exclusion had further ramifications, as it conditioned their appearances in the official record produced by state institutions, which were subsequently read by individuals like Thomas Egerton as they formulated policies and ideas. The increased dependence on written materials in the sixteenth and seventeenth centuries, in turn, tightened the existing inheritance of hierarchies and exclusions.

This chapter has also revealed some of the perspectives and precautions of which historians need to be aware when engaging with the archive. The light that archives shed on the past is no less filtered for modern historians than it was for medieval and early modern searchers and interpreters of the records. Historians using this body of evidence must recognise its innate refractions – both in terms of what was included and what was omitted – for otherwise they risk reifying the perspectives of their creators.[56] This does not mean that there is no way to recover elements of the voices of the lost and marginalised individuals who did not constitute the political elite. Indeed, as this chapter has shown, searching for ephemeral glimpses into their lives and situating them beyond their archival contexts can uncover the experiences and agency of those most marginalised from the political process. But historians must also recognise that even the putative recovery of lost voices relies on an archive that was an agent of marginalisation.[57] The archive whose preservation depended on Goody Walsh's labours was a titration of lived experience, one reliant on social collaborations that it also concealed, much as Elizabeth Ryley disguised her own role in mobilising her husband's papers. Women's political activities can be glimpsed from such records, but only ever in a distorted fashion, through an irrevocably cracked glass.

It is also important to note that the records of the past are material productions that themselves have histories. Considering the conditions of their preservation and use illustrates the broader challenges faced by historians. The dynamics which led to the actions and events of some social actors to be captured in inscription, while others were consigned to oblivion, has also governed the subsequent survival of historical

234 *Nicholas Popper*

records. Nevertheless, it is important to remember that the safe-guarding of these records depended upon the cooperation of those who were both included and excluded from formal political authority. The preservation of the past thus depended upon the collaboration and labour of many whose stories are not present within the records that they painstakingly maintained for future generations.

Acknowledgments

I wish to thank the volume's editors, Kat Lecky, Caylin Carbonell, and Amanda Herbert for improving the chapter considerably through their constructive advice and criticism.

Notes

1 See for example Julia Crick and Alexandra Walsham (eds), *The Uses of Script and Print, 1300–1700* (Cambridge: Cambridge University Press, 2004); Adam Fox, *Oral and Literate Culture in England, 1500–1700* (Oxford: Oxford University Press, 2000); Harold Love, 'Oral and Scribal Texts in Early Modern England', in John Barnard and D.F. McKenzie (eds), *The Cambridge History of the Book* (Cambridge: Cambridge University Press, 2002), 97–121; Noah Millstone, *Manuscript Circulation and the Invention of Politics in Early Stuart England* (Cambridge: Cambridge University Press, 2016).

2 The study of archives as historical objects has flourished in recent years. See Richard Ross, 'The Memorial Culture of Early Modern English Lawyers: Memory as Keyword, Shelter, and Identity, 1560–1640', *Yale Law School Journal of Law and the Humanities*, 10 (1998), 229–326; Nicholas Popper, 'From Abbey to Archive: Managing Texts and Records in Early Modern England', *Archival Science*, 10 (2010), 249–66; Paul Halliday, 'Authority in the Archives', *Critical Analysis of Law*, 1 (2014), 110–42; Liesbeth Corens, Kate Peters, and Alexandra Walsham (eds), *The Social History of the Archive: Record Keeping in Early Modern Europe* (Past & Present Supplement 11, 2016); and Kate Peters, Alexandra Walsham, and Liesbeth Corens, *Archives and Information in the Early Modern World* (Oxford: Oxford University Press, 2018). For the European context, see Randolph Head, 'Knowing Like a State: The Transformation of Political Knowledge in Swiss Archives, 1450–1770', *Journal of Modern History*, 75 (2003), 745–82; Filippo de Vivo, *Information and Communication in Venice: Rethinking Early Modern Politics* (Oxford: Oxford University Press, 2007); R.C. Head, 'Mirroring Governance: Archives, Inventories and Political Knowledge in Early Modern Switzerland and Europe', *Archival Sciences*, 7 (2007), 317–29; R.C. Head (ed.), 'Archival Knowledge Cultures in Europe, 1400–1900', special issue, *Archival Science*, 10 (2010), 191–343; Filippo de Vivo, Andrea Guidi, and Alessando Silvestri (eds), 'Archival Transformations in Early Modern European History', special issue, *European History Quarterly*, 46 (2016), 421–589; Markus Friedrich, *The Birth of the Archive: A History of Knowledge*, trans. John Noël Dillon (Ann Arbor: University of Michigan Press, 2018); and R.C. Head, *Making Archives in Early Modern Europe: Proof, Information, and Political Record-Keeping, 1400–1700* (Cambridge:

Inscription and Political Exclusion 235

Cambridge University Press, 2019). See also James Daybell, 'Gender, Politics, and Archives in Early Modern England', in James Daybell and Svante Norrhern (eds), *Gender and Political Culture in Early Modern Europe, 1400–1800* (London and New York: Routledge, 2017), 25–46.

3 Nicholas Popper, 'An Information State for Elizabethan England', *Journal of Modern History*, 90 (2018), 503–35.

4 For copying in early modern Europe, see Andrew Gordon, '*Copycopia*, or the Place of Copied Correspondence in Manuscript Culture: A Case Study', in James Daybell and Peter Hinds (eds), *Material Readings of Early Modern Culture: Text and Social Practices, 1580–1730* (Basingstoke: Palgrave Macmillan, 2010), 65–81; James Daybell, *The Material Letter in Early Modern England: Manuscript Letters and Culture and Practices of Letter-Writing, 1512–1635* (Basingstoke: Palgrave Macmillan, 2012), 175–216; Andrew Gordon, 'Material Fictions: Counterfeit Correspondence and the Culture of Copying in Early Modern England', in James Daybell and Andrew Gordon (eds), *Cultures of Correspondence in Early Modern Britain* (Philadelphia: University of Pennsylvania Press, 2016), 85–109.

5 For the use of inscription as a means of exclusion see Andy Wood, 'Tales from the "Yarmouth Hutch": Civic Identities and Hidden Histories in an Urban Archive', *Past and Present*, 230, issue supplement 11 (2016), 213–30. For exclusions more broadly see Susan D. Amussen, *An Ordered Society: Gender and Class in Early Modern England* (Oxford: Basil Blackwell, 1988); and Tim Harris (ed.), *The Politics of the Excluded, c.1500–1850* (Basingstoke: Palgrave Macmillan, 2001). On the extent and limitations to which archives illuminate women's lives see Helen M. Jewell, *Women in Medieval England* (Manchester: Manchester University Press, 1996), 1–18; Tim Stretton, 'Women, Legal Records, and the Problem of the Lawyer's Hand', *Journal of British Studies*, 58 (2019), 684–700; and Alexandra Shepard, 'Worthless Witnesses? Marginal Voices and Women's Legal Agency in Early Modern England', *Journal of British Studies*, 58 (2019), 717–34.

6 For a basic overview of the production of such sources see G.R. Elton, *England, 1200–1640* (Ithaca: Cornell University Press, 1969); a critical approach was inaugurated by Natalie Zemon Davis, *Fiction in the Archives: Pardon Tales and their Tellers in Sixteenth-Century France* (Stanford: Stanford University Press, 1987). See also Shannon McSheffrey, 'Detective Fiction in the Archives: Court Records and the Uses of Law in Late Medieval England', *History Workshop Journal*, 65 (2008), 65–78; and Jennifer Bishop, 'The Clerk's Tale: Civic Writing in Sixteenth-Century London', *Past and Present*, 230, issue supplement 11 (2016), 112–30.

7 See Judith Bennett, 'Public Power and Authority in the Medieval English Countryside', in *Women and Power in the Middle Ages* (Athens: University of Georgia Press, 1988), 18–36; James Daybell (ed.), *Women and Politics in Early Modern England, 1450–1750* (Aldershot: Ashgate, 2004), esp. 1–20, 114–31; Anthony Fletcher, *Gender, Sex, and Subordination in England, 1500–1800* (New Haven and London: Yale University Press, 1995), 256–80; Sara Mendelson and Patricia Crawford, *Women in Early Modern England* (Oxford: Oxford University Press, 1998), 345–429; and Andy Wood, *Riot, Rebellion, and Popular Politics in Early Modern England* (Basingstoke: Palgrave Macmillan, 2002), 100–111. More broadly, see Michael J. Braddick and John Walter (eds), *Negotiating Power in Early Modern Society: Order, Hierarchy, and Subordination in Britain and Ireland* (Cambridge: Cambridge University Press, 2001).

236   Nicholas Popper

8 On paperwork as a gendered epistemic technology, see James Daybell, 'Gendered Archival Practices and the Future Lives of Letters', in Daybell and Gordon (eds), *Cultures of Correspondence in Early Modern Britain*, 210–236; Laura Gowing, 'Girls on Forms: Apprenticing Young Women in Seventeenth-Century London', *Journal of British Studies*, 55 (2016), 447–73; and Carla Bittel, Elaine Leong, and Christine von Oertzen, *Working with Paper: Gendered Practices in the History of Knowledge* (Pittsburgh, PA: University of Pittsburgh Press, 2019).

9 The registers from the 1670s are The National Archives (hereafter TNA), C 272/1 and British Library (hereafter BL), Harley MS 6751.

10 On women's work and its invisibility in early modern Britain, see Peter Earle, 'The Female Labour Market in London in the Late Seventeenth and Early Eighteenth Centuries', *Economic History Review*, 42 (1989), 328–53; Ilana Ben-Amos, 'Women Apprentices in the Trades and Crafts of Early Modern Bristol', *Continuity and Change*, 6 (1991), 227–52; Penelope Lane, Neil Raven, and K.D.M. Snell (eds), *Women, Work and Wages in England, 1600–1850* (Woodbridge: The Boydell Press, 2004); Amy Erickson, 'Married Women's Occupations in Eighteenth-Century London', *Continuity and Change*, 23 (2008), 267–307; Natasha Korda, *Labors Lost: Women's Work and the Early Modern Stage* (Philadelphia: University of Pennsylvania Press, 2011), esp. 1–40; Eleanor Hubbard, *City Women: Money, Sex, and the Social Order in Early Modern London* (Oxford: Oxford University Press, 2012); Alexandra Shepard, 'Crediting Women in the Early Modern English Economy', *History Workshop Journal*, 79 (2015), 1–24; and Gowing, 'Girls on Forms', 447–73.

11 Antoinette Burton, *Dwelling in the Archive: Women Writing House, Home, and History in Late Colonial India* (Oxford: Oxford University Press, 2003); Ann Laura Stoler, *Along the Archival Grain: Epistemic Anxieties and Colonial Common Sense* (Princeton: Princeton University Press, 2009); Kathryn Burns, *Into the Archive: Writing and Power in Colonial Peru* (Durham: Duke University Press, 2010); Bhavani Raman, *Document Raj: Writing and Scribes in Early Colonial South India* (Chicago: University of Chicago Press, 2012); Kristen Weld, *Paper Cadavers: The Archives of Dictatorship in Guatemala* (Durham: Duke University Press, 2014); and Marisa Fuentes, *Dispossessed Lives: Enslaved Women, Violence, and the Archive* (Philadelphia: University of Pennsylvania, 2016).

12 See for example Joad Raymond, *Pamphlets and Pamphleteering in Early Modern Britain* (Cambridge: Cambridge University Press, 2013); and Jason Peacey, *Print and Public Politics in the English Revolution* (Cambridge: Cambridge University Press, 2013). Recent work has emphasised that manuscript circulation, and not just print, might engage such publics, see Millstone, *Manuscript Circulation and the Invention of Politics*.

13 Cardinal Wolsey and Thomas Cromwell, for example, might have had comparable archives but it is striking that multiple statesmen and administrators in Elizabethan and early Stuart England possessed such large archives.

14 For Egerton, see Louis A. Knafla, *Law and Politics in Jacobean England: The Tracts of Lord Chancellor Ellesmere* (Cambridge: Cambridge University Press, 1977).

15 Henry E. Huntington Library, Ellesmere Collection, HEH EL 2649 (hereafter HEH EL); HEH EL 2649B; HEH EL 1122; and HEH EL 34/A/9.

16 HEH EL 34/C/4; and HEH EL 35/C/36.

17 HEH EL 2547–2624.

Inscription and Political Exclusion   237

18 HEH EL 1230–1515.
19 HEH EL 1216.
20 HEH EL 2551.
21 HEH EL 456.
22 M.T. Clanchy, *From Memory to Written Record: England, 1066–1307* (London: Blackwell, 1993).
23 See Gowing, 'Girls on Forms', 447–73. For the question of whether and how women's spaces and spheres for public participation changed in the early modern period, see Amanda Vickery, 'Golden Age to Separate Spheres? A Review of the Categories and Chronology of English Women's History', *Historical Journal*, 36 (1993), 383–414.
24 For the Tower Records, see Elizabeth M. Hallam, 'The Tower of London as a Record Office', *Archives*, 14 (1979), 3–10.
25 Tim Stretton, *Women Waging Law in Early Modern England* (Cambridge: Cambridge University Press, 1998), 53.
26 See for example Stretton, *Women Waging Law*; Elaine Chalus, 'Elite Women, Social Politics, and the Political World of Late Eighteenth-Century England', *Historical Journal*, 43 (2000), 669–97; Mendelson and Crawford, *Women in Early Modern England*, 345–430; Barbara J. Harris, *English Aristocratic Women, 1450–1550* (Oxford: Oxford University Press, 2002), 175–209; and James Daybell, *Women Letter-Writers in Tudor England* (Oxford: Oxford University Press, 2006). Evidence of women's agency was more likely to manifest in letters than official records, and thus subject to more vagaries of preservation, see Daybell, 'Gender, Politics, and Archives in Early Modern England', 25–46.
27 Bernard Capp, 'Domestic Exclusions. The Politics of the Household in Early Modern England', 31–41.
28 Stretton, *Women Waging Law*, 68–9. Others, like Frances Dolan have drawn attention to the constructed and fictive nature of legal sources, suggesting that no authentic voice can be found in women's legal testimony, including witness depositions. Frances Dolan, *True Relations: Reading, Literature, and Evidence in Seventeenth-Century England* (Philadelphia: University of Pennsylvania Press, 2013), 123–39.
29 Shepard, 'Worthless Witnesses?', 717–34.
30 TNA C 272/1, f. 10r, 11r.
31 In May 1673 he obtained extracts of escheat rolls concerning the Henrician Earl of Angus Gilbert Umfraville, whose baronial seat and holdings had been in Northumberland. He also returned in this capacity in June 1674 to pay almost £4 for copies of other related escheat rolls and again in November 1674 to search for Stoake Cursy in Somerset, and again in January 1674/5 to search for 'several lands in Northumberland'. TNA C 272/1, f. 83r, 102r, 109r, 113r. The Countess had re-married by the time of Champion's final search.
32 For widows acting as executors, see Amy Louise Erickson, *Women and Property in Early Modern England* (London and New York: Routledge, 1994), 156–61.
33 Morley paid 'for a search of a Rent-Charge of St Marks per Annum settled to the Chappel of Hilton in Libertatu vel Episcapatu Durham' and then for a copy of a related entry from an Escheat Roll. TNA C 272/1, f. 9r, 10r.
34 TNA C 272/1, f. 15r.

238 *Nicholas Popper*

35 On the Ryleys, see John Eglington Bailey, *The Troubles of William Ryley, Lancaster Herald, of his Son, Clerks of the Records in the Tower* (Leigh: Chronicle Office, 1879).
36 TNA SP 29/387, f. 251r.
37 TNA SP 29/251, f. 200r; TNA SP 29/66 f.220; and TNA SP 45/21, f. 82r.
38 TNA SP 29/387, f. 252r.
39 TNA SP 29/387, f. 252v.
40 On women's oversight of household papers see, Stretton, *Women Waging Law*. For the potential power of women as custodians of household archives see Daybell, 'Gender, Politics, and Archives in Early Modern England', 25–46. For a compelling argument for using 'collaboration' as a framework for thinking about women's legal participation see Stretton, 'Women, Legal Records, and the Problem of the Lawyer's Hand', 684–700. For women petitioners in early modern England, see Bernard Capp, *When Gossips Meet: Women, Family, and Neighbourhood in Early Modern England* (Oxford: Oxford University Press, 2004), 306–11; and Amanda Jane Whiting, *Women and Petitioning in the Seventeenth-Century English Revolution: Deference, Difference, and Dissent* (Leiden: Brepols, 2015).
41 TNA SP 29/387, f. 252r.
42 Dolan, *True Relations*, 123–39.
43 For a somewhat similar case of women's relationship to the archive, see Gowing, 'Girls on Forms', 447–73.
44 It should be noted that their son Philip became a prosperous administrator. See the entry for 'William Ryley (d. 1667), herald and writer' in *The Oxford Dictionary of National Biography (ODNB)* (Oxford, 2004) https://doi.org/10.1093/ref:odnb/24423.
45 Note too that patriarchy was predicated on the notion that men could better represent women's interest without the inclusion of women's voices or labour. Dolan, *True Relations*, 123–39.
46 TNA SP 29/143, f. 265.
47 Her last name is also sometimes given as 'Welsh'. BL Harley MS 6751, f. 107v; and TNA C 272/1, f. 127r, f. 127v.
48 For the permeability of ostensibly gendered social spaces in early modern England, see Amanda Flather, *Gender and Space in Early Modern England* (Woodbridge: The Boydell Press, 2007).
49 For other contemporary examples, see Diane Willen, 'Women in the Public Sphere in Early Modern England: The Case of the Working Poor', *Sixteenth Century Journal*, 19 (1988), 559–75. Typical day wages for male labourers in this period were about 20 pence. If she swept once a week, her rate was under 10 pence, but it is unclear how often she worked there or, for example, whether it took the whole day. For such wage rates see Jeremy Boulton, 'Wage Labour in Seventeenth-Century London', *Economic History Review*, 49 (1996), 268–90.
50 TNA C 272/1, f. 124r.
51 BL Harley MS 6751, f. 108v.
52 BL Harley MS 6751, f. 102v.
53 Gadi Algazi, 'Scholars in Household: Refiguring the Learned Habitus, 1480–1550', *Science in Context*, 16 (2003), 9–42; and Alix Cooper, 'Homes and Households', in Katharine Park and Lorraine Daston (eds), *The Cambridge History of Science: Volume 3 Early Modern Science* (Cambridge: Cambridge University Press, 2006), 224–33.
54 TNA C 272/1, f. 128v.

55 TNA C 272/1, f. 127r.
56 See Bonnie G. Smith, 'Gender and the Practices of Scientific History', *American Historical Review*, 100 (1995), 1150–76; Joan M. Schwartz and Terry Cook, 'Archives, Records, and Power: The Making of Modern Memory', *Archival Science*, 2 (2002), 1–19; Antoinette Burton, *Dwelling in the Archive*; McSheffrey, 'Detective Fiction in the Archives', 65–78; and Imtiaz Habib, *Black Lives in the English Archives, 1500–1677: Imprints of the Invisible* (Aldershot: Ashgate, 2008).
57 See especially Fuentes, *Dispossessed Lives*, passim.

Afterword

Andrew Spicer

Early modern society was bound by certain conventions and understandings intended to maintain order and good relations within communities. Transgressing these principles could result in individuals or groups being marginalised or ostracised by the community. A few people appear to have been preternaturally disposed to defying convention, but there were also individuals who found themselves marginalised through no fault of their own. While some principles intended to regulate and maintain order within communities were legally defined, others were determined by relationships or societal norms. As the essays in this volume illustrate, the boundaries of what was considered acceptable or beyond the pale were at times malleable and porous. Social exclusion or inclusion could be negotiable. The application of societal conventions and norms depended on the particular circumstances as well as community attitudes towards the transgressors.

Focusing on these examples of negotiated exclusion and inclusion in early modern England might be summed up by the legal phrase 'the exception proves the rule'. This principle was reinterpreted during the early modern period from the medieval legal proverb, *exceptio probat regulum*.[1] Initially, this was understood in terms of overarching rules that were applied, apart from in anomalous or exceptional cases. The immutability of the general rule in spite of exceptions continued to be a subject for discussion in the early modern period.[2] By the mid-seventeenth century, outside the legal sphere, this understanding of the maxim had changed and came to mean the opposite position. In its translation into English *exceptio* was understood as 'something that is excepted' rather than its original sense of 'the action of excepting'. This redefinition of the phrase has come to justify inconsistencies.[3] The exceptions and the boundaries of early modern English society revealed in the essays in this volume provide some insights into the attitudes towards and limitations of the conventions and principles that governed and regulated communities.

The more serious threats to communal relations were legally defined and enforced through court prosecutions and the judicial punishment of

Afterword 241

offenders. The trial of and subsequent execution of the Earl of Castlehaven by his peers illustrates that even the higher echelons of society were held accountable for their actions.[4] Nonetheless, the application of the law was not always equal or straightforward. English common law could be a blunt-edged sword; lacking some of the nuances and distinctions evident in ecclesiastical and Roman law, which it largely supplanted following the Reformation. The more limited application of common law to describe illegitimate individuals is an example of this.[5] Furthermore, while recourse to the law might be necessary when communities were unable to resolve differences or negotiate accommodations for themselves, its effectiveness was at times compromised and limited. Overlapping and conflicting jurisdictions could hamper magistrates in trial proceedings and in administering justice.[6] There were also inconsistencies in the ways in which cases were conducted, which might result in a different set of exclusions. For example, the need to establish whether there had been consent in prosecutions for rape and sexual assault required more explicit testimony from young girls compared to that of older girls or women.[7] In part, this reflected the difficulty for the courts in determining what had happened and requiring a higher burden of proof, which is also evident in sodomy cases from the mid-eighteenth century.[8]

Legal process privileged male property holders; women had limited agency, and their status was generally subordinate to men, although widows had more access to the law.[9] Proposals put forward by Thomas Egerton, Lord Chancellor under Elizabeth I and James I, sought to limit further women's direct participation in litigation, particularly in cases relating to their honour.[10] Nonetheless, the vexatious lawsuits brought by the scheming Thorold sisters illustrate how women were able to access the courts by bringing cases in the name of their husbands and male relatives.[11] Even so, the reliance on historical precedent, drawing upon the administrative and legal archives of the state, 'amplified the embedded exclusions of these documents', with the result of ingraining these structures of marginalisation into the wider social and political order.[12]

Alongside the secular courts, the Church sought to uphold ecclesiastical law and societal values during this period. Illegitimate children were a particular concern as the religious authorities sought to address sins such as adultery, fornication, and other offences that had led to their births.[13] In establishing the circumstances surrounding these conceptions, the Church authorities regarded bridal pregnancies or infants conceived after a legal betrothal as 'legitimate in the eyes of God and the law'.[14] In the cases where sin had been committed, those concerned were required to perform their penance or pay a fine; the matter was then regarded as settled.[15] For those who failed to repent of their sins, exclusion from the community and excommunication from the

242 *Andrew Spicer*

Church might follow.[16] However, the church courts were abolished in 1641, and although they were restored after the Restoration, their authority was greatly diminished and limited the Church's effectiveness in dealing with transgressors.[17]

Besides the exercise of ecclesiastical and secular law, inclusion and exclusion from early modern communities were influenced by societal conventions and norms, such as patriarchy, kinship, and neighbourliness. Certain obligations and expectations also influenced relations between some groups, such as hospitality and sociability. Although pamphlets were published offering advice, these rules and etiquette had to be learned and acknowledged; failure to recognise and adhere to them carried the risk of being excluded. Across the essays in this volume, we see a number of examples where these societal norms were challenged or negotiated.[18]

Subordination to a patriarchal system was expected in early modern society; women vowed at their weddings to obey their husbands, while the fifth commandment enjoined children to honour their parents. Gender relations were, however, far more complicated than a simple dichotomy of patriarchal men and subordinated women.[19] Although the historical record upheld these hierarchical conventions, in certain circumstances, women could manipulate it to legitimate their actions and status.[20] The less subtle machinations of the Thorold sisters illustrate the determination of some women to assert their authority over their husbands and male relatives, and the failure of the male clergy and lawmakers to put a stop to their schemes.[21] Symbolically and in practice, women wearing breeches was regarded as a violation of godly order, due to the Old Testament condemnation of cross-dressing, and an overt threat to male authority. The fashion for women to don quasi-masculine attire during the early seventeenth century led James I to order ministers to preach against 'the insolencie of our women' and the publication of several diatribes against the practice.[22] In a lighter vein, ballads and jestbooks poked fun at the notion of women dressed as men.[23] Probably the ultimate challenge to the patriarchy was adulterous wives. Early modern comedies, libels, and satires used cuckolds or their signature horns to defame and ridicule the husbands of unfaithful wives. Such challenges to male authority were robustly defended, often in the courts and sometimes with violence.[24]

This volume also makes evident that challenges to the patriarchal system stemmed from the failure of some men to observe social conventions. Charivari or skimmington rides, as depicted in one of the engravings from the series *English Customs* (Figure 8.1), punished men for failing to govern their wives.[25] Besides maintaining order within the family, the patriarch's authority also encompassed their servants. The head of the household was expected to maintain a social distance from the servants and certainly not fraternise with them.[26] As significant as the accusations of rape, sodomy, and sexual debauchery made against the Earl of Castlehaven were, his exclusion resulted from his failure as a patriarch. This was compounded by his defence that presented him as the victim of a conspiracy instigated by his wife and son.[27] While this was a more extreme example, it underscores the failure of some men to preside over their households and uphold the social hierarchy.[28]

Neighbourliness was also a significant factor in determining social acceptance as 'it provided a set of values and expectations that could be appealed to by all – by enforcers of the norm, the mediators of disputes, and those who sought to aid redress'.[29] Although neighbours carefully policed their communities, denouncing those guilty of various misdeeds or expressing their disapproval of wrongdoers, several essays in this volume illustrate the support provided by neighbours and their efforts to maintain harmony within the community.[30] Far from routinely ostracising single mothers, some members of the community would actively prevent their parochial exclusion, sometimes at great personal cost.[31] Relations within the community were constantly being re-assessed. The number of defamation cases brought before the courts, particularly by women, reflected the importance of preserving and upholding reputations. Slanderous accusations and sexual insults were contested, although the pejorative term 'bastard' was not similarly used to defame individuals.[32] The reputation of Dissenting and Catholic women was similarly challenged through their portrayal as a threat to society. Yet, women from Independent and nonconforming back-grounds sought to overcome this stereotype by their expressions of neighbourliness.[33]

The significance of neighbourliness in maintaining community rela-tions can be best illustrated by the obligation of hospitality, which overcame other differences that might have otherwise prompted social exclusion.[34] That it did so does not mean that there was not an under-lying tension between the hosts and their guests. This is evident in a few examples from this volume. Despite their confessional differences, Sir Thomas Hoby provided hospitality for the Catholic William Eure's hunting party, although the raucous guests exploited the opportunity to denigrate their host's faith and impugn his honour.[35] Similar tensions no doubt arose from the dinner claimed by Sir Pexall Brocas and his men from the Lord Mayor of London.[36] Sociability amongst male elites was also important for maintaining personal and political connections. While these might override exclusionary factors, this sociability could be disrupted by political antagonisms and rivalries.[37]

By the eighteenth century, the sophisticated rules and conventions that determined acceptance and behaviour in polite society spawned its own literature to guide the fashionable elite.[38] Nonetheless, some high-ranking women, lacking the necessary education, failed to understand the expected conventions and thereby risked social exclusion.[39] It was an

244 *Andrew Spicer*

environment fraught with anxiety and uncertainty. Even the selection of a young woman's friends brought potential risks lest a former confidante revealed secrets that undermined the individual's reputation or that of her family.[40] Inclusion required women to conform to the social norms in their comportment and politeness.[41] Even the language employed in these circles underscored their social difference and exclusion, where the term bastard might be more readily employed in polite circles to denote a social inferior than an equal.[42]

While entry to these elite circles had to be negotiated, some aspects of sociability and civility conflicted with particular religious beliefs. As gambling and playing cards were regarded to be at odds with a godly life, some individuals chose not to participate, or even withdrew from polite society.[43] For Dissenting women, conscious of their own inherent sinfulness and the need to live exemplary lives, they took particular care to ensure that their behaviour and demeanour did not attract adverse comment.[44] Similar concerns about morality and propriety probably lay behind the efforts of the female donors to the Westminster Infirmary to prevent the admission of patients suffering from venereal disease.[45] The moral concerns of its supporters also combined with a process of institutionalised exclusion on religious grounds. Founded in the early eighteenth century, to restore social order in the capital by addressing the needs of the sick poor, the Westminster Infirmary also sought 'to stifle the threat of religious dissent'. The hospital directed its charitable activities towards those who 'shall give full satisfaction and proof to the Society of their being Protestants', which principally meant Anglicans. This confessional distinction also extended to the hospital staff, as evidenced by the fact that two Catholic nurses were summarily dismissed for fear that they might subvert this Anglican institution.[46]

A number of these essays have illustrated how women challenged and negotiated the prevailing attitudes and circumstances regarding their place and status through analysing particular individuals as well as, more broadly, the role of women in early modern society. This includes thinking about how the agency and presence of women can be revealed, read, and heard in the archives and historical record. To what extent might a similar approach be taken to better understand attitudes to those marginalised by early modern society due to their colour, disability, nationality, and sexuality? Recent research, for example, has drawn attention to the illegitimate children of East India Company employees and Indian concubines who were sent 'home' in the eighteenth century for education, marriage, or employment in Britain.[47] Similarly, illegitimate mixed-race children were sent from the West Indies by their white fathers to be educated in Britain. Probably the most well-known example being Dido Elizabeth Belle, the illegitimate daughter of an African slave in the West Indies and a royal navy captain, Sir John Lindsay, who was brought up by her great uncle, the Earl of Mansfield.[48]

Afterword 245

Nonetheless, Belle and other Anglo-West Indian migrants, like the 're-turning' Anglo-Indian children, had an ambiguous and negotiated po-sition within the household and English society. These were not the black poor of eighteenth-century London, but the children of elite men, whose illegitimacy and racial background meant that their social position and status was complicated.[49] The experience of Belle and others illustrates how mixed-race progeny could be accommodated within English society, although this remains an area for further research.[50]

Engaging with other marginalised communities and individuals offers further perspectives on early modern society, in particular how its parameters were understood and negotiated. Whilst there were sig-nificant conventions and principles that underpinned early modern so-ciety, they were not immutable. As these essays have illustrated, these societal norms were contested and negotiated according to particular circumstances and situations. The boundary between inclusion and ex-clusion was not absolute and clear cut. Some individuals or groups were ostracised, but there were also gradations of social exclusion depending on the attitudes of the local community. Neighbourliness could, on oc-casion, result in social conventions and even the law being flouted and ignored in favour of those who might otherwise be excluded. The ex-amples in this volume demonstrate the complexities of this process of engaging with societal norms, but they also underscore their existence and importance. In this sense, the exceptions do prove the rule.

Notes

1 Paul Hymans, 'Due Process versus the Maintenance of Order in European Law: The Contribution of the *ius commune*', in Peter Cross (ed.), *The Moral World of the Law* (Cambridge: Cambridge University Press, 2000), 88.
2 'exception, n.'. *Oxford English Dictionary Online (OED)*. June 2020. Oxford University Press www.oed.com/view/Entry/65724. Accessed 20 August 2020; Ian Maclean, 'Evidence, Logic, the Rule and the Exception in Renaissance Law and Medicine', *Early Science and Medicine*, 5 (2000), 235–6.
3 'exception, n.'. *OED*; Donald F. Bond, 'English Legal Proverbs', *Proceedings of the Modern Language Association of America*, 51 (1936), 933–4.
4 Cynthia B. Herrup, 'Mervin Touchet, Second Earl of Castlehaven (1593–1631)', *Oxford Dictionary of National Biography (ODNB)* (Oxford, 2004) https://doi.org/10.1093/ref:odnb/66794; Susan D. Amussen, 'Failing at Patriarchy: Gender, Exclusion and Violence, 1560–1640', 184–5.
5 Kate Gibson, 'The Language of Exclusion: "Bastard" in Early Modern England', 47–8, 50. See also Martin Ingram, '"Popular" and "Official" Justice: Punishing Sexual Offenders in Tudor London', in Fernanda Pirie and Judith Scheele (eds), *Legalism: Community and Justice* (Oxford: Oxford University Press, 2014), 201–4.
6 Bernard Capp, 'Domestic Exclusions. The Politics of the Household in Early Modern England', 35–6, 40–1. See also James McComish, 'Defining Boundaries: Law, Justice, and Community in Sixteenth-Century England', in

246 *Andrew Spicer*

Pirie and Scheele (eds), *Legalism: Community and Justice*, 125–49; Ingram, '"Popular" and "Official" Justice', 204–9; Shannon McSheffrey, 'Stranger Artisans and the London Sanctuary of St. Martin le Grand in the Reign of Henry VIII', *Journal of Medieval and Early Modern Studies*, 43 (2013), 545–71.

7 Sarah Toulalan, 'They "Know as Much at Thirteen as If They Had Been Midwives of Twenty Years Standing": Girls and Sexual Knowledge in Early Modern England', 205–14.

8 Netta Murray Goldsmith, *The Worst of Crimes. Homosexuality and the Law in Eighteenth-Century London* (Aldershot: Ashgate, 1998), 34–37, 54–57.

9 Cynthia B. Herrup, 'Law and Morality in Seventeenth-Century England', *Past and Present*, 106 (1985), 108; Garthine Walker and Jenny Kermode, 'Introduction', in Jenny Kermode and Garthine Walker (eds), *Women, Crime and the Courts in Early Modern England* (London, 1994), 6–8; Nicholas Popper, 'Inscription and Political Exclusion in Early Modern England', 226–7.

10 Popper, 'Inscription and Political Exclusion', 227. See Laura Gowing, 'Language, Power, and the Law: Women's Slander Litigation in Early Modern London', in Kermode and Walker (eds), *Women, Crime and the Courts*, 26–47.

11 Capp, 'Domestic Exclusions', 34–5, 37, 40. See also Kermode and Walker (eds), *Women, Crime and the Courts*.

12 Popper, 'Inscription and Political Exclusion', 225, 225–7.

13 Gibson, 'The Language of Exclusion', 47–8; Charmian Mansell, 'Defining the Boundaries of Community? Experiences of Parochial Inclusion and Pregnancy Outside Wedlock in Early Modern England', 144–6.

14 Mansell, 'Defining the Boundaries of Community?', 148, 144–6.

15 Ibid., 145–6, 154–5.

16 Ibid., 141–2, 145–6.

17 See Andrew Thomson, 'Church Discipline: The Operation of the Winchester Consistory Court in the Seventeenth Century', *History*, 91 (2006), 337–59, esp. 350–52.

18 See for example, Carys Brown, 'Women and Religious Co-existence in Eighteenth-Century England', 68–87; Naomi Pullin, 'Failed Friendship and the Negotiation of Exclusion in Eighteenth-Century Polite Society', 88–114; Tom Rose, 'Hunting, Sociability, and the Politics of Inclusion and Exclusion in Early Seventeenth-Century England', 161–78; Kathryn Woods, 'The Negotiation of Inclusion and Exclusion in the Westminster Infirmary, 1716–1750', 117–40.

19 Michael J. Braddick and John Walter, 'Grids of Power: Order, Hierarchy and Subordination in Early Modern Society', in Michael J. Braddick and John Walter (eds), *Negotiating Power in Early Modern Society: Order, Hierarchy and Subordination in Britain and Ireland* (Cambridge: Cambridge University Press, 2001), 17–21.

20 Popper, 'Inscription and Political Exclusion', 221–2, 226, 227–301; Braddick and Walter, 'Grids of Power', 20–21; Gowing, 'Language, Power, and the Law', 42–3.

21 Capp, 'Domestic Exclusions', 31–40.

22 Quoted in Sandra Clark, '"Hic Mulier," "Haec Vir," and the Controversy over Masculine Women', *Studies in Philology*, 82 (1985), 166; Mark Stoyle, '"Give mee a Souldier's Coat": Female Cross-Dressing during the English Civil War', *History*. 103 (2018), 7–13; David Cressy, 'Gender Trouble and Cross-Dressing in Early Modern England', *Journal of British Studies*, 35 (1996), 442–5.

Afterword 247

23 Stoyle, '"Give mee a Souldier's Coat"', 9–11; Rose, 'Hunting, Sociability, and the Politics of Inclusion and Exclusion', 169–70.

24 Amussen, 'Failing at Patriarchy', 188–91. See also Braddick and Walter, 'Grids of Power', 29–30.

25 Amussen, 'Failing at Patriarchy', 191–2.

26 Ibid., 184–87, 193.

27 Ibid., 184–5; Cynthia Herrup, 'Sex and Gender: The Patriarch at Home: The Trial of the Second Earl of Caslehaven for Rape and Sodomy', *History Workshop Journal*, 41 (1996), 1–18.

28 Capp, 'Domestic Exclusions', 29–30, 35–6, 40.

29 Keith Wrightson, 'The "Decline of Neighbourliness" Revisited', in Norman L. Jones and Daniel R. Woolf (eds), *Local Identities in Late Medieval and Early Modern England* (Basingstoke: Palgrave Macmillan, 2007), 32. See also Keith Wrightson, 'Mutualities and Obligations: Changing Social Relationships in Early Modern England', *Proceedings of the British Academy*, 139 (2006), 157–94.

30 Mansell, 'Defining the Boundaries of Community?', 141–2, 148–9; Capp, 'Domestic Exclusions', 35, 38–9. See also Faramerz Dabhoiwala, 'Sex, Social Relations and the Law in Seventeenth- and Eighteenth-Century London', in Braddick and Walter (eds), *Negotiating Power*, 94.

31 Mansell, 'Defining the Boundaries of Community?', 149–54; Amussen, 'Failing at Patriarchy', 192–4.

32 Wrightson, 'Mutualities and Obligations', 173; Gowing, 'Language, Power, and the Law', 26–47; Martin Ingram, 'Law, Litigants and the Construction of "Honour": Slander Suits in Early Modern England', in Cross (ed.), *The Moral World of the Law*, 134–60, esp. 148–57; Mansell, 'Defining the Boundaries of Community?', 145–6; Gibson, 'The Language of Exclusion', 58–60.

33 Brown, 'Women and Religious Co-existence', 72–3, 76–9.

34 Felicity Heal, *Hospitality in Early Modern England* (Oxford: Oxford University Press, 1990), 3–8.

35 Ibid., 13, 198; Rose, 'Hunting, Sociability, and the Politics of Inclusion and Exclusion', 166–8.

36 Amussen, 'Failing at Patriarchy', 186.

37 Rose, 'Hunting, Sociability, and the Politics of Inclusion and Exclusion', 162–5.

38 Pullin, 'Failed Friendship and the Negotiation of Exclusion', 90–4. See also Brown, 'Women and Religious Co-existence', 71–3.

39 Pullin, 'Failed Friendship and the Negotiation of Exclusion', 92–3, 94–5.

40 Ibid., 93.

41 Ibid., 92–4.

42 Gibson, 'The Language of Exclusion', 52–8.

43 Brown, 'Women and Religious Co-existence', 75–7 Rose, 'Hunting, Sociability, and the Politics of Inclusion and Exclusion', 167.

44 Brown, 'Women and Religious Co-existence', 80–1.

45 Woods, 'The Negotiation of Inclusion and Exclusion', 123–4, 131–2.

46 Ibid., 122, 125–6, 127.

47 Durba Ghosh, *Sex and the Family in Colonial India. The Making of Empire* (Cambridge: Cambridge University Press), 125–28; Margot Finn, 'Anglo-Indian Lives in the Later Eighteenth and Early Nineteenth Centuries', *Journal for Eighteenth-Century Studies*, 33 (2010), 59–61; Ellen Filor, 'The Intimate Trade of Alexander Hall. Salmon and Slaves in Scotland and Sumatra, c.1745–1765' and Alistair Mutch, 'Connecting Britain and India. General Patrick Duff and Madeira', in Margot Finn and Kate Smith (eds), *The East India Company at Home, 1757–1857* (London: UCL Press, 2018), 329–31, 341–2.

48 Reyhan King, 'Belle [married name Davinier], Dido Elizabeth (1761?–1804)', *ODNB* https://doi.org/10.1093/ref:odnb/73352. See also Daniel Livesay, *Children of Uncertain Fortune: Mixed-Race Jamaicans in Britain and the Atlantic Family* (Chapel Hill: University of North Carolina Press, 2018), 8–15, 75–7, 101–5, 219–32.
49 King, 'Belle [married name Davinier], Dido Elizabeth', *ODNB*; Livesay, *Children of Uncertain Fortune*, 106–12, 219–32; Finn, 'Anglo-Indian Lives', 59–61.
50 Finn and Smith (eds), *The East India Company at Home*, 12, 20, 430.

Contributors

Susan D. Amussen is Professor of History at the University of California, Merced, and a historian of early modern England, gender, and race. Her books include *An Ordered Society: Gender and Class in Early Modern England* (Basil Blackwell, 1988); *Caribbean Exchanges: Slavery and the Transformation of English Society* (University of North Carolina Press, 2007); and *Gender, Culture and Politics in England, 1560–1640: Turning the World Upside Down* (Bloomsbury, 2017). She is currently pursuing the history of patriarchy as a social formation in early modern England and co-editing the early modern volume of the New Cambridge History of Britain.

Carys Brown is a Research Fellow at Trinity College, Cambridge. She completed her PhD at the University of Cambridge and has also been a Research Associate on the AHRC-funded project *Faith in the Town, 1740–1830*, based at the University of Manchester. She is currently working on her monograph, *Friends, Neighbours, Sinners: Religious Difference and English Society, 1689–1750*, and is beginning a new project on the upbringing of children in eighteenth-century England. She has articles published in *The Historical Journal*, *British Catholic History*, and *Journal for Eighteenth-Century Studies*.

Bernard Capp is Emeritus Professor of History at the University of Warwick, where he taught from 1968 to 2020, and a Fellow of the British Academy. His books include *When Gossips Meet: Women, Family and Neighbourhood in Early Modern England* (2003), *England's Culture Wars* (2012), and *The Ties that Bind: Siblings, Family and Society in Early Modern England* (2018), all published by OUP. He is currently writing a book on British slaves in Barbary.

Kate Gibson is a Research Associate at the University of Manchester, working on the AHRC-funded project, *Faith in the Town: Lay Religion, Urbanisation and Industrialisation in England, 1740–1830*. She has published on the histories of unmarried mothers, extra-marital sex, Catholic marriage, and religious sociability in the eighteenth century in *The Historical Journal*, *Cultural & Social History*, *Journal of Family History, and forthcoming in Past & Present*. She is currently working on a monograph on the experiences of illegitimate individuals in England between 1660 and 1834.

250   *Contributors*

Charmian Mansell is a British Academy Postdoctoral Research Fellow at the University of Cambridge. She is a social and economic historian of early modern England, with particular research interests in gender, work, community, and everyday travel. She has published several articles on female service, including 'The Variety of Women's Experiences as Servants in England (1548–1649): Evidence from Church Court Depositions', *Continuity and Change*, 33 (2018) and 'Beyond the Home: Space and Agency in the Experiences of Female Service in Early Modern England', which is forthcoming in *Gender and History*. She is currently working on a monograph titled *Female Servants in Early Modern England* as well as embarking on a new project titled 'Everyday Travel and Community in Early Modern England'.

Nicholas Popper is Associate Professor of History at the College of William & Mary. He is completing a book examining how the proliferation of archives transformed politics and epistemology in early modern Britain. He is the author of *Walter Ralegh's History of the World, and the Historical Culture of the Late Renaissance* (Chicago, 2012) and numerous articles and book chapters. He is also Book Review Editor of the *William and Mary Quarterly*.

Naomi Pullin is Assistant Professor of Early Modern British History at the University of Warwick. She is the author of *Female Friends and the Making of Transatlantic Quakerism, 1650–1750* (Cambridge University Press, 2018), and has published a number of articles and book chapters on different aspects of early Quaker culture and women's involvement in international religious communities in the seventeenth and eighteenth centuries. She is currently writing a new monograph on the relationship between sociability and solitude in early modern Britain, which is supported by a Leverhulme Early Career Fellowship.

Tom Rose successfully completed a PhD in January 2020 at the University of Nottingham titled 'Hunting in Early Stuart England: Status, Sociability, and Politics'. His research looked at how politics (in its broadest sense) and socialising intersected through an analysis of hunting in the early seventeenth century. He now works in the Civil Service.

Andrew Spicer is Professor of Early Modern European History at Oxford Brookes University and President of the Sixteenth Century Society and Conference. His research focuses on the socio-cultural impact of the Reformation, and he has also published widely on aspects of immigration and refugee communities in early modern England. His publications include *The Place of the Social Margins, 1350–1750* (London and New York: Routledge, 2017) co-edited with Jane Stevens Crawshaw.

Sarah Toulalan is Associate Professor of Early Modern History at the University of Exeter. Her work focuses on the histories of bodies, sex, reproduction, and sexuality in the early modern period. Her monograph, *Imagining Sex: Pornography and Bodies in Seventeenth-Century England*, was published by Oxford University Press in 2007. She is currently completing a second monograph on children and sex in early modern England and has published several journal articles and chapters in books on this subject, including on child rapists in the *Journal of the History of Sexuality*.

Kathryn Woods is Dean of Students at Goldsmiths, University of London. She was previously Director of Student Experience for the Faculty of Arts, and Teaching Fellow in the History of Medicine, at the University of Warwick (2015–20). She was awarded her PhD in History by the University of Edinburgh. She has published research on the social meanings of different aspects of physical appearance in the eighteenth-century Britain in the *Journal for Eighteenth-Century Studies* and *Social and Cultural History*. Her current research focuses on the history of the student experience 1950 to present.

Index

Act of Toleration 6, 41, 68–9
Adair, Richard 45
Addams, William 156
adolescents, in stepfamilies 29
adultery: domestic violence caused by
28; examples of 185–86; language
of 45; legal challenges for 152–53;
libelous attacks for 190; patriarchal
responses to 188; pregnancy outside
wedlock caused by 144
Agarde, Arthur 224
Allen, Charles 104
Anderson, Benedict 11
Anglican church; *see* Church of
England
Anglicanism 74
Anne of Denmark, Queen 169–70
archives 223–24; *see also* Tower of
London Record Office
Armstrong, Ellenor 32
Arrowsmith, Steven 205
Aschheim, Steven 10, 12
Ash, John 50
Astill, Edward 189–90
atheism 79
Athenian Mercury 93
Athenian Society 93
Avyard, John 44

Bacon, Francis 1
'badging of the poor' 6
Bailey, Nathan 49
Baird, Ileana 123
Barrel, William 212
Barry, Jonathan 117
Bartholin, Thomas 49
bastard: in biblical passages 48;
definition of 49; elite child as 54; as
illegitimacy term 44, 48, 52; as

insult 46, 50, 58, 61; natural versus
61; as pejorative term 45–6, 49,
53–4, 59–60; as poverty term 53,
59; prosecution of 58, 60; religious
view of 48–9; shame and 57; as
slander term 58–9; as socio-
economic distinction term 54–5;
synonyms for 48–50, 54, 59
Batchley, Elizabeth 155
Baynham, John 206
Beale, Robert 223
Beauvoir, Osmond 99, 101, 104
Bedell, Capell 171
behavioural expectations, patriarchy
as basis for 7
Belcher, Jane 131
Belle, Dido Elizabeth 244–45
Bennett, Anna Maria 53
Bennett, Judith 222
Bennett, Walter 145
Bentinck, Margaret Cavendish 88
Berryman, John 150
Bessborough, Lady 55
Blackmore, Abigail 77
Blackstone, William 48
Blomfield, Henry 55
Blount, Thomas 49
Borsay, Peter 123
Boswell, James 56
Boult, Eleanor 152
Bourdieu, Pierre 11
Braddick, Michael J. 6, 174
Braithwaite, Richard 168
Brennelcombe, John 147
Brewster, Thomas 189–90
Brickinshaw, Mary 210
Brittlebank, William 54
Broadben, Elizabeth 206
Brocas, Pexall 185–88, 243

Brooke, Katherine 152
Brown, Julian 214
Brydall, John 48
Buckley, Margaret 28
Buckley, Richard 28
Buckley, Robert 28
Burney, Fanny 88, 95, 100

Caesar, Julius 223
Cannon, John 52, 56
Canterbury School 99
Capp, Bernard 7, 78, 142, 154, 227
Carew, George 223
Carter, Elizabeth 88–9, 94–6,
   99–103, 105
Castlehaven, Earl of 184–87, 241
Catholics: hunting by 165–66, 174;
   Lutherans and 5–6; Protestants and
   83, 165–66, 174
Cecil, Robert 162–63
Cecil, William 223
Chalkley, Martha 211
Chamberlain, John 171
Champion, Henry 228
Chapman, Edward 203
Chapone, Hester 99
"Character of a Presbyterian, or a
   Female Hypocrite" 72
Chardon, Roger 141–42
charitable hospitals; see Westminster
   Infirmary
Charitable Society for the Sick Poor
   and Needy 121, 123
charity: description of 13, 78; for
   pregnant unmarried women
   149–54; of Westminster Infirmary
   117–18, 122
charivari 7, 165, 182, 188, 191, 242
Charles I 169, 171
Charles II 229
Cheadle, Thomas 28–9
Chester, Anthony 229
children: see 'bastard'; see 'girls';
   legitimacy of 47; as defendants for
   rape 200–20
childbirth 77
Chorier, Nicolas 203
Church of England 9, 52, 70–1, 79,
   81–2; punishment for extramarital
   sex 145; pregnancy outside wedlock
   and 144–45, 156, 242; repentance
   from 145
Churchman, John 74

Churchman, Mary 78
civility 92
Clanchy, Michael 225
Clare, John 54
Clark, Anna 153
Clark, Peter 123
Clifford, Anne 173
Clifford, Henry 164
Clifton, Gervase 166
Clifton, Sarah 206
Coates, John 211, 213
Cockaine, Thomas 168
Cockburn, Patrick 123
coffeehouse 9
Coleborn, Henry 36, 38
*Commentaries on the Laws of
   England* 48
commercialism 92
communities: belonging purpose of 12;
   cohesion purpose of 12; collective
   identity of 13; conflict and 13;
   Simmel's theory of 12; social
   structures in 6
community organisation 8
community relations, neighbourliness
   in maintaining 240, 243
Congregationalism 74
Cook, Christian 153
Cooper, Alice 154
Cooper, William 35–6
coverture, doctrine of 227
Cowan, Brian 9
Crawford, Patricia 168, 222
Creese, Morgan 147
Crofts, Lady 173
Cromwell, Oliver 32, 38
Crosier, Esther 207
cross-dressing 242
Cuckold's Haven/Cuckold's
   Point 188
cuckolds/cuckoldry 167, 185,
   187–92
Culliford, Francis 146
Culpeper, Nicholas 200

Dabhoiwala, Faramerz 201
Dampire, John 28
d'Arblay, Alexandre 100–1
Davies, Alice 151
Davy, Thomas 57
Dawson, Anne 74–6, 78, 80
Day, Elizabeth 53
Day, John 191

254 *Index*

defamation: declining use of 56; illegitimacy as 58–60; language of 45–6

deism 79

Delaney, Mary 99

Denman, Charles 209

Devereux, Robert 163

Dickenson, John 96–7, 99, 103, 109

Dictionary of the English Language 1

DiGangi, Mario 204

Diocesan courts, morality enforcement by 144

Dissenting women: community relations affected by 78–9; definition of 69; disobeying of husbands by 74–5; Established Church and 79, 81–2; isolation of 77, 82; pious behavior of 82; reading of religious texts by 74; religious standards for 82; social behaviour of 76–7; stereotypes of 73; unpleasantness of 75–6; wealthy ladies and 81

Dixon, Anna 211, 213

Dodsley, Lady 130

Dolan, Frances 83, 230

domestic exclusion: case studies of 29–41; contexts for 27–8; failing marriages as cause of 28; in family structures 29–41; inheritance issues as cause of 27–8; stepfamilies 28–9; by stepmother 29–31

domestic violence 28, 192–94

Donovan, Bill 3

Dore, Marie 148

Douglas, Andrew 88

Douglas, Mary 4

Dover, Hepzibah 210

Duncan, Derek 4

Durkheim, Émile 11–13

East India Company 244

ecclesiastical law 150, 241–42

Edward I 225

Edward III 224

Egerton, Thomas 223–26, 241

Elizabeth I 221

Elizabethan Poor Laws 142; *see also* Poor Laws

empiricism, science and 11

English Customs 191, 242

English Gentleman, The 168

English Gentlewoman, The 168

erotic texts 203–4

Essex, John 72

Established Church; *see* Church of England

Eure, William 166–68, 243

Everesse, Edmund 150

exclusion: definition of 1; in history 2–10; religion and 166; theories of 10–3

Exclusion Crisis 9

exclusionary culture, social structure and 8

exclusionary texts 225–27

extramarital affairs, 53, 144–45, 152

"face-to-face" society 8

factitional politics, hunting and 162–65

failed patriarchs: chastising of 188; cuckolding of 188–92; description of 183; examples of 184–85; exclusion of 242–43; execution for 184–85; insults by 194; marital breakdown as result of 187; punishment for 184–87, 242

falconry 170

families, domestic exclusion in 29–41

Farington, Joseph 44, 53

Farrant, Jane 131

father: disinheritance by 27–8; patriarchy of; *see* patriarchy

Father's Legacy to His Daughters, A 93

Faucet, Mary 209

fear: marginalisation caused by 4

Felmingham, Anne 192

Felmingham, Thomas 192–93

Female Spectator 71

Fenwick, Joshua 59

Field, Jane 211

Finch, Isabella 53

Flather, Amanda 169

Forbes, Ann 207

Ford, Susan 141

Fosse, Edward 189

Fothergill, John 95, 99, 104

Foundling Hospital 46, 56

Foyster, Elizabeth 7

Frances, Edward 190–91

Freeman, Thomas Edwards 94

Friar, Avice 141

friendship: case study of 94–110; dishonour caused by breakdown in 93; in eighteenth-century advice literature 90–4; failed 98–109; importance of 91; intimacy of 98; overview of 88–90; politeness in 89, 91–2, 109; power hierarchies in 104; secrets in 104; as social relationships 90; subordination in 104; women's natural propensity for 93

Game Laws 161
Garner, William 210
Garrioch, David 60
Gascoigne, George 161
Gee, Joshua 120
gender: illegitimacy descriptions affected by 55–6; *see also* women; norms of 182
gender order 183
gendered expectations 68, 71
gendered mediations 228–31
George I 123
George II 123
George III 95
gin 134–35
girls: female body parts as understood by 210–11; *see also* women; literacy of 204; modesty by 208; rape of 201; sexual consent of 205–7, 209; sexual knowledge of 200–5; sexual understanding of 214
Glossographia 49
Gobert, John 189
Godwin, Elizabeth 141
Goodwin, Andrew 35, 38
Goodwin, Wessel 31–41
Gordon, John 190–91
gossip 13
Gouge, William 27, 187
Gough, Richard 51–2
Gould, Joana 154–55
Gowing, Laura 142, 144, 208
Gregory, John 92–3
Greig, Hannah 8, 92
Grey, Elizabeth 172–73
Griffiths, Elizabeth 168
Gurney, Dorothy 169

habitus 11
Hall, Elizabeth 212
Halvorson, Michael J. 12
Hamilton, Mary 88–9, 94–8, 102–5, 107
Hamlyn, Nicholas 155
Hammond, Henry 122

Hanlon, Gregory 13
Hannet, Rachel 206, 207
Hanway, Jonas 56
Harris, Barbara 172
Harris, Jane 207
Harris, Tim 10
Harvey, Karen 7
Hat, John 39
hawking 168–70
Hawkins, Elizabeth 145
Hawkins, William 213
Hawksmoor, Nicholas 122
Haywood, Eliza 71
Heal, Felicity 151, 161
Heigham, Robert 169–70
Heister, Ann 57
Helmholz, Richard 149
Henry, Matthew 48
Henry IV 224
Henry VIII 226
Herbert, Amanda 74
Hewes, Elizabeth 193
Hickes, George 71
Higgens, Martha 146
Highland, Samuel 40
Hilliard, William 167
Hindle, Steve 6, 151
"history from below" 3
Hitchcock, Tim 13
Hitchens, Richard 141
Hobcraft, John 10
Hoby, Thomas Posthumous 166–67, 189, 243
Holmes, Clive 161
Hooper, Jane 153–54
Hopkins, Elizabeth 148
horns, as cuckold sign 188–89
Howard, Frances 163
Hull, Joanne 141–42, 156
Humphreys, Margaret 126
Hunter, John 205, 209
hunting: androcentrism of 161; as elite sport 161; exclusion in 161–62; factitional politics in 162–65; inclusion through 163; as male activity 168; religion and 165–68, 174; social participation in 161–62; social politics of 164–65, 173–74; women in 168–74
hunting chase 169
hunting parties: inclusion through 166–67; social status-related boundaries in 162

256 *Index*

hunting rights 165
hunting sociability: fluidity of 164,
174; overview of 161–62; power
and 174; women in 172
husband: domestic violence by
192–94; governing of wife by 182

illegitimacy: "bastard" as 44, 48, 52;
Church's views on 241; classes of
47; common law view of 48;
contextual descriptions for 54, 60;
as defamation 58–60; elite 53;
experience of 50–8; gender
differences in descriptions of 55–6;
labels used in 46–7, 50–2, 61;
language of 44–6, 52; legislation 48;
lower-status authors' use of 54;
marriage and 46; morality and 56;
"natural" as 44–6, 50, 52–3, 61; in
pauper letters 54–5; personal
relationships and 56; public
identification of 56; reputational
damage of 58–9; Shaw's view of 54;
as sin 241; socio-economic status
effects on 51, 62; stigma/
stigmatisation associated with 44–6,
58, 62; vocabulary of 47–50, 52, 60
"imagined communities" 12
incestuous relationships, bastards as
children of 52
Inchbald, Elizabeth 55
inclusion: exclusion and 1; in history
2–10; hunting and 163, 166–67; of
Independent women 77; in polite
society 110; of pregnant unmarried
women 154–56; religion and 79–81,
166; theories of 10–3; in
Westminster Infirmary 117–37
Independent women: community
relations affected by 78–9;
description of 69–70; devotional
literature 73; exclusion of 73–6;
inclusion of 77; isolation of 82; moral
reputation of 81; neighbourly duty by
77–9; reputation of 80–1; stereotypes
of 72–3; visiting the sick by 78
infanticide 144, 149
Ingram, Arthur 164
inscriptional patriarchy 225–27
insults: bastard as 46, 58, 60–1;
cuckolds 190; gender norms
maintained through 183; language
of 45; violence and 191

Interregnum 69
Irish, Mary 208

Jackson, John 165
Jackson, William 141
James I 224, 242
James II 9
James VI 163
Johnson, Samuel 1, 50, 91
Johnson, Thomas 54
Jones, Benjamin 213
Jones, Catherine 148
Jones, Colin 117
Jones, Edward 33, 35, 37, 40
Jones, Mehetabel 32–5, 38, 40
Jütte, Robert 45

Kaplan, Benjamin J 5
Kiffin, William 33, 39
Knibb, Richard 211
Knight, Katherine 154
Knollys, Hanserd 33–4, 41

Ladies Dictionary, The 93
Lambarde, William 224
land ownership 161
Lane, Peter 147
Langford, Paul 91
language: of adultery 45; of defamation
45–6; exclusion through 45; of
illegitimacy 44–6; moral attitudes
conveyed through 45; of poverty 45;
socio-economic status and 60
Le Strange, Alice 168
Le Strange, Nicholas 169
Leake, Francis 171, 173
Leeming, Benjamin 54
leprosy, witchcraft and 4
Lerry, Elizabeth 145–46
Lewes, Nicholas 148
Lewknor, Edward 169
Lex Spurorium 48
libel 190
libertinism 79
Lindsay, John 244
Link, Bruce 45
Lisle, Alice 228
Locke, John 50
Lolbech, Ann 127
London: beggars in 121; hospitals
in 121; migrants in 120; population
of 8, 120; poverty in 121; unsanitary
living conditions in 120

London Hospital 127
London Journal 121
Long, Elizabeth 212
Lowther, William 59
Loxton, Mary 149
Lutherans, Catholics and 5–6

Macfarlane, Alan 3, 146, 148
Making of the English Working Class 3
Mandeville, Bernard 123
Manners, George 171
Manners, Grace 171–72
marginal groups: charity refusal by 3; fear as cause of 4; historical experience of 3; historiography of 3–4
Maria, Henrietta 169, 171
marital breakdown: domestic violence as cause of 192–94; failed patriarchs as cause of 187
marriage: economic purpose of 100; legal separations 187; Marriage Act (1753) regulations on 52; pregnancy outside wedlock legitimatised through 146–47; secrecy in 99; sociability affected by 100; for unmarried women 146–48; women's status affected by 100
Marriage Act (1753) 52
Marshall, Susan 214–15
Martin, Ann 126
May, Betteridge 213
May, John 213
McIntosh, Marjorie 149
Mears, Martha 202
Meddall, Richard 146
men: domestic violence by 192–94; *see also* patriarchy; as property holders 241
Mendelson, Sara 168, 222
mental illness 133–34
metropolitan elite 92
midwives 200, 202–3
Midwives Book 202
Mills, Agnes 191
Mills, Thomas 191
Monro, Alexander 92
Montagu, Elizabeth 95
Montagu Wortley, Mary 51, 55
Moor, Sam 134
Moore, Robert 4
More, Hannah 88

multiconfessionalism 5
Murgatroyd, John 59
Mytens, Daniel 169

Naphy, William G. 4
natural: as illegitimacy term 44–6, 48, 50, 52–3, 61
neighbourliness 243; *see* community
neighbourly duty 77–9
New and Complete Dictionary of the English Language 50
Noble Arte of Venerie or Hunting, The 161
Norton, William 186–87
Notes of a Journey 88

Of Domesticall Duties 27, 187
Oglander, John 170
O'Hara, Diana 147
Orlin, Len Cowen 149
Outram, Robert 52

Page, William 209
Pagitt, James 29–31, 41
Pagitt, Justinian 29–31, 41
Parliament of Women, The 200, 203–4
Parrett, Richard 148
patriarchy: adultery and 188; behavioural expectations based on 7; boundaries of 189; description of 181; enforcement of 181–82; execution used to ensure conformity to 185; inequality in 91; inscriptional 225–27; norms of 7; policing of 194; rejection of norms 185–87; responsibilities of 185; social expectation of 187; social rituals used to maintain 7; subordination to 242; violence 192–94
Paw, Alice 147
Pearce, Mary 135
Pearce, Thomas 147
Pepys, Samuel 52, 57
Percival, Viscount 52
Percy, Elizabeth 228
persecution: of marginal groups 4; of religious groups 5; religiously motivated 4; toleration and 4–5
Pettegree, Andrew 5
Petty, William 121
Petyt, William 228

258 *Index*

Pexall, Richard 185
Phelan, Jo 45
Phesey, Alice 189
Philp, Mark 100
Pickering, Joanne 147
Pigeon, Elizabeth 33–6, 39–40
Pigeon, John 33, 36, 38–9
Pight, Robert 133
Pile, John 131
Piozzi, Gabriel 100
Pitt, Christopher 193
Pitts, Grace 205, 209–10
Placita Parliamentaria 229
Plumbley, Marie 154
Pocock, David 11
polite femininity 89
Polite Lady, The 104
polite society: exclusion from 88–110;
    inclusion in 110; language of 45
polite spaces 8
politeness 8, 68, 89, 91–2, 94–8, 109
political practice: archives in 223–24;
    paperwork and 223–25
Poor Laws 142; *see also* Elizabethan
    Poor Laws
pornographic texts 203–4
Porter, Roy 3, 6, 134
poverty: bastard as term of 53, 59;
    language associated with 45; in
    London 121; stigma of 62
Powell, Jane 148
Practical Part of Love, The 200
pregnancy outside wedlock: adultery
    as cause of 144; case study of 141;
    church court depositions regarding
    144–45, 156, 242; community
    effects of 143; community exclusion
    because of 142; extramarital affairs
    as cause of 144, 146; marriage for
    legitimatising of 146–47; marriage
    opportunities affected by 143;
    penance for 145; reputation affected
    by 142; vulnerability of women in
    144; witnesses in 146
pregnant unmarried women:
    acceptance of 154–56; charity for
    149–54; compassion for 150;
    harboring of 150–51; inclusion of
    154–56; legal support for 152–53;
    marriage for 148–49;
    neighbourhood support for 149–54,
    156; respectability of 155

Presbyterian women: community
    relations affected by 78–9;
    description of 69–70; devotional
    literature 73; exclusion of 73–6;
    gendered expectations for 72;
    inclusion of 77; isolation of 82;
    marginalisation of 73–6; moral
    reputation of 81; neighbourly duty
    by 77–9; religious dissent by 75;
    reputation of 80–1; social behaviour
    of 77; stereotypes of 72–3, 75;
    visiting the sick by 7
Prescott, Henry 78–9
Privy Council 39
prostitutes 203
Protestants: Catholics and 83, 165,
    174; hunting by 165–66, 174;
    see also Church of England
puberty 209
punishment: for failed patriarchs
    184–87, 242; patriarchal
    enforcement through 181–82
Pupil of Nature, The 202
Pye, Thomas 53

Quakerism 5, 69
Quarman, Thomas 149

Raleigh, Walter 1
Ramsden, John 165
rape: age of consent and 208–9;
    definition of 213; description of 7,
    182, 185; by schoolmasters 204
rape trials: court testimony in 207–14;
    deception in 206; depositions in
    201–2; penetration and 215;
    seminal emission questions in
    212–13; sexual consent and 205–7;
    sexual knowledge by girls in 205–14
Regicide, the 69
religion: exclusion caused by 4, 166;
    hunting and 165–68, 174; inclusion
    based on 166; persecution
    motivated by 4; toleration of 5–6
religious coexistence 5–6; women
    and 68–83
reputation: illegitimacy effects on
    58–9; of Independent women 80–1;
    sexual immodesty and 201
Reynolds, Joshua 88
Rich, Henry 163–64
Richardson, Samuel 99

Index 259

Riches, Isott 152
Riley, William 130
Rimer, Richard 58
Risse, Guenter B. 126, 130, 132
Robbins, William 210
Roberts, Penny 4
Roberts, Philip 207
Robertson, Sarah 213
Robinson, Hannah 193
Robinson, John 183
Robinson, William 189
Roe, Gilbert 152–53
Rosyer, Nicholas 191
Rousseau, Jean-Jacques 50
rural life 6–7
Ryley, Elizabeth 228–30, 233
Ryley, William Jr. 228–29

Sabean, David 13, 136
Sadler, Margaret 146
Savage, Sarah 74–5, 77, 80
Savile, George 92
Savile, John 162, 164–65
Say, Samuel 75
Say, Sarah 75
Scholsy, Samuel 44
science, empiricism and 11
scolding 184
scold's bridle 7
Scrope, Emanuel 169
secrets 104
Seelye, John 146
sensibility 53
Serjeant, William 27–8
servants: intimacy with 193; literacy of
    204; patriarch's distancing from 242
sexual assault 200–1
sexual consent 205–7, 209
sexual deviancy 145
sexual intercourse 208, 214
sexual knowledge: age differences in
    207–14; court testimony and
    207–14; cultures and exchange of
    202–5; impudence and 206–7;
    literacy and 204; by midwives
    202–3; origins of 203–4;
    pornographic texts 203–4; rape
    trials affected by 205–6; sources of
    202–4; of young women 203
sexual misdemeanours 155
sexual promiscuity 40
shame: "bastard" used to express 57;
    description of 7

Sharp, Jane 202
Sharpe, Fane William 94
Sharpe, J.A. 58
Sharpe, Mary: biographical data about
    94; description of 88–9; failed
    friendship and 98–109; Osmond
    Beauvoir marriage 99, 101, 104; in
    polite society 94–5; social circle
    of 94–8
Shaw, Benjamin 51, 54
Sheils, Bill; *see* Sheils William
Sheils, William 6, 166
Shepard, Alexandra 7, 12, 184
Shepherd, William 150
Sheppard, Margaret 81
Sherwood, Elizabeth 154–55, 156
Shirley, Margaret 185
Shoemaker, Robert 56
Short Treatise of Hunting 168
Sibley, David 11
siblings 28
Sidney, Barbara Gammage 173
Siena, Kevin 127–28
Simmel, Georg 12–3
Sims, Dorothy 150
skimmington rides 7, 182, 191–92,
    242; *see also* charivari
Slack, Paul 122
Sliden, Maria 148
Smith, John 212
Smith, Mary 55
Snell, Keith 142
sociability: description of 8, 92;
    hunting; *see* hunting sociability;
    marriage effects on 100; political
    consequences of 164; religious
    beliefs and 244; societal power
    and 162
social acquaintances 88
social circles 8–9
social exclusion 8, 10
social relations, political influences
    on 9
social rituals 7
social structures: in communities 6;
    exclusion's role in 11; inclusion's
    role in 11; social rituals used to
    maintain 7; socio-economic
    developments that affected 8
Societies for the Reformation of
    Manners 79–80
Society for Promoting Christian
    Knowledge 122

260 *Index*

Spacks, Patricia Meyer 104
Spectator, The 88
Spierling, Karen E. 12
St Bartholomew's Hospital 121, 131
St George's Hospital 127
St Margaret's Workhouse
  Infirmary 128
St Thomas's Hospital 121
Star Chamber cases 185–86, 189
Steele, Richard 88
stepfamilies 28–9
stepmothers: domestic exclusion by
  29–31; domestic exclusion of 29
Stevens, Cath 130
Stringer, William 211
Sutton, Samuel 130
Sweet, R.H. 92

Tabor, Mary 210
Tadmor, Naomi 49, 91
Talbot, Catherine 95
Tanner, John 148
Tarantino, Giovanni 5
Taylor, John 188
theft 135
Thomas, Keith 8
Thomason, George 37
Thompson, E.P. 3
Thorold, Edward 38
Thorold, John 33
Thorp, John 59
Thrale, Hester 100
Throckmorton, John 173
toleration: dissenting groups advocacy
  for 5; historiography of 4;
  persecution and 4–5; religious 5–6
Toleration Act 6, 41, 68–9
Tories 9
Tower of London Record Office:
  clerks in 231–32; description of
  221–23; labour within 231–33;
  male employees in 232; visitors to
  226; women in 228–29, 231–32
Town, Daniel 29
Treatise of the Pleas of the Crown 213
*Treatise on the Improvement of
  Midwifery* 203
Trepan, The 37, 40
trepan/trepanning 31–2, 40
Tucker, Richard 147
Turner, George 55
Turner, Thomas 51–3, 56–7
Tyler, Sarah 52

unmarried women: marriage for
  146–47; *see also* pregnant
  unmarried women
Upington, Elizabeth 209

van Reyney, Adrien 127
Van Somer, Paul 169
Vane, Lady 81
Vavasour, Thomas 165
venereal disease 131–32, 212, 244
Vernon, Samuel 32, 36–9
Vesey, Elizabeth 88
Vincent, David 99, 106
violence: cuckoldry and 187–92;
  disorderly types of 182; insults and
  191; methods of 182; patriarchy
  enforcement through 181–82
Vyolett, Susan 193–94
Vyolett, Thomas 193–94

Walker, Benjamin 147
Walker, Clement 193
Walker, Garthine 201
Walker, Thomas 151
Walpole, Horace 51, 53–4, 57, 88
Walsal, Francis 33
Walsh, Goody 232–33
Walsham, Alexandra 5, 6
Walsingham, Francis 223
Walter, John 6, 174
Ward, Ned 73
Warnett, Mary 213
Webb, Joanne 147
Wentworth, Thomas 164–65
Wesley, John 49
Westminster Infirmary: admission to
  126–32; as Anglican institution 126;
  location of 131; charity of 117–18,
  122; committees of 132; contagious
  diseases excluded from 128;
  description of 8; discharge from
  132–36; donor stakeholders of
  123–26, 129, 137; establishment of
  117–18; exclusion from 117–37;
  female subscribers of 123; gin
  consumption in 134–35; inclusion in
  117–37; letters of recommendation
  for treatment at 129, 131; matron of
  125; medical staff of 124–25; nurses
  in 125–26; patients in 120, 127;
  physician examination of patients at
  130; physicians in 124–25; purpose
  of 136; recommending of patients

for treatment at 129–30; records of 128, 129, 131; relocation of 118; rules of 134; sick poor in 127, 136; social order and 120–22; staff of 123–26; subscribers of 123; theft in 135; and venereal disease 131–32, 244

Whigs 9

Whittle, Jane 168

Whole Duty of Man, The 122

Whyman, Susan 162

Wiesenthall, Charles 206

Wilkes, Wetenhall 72

Williamson, Joseph 229–30

Willoughby, Lady 81

Winnington, Rob 134

Winwood, Lady 171

witchcraft: leprosy and 4; neighborhoud disputes as origin of accusations 3; violence in 183

Witham, Robert 123

Withington, Phil 12, 162

wives: correction of 182, 193; governing of, by husbands 182; patriarchal failure to control 183; skimmingtons against 191–92; violence against 192–94

Wogan, William 123

women: as agents 228, 244; *see also* girls; *see also* wives; "as weaker sex" 7; behavioural ideals of 7; cheerfulness of 72; community relations affected by 78–9; cross-dressing of, as men 242; disorderly 183; in Established Church 70–1; in falconry 170; gendered categorisations for 83; gendered expectations for 68, 71; in hawking 170; in hunting 168–74; in hunting sociability 172; ideals for 71–3; Independent; *see* Independent women; in law courts 227; moral standards for 80; neighbourly duty by 77–9; patriarchal enforcement for 181; in polite culture 68; pregnant unmarried; *see* pregnant unmarried women; in public political spheres 227; religious coexistence and 68–83; religious modesty of 71–2; reputation of 58–9, 81, 201; stereotypes for 71–3; in Tower of London Record Office 226, 228–29, 231–32; unruly 183

Wood, Andy 9

Wood, Jan 129

Worsley, Elizabeth 209

Worsley, Joseph 209

Wright, Christopher 44

Wright, Gillian 74

Wrightson, Keith 142

Yard, Frances 152

Ylivuori, Soile 89, 105

York, Joseph 212

York Cause Papers Database 47, 58

Young Lady's Companion 103

Zika, Charles 5

Printed in the United States
By Bookmasters